SO-AWJ-452

The rough guide to

PERU

=The= rough guides

Other Rough Guides available include:
TUNISIA, SPAIN, PORTUGAL, GREECE, MEXICO, HOLLAND, FRANCE, MOROCCO and **YUGOSLAVIA.**

Forthcoming
KENYA, ITALY, EASTERN EUROPE, CHINA, PARIS and **NEW YORK**

Series Editor
MARK ELLINGHAM

Thanks for material, contributions and inspiration to Carlos Montenegro, Howard Davis, Alonso Zarzar, Rafael El Gordo, Zane Williams, Mr Harrison of the British Tourist Authority in Lima, Lynn Meisch, Peter Frost, Hilary Bradt, *Journey Latin America* (London), *Explorandes* (Lima), Lilly, Badger, and most importantly to Claire and our two daughters – Tess 'n' Bethan.

First published in 1985
Reprinted in 1986
by Routledge & Kegan Paul plc
11 New Fetter Lane
London EC4P 4EE

Published in the USA by
Routledge & Kegan Paul Inc
in association with Methuen Inc
29 West 35th Street, New York, NY 10001

© 1985, 1986.

Set in Linotron Helvetica and Sabon
by Input Typesetting Ltd, London
and printed in Great Britain
by Cox and Wyman
Reading, Berks

© Dilwyn Jenkins 1985

Library of Congress Cataloging in Publication Data

Jenkins, Dilwyn.
  The rough guide to Peru.
  (The Rough Guides)
  Includes index.
  1. Peru — Description and travel — 1981–
Guide-books. I. Title. II. Series.
F3409.5.J46 1985   918.5'04633   85–2474

British Library CIP data also available

ISBN 0–7102–0058–7

The rough guide to
PERU

Written and researched by

DILWYN JENKINS

with additional research and accounts by Peter Schoonmaker, Mike Paul, Ted Bowden, Duncan Corpe and Peter Cloudesley

Maps by
CHRIS RICKETTS

Drawings by
KATE WILKINSON

Edited by

DILWYN JENKINS

WITH MARK ELLINGHAM & JOHN FISHER

Routledge & Kegan Paul
London and New York

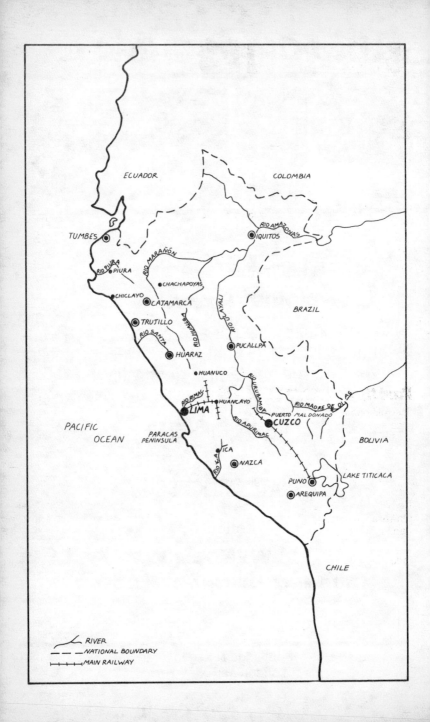

ECUADOR

COLOMBIA

TUMBES

RIO AMAZONAS

IQUITOS

RIO PIURA

PIURA

RIO MARAÑÓN

CHACHAPOYAS

CHICLAYO

CATAMARCA

RIO UCAYALI

BRAZIL

TRUJILLO

RIO HUALLAGA

RIO SANTA

PUCALLPA

HUARAZ

HUANUCO

RIO URUBAMBA

PACIFIC

RIO RIMAC

HUANCAYO

RIO MADRE DE DIOS

OCEAN

LIMA

PUERTO MALDONADO

PARACAS

PENINSULA

CUZCO

RIO APURIMAC

BOLIVIA

RIO ICA

ICA

NAZCA

LAKE TITICACA

PUNO

AREQUIPA

CHILE

⌐ RIVER

– – – NATIONAL BOUNDARY

+–+–+ MAIN RAILWAY

CONTENTS

Part one **BASICS** 1

Peru: where to go and when / Getting there / Red tape / Costs and money / Health and insurance / Maps and information / Getting about / Sleeping / Food and drink / Communications – post, phones and media / Ancient sites, museums, churches and national parks / Fiestas and public holidays / Music and film / Police and thieves / Sexual harassment / Other things / Peruvian terms: a glossary

Part two **THE GUIDE** 25

Part three **CONTEXTS** 263

To self-determination and the recognition of land rights for the Campa-Ashaninka and all other indigenous tribal groups

A percentage of author's and editor's royalties on this book will be donated to *Survival International*'s work in Peru. Survival International work for the rights of threatened tribal peoples worldwide, for details of their activities and an account of the situation in Peru see p. 294

Part one
BASICS

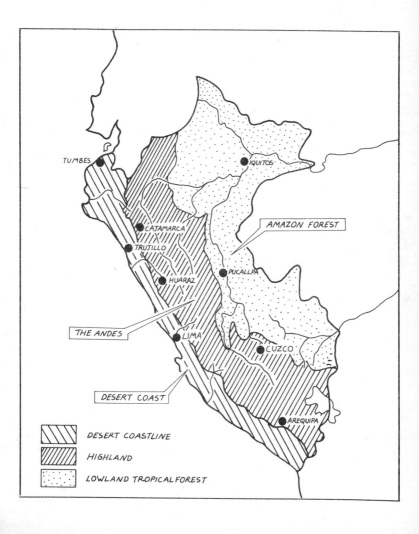

TUMBES

IQUITOS

AMAZON FOREST

CAJAMARCA

TRUJILLO

PUCALLPA

HUARAZ

THE ANDES

LIMA

CUZCO

DESERT COAST

AREQUIPA

DESERT COASTLINE

HIGHLAND

LOWLAND TROPICAL FOREST

PERU: WHERE TO GO AND WHEN

Peru – for travellers – is the most varied and exciting of all South American experiences. Most people visualise the country as mountainous, and are aware of the great Inca relics, but the splendour, both of the immense desert coastline and of the vast tracts of tropical rainforest, often comes as a complete surprise. Dividing these contrasting environments, chain after chain of breathtaking peaks – over 7km high in places and spread across 400km – ripple the entire length of the nation: *the Andes.*

Racially, too, Peru is diverse. Still very much dominated by the Spanish and *mestizo* descendants of Pizarro, more than half the population is nevertheless of pure Indian blood. In the country, native life can have changed little in the last four centuries. But 'progress' is gradually transforming Peru – already the cities wear a distinctly Western aspect, and roads and tracks now connect almost every corner of the Republic with the industrial *urbanizaciones* which dominate the few fertile valleys along the coast. Only the Amazon jungle – nearly two-thirds of Peru's landmass but with only a tiny fraction of its population – remains beyond their reach, and even here lumber companies and settlers are taking an increasing toll.

Frantic as it sometimes appears on the surface, the laid-back calmness of the Peruvian temperament continues to underlie life even in the cities. Lima may operate at a terrifying pace at times – the traffic, the money-grabbers, the political situation – but there always seems to be time to talk, for a *ceviche,* another drink. . . . It's a country where the resourceful traveller can break through barriers of class, race and language far more easily than most of its inhabitants can. And where the limousines and villas of the elite remain little more than a thin veneer on a nation whose roots lie firmly in its ethnic traditions.

With each region offering so many different attractions, it's hard to generalise about which places are best to visit first. **Cuzco** seems the most obvious place to start – a beautiful and bustling colonial city, the ancient heart of the Inca Empire, it's surrounded by some of the most spectacular mountain landscapes and palatial ruins in Peru, and by magnificent hiking country. Yet along **the coast,** too, there are fascinating archaeological sites – the bizarre *Nazca Lines* south of Lima, the great adobe city of *Chan Chan* in the north – and a rich crop of sea life, easiest accessible around the Paracas National Park. The coastal towns, almost all of them with superb beaches, also offer nightlife and great food. For mountains and long-distance treks there are the stunning glacial lakes, snowy peaks and little-known ruins of the **northern sierras** – around **Huaraz** and **Cajamarca.** And if it's wild-life you're into – although there's an abundance almost everywhere – **the jungle** provides startling opportunities for close and exotic encounters. From the comfort of tourist lodges in **Iquitos** to the more exciting river excursions around **Puerto Maldonado,** the fauna and flora of the world's largest tropical forest can be experienced first hand with relative ease.

The attractions of each area are discussed in greater detail in the chapter introductions. Picking **the 'best' time to visit** any of them, however, is complicated by the country's physical characteristics. Summer along the **desert coast** more or less fits the expected image of the Southern Hemisphere – extremely hot and sunny from December to March (especially in the north), cooler and with a frequent hazy mist between April and November. But only in the polluted environs of Lima does the coastal winter ever get cold enough to necessitate a sweater: swimming is possible all year round, though the water itself (thanks to the Humboldt Current) is cool to cold at the best of times. To swim or surf for any length of time you'd need to follow local tradition and wear a wetsuit. Apart from the occasional shower over Lima it hardly ever rains in the desert. The freak exception, every ten years or so, is when the shift in ocean currents of *El Niño* causes torrential downpours, devastating crops, roads and communities all down the coast. Since it last broke in 1983 there seems no immediate danger.

In the Andes seasons are more clearly marked, with heavy rains from December to March and a warm, relatively dry period from June to

	SUNNY SEASON	RAINY SEASON	APPROX. TEMP.(°C) Jan.	July	ANNUAL RAINFALL
COAST	Dec.-March	Rare	18–30	13–20	0.50mm
ANDES	May-Sept.	Dec.-March	5–15	0–10	400–1,000mm
JUNGLE	May-Oct.	Nov.-April	20–30		1,000–2,000mm

September. Inevitably, though, there are always some sunny weeks in the rainy season and wet ones in the dry. A similar pattern dominates the **jungle,** though rainfall in the *selva* is heavier and more frequent, and it's hot and humid all year round. Ideally, then, the coast should be visited around January while it's hot, and the mountains and jungles are at their best after the rains, say June to September. Since this is hardly likely to be possible there's little point in worrying about it – the country's attractions are invariably enough to override the need for guarantees of good weather.

Terrorism, which has made the world news and worries some potential visitors, is an increasing problem for Peru. But it's localised and certainly not aimed at travellers. Keep away from the danger zones, (in some of which travel is restricted anyway) and it shouldn't affect you in the least. Even here you're more likely to be held on suspicion of being a guerilla than actually to encounter one.

GETTING THERE

By air
There are a wide variety of flights direct to Peru from the States, slightly fewer from Europe, and only indirect routings from Australia or New Zealand. Their prices can vary enormously – depending not so much on the distance travelled as on who is selling the ticket.

From the States, for example, *Avianca* (320 E. Flagler St, Miami, Fla. 33126; tel. 305–883 4291) charge around $900 for a Miami-Lima return and $1200 from New York. But with the Peruvian airline *Faucett* (3095 NW 77th Av., Miami, Fla. 33126; tel. 305–591 7575, or toll free 800–327 1343) you can get a Miami-Lima return for around $450 and if you ask for the special ticket can also stop off in Iquitos, Cuzco or Arequipa. *Air Panama* is also cheap on the Miami-Lima route. The only answer is to shop around and carefully compare what's on offer.

From Europe flights go for anything from £400 upwards: the cheapest options usually being scheduled flights from London, Paris or Madrid with the South American airlines (*Avianca* – 2 Hanover St, London W1, tel. 01–408 1889: *Faucett* – 27 Cockspur Street, London SW1; or *Viasa* and others); or stand-by to Miami and on by scheduled flights from there. In Britain, the best deals will usually be found advertised in the London magazines *Time Out* and *LAM* or, nationally, in the *Sunday Times, Observer* or *Private Eye*. *Journey Latin America* (10 Barley Mow Passage, London W4; tel. 01–747 3108) and *STA* (74 Old Brompton Road, London SW7; tel. 01–581 1022) are probably the cheapest and most reliable operators. In Paris *UNICLAM* (63 rue Monsieur le Prince, Paris 75006; tel 325 7965) are a major charter and tour operator.

Two possible routes will get you to Lima **from Australia and New Zealand:** either to Tahiti with *Air New Zealand* and *LAN-Chile* on from there, or *Qantas* to the States and down by scheduled flight. Neither could be described as cheap.

In any event it's best to avoid buying international **air tickets in Peru,** where they are inflated by a 23 per cent government tax: if you're uncertain of your schedule the extra expense of an open-ended return is probably worth it. Remember too that on flying out of Lima you'll have to pay a $10 **departure tax.**

Overland
There are three main overland routes into Peru.

From the north, it's possible to travel virtually all the way from the USA via Mexico, Central America, Colombia and Ecuador on buses. If you follow this route, be prepared to cross through politically volatile areas of Central America and remember that it's virtually impossible to travel overland from Panama into Colombia, where there's still no road through the undeveloped Darien Gap. Some people hike through and a few even try it by jeep, but it's far easier to take the ferry or a short flight.

From Brazil, you can take the amazing boat ride up the Amazon from Manaus to Iquitos – around ten days' ride which, if you're prepared for a few discomforts, can prove a fabulous experience. Take a hammock and plenty of reading material.

The third overland route arrives in the south of Peru **from Bolivia** (you can also get in via Chile from either Bolivia or Argentina, but it seems rather a long way round). The final section across the high *altiplano* to Lake Titicaca is by bus or truck, and though the lake itself can be crossed by ferry or even hydrofoil, the majority of travellers stick to the bus (which is cheaper).

By sea
The *Pacific Steam Navigation Company* used to take passengers from Europe to Lima, but no more. In fact the age of sea travel is virtually over, with only two remote possibilities: you can attempt to **work your passage** (union rules allowing) from a major European port such as Hamburg to Brazil; or you can hang around in Panama or the Caribbean hoping to find a **private yacht** sailing in this direction. Good luck!

Package tours
Many of the bigger travel companies – like *Thomas Cook* – organise standard holiday tours to Peru. These all-in packages are invariably very expensive and mostly extremely limiting – you'll see only what they want you to see. But of course they do provide a considerable degree of comfort and peace of mind. Full details from any good travel agent.

More exciting are several companies in Europe and North America which specialise in **treks** and organised **overland travel.** Still expensive, this type of tour – often based around some special interest theme – offers a far closer encounter with the country. Some of the best operators are listed below, and many of them are also good for cheap tickets out:

Journey Latin America (tours and tickets)
    –10 Barley Mow Passage, London W4 (01–747 3108)
STA (tours and tickets)
    –74 Old Brompton Rd, London SW7 (01–581 1022)
Exodus Expeditions (treks and tours)
    –100 Wandsworth High St, London SW18 (01–870 0151)
Encounter Overland (tours)
    –267 Old Brompton Rd, London SW5 (01–370 6845)
Trailfinders (tours and tickets)
    –42–48 Earls Court Rd, London W8 (01–603 1515)
Mountain Travel (treks)
    –1398 Solano Av., Berkeley, California 94706 (415–527 8100)
Wilderness Adventures (treks)
    –1760 Solano Av., Berkeley, California 94707 (415–524 5111)
Peruvian Andean Treks
    –707, 6223–31 Av. NW, Calgary, Canada (403–286 2286)

RED TAPE

All nationalities need a **tourist card** to enter Peru – they are issued at the frontiers or on the plane before landing in Lima. In most cases this will be valid for 90 days, though the period can be as little as 60 or 30 days. In theory you have to show an outbound ticket (by air or bus) before you'll be given a card, but this is not always checked. One copy of the tourist card must be kept with your passport at all times.

Should you want to **extend your stay,** there are two basic options – either cross one of the borders or spend several days going through the bureaucratic rigmarole at a *Migraciones* office. These (in Lima and Cuzco) rarely give more than 60 days for a renewal and charge $20: for a second renewal you'd probably get only 30 days. In short it's normally easier to leave the country where in practice you only need to spend a night over the border before coming back and getting another 90 days.

Peruvian embassies abroad include:

Australia – 111 Monaro Crescent, Red Hill, ACT 2603

Britain – 52 Sloane Street, London SW1 (01–235 1917)

Canada – 539 Island Park Drive, Ottawa, Ontario (722 7186)

Netherlands – Van Alkemadelaan 189, 2597 AE, The Hague

Sweden – Brunnsgatan 216, 111 38 Stockholm (110019)

USA – 1700 Massachusetts Avenue NW, Washington D.C. 20036 (833 9860)

COSTS AND MONEY

Peru is certainly a very much cheaper place to live than Europe or the States, but how much so will depend very much on where you are and when. **Inflation** is currently running at an incredible 150 per cent, and if you've been before it can be a nasty shock the first time you pay for anything in Peruvian *soles*. Chances are you're not being ripped off, and if you examine the dollar equivalent you'll find that the cost to you hasn't changed that much (although for Peruvians it may have soared even in real terms). For this reason prices throughout this book are quoted in dollars, far the most widely acceptable and easiest foreign currency to take, and against which costs seem to remain relatively stable.

As a general rule you should – with care – be able to get by on around $6–7 a day. A good **meal** can always be found for under $1, **transport** is very reasonable, an adequate double **room** $2–3 a night, and **camping** costs nothing. Expect to pay a little above the odds in the larger towns and cities, and especially in the jungle where most food supplies have to be imported by truck from other regions. In the villages and rural towns, on the other hand, things come cheaper – and by roughing it out in the *campo*, buying food from local villages or the nearest market, you can live well on next to nothing.

Costs in the more popular parts of Peru vary considerably with the seasons. Cuzco, for instance, has its best weather from June to August and, crowded with *gringos*, doubles many of its prices. The same thing happens at fiesta times – although on such occasions you're unlikely to resent it too much. As always, if you're travelling alone you'll end up spending considerably more than you would in a group of two or more people: sharing rooms and food saves considerably. If you have some kind of international **student card,** it's worth taking along for the occasional reduction.

For safety's sake the bulk of your money should be carried as **traveller's cheques** – preferably of two different types. From time to time rumoured forgeries will make one type of cheque difficult to unload. *American Express* may be the best bet since they have their own offices in Lima and Cuzco, and also offer an efficient poste restante service. Large denominations – in notes or traveller's cheques – should be avoided; you'll find them hard to change anywhere in South America.

Your money should also be in **dollars** – anything else will almost certainly prove a constant annoyance, and even the major European currencies are hard to get rid of outside Lima. Always keep some **cash** for emergencies: there will inevitably be someone – a hotel owner or shopkeeper – who wants to buy a few US dollars since, despite 90 per cent interest on bank savings, they are the only safe counter against inflation.

Peruvian currency – *soles de oro* – can pose the occasional problem for unwary tourists. Banknotes range from 50,000 *soles* down to 500. It's particularly hard to change the larger ones in jungle towns, but even in Cuzco and Lima shopkeepers and waiters are often reluctant to accept them, or if they do, will end up running around trying to find change. It's best to break up any large notes at every opportunity – in large shops, bars, post offices etc. If you hang on to the 1,000 and 500 *sole* notes you'll have few difficulties in even the smallest villages. Another common source of confusion is linguistic; in particular the frequent use of the term *libra* (literally a pound) to refer to 10 *soles*. This is something you simply have to get used to.

Banks are open weekdays from 8.45 until 12.15 (some change to 9.15–12.45

in the winter, April to November). The *Banco de la Nacion* is the one which officially deals with foreign currency, but most banks seem to deal with dollar traveller's cheques, and there is often less of a queue in the *Banco Continental*. The rate of exchange varies daily, and you're invariably better off changing a little at a time. On the other hand, there's an enormous amount of paperwork involved in even the simplest transactions – some places fill out seven copies of each form – and inevitably a good deal of time. You'll always need to show your passport. For convenience there's a lot to be said for the **Casas de Cambio** which can be found in just about any town on the tourist circuit. They open all day, there's rarely a queue, and the rate of exchange is often better too.

The very best exchange rates are found on the **black market.** In Peru the difference is never as dramatic as it is in, say, Bolivia, but it is possible to gain as much as 20 per cent. Black market is a rather nebulous term encompassing any buyer from hotel clerks and shopkeepers to the small men in suits clutching briefcases who constantly attempt to catch tourists' attention without drawing attention to themselves. The latter usually offer the best rates and

can be spotted in the commercial or tourist centre of any large town – behind the *Hotel Bolivar* in Lima – and at all border crossings. Theft of signed or unsigned traveller's cheques, sometimes under threat of violence, is always a slight risk, particularly in Lima: when changing on the street in this way, play it safe – and never hand over your cheques until given the cash. Going into unfamiliar buildings (with hidden back-staircases) 'to negotiate' is inadvisable.

Credit cards are accepted in the more expensive restaurants and hotels as well as for car-hire. The better known ones (including *American Express, Diners* and *VISA*) can also be used with the larger travel companies, but not to pay for bus or train journeys. It's probably worth checking if your credit company has connections with Lima. For **emergency cash** the quickest method is direct transfer from an account in the States or Europe. The people to see for this are the *Bank of London and South America* (Lloyds International): branches in Jr. Lampa (between the two main plazas in the centre of Lima) or at Larco, Miraflores. The money is usually transferred in dollars and if you ask for a telex transfer takes only five working days.

HEALTH AND INSURANCE

At the moment there are no required **inoculations** for Peru, but it's a good idea to check with the embassy or travel agent a couple of months before you go. Your doctor will probably advise you to have some anyway: typhoid, cholera and yellow fever jabs are a sensible precaution, as is ensuring that you're up to date with such things as polio and tetanus boosters. *Gamma-globulin* against hepatitis is also usually recommended, but if you're travelling long term you should be aware that the effects are relatively short-lived and you may end up more vulnerable once it's worn off than you were before you had it. You can, of course, get boosters in Peru.

In Britain these can all be obtained from your local doctor or Health Authority or, in a hurry, from the *British Airways Medical Centre* (75 Regent St, London W1; tel. 01–439 9584 – Mon. to Fri. 8.30–4.30) or the *Thomas Cook Vacci-*

nation Centre (45 Berkeley St, London W1; tel. 01–499 4000 – Mon. to Fri. 8.30–6, Sat. 9–12). Information **in the States** from the local Public Health Service or Department of Health. In Los Angeles there's a similar place for jabs in a hurry – the *Convenience Care Center* (World Trade Center, 350 S. Figueroa St, L.A., CAL 90071).

The illnesses most commonly encountered are **typhoid** or **hepatitis. Rabies** does exist but it's a relatively remote possibility. **Soroche** or mountain sickness is much more probable. The best way to prevent it is light meals, plenty of rest and coca tea for the first few days at a high altitude, but a thorough acclimatisation to any altitude above 2,500m is the only sure preventive measure. Take it easy for a few days before trying anything even vaguely strenuous. Anyone who suffers from headaches or nausea should rest; more seriously, a sudden bad cough at altitude necessitates immediate descent and medical advice. *Soroche* can kill. Quite a few people suffer from *soroche* on trains crossing high passes; if this happens, don't panic, just rest and stay with the train until it descends. Most trains are equipped with oxygen bags which are brought round by the guard for anyone in need.

If you intend going into jungle regions, **malaria tablets** (*Maloprim* once a week or *Paludrin* daily) should be taken – starting a few weeks before you arrive and continuing for some time after.

For **minor ailments** you can buy most drugs in *farmacias* without a prescription. Antibiotics and malaria pills can be bought over the counter, as can antihistamines (for bite allergies) or medication for an upset stomach (try *Lomotil, Kaolin and Morphine* or *Streptotriad*). The only drugs you may need to take out with you are **contraceptives** (expensive), any special or unusual medicines, water purifying tablets and insect repellents. **Doctors, dentists** and **hospitals** (detailed for Lima on p. 53) can be found easily in the phone book, or simply by relying on a taxi driver.

Food is frequently condemned as a health hazard. Personally I relish eating almost anything bought from street stalls and have never had any problems. Drinking bottled **water,** though, is always a sensible precaution, as is avoiding lettuce.

In any event you should invest in some form of **travel insurance;** a good policy should cover not only medical expenses but also theft and loss of baggage or money. It can be arranged through any travel agent or broker. Even with insurance, most Peruvian clinics will insist on cash up front except in really serious hospital cases – an emergency stash is again a good idea. Keep all receipts and official papers involved with any claim you're going to want to make; in the case of theft this would ideally include a copy of the police report (*denuncia*).

Alternative medicines have a popular history going back at least 2,000 years in Peru and the traditional practitioners, *herbaleros, hueseros* and *curanderos,* are still commonplace. *Herbaleros* sell curative and magical plants, herbs and charms on the streets and in the markets of most towns. They lay out vast arrays of ground roots, liquid tree barks, flowers, leaves and creams – all with specific medicinal functions and much cheaper than the wrapper-orientated *farmacias*. If told the troublesome symptoms, a *herbalero* will be able to select remedies for most minor and apparently some major (cancer) ailments. The *hueseros* are physiotherapeutic consultants who treat diseases and injuries by bone manipulation (if you can't find them in the phone book ask a taxi driver). *Curanderos* claim magic diagnostic, divinatory and healing powers and have had long lists of customers since pre-Inca days. They tend to live on the outskirts of town and hardly ever advertise – so, again, get a taxi driver to take you. For further information see the CONTEXTS section (p. 282). **Homeopathy** and **Shiatzu** are growing in popularity in Peru (mostly in Lima) – again, you'll find addresses for these in the phone book.

MAPS AND INFORMATION

Peru has no official **tourist offices** abroad. However you can get a range of information from most tour companies (see p. 5) and also, to a limited extent, from Peruvian consulates. In Peru you'll find some sort of a **tourist office** in most towns of any size, which can help with information and perhaps free local maps. As often as not, though, they are simply fronts for tour operators, and are only really worth bothering with if you have a specific question – about fiesta dates or local bus timetables for example. In Lima the main branch of the official organisation is located in an arcade at Belen 1000, near the Plaza San Martin. Even this one is not particularly helpful, though they do have free maps of the city centre.

Maps of Peru fall into four basic categories. A standard **road map** should be available from a good map seller just about anywhere in the world, or in Peru itself from street vendors or *librerias*. **Departmental maps,** covering each *departmento* in greater detail, but often badly out of date, should also be fairly widely available. **Ordnance survey type** maps (usually 1:100,000) extend over the entire coastal area and most of the mountains: they can be bought in Peru from the *Instituto Geografico Militar* (in Lima, Nicolas de Pierola 947, Plaza San Martin). A few **maps for hikers,** in still greater detail, are produced by the *South American Explorers' Club* (see below), though these only cover the most popular trekking zones. In Britain the best **sources** for all these are *McCarta* (122 King's Cross Rd, London WC1; tel. 01–278 8278), *Stanfords* (12 Long Acre, London WC2; tel. 01–836 1321) and above all *Bradt Enterprises* (mail order only – 41 Nortoft Rd, Chalfont St Peter, Bucks; tel. 02407 3478). In the States the *South American Explorers' Club* (2239 E. Colfax Av. No. 205, Denver, CO 80206; tel. 320 0308) or *Bradt Enterprises* (95 Harvey St, Cambridge, MA 02140).

The **South American Explorers' Club** is a non-profit-making organisation founded in 1977 to support scientific and adventure expeditions, to produce a magazine and provide services to travellers. In return for membership ($25) the Club offers four copies of the magazine; use of their facilities in Lima; use of library and map collections; discounts on maps, guidebooks, leg pouches etc; information on visas, doctors and dentists; and an 'emergency crash pad'. In Lima their address is Av. Portugal 146, between Av. Bolivia and Av. España (tel. 314488), or by post to Castilla 3714, Lima 100.

GETTING ABOUT

By road

Buses are good value and go virtually everywhere. There are several varieties from the swish coastal 'luxury' coaches of *Ormeño* to the beaten-up reject 'school' buses used on local runs throughout Peru. Long-distance bus journeys cost around $1 per hour (i.e. 60 or 70km) on the fast coastal highway and half this on the slower mountain and jungle tracks. It's best to buy tickets in advance for inter-city rides, making sure you avoid sitting over the wheel arches. Services are efficient in that you always arrive some time, if often slowed down by punctures, arguments and landslides. At least one bus station/stop can be found in the centre of any town; since they are the only public means of transport available to most of the population, buses run with surprising regularity. Failing this, you can wait for them at the police *control* on the edge of town, or hail one down virtually anywhere.

Shared taxis (*colectivos*) also connect the coastal towns and many of the larger centres in the mountains. Like the buses, they are usually ancient imports from the USA – huge old Dodge Coronets with the Virgin Mary dangling from the rearview mirror. The drivers are safe enough, though, and it's certainly a faster form of travel than the bus, if almost twice as expensive. Most manage to squeeze in about six people plus the driver (three in the front and four in the back).

Colectivos can be found either in the centre of a town (near the main plaza) or on the road-exit in the direction one wants to go. If there is more than one ready to leave, it's worth asking for a few quotes as the price is often negotiable.

Trucks and **hitching** usually amount to the same thing. It's very rare that a private car will stop (although I have had rides of over 1,000km this way) and most people who give lifts (particularly truck drivers) will ask for a set payment. With most trucks you won't have to pay before setting off – but there are stories of drivers stopping in the middle of nowhere and demanding higher than usual sums (from *gringos* and Peruvians alike) before going any further. Trucks can be flagged down anywhere but there is greater choice around markets, at police *controls* or petrol garages on town outskirts. You may end up sitting on top of 5 tons of potatoes or bananas since trucks travel the roads that buses won't touch. Hitching without paying can work but waits are often long.

Driving your **own car** or riding **motorbikes,** or **bicycles** is a good way of getting to places off the beaten track but involves a lot of responsibility. Spare parts, particularly tyres, will have to be carried as well as a tent, emergency water and food. The chance of theft increases dramatically – the vehicle, your gear and accessories are all vulnerable when parked. What few traffic signals there are are either completely ignored or used at drivers' 'discretion'. The pace is fast and roads everywhere are in a bad way: only the Pan American Highway, running down the coast, and a few short stretches inland are paved. **Mechanics** are generally good and always ingenious – they have to be due to a lack of spare parts! The 95 octane **petrol** is much cleaner than the 84.

Hiring a car is expensive by American and European standards. The major car-hire firms all have offices in the larger towns and there are one or two Peruvian companies. In the jungle towns it's usually possible to **hire motorbikes** or **mopeds** by the hour or by the day: a good way of getting to know a town or for shooting off into the jungle for a day.

Taxis can be found anywhere at any time in the towns. Always fix the price in advance since none have functioning meters. Any car can become a taxi simply by sticking a taxi sign up in the front window; a lot of people, especially in Lima, take advantage of this to supplement their income. In Lima the minimum fare is $0.75, but its much cheaper elsewhere.

By rail
Peru's **railways** are in themselves one of the country's major attractions – the highest standard gauge tracks anywhere in the world. At least one major train journey should certainly form part of your plans, and the rails felicitously connect many of the major tourist attractions. All are spectacular.

The **Central Railway** climbs and switchbacks its way up from Lima into the mountains as far as Huancayo and Huancavelica. The **Southern,** starting on the south coast at Arequipa, heads inland to Lake Titicaca before curving back towards Cuzco. And from Cuzco a line heads out down the magnificent Urubamba Valley, past Machu Picchu, and on into the fringes of the Amazon forest. The trains move slowly and there's ample time to contemplate what's going on outside. On the other hand, you do have to keep one eye on events inside where the carriages – often extremely crowded – are notorious for **petty thefts.** If you want to know something of this less pleasurable side of Peruvian rail travel – and intimate details of being sick on board – try Paul Theroux's *Old Patagonian Express.*

All the major legs (Lima-Huancayo,

Arequipa-Puno and Puno-Cuzco) seem to last about 12 hours, for which you pay around $6. Wherever possible **tickets** should be bought in advance: the day before or very early on the morning you plan to leave.

By air
Some places in the jungle can only sensibly be reached by air and Peru is so vast that the odd flight can save a lot of time. There are two major companies – **AeroPeru** and **Faucett** – which both fly regularly to all the main towns on the coast, in the mountains and in the jungle. Tickets can be bought from travel agents or the airline offices. The most popular routes, such as Lima-Cuzco, are on the expensive side for a tourist at around $80 (nationals and residents pay less) and usually need to be booked at least a few days in advance. Others, less busy, also tend to be less expensive. **Grupo Ocho,** the Peruvian airforce, carry passengers on some of their standard flights. Less regular or reliable, these compensate by being very much cheaper: you'll need to check availability at their offices at all the major airports.

On all flights it's important to **reconfirm** your booking the day before departure. They are often cancelled, delayed or even leave earlier than scheduled – especially in the jungle where the weather can be a problem. If a passenger hasn't shown up within 20 minutes of the flight then the company can give the seat to someone on the waiting list; so it's as well to be on time whether you're booked or merely hopeful. The luggage allowance is 16 kilos not including hand-luggage.

There are also **small planes** (6 and 10 seaters) serving the jungle and certain parts of the coast. *SASA* and *Aguila* operate scheduled services between jungle towns at quite reasonable rates. But for an *expresso* service (which will take you to any landing strip whenever you want) the price is over $200 per hour and all calculations include the return journey, even though you may just want to be dropped off somewhere.

By river and lake
There are no coastal boat services in Peru, but in many areas – around Lake Titicaca and especially in the jungle – water is the obvious means of getting around.

In the jungle motorised canoes come in two basic forms: those with a large outboard motor and those with a Briggs and Stratton *peque-peque* engine. The outboard is faster and more manoeuverable, but it costs a lot more to run. Occasionally you can hitch a ride in one of these canoes for nothing, but this may involve waiting around for days or even weeks and, in the end, most people expect some form of payment. More practical is to **hire a canoe** along with its guide/driver for a few days. This means searching around in the port and, from around $35 per day for a *peque-peque* canoe, will invariably work out cheaper than an organised tour, as well as giving you the choice of guide and companions. The more people in the boat, the cheaper it will be individually.

If you're heading downstream it's always possible in the last resort to buy, borrow, or even make, a **balsa raft.** Most of the indigenous population still travel this way so it's sometimes possible to hitch a lift, or to buy one of their rafts. Riding with someone who's going your way is probably better since rafting can be dangerous if you don't know the river well. For more details see Chapter 7.

From Puno on **Lake Titicaca** you can get across to Bolivia by ship or hydrofoil. There are also smaller boats which take visitors to the various islands – floating and real. These aren't expensive and a price can usually be negotiated down at the docks.

On foot

Even if you've no intention of doing any serious hiking, there's a good deal of walking involved in checking out many of the most enjoyable Peruvian attractions. Climbing from Cuzco up to the fortress of Sacsayhuaman, for example, or wandering around at Machu Picchu, involve rather more than a Sunday afternoon stroll. Bearing in mind the rugged terrain throughout Peru, the absolute minimum footwear if you hope to do anything more energetic than these is a strong pair of baseball boots. Better still, a proper pair of walking boots which support the ankle.

Trekking – whether in the desert, the mountains or the jungle – can be an enormously rewarding experience, but you should go properly equipped and bear in mind a few of the **potential hazards.** Never stray too far without

food, something warm and something waterproof. The weather is renowned for its dramatic changeability, especially in **the mountains,** where there is always the additional danger of *soroche* (altitude sickness – see p. 7). In **the jungle** the biggest danger is getting lost. If this happens, the best thing to do is follow a water course down to the main stream, and stick to this until you reach a settlement or get picked up by a passing canoe. If you get caught out in the forest at night, build a leafy shelter and make a fire or try sleeping in a tree.

In the mountains it's often a good idea to rent a **pack animal** to carry your gear. *Llamas* only carry about 25 kilos and move slowly; a *burro* (donkey) carries around 80 kilos, but **a mule** will shift 150 with relative ease. Mules can be hired from upwards of $3 a day, and they normally come with an *arriero,* a muleteer who'll double as a guide. It is also possible to hire mules or horses for **riding** but this costs a little more. With a guide and beast of burden it's quite simple to reach even the most remote valleys, ruins and mountain passes, travelling in much the same way as Pizarro and his men over 400 years ago.

With an organised tour

There are far too many **travel agents** and **tour operators** in Peru – so much so that their reps are forced to hunt out customers on trains and in the streets. Everything on offer seems expensive when you consider the ease with which you could do it yourself. Nevertheless, organised excursions can be a quick and painless way to see some of the more popular sites, while a prearranged trek can take much of the worry out of camping preparations. Some are positively adventurous – they include:

Explorandes (one of the best)
— Bolognesi 159, Miraflores, Lima (tel. 469889)
— Calle Procuradores 372, Cuzco (tel. 226671)
Mayoc Expediciones (river running and treks)
— Procuradores 354, Cuzco (postal:- Apartado 596, Cuzco)
Peruvian Andean Treks (treks, guides and outfitters)
— Av. Pardo 575, Piso 2, Cuzco (tel. 225701)
Percy Tapia, Casilla 3074, Lima 100

Yachay (scientific and cultural treks)
 – San Martin 453, Barranco, Lima
(tel. 670810)

Hirca (educational/adventure travel)
 – Miguel Dasso 126, Of.203, San
Isidro, Lima (tel. 224487)

SLEEPING

Peruvian **hotels** may describe themselves as *Hostals, Residencials, Paradors* or just plain *Hotels* – distinctions which for the most part are fairly meaningless. Nor is there any standard or widely used rating system. The only way to tell a hotel is to walk in and ask to take a look at it – they rarely mind this, and you soon get used to spotting places with promise.

The **cheaper hotels** are generally old – sometimes beautiful in this, converted from colonial mansions with rooms grouped round a patio – and tend to be within a few blocks of a town's central plaza, general market or bus or train station. In the **cheapest,** which can be fairly basic with collective rooms and a communal bathroom, you can usually find a bed for between $2–4, occasionally even less. Go **slightly upmarket,** with good, clean, single or double rooms with bath, and you'll be paying around $4–12 per person. A little **haggling** rarely goes amiss, and if you find one room too pricey, another, perhaps identical, can often be found for less. The phrase for 'Have you a cheaper room?' is *Tiene un cuarto mas barato?*. Savings can invariably be made, too, by sharing rooms – many have two, three, even four or five beds. A double-bedded room (*casa con matrimonial*) is invariably cheaper than one with two beds (*con dos camas*).

One additional category of hotel, which you'll find in all larger Peruvian resorts, and some surprisingly offbeat ones, is a **State hotel,** or *Hotel de Turistas*, often with a swimming pool and invariably among the flashiest places in town. Out of season some of these can be relatively inexpensive (from around $6), and if you like the look of a place it's often worth asking. Consistently good bets – along with hotels in all the cheaper categories – are detailed in the main text of the guide.

Camping is possible almost anywhere in Peru. With a population of less than 18 million and a land area ten times the size of England it's not difficult to find space for a tent. It is usually alright to camp on the outskirts of any urban area by asking permission and advice from the nearest farm or house. Apart from a few restricted areas, Peru's enormous sandy coastline is any man's land – the real problem not being so much where to camp as how to get there; some of the most stunning areas are very remote. The same can fundamentally be said of both the mountains and the jungle – camp anywhere with local permission, if there are any locals. On the coast it's normally warm and dry enough to sleep out. It is always cold enough for a tent in the mountains. In the jungle it's really too hot for a tent but very handy when it rains. Camping is free since there are only one or two organised camp sites in the whole country; it is probably also the most satisfactory way of seeing Peru. With a tent it is possible to go anywhere without worrying if you'll make it to a *hostal*; and some of Peru's most fantastic places are quite off the beaten track.

In recent years there have been reports of tourists being attacked for money and goods while camping in fairly **remote areas.** Personally I've never come across any hostility, nor have I met anyone who has suffered an attack while camping – but it does happen. There are three basic precautions that one can take; firstly, always let someone know where you intend to go camping; secondly, try to go with a friend or two; and, thirdly, show respect and communicate with any locals you may meet or be camping near.

FOOD AND DRINK

As with almost every activity, the style and pattern of eating and drinking varies considerably between the three regions of Peru. Depending on the very different ingredients available locally, food in each area is essentially a *mestizo* creation, combining indigenous Indian cooking with 400 years of European – mostly Spanish – influence. In the past 20 years, with the wave of North American interests in the country, fast food has become commonplace: you'll find *Kentucky Fried Chicken* in Lima and hamburgers are more readily available than guinea-pig in any large town. Nevertheless, a wealth of good traditional food remains.

Along **the coast,** not surprisingly, **seafood** is the speciality. The Humboldt Current keeps the Peruvian ocean extremely rich in plankton and other microscopic life-forms. Plankton attracts fish which attract fishermen.

Ceviche is the ultimate sea dish – depending on what you choose (fish, prawns, scallops, squid, or a mixture) it will be marinated in lime juice and chili peppers, then served 'raw' with corn and sweet potato and onions. Raw seafood with a bit of chili has probably been a Peruvian snack for over 2,000 years. Ceviche, fried fish and fish soups can be found in most restaurants on the coast for around $1. There are also good salads such as *huevos a la rusa* (egg mayonnaise), *palta rellena* (stuffed avocado), or straight tomato. *Papas a la Huancaina* are great too, a cold starter of potatoes covered in a spicy light cheese sauce.

Even in the villages you'll find cafes and restaurants which double up as bars. These stay open all day and serve anything from a coffee with bread to steak and chips or lobster.

Mountain food is more basic – a staple of potatoes and rice with the meat stretched as far as it will go. *Lomo saltado,* or diced 'prime' cut sautéed with onions and peppers, rice and a few chips, is served anywhere at any time. Trout is also widely available. A delicious snack from street vendors and in cafes is *papa rellena,* a potato stuffed with vegetables and then fried. Cheese, ham and egg sandwiches are also available in most places. *Chicha* is a maize beer drunk throughout the *Sierra* region and on the coast in rural areas. It is very cheap and has a pleasant tangy taste.

In the **jungle** food takes on new proportions. Bananas and plantains figure highly, along with *yuca* (a manioc rather like a yam), rice and plenty of fish. There is meat as well, mostly chicken supplemented occasionally by game –

deer, wild pig or monkey. Every settlement big enough to get on the map has its bar or cafe, but in remote areas it's more a matter of eating what's on offer and drinking coffee or bottled drinks if you don't fancy the *masato* (manioc beer) they make themselves.

Most larger towns will offer a fair choice of **restaurants** and a varied menu. Among them *chifa* (**Chinese**) places have always featured, and nowadays there are a fair number of **vegetarian** restaurants too. Almost all open early and close late. Usually they will offer a *cena,* or **set menu,** from morning through to lunchtime and another in the evening. Ranging in price from $0.50 to $2, these most commonly comprise three courses: soup, a main dish and a cup of tea or coffee to follow. Every town, too, seems now to have at least one restaurant which specialises in *pollos a la brasa* – spit-roasted chickens. **Tipping** is normal – rarely more than about 20 US cents – but in no way obligatory. In the fancier places you may have to pay a **cover charge** – up to $2 if there's some kind of entertainment on offer, around 50 cents in the flashier restaurants in major town centres.

For less formal eating there's a good variety of traditional **fast foods and snacks** such as *salchipapas* (chips with sliced sausage covered in various sauces), *anticuchos* (a shish-kebab made from marinated lamb or beef heart), and *empanadas* (meat-or cheese-filled pasties). These are all sold on street corners until late at night. The most popular **sweets** in Peru are made from either *manjar blanco* (sweetened condensed milk) or fresh fruits.

In general, the **market** is always a good place to head for – you can buy food ready to eat on the spot or to take away and prepare, and the range and prices will be better than in any shop. Most food prices are fixed, but the vendor may throw in an orange, a garlic or some coriander leaves for good measure. Markets are the best places to stock up for a trek, for a picnic, or if you just want to live cheaply. Smoked meat, which can be sliced up and used like salami, is normally a good buy.

Beers, wines and **spirits** are served in almost every bar, cafe or restaurant at any time; but there is a deposit on taking beer bottles out (canned beer

Basics

Arroz	Rice	– pasado	– boiled
Avena	Oats (porridge)	– revuelto	– scrambled
Galletas	Biscuits	Mermelada	Jam
Harina	Flour	Miel	Honey
Huevos	Eggs	Mostaza	Mustard
– duro	– hard boiled	Pan (integral)	Bread (brown)
– frito	– fried	Queso	Cheese

Soups (sopas) and starters

Caldo	Broth	Palta	Avocado
Caldo de gallina	Chicken broth	Palta rellena	Stuffed avocado
Causa	Mashed potatoes and shrimp	Papa rellena	Stuffed fried potato
		Parihuela	Mixed fish soup
Conchas a la parmesana	Scallops with parmesana	Sopa a la criolla	Noodles, veg and meat
Huevos a la rusa	Egg mayonnaise		

Seafoods (mariscos) and fish (pescado)

Calamares	Squid	Jalea	Large fish with onion sauce
Camarones	Shrimp		
Cangrejo	Crab	Langosta	Lobster
Ceviche	Marinated seafood	Langostino	Cray fish
Chaufa de mariscos cojinova	Chinese rice	Lenguado	Sole
		Paiche	Large jungle river fish
Corvina	Sea bass		
Erizo	Sea urchin	Tollo	Small shark
		Zungarro	Large jungle fish
		– a lo macho	– in spicy shellfish sauce

Meats (carne)

Adobado	Meat/fish in red sauce	Jamon (Ingles/Pais)	Ham (English/national)
Aji de gallina	Chicken in chili sauce	Lechon	Pork
		Lomo asado	Roast Beef
Anticuchos	Skewered kebabs	Lomo saltado	Sautéed Beef
Biftek (bistek)	Steak	Pachamanca	Meat and veg, roasted over open fire
Cabrito	Goat		
Carne a lo pobre	Steak, chips, egg and banana	Parillada	Grilled meat
Carne de res	Beef	Pato	Duck
Carpulcra	Pork, chicken and potatoes	Pavo	Turkey
		Pollo (a la brasa)	Chicken (spit-roasted)
Chicharrones	Deep fried portions		
Conejo	Rabbit	Tocina	Bacon
Cordero	Lamb	Venado	Venison
Cuy	Guinea-pig (traditional dish)	– picante de..	– spicy dish of..
Higado	Liver		

Vegetables (legumbres)

Aji	Chili	Lechuga	Lettuce
Camote	Sweet potato	Papas	Potatoes
Cebolla	Onion	– a la Huancaina	– in spicy cheese sauce
Choclo	Corn on the cob		
Fideos	Noodles	– rellena	– stuffed and fried
Frijoles	Beans	Tallarines	Spaghetti noodles

Hongos	Mushrooms	*Tomates*	Tomatoes
		Yuca	Manioc (like a yam)

Sweets (*dulces*)

Barquillo	Ice cream cone	*Manjar blanco*	Sweetened condensed milk
Flan	Flan		
Helado	Ice cream	*Mazamorra morada*	Fruit/maize jelly
Keke	Cake	*Panqueques*	Pancakes
		Picarones	Doughnuts with syrup

Snacks (*bocadillos*)

Castanas	Brazil nuts	*Sandwich de butifara*	Ham and onion sandwich
Chifles	Fried crisps of bananas or sweet potatoes	*Sandwich de lechon*	Pork and salad sandwich
Empanada	Meat or cheese pasty	*Tamales*	Stuffed maize-cakes
Hamburguesa	Hamburger	*Tortilla*	Omelette cum pancake
Salchipapas	Chips, sausage and sauces	*Tostados*	Toast

Fruit juices (*jugos*)

Especial	Fruit, milk and sometimes beer	*Papaya*	Papaya
		Pina	Pineapple
Fresa	Strawberry	*Platano*	Banana
Higo	Fig	*Surtido*	Mixed
Manzana	Apple	*Toronja*	Grapefruit
Melon	Melon	*Zanahoria*	Carrot
Naranja	Orange		

Drinks (*bebidas*)

Agua	Water	*Limonada*	Real lemonade
Agua Mineral	Mineral water	*Masato*	Fermented manioc beer
Algarrobina	Algarroba-fruit drink	*Pisco*	White grape brandy
Cafe	Coffee		
Cerveza	Beer	*Ponche*	Punch
Chicha de jora	Fermented maize beer	*Ron*	Rum
		Te	Tea
Chicha morada	Soft maize-drink	*– con leche*	– with milk
Chilcano de pisco	Pisco with lemonade	*– de anis*	aniseed tea
		– de limon	Lemon tea
Chop	Draught beer	*– hierba luisa*	lemon grass tea
Cuba libre	Rum and coke	*– manzanilla*	camomile tea
Gaseosa	Soft fizzy drink		
Leche	Milk		

was one of the worst inventions to hit Peru this century – some of the finest beaches are littered with empty cans). **Peruvian beer** – except for *cerveza malta* (black malt beer) – is mostly bottled lager, and extremely good. *Cuzqueña* (from Cuzco) is one of the best, but not universally available; you won't find it on the coast in Trujillo, where they drink *Trujillana*. **Soft drinks** range from mineral water through the ubiquitous *Coca Cola* and *Fanta* to home-produced novelties like *Inca Cola* (gold-coloured with a taste like dandelion and burdock) and *Cola Inglesa* (red and extremely sweet). Fruit juices (*jugos*), most commonly payaya or orange, are prepared fresh in most places, and you can get coffee and a wide variety of herb and leaf teas almost anywhere.

Peru has been producing **wine** for over 400 years, but with one or two exceptions it is not all that good. Among the better ones are *Vista Alegre* (tipo familiar) – not entirely reliable but only around $1 a bottle – and most notably *Tacama Gran Vino Blanco Reserva Especial* for about $3 a bottle. Good Argentinian and Chilean wines run from about $5.

As for **spirits,** Peru's sole claim to fame is *Pisco.* It's a white grape brandy with a unique, powerful and very palatable flavour – the closest equivalent elsewhere is probably *tequila.* Almost anything else is available as an import – whisky is cheaper in Lima than in London – but beware of the really cheap imitations which can remove the roof of your mouth with ease.

COMMUNICATIONS – POST, PHONES AND MEDIA

Peruvian postal services are reasonably efficient. Letters from the US or Europe generally take around two weeks – occasionally less – and with a little patience you can make international phonecalls from just about any town in the country.

You can have mail sent to you **poste restante** at any principal post office (*Correo Central*) and on the whole the system works quite smoothly. Have letters addressed:

SURNAME (IN CAPITALS), Lista de Correos, Correo Central, CITY. To pick up mail you'll need to take your passport along, and you may need to urge that the files for the initials of all your names (including Ms, Mr, etc.) are checked. Rather quirkily, letters are sometimes filed separately by sex, too – in which case it's worth checking both piles. An alternative to the official *lista* is to use the **American Express** mail collection service, their two main offices in Peru are:

LIMA: Belen 1040.
CUZCO: Av. El Sol.

Officially, Amex charge for collection unless you have one of their cards or use their cheques – though I've never known then to do so.

Sending letters airmail to the US or Europe should take between ten to fourteen days. **Parcels,** however, are a different matter. They are very vulnerable to being opened en route – in either direction – and expensive souvenirs can't be sure of going beyond the building where you post them. Likewise, Peruvian postal workers are always happy to 'check' incoming parcels which contain cassettes or interesting foods. Don't assume (or even hope) otherwise.

All towns have a **telephone exchange** (*Telefonos*), which is usually the most productive place to try putting through an **international call.** It's impossible to estimate how long this will take – 3 minutes is quite common, 3 hours not unknown. All international calls are at present made through the international operator – dial 08. If you want to make a collect (reverse charge) call you'll need a deposit – $1 at the Lima exchange but often $25 or so elsewhere. Calls within Peru are quite straightforward: just go to any local phone office (or in Lima to a phonebox on the streets).

As for **news services,** there is an English language newspaper, the weekly **Lima Times,** which gives summaries of national and world events – slanted towards how it affects industry, culture and English speaking expatriates in South America. Published every Friday, it's widely available throughout Lima, and sporadically in Cuzco. The *Times* is useful for listings of events, and for its ads. For more serious, in-depth coverage they also produce an economic and political review called the *Andean Report* – recommended if you've any interest in Peruvian (and Andean) developments.

If you can read Spanish – which is a lot easier than speaking it – you'll have access to the **Peruvian press,** too. The two most established (and establishment) papers are *El Commercio* and *La Prensa.* Commercio's 'Section C' has the most comprehensive cultural listings of any paper – good for just about everything going. Among the other nationals are *El Expresso,* which devotes vast amounts of space to anti-Communist propaganda; *La Republica,* middle of the road and sensationalist; *El Observador,* slightly left of centre; and *El Diario,* probably the most intelligent and analytical for both national and international coverage, again left of centre. Best of the magazines is the liberal *Caretas,* which (in 1985) offers critical support to Belaunde. And finally, if you're really intrigued by the Peruvian political scene, there's a satirical weekly called *Monos y Monedas* ('Monkeys and Moneys').

Although Peru has a population of some 18 million the actual readership of all these papers is very small. Illiteracy is still widespread and, travelling around, you'll notice many Peruvians prefer to read comic books. And why not? Inevitably, too, they watch a lot of **television** – most addictively, football and soap operas, though TV is also a main source of news. Most programmes shown come from Mexico, Brazil and the US, with occasional (and often eccentric, viz *Upstairs Downstairs*) selections from Britain. There are five main channels – all crammed with adverts – and also a cable company, *Channel 27,* which most

people pick up quite happily just by tuning in their sets. *Channel 5* often shows British and German soccer at weekends, a prestigious time for Brits to be watching.

If you've a **radio** you can pick up the **BBC World Service** at most hours of the day – frequencies shift around on the 19m, 25m and 49m short wave bands. For a schedule contact the British Council in Lima. Alternatively, turn the dials and you'll be confronted by a quite incredible mass of **Peruvian stations,** nearly all of them music and advert based. *Radio Miraflores* (96FM) is one of the best, playing mainly disco and new US/British rock, though also with a good jazz programme on Sunday evenings and an excellent news summary every day from 7 to 9am. *Radio Cien* (100FM) has the occasional programme in English – there's one on Sunday mornings. Most Andean music comes over on AM tuning.

ANCIENT SITES, MUSEUMS, CHURCHES AND NATIONAL PARKS

Very few of Peru's **ancient sites** are fenced off, though you normally pay a small admission fee to the local guardian – who may then walk round with you, pointing out aspects you'd otherwise miss. Only Machu Picchu, the big tourist attraction of Inca Peru, charges more than a couple of dollars – and this is one site where you may find it worth flashing a student card (which generally gets half price reduction on state museum/site admissions). **Opening hours** generally coincide with daylight – from around 7am to 5 or 6pm daily – for the more important ruins. Smaller sites are nearly always accessible.

Of the great many **museums** in Peru, some belong to the State, others to institutions and a few to individuals. Most charge a small admission fee and stay open from 9 to 12 in the mornings and from 3 to 6 on weekday afternoons. The highlight for most travellers – and a good place to get to know before setting out to the sites – is the *Museum of Archaeology and Anthropology* in Lima, with its fabulous collections of ancient ceramics. But throughout the country there are smaller, equally fascinating displays. The *Larco Herrera Museo* (again in Lima) has prob-

ably the world's finest exhibition of erotic art, mainly from pre-Inca cultures; the *Ica Regional Museum* is superb on the pre-Columbian coastal cultures, with spectacular Paracas textiles, bizarre trophy heads and well-preserved mummies; while in Cuzco and Arequipa you'll find some excellent colonial art. **Churches** – again at their best in Arequipa and around Cuzco – open in the mornings for mass, after which the smaller ones close. The more interesting for tourists, however, stay open through the day, or at least re-open from, say, 3–6pm. Very occasionally there's an admission charge to churches, and more regularly to monasteries (*monasterios*). Try to be aware of the strength of religious belief in Peru, particularly in the Andes, where churches have a rather heavy, sad atmosphere. You can enter and, usually, look around in all churches, but in the Andes especially refrain from taking photographs. People don't like it, which is easy enough to understand.

To visit **National Parks,** or nature reserves, there's usually a small charge. Sometimes, as at the *Manu National Park* (near Cuzco), this is a daily rate; at others, like the *Paracas Reserve* on the coast, you pay a fixed sum to enter. If the park is in a particularly remote area, permission may also be needed – either from the *National Institute of Culture* or the *Ministry of Agriculture, Flora and Fauna* (for details check with the South American Explorers' Club in Lima or the local tourist office). Keep in mind that the parks and reserves are enormous zones, within which there is hardly any attempt to control or organise nature. Beginning in 1972, the *National System for Conservation Units* (*SNCU*) has organised and developed a number of parks, reserves and sanctuaries with the idea of combining conservation, research and, in some cases, such as the Inca Trail, recreational tourism. The term 'park' probably conveys the wrong impression about these huge, virtually untouched areas.

FIESTAS AND PUBLIC HOLIDAYS

Public holidays, Carnival (February) and **local fiestas** are all big events in Peru – celebrated with an openness and intensity that make them great times to travel, despite the wholesale closure of banks, post offices, tourist offices and museums.

The main **national fiestas** take place over **Easter, Christmas** and during the month of **October,** in that order of importance. **Cuzco** is the great place to be for both Catholic celebrations, and also for the 'Inca' festivals like *Inti Raymi* during June. In October **Lima,** and especially its suburb of La Victoria, takes centre stage, with processions dedicated to *Our Lord of Miracles* – striking and impressive collective memories of the ever present earthquake danger, in atonement for which many women dress only in purple for the whole month. Carnival time is lively almost everywhere in the country, with fiestas held every Sunday – a wholesale licence to throw water at everyone and generally go crazy.

National festival days/public holidays include:

January 1   *New Year's Day,* public holiday.
February   *Carnival.*
March/April *Holy Week.* Main processions on *Good Friday* and the night of *Easter Saturday/Easter morning.* Easter Saturday is a public holiday.
May 1   *May day* (May 1, public holiday), followed by the *Fiesta de la Cruz* (May 2–3).
June 24–30 *Inti Raymi* (Cuzco week).
29   *St Peter's Day,* fisherman's fiesta on coast.

July 28–29 *National Independence Day* (military and school processions), public holiday.
August 30   *St Rosa of Lima,* public holiday.
September 24 *Virgin of Mercy,* Armed Forces patron.
October 9   Autumn public holiday.
18–28   *Lord of Miracles* festival (processions in Lima). Bullfights and celebrations throughout the month in Lima.
November 1 *All Saints Day,* public holiday.
12–28   *Pacific Fair* in Lima (bi-annually, 1986, 1988 etc.).
December 8 *Immaculate Conception,* public holiday.
25 *Christmas Day,* public holiday.

In addition to these – and often locally far more important – nearly every community has its own saint or patron figure to worship at town or **village fiestas.** Processions, music, dancing in costumes, eating and drinking form a natural part of these parties. In some cases the villagers will enact symbolic dramas with Indians dressed up as Spanish colonists wearing hideous blue-eyed masks with long hairy beards. The symbolism is even clearer in one area where they celebrate the *Yawar Fiesta.* This involves such feats as capturing a wild condor (representing the Andean Indians) and tying it to the back of a village bull (symbol for the Spanish conquerors who brought bulls to Peru). The climax is the inevitable battle – the condor usually killing the bull.

Walking up in the hills around towns like Huaraz and Cuzco it's relatively common to stumble into a village which is enjoying a fiesta, and with the explosion of human energy and noise, the bright colours and the uneasy mixture of pagan and Catholic symbolism, this may prove a highlight of your travels. Personally, though, I've always thought it a liberty to publicise *fiesta* dates for fairly remote communities – they may after all not want to be invaded by gringos waving cameras and expecting to be feasted for free. Those dates that I have given in the text are all established events, already to some extent on the Peruvian tourist map.

It is probably worth mentioning here, too, that in many coastal and mountain *haciendas* (estates) **bullfights** are often held at fiesta times. So too, in less organised fashion, at many of the country's villages – though here often without a bullring, the bull being left to run through the village until it's eventually caught and mutilated by one of the men. This is not just a sad sight – it can be dangerous for you, as an unsuspecting gringo, if you happen to wander into an apparently evacuated village! The Lima bullfights in October, in contrast, are a very serious business; even Hemingway was impressed.

MUSIC AND FILM

It's not possible to talk of a Peruvian national **music** – or culture – since the country has such a multitude of different forms, each closely bound up in ties of region, history, ethnicity, and often class. In Lima, however, you can come upon most forms, and travelling about the country you're bound to get addicted to at least one.

The music people most commonly associate with Peru is **Andean folk** – lively tunes played on instruments such as cane flutes, pan-pipes, simple drums and the *churrango* (a kind of mandolin, with the sound box made from an armadillo's shell). The music is an effective blend of sad songs with plucky singing and whooping; the dances, usually communal, are highly stylised. There are a large number of Andean folkloric groups and as a tourist this is the sort of music that you will come across most often – either in restaurants, folklore clubs (peñas) or, the real McCoy, at village festivals.

Peñas – which range from flashy dining clubs to spit-and-sawdust taverns – are also the places to hear **criolla,** or creole, music. Played on Spanish guitars and percussive *cajones*, this is a thoroughly hybrid, romantic form – based around love ballads, but combining everything from African coastal rhythms to Viennese waltzes. There is also a certain amount of regional variation and each dance comes from a specific area – the *Marinera*, for instance, is traditionally from the North coast.

Chicha music, which developed in Colombia, is faster – the songs full of lyrical cheek, with energetic percussion and very twangy electric guitar backing. Although you hear chicha quite a lot in the mountains it's really based in the jungle and the best way to sample it is at a live Saturday night fiesta in one of the larger jungle settlements. Similar in tempo, and a unifying factor throughout Latin America, is **Salsa** – though with international stars (most of whom now live in New York or Miami), this is considerably more sophisticated. Like criolla, it's best heard in the Lima clubs, many of which, known as *salsadromos,* devote themselves exclusively to the music.

Less expected generally – but an equally concrete cultural force on the Peruvian coast – is **musica negra,** black music with roots in the old slave communities, shipped into the plantations from the C16–19 by the Spanish. Sometimes linked with social protest, musica negra portrays the daily life of the communities. There are a large number of black music bands and several dance groups – led by a troup of 30 calling themselves *Peru Negro* who have performed in Panama, Cuba, Mexico and Spain – and an annual **Festival of Black Music and Dance** has just begun in Lima. One of the liveliest and most popular dances is the *Alcatraz* in which successive pairs of dancers (one male and one female) try to set light to paper napkins hanging from behind their waists as they twist and turn. It's quite normal for members of the audience to get roped into this number – so be warned! There are also black songs and dances based on the jingles sung by *pregoneros* (negro street vendors) who have wandered Lima's streets calling out their wares for well over 100 years: *Tamales! Tamales! Tamales! Pan dulce! Pan dulce!* Musica negra is generally performed in peñas on the coast, and occasionally in concert. Keep your eyes open for posters advertising either *Peru Negro* or the *National Folk Ballet* (which specialises in both black and Andean folk dance).

In more recent years there has been some interest on the jazz and rock front. Little pure **jazz** reaches Peru but once in a while one of the foreign cultural institutions invites an artist to play in Lima. There is an afro-jazz group called *Los Chonducos* which plays quite regularly and there are a few small groups of avant-garde jazz (notably Enrique Luna's band). Most are formed by wealthy young intellectuals since the market is too small to make a living. There are also one or two **protest ballad** singer-songwriters who follow in the path of the Cuban Pablo Milanes and the Chilean Victor Jara. **Rock,** as a form of musical expression, bears almost no relation to Peruvian culture except as a modern influence on the young rich (those with cosmopolitan contacts) and as a popular influence on the radio stations (mostly stuff like the Beatles and Queen). In the first few years of the 1980s three Peruvian 'new wave' groups have become quite well known in Lima: *Fragil, Toilet Paper* and *Dr No.* They're not bad. For concerts check newspapers – particularly *El Commercio* – and keep an eye out in Lima for bill stickers, particularly in the streets of Miraflores.

Cinemas in Peru are extremely cheap. Most films are shown in the original language (usually English or Italian) with Spanish subtitles. South America is seen by film distributors as part of the American market, so new films from the USA arrive quickly to Lima – often long before they get to Europe. Peru itself really started making full-length films only five or six years ago when various producers and directors got together and, with the help of distributors, managed to propose a new cinematic law. This required assistance in the form of obligatory distribution, i.e. all full-length or short films made by Peruvians or with Peruvian money should be guaranteed showing for 18 months in Peruvian cinemas after passing the censorship committee. Most films made in Peru are only 15 or 20 minutes long and are shown before the full-length feature. The censorship committee's taste has also meant that a lot of them are thematically (and ideologically) unsound as well as often pretty ropey technically. There are, however, two very promising young directors, Francisco Lombardi and Chicho Duran, who have both made interesting feature films dealing with important sociological and political issues. These, if you get the chance to see them, are *Maruja en el Infierno* (Lombardi) and *Ojos de Pero* (Duran). In recent years a few cine clubs have sprung up around Lima, giving the public a chance to become a more critical audience and to see less commercially orientated films.

POLICE AND THIEVES

Most contact with the **police** will be at frontiers and controls. Depending on your personal appearance and the prevailing political climate the police at these posts (*Guardia Civil* and *Policia de Investigaciones*) may want to search your luggage; although this seldom happens it can be very thorough. Occasionally, too, tourists are required to get off buses and register documents at the police controls which regulate the traffic of goods and people from one *Departmento* of Peru to another; these are usually situated on the outskirts of large towns on the main arterial routes but you sometimes come across a control in the middle of nowhere. Always stop, and always be scrupulously polite – even if it seems that they're trying to make things difficult for you. In general the police tend not to bother travellers but there are certain sore points. The possession of (let alone trafficking in) either soft or hard **drugs** (basically grass or cocaine) is considered an extremely serious offence in Peru – usually leading to at least a ten-year sentence. There are many gringos languishing in Peruvian jails – some of whom have been waiting two years for a trial; if you have time to visit one of them you can get details from your respective embassy. There is no bail on serious charges. Apart from drugs, the police have a tendency to follow the media in suspecting gringos of being **political subversives** and even gun-runners or terrorists; it's a little unwise to carry Maoist or radical literature. If you find yourself in a tight spot, don't make a statement before seeing someone from your embassy, or without the services of a reliable translator. It's not unusual to be given the opportunity to pay a **bribe** to the police (or any other official for that matter) even if you've done absolutely nothing wrong. You'll have to weigh up this situation as it arises – but remember bribery is seen as an age-old custom rather than a dirty habit in South America and can work to the advantage of both parties, however annoying it might seem. It's also worth noting that all police carry either a revolver or a submachine gun and will shoot at anyone who runs.

The one big problem of travelling in Peru, however, is **thieves** – for which the country is beginning to gain perhaps the worst reputation in South America. On one particular train journey (Arequipa-Puno at night) an estimated 80 per cent of tourists are robbed. The usual places, however, are crowded markets, bus depots and railway stations, where *ladrones* working in pairs cut bags open with razor blades or just whip the whole thing from your shoulders. Objects left on restaurant floors in busy parts of town or in unlocked hotel rooms are also liable to take a walk. Peruvians and tourists alike have even had pierced earings pulled viciously out.

You'd need to spend the whole time completely watchful and paranoid even to be 90 per cent sure of not losing your gear, but a few simple **precautions** can make life a lot easier. The most important is to keep your ticket, passport, money and traveller's cheques on your person at all times (under your pillow while sleeping). Belt wallets are a good idea for traveller's cheques and tickets (as long as you don't leave them exposed or in a shoulder bag). Another holder for your passport and money can be hung either under a shirt around the neck, or from a waist belt under trousers or skirts. Some people go as far as lining their bags with chicken wire (called *maya* in Peru) to make them knife-proof, and wrapping wire around camera straps so that they lose their head rather than their camera! I've never encountered problems camping – even when my gear has been left all day in an unguarded tent – but, again, some people do lose stuff. The secret is probably to get on as good terms as possible with local people; if you become friendly with someone who allows you to camp nearby it's very unlikely that anyone else will touch your gear.

SEXUAL HARASSMENT

So many oppressive limitations are imposed on women's freedom to travel together or alone that any advice or warning seems merely to reinforce the situation. That said, *machismo* is well ingrained in the Peruvian mentality, particularly in the towns, and the *gringa* (female foreigner) is almost universally seen as liberated and therefore sexually available. On the whole this is more an annoying than a dangerous problem, with frequent whistling and hissing in the **cities,** sometimes comments or touching on buses etc. Mostly these are situations you'd deal with routinely at home – as *Limeno* women do here in the capital – but they can seem threatening without a clear understanding of Peruvian Spanish and slang. To avoid getting further in, provocation is best totally ignored.

In the more **remote,** predominantly Indian, **areas** there is less of an overt problem – though this is actually where most physical assaults take place. They are not common, however – you're probably safer hiking in the Andes than in most American or European cities. Two obvious, but enduring, pieces of advice are to travel with friends (being on your own is your main vulnerability), and if you're camping, to be quite open about it. Making yourself known to locals gives a kind of acceptance and insurance, and may even lead to the offer of a room – Peruvians, particularly those in rural areas, can be incredibly kind and hospitable.

OTHER THINGS

ADDRESSES in Peru are frequently written with just the street name and number (as: Pizarro 135). Officially, though, they're usually prefixed by *Calle* or *Jiron* (street), or *Avenida*. The first digit of any street number (or sometimes the first two digits) represents the block number within the street as a whole. Note too that many of the major streets in Lima have two names – a relic of the military governments of the 1970s.

ARTESÁNIA, traditional craft goods from most regions of Peru, can be found in markets and shops in Lima. Woollen and alpaca products, though, are usually cheaper and often better quality in the *sierra* – particularly in Juliaca and Puno; carved gourds are imported from around Huancayo, while the best places to buy ceramic replicas are Trujillo, Huaraz and Nazca. Oxfam's *Antisuyo* shop in Lima (see p. 53) is good for jungle crafts.

BARGAINING for artesania in markets and with taxi drivers (always before getting in) is generally expected. It's also sometimes possible to haggle over the price of hotel rooms if you're travelling in a group. Food and shop prices, however, tend to be strictly fixed.

CAMPING EQUIPMENT is difficult to find and relatively expensive. One or two places sell, rent or buy second-hand gear: the *South American Explorers' Club* in Lima; the *Hotel Barcelona* in Huaraz; and a couple of shops and tour/trek agencies can outfit you in Cuzco, near the Plaza de Armas. It's worth checking the notice boards in the popular gringo hotels and bars for gear that is no longer needed or for people looking for trekking companions. Camping gaz bottles are available from most of the above places and from some *ferreterias* (ironmongers) in the more important tourist resorts.

CONDOMS are available from street vendors and some *farmacias* (chemists). Rumour has it that these are another example of US rejects being sold to a less discriminating and less informed market.

CUSTOMS regulations stipulate that no items of archaeological or historical value/interest may be removed from the country.

ELECTRIC CURRENT AC 200 v./60 cycles is the standard except in Arequipa where it is AC 200 v./50 cycles.

EXTRAS you may want to bring include: **film** (expensive in Peru); a **padlock** (additional security in hotel rooms); **glucose tablets** (useful against the milder effects of altitude sickness); **gifts** for kids and adults, particularly if you're hiking (small coins, stamps, pens, pencils, photos, postcards from home are often appreciated). See also HEALTH (pp. 7–8).

FEMINIST MOVEMENT Still relatively new to Peru – and inevitably urban. However, there are two major feminist organisations: *Flora Tristan* (Av. Arenales 601, Lima) and the less radical *Peru Mujer*. The former is allied to the United Left and its basic tenet is 'first socialism, then the feminist revolution'. There is one feminist magazine, *Mujeres y Sociedad* (Women and Society), produced three or four times a year. For help, literature or advice try *Flora Tristan*, the *Libreria de la Mujer* bookshop (near the start of Av. Arenales, Lima), or the *Women's Centre* which is run by nuns near the centre of Lima (in Quilca just half a block from Av. Wilson).

GAY LIFE is still pretty much underground but in recent years Lima has seen a liberating advance (in a still very *macho* society); Transvestites can now walk the streets in relative freedom from abuse and there are one or two gay clubs. Beyond Lima there is no organised gay life.

INSECTS are more of an irritation than a serious problem but on the coast, in the jungle and to a lesser extent in the mountains, the **common fly** is a pest. Although it can carry typhoid, there is little one can do; you might spend mealtimes successfully fighting flies from your plate but even in expensive restaurants it's difficult to regulate hygiene in the kitchens. A more obvious problem is the **mosquito.** In some parts of the lowland jungle this carries malaria. Repellents are of limited value – it's better to cover your arms, legs and feet with a good layer of clothing. Mosquitoes only tend to emerge after dark. The daytime holds worse biting insects in the jungle regions, among them the **Manta Blanca** (or white blanket), so called because in bad spots they swarm as a blanket of tiny flying insects. They don't hurt while biting but itch like crazy for a few days. Antihistamine tablets relieve the sting or itchiness of most insect bites. Try not to scratch them and if it gets unbearable ask the locals or go to the nearest *farmacia* for advice.

INSULTS are sometimes hurled at gringos by Peruvians who begrudge the apparent relative wealth and freedom of tourists. Remember, however, that the terms 'gringo' or 'mister' are not generally meant in an offensive way in Peru.

LAUNDRY can be done in the communal washrooms of most basic hotels; failing this the price of labour is so cheap that it's no real expense to get your clothes washed by the hotel or in a *lavandaria* (laundry). Things tend to disappear from public washing lines so be careful where you leave clothes drying.

NATURAL DISASTERS Peru has more than its fair share of avalanches, landslides and earthquakes – and there's not a lot you can do about any of them. If you're naturally wise or cautious you might want to register on arrival with your embassy – they like this, and it does help them in the event of a major quake (or an escalation of the current terrorist activity). Landslides – *huaycos* – devastate the roads and railways every rainy season, though alternative routes are usually found surprisingly quickly.

PHOTOGRAPHY The light in Peru is very bright with a strong contrast between shade and sun. This can produce a nice effect and generally speaking it's easy to take good pictures. One of the more complex problems is how to take photos of people without upsetting them! You should always talk to a prospective subject first, and ask if s/he minds you taking a quick snap (*una fotito*); most people react favourably to this approach even if all the communication is in sign language. Film is expensive to buy, so take as much as you think you'll need with you. I wouldn't recommend getting films developed

until you get home – they tend to get badly scratched even in the Lima Kodac laboratory.

PUNCTUALITY is unimportant in Peru except where public transport is concerned. The bus, train or aeroplane won't wait a minute. People, however, almost expect friends to be an hour or more late for an appointment (don't arrange to meet a Peruvian on the street – make it a bar or cafe). The Peruvians stipulate that an engagement is *a la hora Inglesa* (by English time) if they genuinely want people to arrive within half an hour of the time they fix.

TAMPAX are available – though expensive – at *farmacias*.

TIME Peru keeps GMT + 5 – the same hours as New York, 6 (generally) behind Britain.

WATER is usually drinkable but if you've just arrived in South America it's best to stick to the bottled stuff, and in remote areas to ask if it's safe (*es potable?*). Occasional outbreaks of water-related hepatitis do occur.

WORK is generally available for **English teachers** in Lima, and sometimes in Arequipa or Cuzco, though not much ever turns up in other fields. In the more remote parts of the country it may sometimes be possible to find board and lodging in return for a little **building work** – but it's all really a question of keeping your eyes open and making contacts. There is an enormous amount of **bureaucracy** involved if you want to work (or live) officially in Peru. Two possibilities exist, however, for **arranging work before you go.** In Britain, the *TLS* and Tuesday's *Guardian* sometimes advertise **teaching posts** (as does *El Commercio* in Peru). And for **biology graduates** there's a chance of free board and lodging if you're willing to work for three months or more as a tour guide in a jungle lodge: for this 'Resident Naturalist' scheme contact *Peruvian Safaris S.A.*, Garcilazo de la Vega 1334, Lima (tel. 313047).

PERUVIAN TERMS: A GLOSSARY

ALLYU   kinship group, or clan
ARRIERO   muleteer
BARRIO   suburb (sometimes a shanty town)
BURRO   donkey
CACIQUE   headman
CALLEJON   corridor, or narrow street
CEJA DE LA SELVA   edge of the jungle
CHAKRA   cultivated garden or plot
CHAQUIRAS   pre-Columbian stone or coral beads
CORDILLERA   mountain range
CURACA   chief
CURANDERO   healer
EMPRESA   company
ENCOMIENDA   colonial grant of land and native labour
FARMACIA   chemist
GRINGA, GRINGO   European or North American (male/female); a very common term, occasionally replaced by EXTRANJERO (foreigner)
HACIENDA   estate

HUACA   sacred spot or object
HUACO   pre-Columbian artifact; hence HUAQUERO, someone who digs   or looks for *huacos*
LOMAS   place where vegetation grows with moisture from the air   rather than from rainfall or irrigation
MAMACONA   Inca Sun Virgin
PEÑA   nightclub with live music
POBLADO   settlement
PUEBLOS JOVENES   shantytowns
PUNA   barren Andean heights
QUEBRADA   stream
SELVA   jungle; hence SELVATICO/A, jungle dweller
SIERRA   mountains; hence SERRANO, mountain dweller
SOROCHE   altitude sickness
TAMBO   Inca highway rest-house
TIENDA   shop
TRAMITES   red tape, bureaucracy
UNSU   throne, or platform

Part two
THE GUIDE

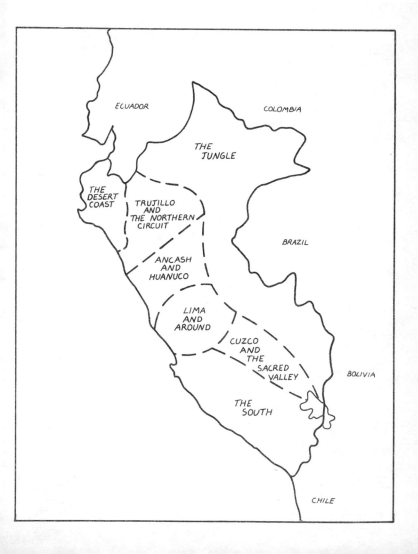

Chapter one

LIMA AND AROUND

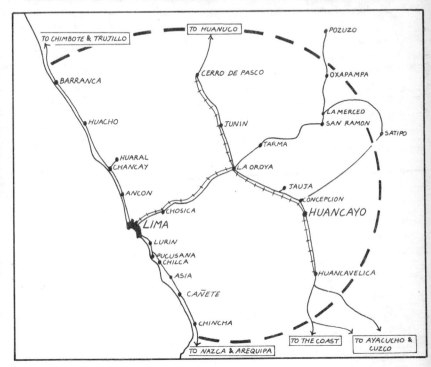

Very few travellers consider **Lima** an important goal in itself and on the whole they're probably right. Long established as capital, and once reputed to be the most beautiful city of Spanish America, Lima is today a rather daunting, shapeless sprawl of modern suburbs and *barriadas* – shanty towns which run for miles in each direction along the Pan American Highway. Which is not to say that you can't enjoy it – Limeños are generally very open, and the way of life here (with its incredibly complex status system) individual and compelling – but it's important not to come expecting the wrong things. Lima is not exotic and most of the downtown areas are thoroughly Western in style. It does have a certain elegance still in the old colonial centre, along with a string of excellent and important museums, but it's not really a city to sightsee. You have to look hard for its beauties.

One compensation to all of this, and reason in itself to delay the usual progress on to Arequipa or Cuzco, is the area immediately **around the city**. Just an hour or so's drive – to the north at **El Paraiso**, to the south about **El Silencio** – are a series of near perfect beaches. And in the neighbouring Rimac valley there are the pre-Incaic sites of **Puruchuco** and **Cajamarquila**, and, poised above a sandstone cliff at the edge of the ocean, the ancient pilgrimage centre and temple complex of **Pacachamac**. Further afield, the **Lima-Huancayo railway** takes you into the Andes, always a startling journey and one that you can extend by going on to the jungle towns of **Pozuzo** or **Satipo**. This, if you've the time, is a rewarding trip, well off the standard tourist circuits. If you're adventurous, too, you can complete a circuit through the mountains from **Satipo to Huancayo**, or even fly on to **Atalaya**, where there are occasional boats downriver through the jungle to **Pucallpa**. The rail and road link beyond Huancayo and Huancavelica **towards Ayachuco and Cuzco**, once a popular highland route, is, however, not currently feasible due to the accelerating guerilla activity of *Sendero Luminoso* (see p. 276). Heading for Cuzco from Lima, the usual approaches are now either up from the coast around Nazca or by rail from Arequipa – or, of course, if you've the money, by air.

LIMA

LIMA spreads out over a large and arid river valley, inhabited since well before the Incas controlled the land, and now a city of some 6 or 7 million. It can at times seem a nightmare. The main plazas, once attractive meeting places, are now dangerously thick with pick-pockets, exhaust fumes and, not infrequently, riot police. It's hard to find anything of quality in the shops or even among the *ambulantes*, Lima's traditional street sellers who have recently been herded into a small zone behind the post office, next to the uninviting Rimac river. And, perhaps overriding everything else, the climate seems to set the mood: outside the four summer months (December to April), a low, heavy mist descends over the city, forming a solid grey blanket from the beaches up as far as Chosica in the foothills of the Andes – a sometimes depressing phenomenon which is undoubtedly worsening along with the critical pollution problems.

The positive side of this is sometimes difficult to pin down. On a strictly guidebook level there are the museums (best of all the pre-Incaic treasures of the Gold and Archaeological collections), the Spanish churches in the centre, and some distinguished mansions in the wealthy suburbs of Barranco and Miraflores. And in their own way, too, there's a powerful atmosphere in the *barriadas* – future hope of Peru's landless peasants. Personally, staying and working in the city, I've always found my frustration with it – and its own noisy, fast-moving, inherent craziness – mellowed by the presence of the sea and the beaches, and by the mix of lifestyles and image. These range through a kind of snappy, creole – all big, fast, American cars, cruising down the streets – to a ridiculously easygoing, happy-go-lucky attitude that can come like a godsend when you're trying to get through some bureaucratic hassle. And as anyone who stays here more than a week or so finds, Limeñan hospitality and kindness are almost infinite once you've established an initial rapport . . .

Some history

Even if you don't have the time or the inclination to search out and savour the delights and agonies of Lima, it is possible to get a good feel for its history in only a few days. Out at Ancón, now a popular beach resort just north of Lima, an important **pre-Inca** burial site shows signs of occupation – including pottery, textiles and the oldest known bow in the entire Americas – going back at least 3,000 years. Although certainly one of the most populous valleys, the Rimac area first showed indications of true urbanisation around AD 1200 with the appearance of a strong, independent culture – the **Cuismancu State** – in many ways parallel to, though not as large as, the contemporary Chimu Empire which bordered it to the north. *Cajamarquilla*, a huge, somewhat crowded, adobe city-complex associated with the Cuismancu, now rests peacefully under the desert sun only a few kilometres beyond Lima's outer suburbs. Dating from the same era, but some 30km south of the modern city, is the *temple of Pachacamac*. For hundreds of years, until ransacked by the Conquistadores, this shrine attracted thousands of pilgrims from all over Peru, the Incas being the last in a series of dominant groups to adopt Pachacamac as one of their own major *huacas*.

When the Spanish first arrived here the valley was dominated by three important **Inca** controlled urban complexes: *Carabayllo* to the north near Chillón; *Maranga* situated these days between the modern city and the port of Callao (and now partly destroyed by the tarmacked Avenida La Marina); and *Surco* which is now a suburb within the confines of greater Lima but where, until the mid-seventeenth century, you could still see ancient chiefs' adobe houses lying empty yet painted in a variety of colourful images.

Francisco Pizarro founded **Spanish Lima**, 'City of the Kings', in 1535 – only two years after the invasion. Evidently recommended by shrewd mountain Indians as a site for a potential capital (this part of the coast doesn't have a very healthy climate at the best of times), it proved essentially a good choice offering a natural harbour nearby, a large well-watered river valley, as well as relatively easy access up into the Andes. By the 1550s the town had grown up around a rather large plaza with wide streets leading through a fine collection of mansions all elegantly adorned by wooden terraces, and well-stocked shops run by wealthy merchants. Since the very beginning Spanish Lima has always been separate and quite different to the more popular Peruvian image: it looks out away from the Andes and their past towards the Pacific for contact with the world beyond.

Lima rapidly developed into the capital of a viceroyalty which encompassed not only Peru but also Ecuador, Bolivia and Chile. The University of San Marcos, founded in 1551, is the oldest in the continent and Lima housed the headquarters for the Inquisition from 1570 until 1813. It remained the most important, the richest and, if hardly credible today, the most beautiful city in South America until the wave of independence radically altered the balance of power during the early nineteenth century.

Perhaps the most prosperous era for Lima was the **seventeenth century**. By 1610 its population had reached a manageable 26,000 made up of 40 per cent coloured (mostly slaves), 38 per cent Spanish, no more than 8 per cent pure Indian, another 8 per cent living under religious orders and less than 6 per cent of mixed blood (now probably the largest proportion of inhabitants). The centre of Lima was crowded with shops and stalls selling quality products such as silks and fancy furniture from as far afield as China. Even these days it's not hard to imagine what Lima must have been like in the seventeenth century. A substantial section of the colonial city is still preserved – many of its streets, set in regular blocks 120m square, are overhung by ornate wooden balconies, and elaborate baroque facades bring some of the older churches to life, regardless of the din and hassle of modern city living. *Rimac*, a suburb just over the river from the Plaza de Armas, and the port area of *Callao*, developed as satellite settlements – initially catering for the very rich though now predominantly 'slum' sectors.

The eighteenth century, a period of relative stagnation for Lima, was dramatically punctuated by the spectacular **earthquake** of 1746 which left only 20 houses standing and killed nearly 7 per cent of the population – by then some 60,000. From 1761–76 Lima and Peru were governed by Viceroy Amat. Although more renowned for his relationship with the 'beautiful and witty' actress, *La Perricholi*, Amat is also remembered as the instigator of Lima's **rebirth**. Under him the city lost its cloistered atmosphere, opening out with broad avenues, striking gardens, rococo mansions and palatial salons. Influenced by the Bourbons, Amat's designs for the city's architecture went hand in hand with transatlantic reverberations of the Enlightenment.

Expanding from its colonial heart out into the east and south towards the end of the last century, Lima created the suburbs of *Barrios Altos* and *La Victoria* – designed for the ever-growing poor sectors of the population. At the same time, the rich developed residential zones above the beaches at *Magdalena, Miraflores and Barranco* – all separated from the centre by several kilometres of farmland, then still studded with fabulous pre-Inca *huacas* and other adobe ruins.

It was **President Leguia** who revitalised Lima by 'cleaning up' the central areas between 1919 and 1930. Plaza San Martin's attractive colonnades and the Gran Hotel Bolivar were erected then, the Presidential Palace was rebuilt and the city was supplied with its first ever drinking water and sewerage systems. From then on Lima exploded into the modern era of ridiculously **rapid growth**. The 300,000 inhabitants of 1930 mushroomed into over 3,500,000 by 1975 and has nearly doubled again in the last ten years. Most of this growth is accounted for by massive emigration of peasants from the provinces into the *barriadas* or pueblos jovenes – 'young towns' – now pressing in on the city along all of its landbound edges. Today the city is as cosmopolitan as any other in the Third World, its thriving middle classes seeking 'higher standards of living' comparable to those of the West or better. The majority, however, scrape meagre incomes while being spatially, ethnically and economically considered as marginals. The fact that they form the core and very essence of modern Lima is something easy to realise as a visitor.

Arriving and rooms – some practicalities

Arriving in Lima, whether by air from another continent or overland from some other region, can be disorientating. At ground level there are few landmarks even to register which direction the centre of town lies in. Set out as it is in a wide, flat alluvial plain, Lima fans out in long, straight streets from its old colonial heart; one, **Avenida Benavides**, stretches out towards the harbour area around Callao and the airport, while at 90° to this, another arm, **Avenida Arequipa**, reaches for downtown **Miraflores** and the old beach resort of **Barranco**. Initially, everywhere looks the same – dusty shanty settlements surrounding increasingly more permanent constructions as you get closer to the central **Plaza de Armas**.

Coming into Lima **by air** it's possible, on a clear day, to get some perspective on the city. After crossing the high Andes, the flight path follows a narrow desert strip bordering the Pacific Ocean – extremely desolate from above, its only relief small yellow studs or foothills rising toward the east; as the city appears you can usually make it out, crowded into the mouth of a river valley with low sandy mountains closing in around the outer fringes. After landing and going through the usual passport and customs checks you're thrown, almost unexpectedly, into the middle of a bustling, very modern airport concourse. The immediate urge, and a sensible one, is to get out as quickly as possible. **Taxis** to the centre will cost around $5, or $8 to downtown Miraflores. A much cheaper, very efficient alternative is to take the **airport bus** which sells tickets from a little office just beyond customs; for a flat rate this will take you to a hotel of your choice anywhere in Lima.

If you're **arriving overland**, the chances are you'll end up in the old, more central areas of town, around Parque Universitario, the Hotel Sheraton, or La Victoria. Whichever of these, it's unwise to wander off looking lost or bemused by a new exciting environment – thieves abound at bus terminals. The best move is to hail the first **taxi** you see, name a hotel and fix a price.

Getting to know Lima and **finding your way around** takes some time. In the **old centre**, the obvious points of reference are the **Plaza de Armas** and the more modern **Plaza San Martin** – separated by some five blocks of the **Jiron de la Union**, Lima Centro's main shopping drag. Plaza de Armas, at its river end, is fronted by the Cathedral and Government Palace, while around Plaza San Martin revolves the commercial centre – offices, large hotels and the major airline offices. Once you've got to know these two squares and the streets between them you're unlikely to get seriously lost in the old part of town.

From here to the modern centre, **Miraflores**, it's a haul of some 7 or 8km down the broad, tree-lined Avenida Arequipa; big yellow buses (No. 2) and beaten up colectivos leave all day from the corner of Plaza San Martin, between the Faucett and Aero Peru offices. A cliff-top, mini-metropolis, very distinct to the old town, Miraflores is slick, fast-moving and quite ostentatious – a commercial and shopping zone, and popular meeting place for the wealthier sector of Lima society.

After getting to know Lima Centro and mastering the bus or colectivo to Miraflores, it's a fairly simple matter to find your way around the rest of this huge, spread-eagled city. Almost every corner of it is linked by a regular **municipal bus service**, known to everyone as *El Bussing* and with flat rate tickets bought from the driver as you go in. In tandem with these there are also privately owned **microbuses**, older and smaller but again flat rates. For routes and destinations covered in this chapter you'll find the number or suburb-name (written on the front of all buses) specified; if you're planning to explore in depth, or stay some time, you might want to get hold of the *Guia de Transportes*, a bus map-guide, cheap and up to date, which you can buy from most of the stalls around Plaza San Martin and Avenida Nicolas de Pierola.

A similar guide, **Lima: Guia de Calles** (available from the same sources), covers every named street with an index and a map – something difficult to do without if you intend visiting many places in and around the capital.

There are no trams serving the citizens of Lima these days, but there is an amazing **railway line** connecting the city to the high Andes as far as Huancayo and Huancavelica. The railway station, *Desamperados*, is an impressive nineteenth-century building situated just behind the Government Palace and opposite the *El Cordano* cafe, an eating or drinking house straight from the past.

Finding a room
There are two main areas to look for rooms – **Lima Centro**, where you'll find hotels in just about every category imaginable, and **Miraflores**, which with few exceptions is resolutely upmarket. There are no campsites, official or otherwise.

LIMA CENTRO
Most travellers **on a tight budget** seem to end up in one of three traditional gringo dives around Desamperados railway station. The *Hotel Europa* is by far the best of these, opposite San Francisco church at Jiron Ancash 376. The others – *El Commercio* and *Hotel Pacifico* – are cheap but leave a lot to be desired; both are situated opposite the right-hand side of the Government Palace in Jr. Agostino N. Wiese. More impressive looking, though still seldom offering hot water, is the *Hotel Richmond*, an old mansion, cheap, with plenty of rooms, and in a very central location at Jr. Union 706. Also within a few blocks of the Plaza de Armas are the *Hostal Machu Picchu* (Cailloma 231), quite basic but good value, and the easy-going *San Sebastian* (Jr. Ica 712). For rather better facilities you might also try the *Hostal Belen*, again well situated – on Belen, just below the Plaza San Martin.

Slightly upmarket, the *Hostal Roma* is a very pleasant place to stay, with communal or private bathrooms and a left luggage service (Jr. Ica 326; tel. 277576 – from around $5 single). Or, relatively expensive from around $18 a night for a double room, there's the elegant *Hotel La Casona* (Moquegua 289), excellent value if you can afford it, with the attraction of rooms set around a pretty colonial courtyard.

MIRAFLORES AND THE SUBURBS
There are no cheap places to stay in **Miraflores**, though the *Residencial Pardo* (Av. Pardo 453) is more or less reasonable; very clean, it serves good local food. Nearer the top of the range, the *Pension Alemana* (Av. Arequipa 4704; tel. 453092) offers superb accommodation, excellent service and is on the main colectivo/bus route connecting Miraflores with Lima Centro.

If you really want to stay outside Lima Centro but can't budget for these places (you would need at least $10 a night), it might be worth trying the modern **youth hostel** (*Albergue Je Juventud*, Av. Larco 1247;

tel. 475374) which is near to the cliff-top with views over the ocean. Alternatively, or if you intend staying in Lima for some length of time, it's often worth checking the ads in *El Commercio* or the *Lima Times* for the addresses of **private householders** looking to rent rooms out to gringos passing through.

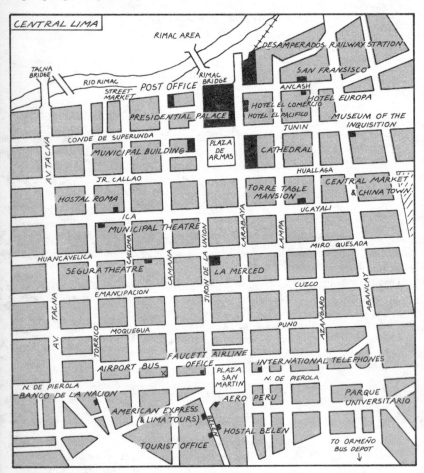

Lima Centro: the old city

Since its foundation, Lima has expanded steadily out from the Plaza de Armas – virtually all of the Rio Rimac's alluvial soils are now built on and even the sand-dunes beyond are rapidly filling up with migrant settlers. When Pizarro arrived here he found a valley dominated by some

400 temples and palaces, most of them pre-Incaic and well spread out to either side of the river; the natives were apparently peaceful, living mostly by cultivating gardens, fishing from the ocean or catching freshwater crayfish. As usual, Pizarro's choice for the site of this new Spanish town was related as much to politics as it was to geography: he founded Lima next to the Rimac on the site of an existing palace belonging to *Tauri Chusko*, the local headman who had little choice but to give up his residence and move away.

Today in the **Plaza de Armas**, or 'armed plaza' (*Plaza Armada*) as the early Conquistadores preferred to call it, not a sign remains of Indian heritage. Standing on Tauri Chusko's palace is the relatively modern Government Palace; while the Cathedral occupies the site of an Inca temple once dedicated to the Puma deity; and the Municipal Building lies on what was originally an Inca envoy's mansion. The **Presidential Palace** was Pizarro's house long before the modern edifice was conceived of. It was here that he spent the last few years of his life and was eventually assassinated in 1541. Its ground might even be considered somewhat 'sacred' since as he died, his jugular severed by an assassin's rapier, he fell to the floor, drew a cross, then kissed it. What you can see today, however, was completed in 1938. It's a clean, almost impressive building, though nothing special. Around midday it's possible to watch the *changing of the guards* – not a particularly wonderful spectacle but immediately afterwards there are usually *guided tours* of the Palace (starting from the visitor's side entrance in Jr. Union).

Less than 50m away, the **Cathedral** (open 10–4, daily; small charge), squat and austere, was modelled on that of Jaen in Spain. Like Jaen, it has three naves following the Renaissance design adopted by Francisco Becerra. When Becerra died in 1605, however, it was still far from completion. The towers weren't finished for another 40 years and, in 1746, the ultimate frustration arrived in the guise of a devastating earthquake. The 'modern' building, essentially a reconstruction of Becerra's design, is primarily of interest for its *Museum of Religious Art and Treasures* and, in the first chapel on the right, some human remains thought to be *Pizarro's body* (quite fitting since he placed the first stone shortly before his death). Although gloomy, its interior retains some of its appealing churrigueresque – highly elaborate baroque – decor. The stalls are superb and, even more impressive, the choir was exquisitely carved in the early seventeenth century by a Catalan artist. The Archbishop's Palace next door was rebuilt as recently as 1924.

Directly across the square, the **Municipal Building** (open 9–1, Mon.-Fri.; free) is a typical example of a half-hearted twentieth-century attempt at something neo-colonial. A brilliant white on the outside, its most memorable features are permanent groups of heavily armed guards and the odd armoured car waiting conspicuously for some kind of action.

Inside, the *Pinacotea Museum* houses a selection of Peruvian paintings, notably those of Ignacio Merino from the nineteenth century. In the library (*la biblioteca*) you can also see the City's Act of Foundation and Declaration of Independence.

Between the Municipal Building and the post office, set back from one corner of the main square, is the church and monastery of **Santo Domingo** (open 9–1 and 4–8; monastery closes at 5.30 pm; small charge). Completed in 1549, Santo Domingo was presented by the pope, a century or so later, with an alabaster statue of Santa Rosa de Lima. Rosa's tomb, and that of San Martin de Porras are its great attractions – and much revered. Otherwise it's not of great interest, nor architectural merit although it is one of the oldest religious structures in Lima, built on a site granted to the Dominicans by Pizarro in 1535.

It's a short walk from here to the **Puente de Piedra**, Rimac's 'stone bridge' which arches over the river, usually no more than a miserable trickle, behind the Government Palace. Initially a wooden construction, today's bridge was built in the seventeenth century using eggwhites to improve the consistency of its mortar. Its function was to provide a permanent link between the centre of town and the district of San Lazaro, known these days as **Rimac**, or, more popularly, as *Bajo El Puente* (Below the Bridge). This zone was first populated in the sixteenth century by African slaves, newly imported and awaiting purchase by big plantation owners; a few years later Rimac was beleagured with outbreaks of leprosy. Although these days its status is much improved, Rimac is still one of the most run-down areas of Lima and can be quite an aggressive place at night – a drag since some of the best peñas can be found here. The city's most famous bullring, *Plaza de Acho*, is in Rimac, and a few blocks to the right of the bridge, leading to the foot of a distinctive hill, Cerro San Cristobal, you can stroll up the **Alameda de los Descalzos**, a fine tree-lined walk designed for courtship and an afternoon meeting place for the early seventeenth-century elite. A favourite out-of-doors dive for the wealthy, it remained popular well into the Republican era. Although in desperate need of renovation, it still possesses 12 appealing marble statues brought from Italy in 1856, each one representing a different sign of the zodiac.

At the far end of the Alameda a fine, low Franciscan monastery, **El Convento de los Descalzos** (open Mon.-Sat. 9–5.30; small charge), houses a quantity of colonial and Republican paintings from Peru and Ecuador. A little museum depicts early monastic works and the Chapel of El Carmen possesses a beautiful baroque gold-leaf altar. Founded in 1592, the monastery was sited in a then secluded spot beyond the town, protected from earthquakes by Cerro San Cristobal.

Back on the main side of the river, Ancash leads away from the Government Palace and Desamperados railway station towards one of Lima's most attractive churches – **San Francisco** (open 9–12, 3–6, daily). A large seventeenth-century construction with an engaging stone facade, San Francisco's vaults and columns are elaborately decorated with *mudejar* (Spanish Moorish-styled) plaster relief. It's a majestic building which has withstood well the passage of time and devastation of successive tremors. Guided tours are offered (around 1 and 5pm) of the monastery and its *catacombs*, both worth timing a visit. Discovered only in 1951, these vast crypts contain the skulls and bones of some 70,000 persons. Opposite San Francisco, at Ancash 390, is **La Casa Pilatos** (open Mon.-Fri. 11–1.30pm), now the home of the *Instituto Nacional de Cultura* and one of several well-restored colonial mansions in Lima. Quite a simple building, and no comparison to Torre Tagle (see below), it has an attractive courtyard with an unusual stone staircase leading up from the middle of the patio.

A couple of blocks away, the **Museum of the Inquisition** (Junin 548) faces out onto Plaza Bolivar. Behind a facade of 'Greek' classical columns, the museum (open Mon.-Fri. 9am–8pm, Sat. 9–1; free) contains the original tribunal room with a beautifully carved mahogany ceiling. Underneath are dungeons and torture chambers with a few life-sized human models to show what it was really like. From 1570 until 1820 this was the headquarters of the Inquisition for the whole of Spanish-dominated America. The few blocks behind the Museum of the Inquisition and Avenida Abancay are devoted to the **central market** and **Chinatown**. Perhaps one of the most fascinating sectors of Lima Centro, the market is large and colourful (if a bit smelly and rife with pick-pockets). An elaborate Chinese gateway crosses over one of the main streets, a perfect reference point for the best and cheapest *chifa* restaurants.

Torre Tagle Palace, pride and joy of the old city, can be found at Ucayali 363, between Chinatown and the Plaza de Armas. Now the home of Peru's Ministry for Foreign Relations, Torre Tagle is a superb mansion built in the 1730s and now beautifully maintained. Externally it is embelleshed with a decorative facade and two wooden balconies – typical of Lima in that one is longer than the other. The porch and patio, like the first floor, are distinctly Spanish-Andalucian, although some of the intricate wood carvings on pillars and across ceilings display a visionary native influence; the *azulejos*, or tiling, too shows a strong fusion of styles – this time a combination of Moorish and Limeño *tastes*. In the left-hand corner of the patio you can see a set of scales to weigh merchandise during colonial times, and the house possesses a magnificent sixteenth-century coach complete with mobile toilet. Originally, mansions such as Torre Tagle served as refuges for outlaws – the authorities being unable to enter without written and stamped permission. Being offices today, the afternoons are the best time to visit.

The largest area of old Lima is the stretch **between the Plaza de Armas** and **Plaza San Martin**. Worth a quick look here is the church of **San Augustin** (open daily 8.30–12, 3.30–5.30) on the corner of Ica and Camana. Severely damaged by earthquake activity, only the small side chapel can be visited nowadays but it has a glorious facade, one of the most complicated examples of *churrigueresque* inspiration in Peru. Close by, at Jiron Union 224, is the **Casa Aliaga**, an unusual mansion renowned as the oldest in South America – and occupied by the same family since 1535. You can arrange to visit through a tour company (try *Lima Tours* on Belen). It's one of the most elaborate mansions in the country, with sumptuous reception rooms full of Louis XVI mirrors, furniture and doors. Around the corner, at Camana 459, the **Casa de Riva-Aguero** (open Mon.-Fri. 5–8pm; free) is more accessible to unorganised visiting. A typical colonial house, its patio has been laid out as an interesting *folk-art museum.*

Perhaps the most noticed of all religious buildings in Lima is the **Church of La Merced** (open 7–12, 4–8, daily) just two blocks from the Plaza de Armas along the busy commercial street of Jr. Union. Built on the site where the first Latin mass in Lima was celebrated, the original church was demolished in 1628 to make way for the present building. Its most elegant feature, a beautiful colonial facade, has been adapted and rebuilt several times – along with the broad columns of the nave – to protect the church against tremors. But by far the most lasting impression is made by the *Cross of the Venerable Padre Urraca*, whose miraculous silver staff is smothered by hundreds of kisses every hour in exchange for favours and prayers from a constantly shifting congregation. The attached *cloisters* (open 8–12, 3–6) are less spectacular though they do have a historical curiosity – it was here that the Patriots of Independence declared the Virgin of La Merced their military Marshall.

Of the other churches worth visiting in Lima Centro, San Pedro and Jesus Maria are the most central. San Pedro (open 7–1, 6–8.30), near the Torre Tagle on the corner of Azangaro and Ucayali, was built by and occupied by the Jesuits until their expulsion in 1767. Richly decorated and dripping with art treasures it's a typical colonial temple. Jesus Maria (open 7–1 and 3–7) is down towards Plaza San Martin at Camana/Moquegua; the home of Capuchin nuns from Madrid in the early eighteenth century, its sparkling baroque gilt altars and pulpits are quite outstanding.

Two more interesting sanctuaries can be found on the edge of old Lima, along the Avenida Tacna – Santa Rosa and Las Nazarenas. The **Sanctuary of Santa Rosa de Lima** (open 9.30–1, 3.30–6.30) is named in honour of the first saint created in the Americas. The construction of Avenida Tacna took away a section of the already small seventeenth-century church, and what remains is fairly plain, but in the patio next door you can see the saint's *hermitage*, a small adobe cell, and, just off this, a fascinating *Ethnographic Museum*. At the junction of Tacna/Huancavelica, the church of **Las Nazarenas** (open 7–12, 4–8, daily) is again small and outwardly undistinguished but with an interesting history. After the severe 1655 earthquake a mural of the the crucifixion, painted by an Angolan slave on the wall of his hut, was apparently the only upstanding object in the district. Deemed a miracle, and the cause of popular processions ever since, it is on this site that the church was founded. The processions for the Lord of Miracles, to save Lima from another quake, take place every October (18th, 19th, 28th and 1st of November), based around a silver litter which carries the original mural.

In many ways more typically Limeño, and more expressive of the city's contemporary personality than its churches, are the **parks and gardens**. The most central of these, **Parque Universitario**, just a few short blocks from the Plaza San Martin, is now the site for numerous colectivo companies and street hawkers. The home of South America's first University, San Marcos, today it's obscured by a jumble of cars and busy people. Though no longer even an important annex for the University, it's worth a wander if only to check out the small archaeological museum. A larger park, quite poorly maintained and outside of the centre, is the **Parque de la Exposisíon**, created for the International Exhibition of 1868. Situated between Paseo Colon and Avenida 28 de Julio, and below the towering Hotel Sheraton, it seems mainly to attract courting couples who have nowhere else to go in the evenings or on Sundays (servants' day off). To the north of this park is another, the **Parque Neptuno**, well-shaded and with the small **Museum of Italian Art** within its boundaries. Nearby, the former International Exhibition Palace houses the **National Museum of Art** (Paseo Colon 124; open 9–7 daily; small charge), an excellent public collection covering art and crafts from pre-Columbian times through colonial to modern. Film shows and lectures are also offered on some weekday evenings (for details check posters at the museums or listings in *El Commercio*).

Finally, some eight blocks west of the Plaza San Martin, on the site of an old city gate dividing Lima from the road to Callao, **Plaza 2 de Mayo** still greets visitors (now from the airport) as they enter the city. An important square, it was built to commemorate the repulse of the Spanish fleet in 1866, Spain's last attempt to regain a foothold in South America. These days it's probably one of the most air-polluted spots in Lima.

Downtown Lima: Miraflores and around

Strictly speaking **Miraflores** alone is downtown Lima. To its east is **San Isidro**, a very plush suburb with a golf-course surrounded by sky-scraping apartment blocks and super-modern shopping complexes, and many square kilometres of extraordinarily smart housing estates. To its south begins the ocean-side suburb of **Barranco**, one of the oldest parts of the city and now one of its most attractive above the steep sandy cliffs of the **Costa Verde**. But if you're going downtown in search of action or nightlife (detailed in the section on p. 49), these two are much less relevant. Lined with street cafes and the capital's flashier kind of shops, Miraflores is your place, and until you've experienced it, it's hard to grasp what this city is about.

Although still connected to Lima Centro by the long-established Avenida Arequipa, another highway – Paseo de La Republica (or more familiarly *El Zanjon*, 'the great ditch') – now provides **Miraflores** with an alternative approach. Coming out here on the yellow no. 2 bus, get off at the stop just before Miraflores central park. A good place to make for first, and to get some bearings across the whole downtown area is the **Huaca Juliana**, a vast pre-Incaic adobe mound which continues to dwarf all but a handful of skyscrapers. To get there it's a 2–minute walk from the Avenida Arequipa, to the right as you come from Lima Centro at block 44. One of a large number of *huacas* – sacred places – and palaces that once stretched across this part of the valley, little is known about the Juliana, though it seems likely that it was originally named after a pre-Incaic chief of the area. At the time of writing it is undergoing restoration and nobody seems quite sure what's going to happen – there are rumours that it may be landscaped or even flattened completely. Interestingly, it has a hollow core running through its cross-section and is thought to have been constructed in the shape of an enormous frog. With the frog as rain-god, this huaca evidently spoke to priests who heard the voices of the gods through a tube connected to the cavern at its heart. As an important ritual centre, Juliana may well have been the mysteriously unknown oracle after which the Rimac (meaning 'he who speaks') valley was named; a curious document from 1560 affirms that the 'devil' spoke at this mound.

From the top of the huaca you can see over the towering offices and across the flat rooves of multi-coloured houses in downtown Miraflores. Its central area focuses on the small, almost triangular **Parque Miraflores** – at the end of the Avenida Arequipa. Flashy cafes and bars surround the park, where, during the day, the streets are crowded with busy shoppers, flower-sellers and young men washing other people's big cars. In the park, particularly on Sundays, there are artists selling their canvasses – some are good, most are aimed purely at a tourist market. The main streets radiating from the junction at the end of Avenida Arequipa are **Larco** and **Diagonal**, both fan out along the park en route to the ocean less than 2km away. Miraflores has one important mansion open to the public – the **Casa de Ricardo Palma** (open Mon.-Fri.

10–12.30, 2–7) at General Suarez 189. Palma, probably Peru's greatest historian, lived here for most of his life.

Barranco is a much quieter place than Miraflores, its central park a really pleasant spot to while away some of the afternoon. Overlooking the ocean, and scattered with old mansions, this was the capital's seaside resort in the last century and is now a kind of Limeño Greenwich Village. Increasingly trendy with young artists and intellectuals taking over many of the older properties. There's little specific to 'see', though you might at some stage wander over to take a look at the cliff-top remains of a funicular railway, which used to carry aristocratic families from their summer resort straight down to the beach. Within a block of here, an impressive white church sits on the cliff with gardens to the front and an old wooden bridge crossing over a gully filled with attractive and exotic dwellings. Undoubtedly Lima's most appealing suburb, if there were hotels in Barranco this would be the place to stay.

Down beside the pounding rollers, the **Costa Verde** magestically marks the edge of a continent, so named because of vegetation clinging to the steep, sandy cliffs which overshadow any human endeavours. A bumpy road follows their line from an exclusive Regattas Club and the *Chorrillos* fishermen's wharf along past both Barranco and Miraflores, then a few kilometres further, almost to the suburb of Magdelena. The sea is cold and not so clean – and there's nothing here really, other than sand, pebbles, a couple of beach clubs, a few restaurants and a resident surfing crowd – but downtown Lima would seem quite spare without it and swimming in the surf seems as good a way as any to extend a day mulling about Barranco and Miraflores. As everywhere in Lima, however, keep a sharp eye on your clothes and any valuables.

Unless you're shopping, looking for a sauna, trying to find a disco, or visiting someone, there are few good reasons to stop off in **San Isidro**. One, though, might be to take a stroll through the Bosque El Olivar, just 150m (to the right, going away from Lima Centro) off block 34 of the Avenida Arequipa. A charming grove first planted in 1560, it's now rather depleted in olive trees but you will find the old press and millstone as well as a stage where concerts and cultural events are often held. Only a few blocks away, at Avenida El Rosario, there is also an impressive reconstructed adobe huaca, **Huayamarca** – like Juliana dating from pre-Inca days and now sitting neatly surrounded by wealthy suburbs. The ruins have their own site museum (open 9–11.30, 3–5.30, except Mondays) containing funerary masks and art work – including textiles oddly reminiscent of Scottish tartans. Again, San Isidro has one colonial mansion worth checking out, the *Casa de La Tradicion* (open 2.30–5pm, Mon.-Fri.; small charge) at Avenida Salaverry 3032; a rather elegant old house, this has a private collection of artifacts and pictures covering the history of Lima.

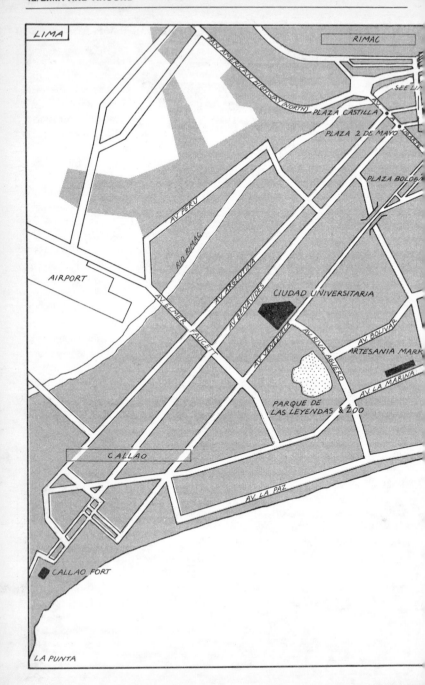

PLAZA DE ACHO (BULL RING)

HIPODROMO

NTRO PLAN

MERCADO MAYORISTA

AV. GRAU

AV. 28 DE JULIO

AV. CAPAC

PAN AMERICAN HIGHWAY SOUTH

AV. MEXICO

ART MUSEUM

ESTADIO NACIONAL

PRADO ESTE

AV. JAVIER

GOLD MUSEUM

AV. AVIACION

AV. AREQUIPA

PASEO

AV. AMOS

DE

AV. ANGAMOS

LA

AV. REPUBLICA

AV. THOMAS MARSANO

USEUM OF ARCHAEOLOGY
ANTHROPOLOGY

SAN ISIDRO

LA HUACA JULIANA

REPUBLICA

MIRAFLORES

AV. SALAVERRY

AV. SANTA CRUZ

DE

PANAMA

CLINICA
ANGLO-AMERICANA

AV. J. PARDO

AV. LARCO

AV. EJERCITO

MIRAFLORES
CENTRAL PARK

BARRANCO

COSTA VERDE

PACIFIC OCEAN

PLAYA HERRADURA (BEACH)

Callao and La Punta

Stuck out on a narrow boot-shaped peninsula, Callao and La Punta ('The Point') form a natural annex to Lima, one that looks out towards the ocean and worldwide communication. Originally quite separate, they were founded in 1537, and were destined to become Peru's principal treasure-fleet port before eventually being sucked in by Lima's other suburbs during the twentieth century.

Now the country's main commercial harbour on the Pacific, and one of the most modern ports in South America, **Callao** lies about 14km west of Lima Centro (easily reached on bus 25 from Plaza San Martin, which runs all the way there – and beyond, past the fort, to La Punta). It's none too alluring a place – indeed its suburbs are considered virtually 'no-go' areas for the city's middle classes being slum zones rife with prostitution and gang-land assassins. However, if you're unworried by such associations, you will find some of the best *Ceviche* restaurants anywhere in the continent.

Further along, too, away from the heavier quarters and dominating the entire peninsula, is the great **Castle of Real Felipe**. Built after the devastating earthquake of 1746, which washed ships ashore and killed nearly the entire population of 5,000 in Callao, this is a superb example of the military architecture of its age, designed in the shape of a pentagon. Although built too late to protect the Spanish treasure fleets against European pirates like Francis Drake, it was to play a critical role in the battles for Independence. Its fire-power repulsed both Admiral Brown (1816) and Lord Cochrane (1818), though many Royalists starved to death here when it was besieged by the Patriots in 1821, just prior to its surrender. The fort's grandeur is only marred by a number of store-houses, built during the late nineteenth century while it was used as a custom's house. Inside, the *Military Museum* (open 9–12, 3–5 Tue., Wed. and Thur.; 2–5.30 Sat. and Sun.; free) houses a fairly complete collection of eighteenth and nineteenth-century arms and various rooms dedicated to Peruvian war heroes.

Out at the end of the peninsula, what was once the fashionable beach resort of **La Punta** is now overshadowed by the Naval College and Yacht Club. Many of its old mansions, however, still remain, some of them very elegant, others extravagant monstrosities. Right at the very point an attractive promenade offers glorious views and sunsets over the Pacific, while at the back of the strand there are some excellent restaurants serving traditional local food (many of these are difficult to find, being in what look like private houses – probably best to ask someone to point one out).

Lima's museums

Not surprisingly, given Peru's rich history, Lima abounds in museums, most of them fascinating, and a few, like Larco Herrera and Amano, specialising in specific categories of art or culture. Their generally scattered locations throughout the city, however, make it difficult to visit more than three or four without it turning into a full-time occupation. At the most brutally selective don't miss either the Gold Museum or Archaeological and Anthropological Museum, both of them fairly tricky to find in their respective suburbs but well worth all the effort.

Gold Museum
(10–7 daily; $5)
Isolated way out of town in the well-to-do suburb of Monterrico, Lima's Gold Museum, owned by the high society Mujica family, is a must. On its ground level it boasts a vast display of **arms and uniforms**, many of them incredible antiques which help bring to life some of Peru's bloodier history. But it's the safe-room downstairs which contains the real gems. Divided into several sections, these basements are literally crammed with treasured objects and beautiful craft goods from **pre-Columbian** times. Most of the **gold and silver jewellery** is in the metalwork rooms, but more fascinating perhaps are the pre-Inca weapons and wooden staffs, or the amazing Nazca yellow-feathered poncho designed for a noble's child. One thing that generally causes a stir, too, is a skull enclosing a full set of pink quartz teeth – in the corner on the right as you enter the main room from the stairs.

The best way to **get out here** is by catching a colectivo from Miraflores or Lima Centro along the Av. Arequipa to block 48, then switching to Av. Angamos to take the No. 72 *Microbus* (yellow and red) as far as Monterrico's *Centro Commercial* shopping centre at the very end of Angamos. From here it's a short walk of three blocks up Av. Primavera, two to the right along Santa Elena – a Fort Knox type building set back in the shade of tall trees.

Archaeological and Anthropological Museum
(Tue.-Sun. 10–6; small charge)
Although much of this museum's immense collections have been rotting in store for decades, the selection on display must still be the most complete and varied exhibition of pre-Inca artifacts anywhere. They also give a detailed and accurate perspective on Peru's pre-history, a vision which comes as a surprise if you'd previously thought of it just in terms of Incas and Conquistadores.

Divided into a number of **collections**, around two colonial-style courtyards, the exhibits begin with evolution and the populating of America.

The earliest Peruvian pieces are stone tools some 8,000 years old. One of the finest rooms is that showing carved **Chavin stones** such as the magnificent *Estela Raymondi*, a diorite block intricately carved with feline, serpent and falcon features, or the *Tello Obelisk*, a masterpiece in granite. The *Manos Cruzados*, or 'Crossed Hands' stone from **Kotosh** is also on display, evidence of a mysterious cult 5,000 years ago. The **Paracas room** is rich in amazing weavings and replete with excellent examples of deformed heads and trepanated skulls; one shows post-operational growth; in another of the cases sits a male mummy, 'frozen' at the age of 30–35 and with fingernails still visible, the fixed sideways glance from his misshapen head enough to send shivers down a snake's spine. The **Nazca room**, stuffed full of incredible ceramics, is divided, interestingly, according to what each pot represents – marine life, agriculture, flora, wildlife, trophy-heads, mythology, sexual and everyday life, etc. The **Mochica** and **Chimu rooms** are also well stocked; there's one entirely devoted to music and dance, containing remarkable ceramics depicting musicians, even birds playing the drums; and, lastly, a room devoted to the **Incas** – a useful initial overview with impressive models of the main ruins like Machu Picchu and Tambo Colorado.

Next door to the Archaeological and Anthropological Museum, the **National Museum of History**, essentially designed as a period nineteenth-century house, possesses dazzling antique clothing and extravagant furnishings, complemented by early Republican paintings. The liberators San Martin and Bolivar both made homes here for a while (open Mon.-Fri. 9–6.30, Sun. 10–5; small charge).

Again not easy to find, the Archaeological and anthropological museum is **currently situated** out of the centre in the suburb of Pueblo Libre on the Plaza Bolivar; the best microbus is No. 41 (white and blue) which you can take from the corner of Cuzco and Carabaya in Lima Centro. A **new site** has been chosen for the museum beside the Parque de las Leyendas, fittingly next to the *Huaca Cruz Blanca* (once the heart of the Maranga culture). Estimated to cost around $40 million, half of the money coming from the Inter-American Development Bank, it was apparently President Belaunde's brainchild but was shelved for 12 years by the Military Revolution in 1968. Since some 15,000 archaeological pieces are confiscated at Lima airport every year, a larger museum has long been needed – it *might*, by the time you read this, be open.

Museo Rafael Larco Herrera
Bolivar 1515; Pueblo Libre (Mon.-Sat. 9–1 and 3–7; $5)
Undoubtedly the city's most unusual museum, this contains over 400,000 excellently preserved ceramics, many of them Chiclin or Mochica pottery from around Trujillo. Its most unique collection, however, is an intriguing collection of **pre-Inca erotic art**. Take either bus No. 23 (from Av. Abancay) or a micro 37 (green) from Av. Nicolas de Pierola.

MOCHICA DRINKING VESSEL

Amano Museum
Calle Retiro 160 (hours by appointment, tel. 412909; free)
A close rival to the above, this has a fabulous exhibition of **Chancay weavings**, as well as bountiful **ceramics**. Reached on a micro No. 13 (red and cream) from Avenida Tacna down to Santa Cruz, Calle Retiro is off block 11 of Angamos Oeste.

Museum of Natural History
Av. Arenales, block 12 (Mon.-Fri. 8–6, Sat. 9–12)
Little visited though quite fascinating, its main attraction, a 'sun fish', is one of only three known examples on this planet. Take a micro No. 13 (red and cream) from Av. Tacna.

National Museum of Peruvian Culture
Av. Alfonso Ugarte 650 (Mon.-Sat. 10–7; small charge)
For material artifacts like carved gourds, costumes and ceramics from most corners of Peruvian history, this is the best place. It's easily enough found, near Plaza 2 de Mayo. Along the same lines, though concentrating more on modern pottery, the private collection of Lima's **Museum of Contemporary Peruvian Folk art** is also worth checking out. It is located at Saco Oliveros off the third block of Av. Arequipa (open Tue.-Fri. 2.30–7, Sat. 8.30–12; donations welcome).

Peruvian Health Sciences Museum
Av. Grau 1541 (Mon.-Fri. 9–12; small charge)
An interesting collection despite the dreadful name, covering pre-

Conquest medical, sexual and magico-medical activities. Take a bus No. 20 from Miro Quesada, entrance next to the emergency doors of Hospital 2 de Mayo.

Philatelic Museum
Camana (Mon.-Fri. 8.30–12 and 3–6; free)
Hidden away in Lima's central post office, near the government palace – and possessing a myriad of antique stamps as well as displays on the Inca postal system. For coin enthusiasts, and on a similar note, just a short stroll away at Cuzco 245, you can find the **Numismatic Museum** on the second floor of *Banco Wiese* (open 9–1, Mon.-Fri.; free).

Bullfight Museum
Plaza de Acho (bullring), Hualgayoc 332, Rimac (Mon.-Fri. 9–1 and 3–6, weekends 9–1)
Houses some original Goya engravings, several interesting paintings and a few relics of bullfighting contests.

Museum of Italian Art
Paseo Colon 125 (Tue.-Sun. 9–7; free)
Located inside an unusual Renaissance building on the second block of the Paseo de la Republica (next to the *Hotel Sheraton*). Exhibits some **contemporary Peruvian art** as well as reproductions of the Italian masters.

Museum of the Inquisition (Junin 548) Pinacoteca Museum (on the Municipal Building); **National Museum of Art** (Paseo Colon 125); **Military Museum** (Callao fort)
These have already been detailed in the text, see pp. 37, 39 and 44. The military museum can be combined with a visit to the **Naval Museum** on Av. Jorge Chavez, off Plaza Grau in Callao (open Mon., Wed., Fri., Sat. 9–12.30 and 3–5.30; free).

The zoo
(Tue.-Sun. 9–5; nominal charge)
In a relatively deserted spot between Lima Centro and Callao, on the sacred site of the ancient Maranga culture, now stands the *Parque de las Leyendas*, home for **Lima's Zoo**. Although quite far from town, the yellow bus No. 48 goes there from the Plaza de Armas. The park and zoo are laid out, very roughly, according to the three regions of Peru – costa, sierra and selva – though there's little attempt to create the appropriate habitats. It's nothing special, just animals in cages – condors, pumas, penguins, even elephants and many more fascinating species. A fine place for a picnic, there are also good artesania stalls outside the park, particularly hot on cases of magnificent, if dead, insects.

Music, movies and cultural events

For listings of music, film and theatre events – indeed everything detailed below – much the best source is the daily El Commercio, *whose 'Section C' is usually pretty comprehensive. In English, a much less complete selection is printed in the* Lima Times.

All forms of **Peruvian music** can be found at their best in Lima, and as a modern city it has also got an interesting range of clubs and discos. As far as the **live scene** goes, though, you're really spoilt for choice in the variety of traditional and hybrid sounds – which for me at least is one of the most enduring reasons for staying in, and returning to, the capital. As usual, things are at their liveliest on Friday and Saturday nights, particularly among the folk group *peñas* and the burgeoning *salsadromos*.

Among the peñas – some of which only open for the weekend – the surest bet for authentic **Andean folk music**, and one of the cheapest, is *Peña Hatuchay*, just over the bridge into Rimac at Trujillo 228; *Peña Wifala*, though more tourist orientated and a small venue, is also quite good – Cailloma 633, off Nicolas de Pierola. If you're into pure **musica negra**, excellent coastal 'roots' music, *La Valentina*, in Av. Iquitos (La Victoria district), is the most popular. Like the peñas it usually gets going around 10pm, though you can often find things just as lively at 5 the following morning. **Creole music**, lying somewhere between Andean folk and negra and incorporating a lot of Spanish influence, is generally pretty good at *La Palizada*, quite a big peña at Av. Ejercito 800 in Miraflores (tel. 410552).

Lima is also an excellent place for **salsa music**, and there are *salsa-dromos* scattered around many of the suburbs – *Sarava* in Surquillo; *Bertoloto* in Magdalena; *La Maquina de Sabor* in Balconcillo; and the *Havana Club* in Miraflores. There's also a relatively new disco-salsa group called the *Hermanos Silva Band*, well worth keeping an eye open for. Virtually everywhere in Lima that has live music also serves **food**, many places – such as Hatuchay – include the price of a meal on the entrance ticket.

Of the numerous **discos** in Lima, many have a members only policy, though if you can provide proof of tourist status (a passport for instance) you usually have no problem getting in. Most of them are in **San Isidro**: *Up and Down*, a new-wave, rock and reggae joint in Augusto Tamayo (opposite Sears); the English-run *Percy's Bar*, more of a drinking place than for dancing, also in Augusto Tamayo; *Mediterraneo*, a trendy, new-wave, rock and disco dive, opposite the Camino Real Shopping Centre; and *La Manzana*, mostly disco, at Miguel Dasso 143. In **Miraflores**, *La Miel* is the most central, popular with sailors and touring sports teams it plays lots of disco, a little salsa, and often levies a heavy cover charge

– Jose Pardo 120 (underneath the Indianapolis Restaurant). Just over the road, above El Pacifico cinema, another disco – *Arizona Colt* – blasts rock and disco onto a rather dimly lit dance floor. For less stereotyped evening out there are a few **bars** in Miraflores, mostly done up like English pubs – *Sergeant Peppers* (San Martin, off Larco) and the *Lion's Club* (Plaza Bolognesi) are among the best, each sometimes offering live music; drinks, however, are expensive.

Movie-going is still an important part of life in Lima and there are major clusters of **cinemas** all around the Plaza San Martin, Jiron Union and Av. Nicolas de Pierola in Lima Centro, and on the fringes of the park in Miraflores – notably *El Pacifico* by the Haiti Cafe, and *Romeo and Julietta* at the ocean end of the park. The *Cine Roma*, which often shows quality films from all over the world, can be found off block 8 of the Avenida Arequipa. For any film which might attract relatively large crowds, it's advisable to buy tickets in advance; alternatively, be prepared to purchase them on the 'black market' at inflated prices – queues are often long and large blocks of seats are regularly bought up by the first in line. For information on film-making in Peru, see p. 20.

Though it's not always so accessible, Lima also has a **theatre** circuit and in addition to regular venues, short performances sometimes take place in theatre bars. The country's major prestige companies, however, are the **National Ballet Company** and **National Symphony**, both based on seasons at the **Teatro Municipal** in downtown Lima. Here, too, there are quite frequent performances by international musicians and companies, often organised by the foreign cultural organisations. The **British Council** are quite active in this line – and surprisingly imaginative – and they also show British-made films at their building on the Av. Arequipa.

Bullfighting has been a popular pastime among a relatively small, wealthy elite from the Spanish Conquest to the present day – despite 160 years of independence from Spain. Pizarro himself brought out the first *lidia* bull for fighting in Lima, and there is a great tradition between the controlling families of Peru – the very same families who breed bulls on their *haciendas* – to hold fights in Lima during the months of October and November. They invite some of the world's best bullfighters from Spain, Mexico and Venezuela, offering the cream up to $25,000 for an afternoon's sport at the prestigious **Plaza de Acho** in Rimac. To get tickets, if you feel the need to observe such spectacle, you'll do best to buy them in advance from the ticket-office (block 2 of Huancavelica) or, failing that, on the door an hour or so before the fights (usually on Saturday and Sunday afternoons – particularly during October).

If you're in Lima for April, an interesting day trip would be to visit the National Concourse of **Pacing Horses** (*Caballos de Paso*) out in the tourist recreation centre at Pachacamac on the Pan Americana South (usually between the 23rd and 29th). Lima's high society is always there in full force, sometimes making the trip a fascinating one, regardless of the horses' antics.

November is the month for the **International Fair of the Pacific** held once every two years (next in 1986) – see billboards for actual dates. Normally held out on the Avenida La Marina, this is essentially aimed at the world of commerce and high technology, though it is considered a cultural event too and is generally accompanied by *fiestas* throughout the city.

Eating and drinking

Of all South American capitals, Lima probably has the widest variety of **restaurants** and an equally broad range of prices. Regardless of class or status, virtually everyone eats out regularly, and although it's considered no great shakes, it usually ends up as an evening's entertainment in itself. Restaurants of every type and size, from expensive hotel dining rooms to tiny set-meal street stalls, seem to crowd every corner of the city. There are no *best* places, since it's ultimately a matter of taste, though there are plenty worth recommending.

In and around **Lima Centro** the choice is almost limitless. *El Cordano* is rich in style, very cheap, has a fast waiter service and is also something of a drinking dive (opposite Desamperados railway station, behind the Government Palace). In the *Hotel Crillon* (Av. Nicolas de Pierola), the *Sky Room* has good fixed-price meals and offers an excellent view across the city – rather plush and quite expensive though. *L'Eau Vive*, Ucayali 390 (opposite Torre Tagle Palace) is very reasonable, serving superb French food cooked by nuns; set menu for lunch and evening meals, closing at 10pm after a chorus of Ave Maria. The *Restaurant Campari* is a nice place to chat over a drink or snack and is very central, only 100m from Plaza San Martin at Apurimac 286. More or less opposite the modern Hotel Crillon, *Chalet Suisse* serves pretty reasonable international food (Av. Nicolas de Pierola 560).

Chinese food, or *chifa*, is one of Lima's finest specialities, the principal zone for this being in the streets around the central market; although a slightly more expensive place, complete with amazing panoramas of the city *El Dorado* is a sky-scraping chifa restaurant at Avenida Arequipa 2450 (tel. 221080). Lima also caters quite well for **vegetarian food** these days: *La Natural* (near the corner of Moquegua and Torrico) has a co-op shop and restaurant around an attractive patio – very cheap lunches and excellent stuff (open 8am–8.30pm); another veggie, *El Girasol* (Camana 327), also takes great care to serve quality food, or for really inexpensive meals you could try the stalls and snack-sellers in the central market.

A few restaurants in **San Isidro** are worth a mention: *Jose Antonia* (Monteagudo 21) has live entertainment and serves typical Peruvian dishes; and *La Barca*, on the corner of Av. Ejercito and Av. Salaverry, produces some of the best seafood around. **Miraflores**, however, has more to offer, even if its nearly all on the expensive side. Along the park, on Diagonal, there are several places to choose from: the *Haiti* is OK for snacks, drinks and soups, and is Lima's number one meeting place; the *Roxy*, further down the street, is hard to beat for pastas (if you can afford them); or for pizzas there's *La Pizzaria*. There are also plenty of restaurants-cum-bars on Larco – *Manolo*'s probably being the most popular – though approaching the ocean from here they tend to be more reasonably priced. Along Schell, the road going away from the park below *Roxy* and at right-angles to Diagonal, there are a few places worth checking out; *La Colina* (No. 727) offers local dishes at very good rates and doesn't mind you sitting around for a few drinks if you're not hungry; *Bircher Berner* (No. 598) has a few **vegetarian** specialities; and a couple of doors beyond *La Colina* there's an excellent *cevicheria*.

Barranco has a good collection of cheaper restaurants (geared more to the locals than a tourist market), most of them spreading out from the municipal park. The best one, however, which is quite pricey, is *El Otro Sitio* (Calle Sucre 315) with a wide range of typical dishes in the pleasant surroundings of a colonial house. Below Barranco, along the **Costa Verde**, you'll also find shacks cooking *anticuchos* and seafood and which, strangely, hire transvestites and bisexuals to wave in customers as they drive past along the coastal road. Much more upmarket are two very plush beach-side restaurants: the *Costa Verde*, which includes turtle on its menu; and the relatively new *Rosa Nautica*, which cost over one million dollars to set up, opened in September 1983, and generally costs around $25 per person – calling itself a tourist restaurant it's constructed on a platform over the sea and at night surfers are hired to hold curling waves under spot-lights.

One place which rarely sees gringos is *Latin Brothers* restaurant in the **suburb of Lince** (Av. Jose Leal 1277–81; tel. 710260). Specialising in enormous communal platters of delicious seafoods, Latin Brothers is a large 'spit and sawdust' eating house whose image is represented on the walls in hallucinogenic paintings of the great salsa artists. Loud salsa music often accompanies the meals.

Consuming business

Airlines   Offices are nearly all on the Plaza San Martin or along Avenida Nicolas de Pierola in Lima Centro.

Airport buses   Leave regularly from outside their office in Camana, near the corner with Nicolas de Pierola and behind the Hotel Bolivar.

American Express   Post restante/cheques, etc. from the main branch *Lima Tours* at Belen 1040 (tel. 276624), near the Plaza San Martin.

Artesania shopping   Is best done in the markets on blocks 3 and 10 of the Av. La Marina in Pueblo Libre; jungle artifacts are excellently selected and sold by *Antisuyo* in San Isidro (Llano Zapata 120), while *La Gringa* (La Paz 522) in Miraflores is also one of the better all-round artesania shops.

Banks   *Banco de la Nacion*, just off Nicolas de Pierola, usually has the quickest service.

Beaches   COSTA VERDE has the nearest beaches, though HERRA DURA (out on the point beyond Barranco and Chorrillos) is much nicer for swimming and quite clean. ANCÓN to the north and EL SILENCIO to the south (both about 30km away) are the most fashionable. More details in the following section.

Black market cash   Peruvian currency can be bought for cheques or cash from guys hanging around behind the Hotel Bolivar or in some of the smaller hostels.

Books   A few shops on Nicolas de Pierola stock English books (try the one at 689), and *The Book Exchange*, just around the corner at Ocoña 211, sells or swops a large quantity of second-hand paperbacks.

Buses   Most bus terminals and offices are between the Hotel Sheraton and Parque Universitario, or in the district of La Victoria along Av. 28 de Julio and Prolongacion Huanuco. For a complete list see Lima's yellow pages telephone guide. Among those companies offering services to a **variety of destinations** are: *Morales Moralitos* (Av. Grau 141; tel. 286252); *Tepsa* (Av. Paseo de la Republica 129 – opposite the Sheraton; tel. 289995); *Leon de Huanuco* (Av. 28 de Julio, La Victoria 1520; tel. 329088); *Ormeño* (Carlos Zavala 145, near Parque Universitario; tel. 275679); and – for **Huaraz and Chavin** only – *Condor de Chavin* (Montevideo 1039; tel. 288122).

Camping gear   Try the *South American Explorers' Club* (Av. Portugal 146; tel. 314480 – English spoken) or failing that buy equipment in Huaraz or Cuzco.

Car rental   Expensive but available through: *Budget* (La Paz 522, Miraflores; tel. 454685); *Hertz* (Jr. Ocoña 262, Lima; tel. 286330); *National* (Av. España 449, Lima; tel. 232526); *Dollar* (Mexico 333, Lima; tel. 725565); *ABC* (Av. Tacna 542, Lima; tel. 335922); and *Avis* (Sheraton Hotel; tel. 327245).

Casas de cambio   Mostly along Nicolas de Pierola between the Plaza San Martin and Plaza 2 de Mayo.

Cock-fighting   Traditional Spanish-American bloodlust – still enacted at weekends in the *Coliseo de Gallos*, Sandia 150.

Dentists and doctors   Ask your embassy for a list of addresses.

Embassies   include AUSTRALIA – Natalio Sanchez 220, Piso 6, Plaza

Washington (tel. 288315): BRITAIN – Natalio Sanchez 125, Piso 12, Plaza Washington (tel. 283830); CANADA – Calle Libertad 130, Miraflores (tel. 463890); FRANCE – Plaza Francia 234 (tel. 238618); ITALY – Av. Petit Thouars 369, Santa Beatriz (tel. 233477); NETHERLANDS – Av. Arequipa 1155, Santa Beatriz (tel. 721925); SWEDEN – Las Camelias 780, Piso 9 (tel. 406700); USA – Av. Garcilaso de la Vega 1400 (tel. 286000).

Emergencies Phone the tourist police on 237225 or 246571. If you can travel safely don't wait for an ambulance – get a taxi straight to the hospital address that they give you.

Health food Best places are the *Natural Co-op* on Moquegua (near corner with Torrico) and *El Girasol* at Camana 327 (not far from the Plaza de Armas).

Hiking information Look in at the *South American Explorers' Club*, Av. Portugal 146 (tel. 314480), for advice, trail maps, etc. For **mountain-climbing** the *Club Alpino Peruano* (Las Begonias 630, San Isidro) are helpful. See also 'trekking' below.

Horse-racing The Hippodromo on Prolongacion Javier Prado, out in Monterrico, is active most evenings except Mondays.

Hospitals The following are all well-equipped: *Clinica Anglo Americana* (Av. Salazar, San Isidro; tel. 403570); *Clinica Internacional* (Washington 1475; tel. 288060); and *Clinica San Borja* (Av. del Aire 333, San Borja; tel. 413141). All have emergency departments which can be used as an 'outpatients' or you can ask for house-calls by telephoning.

Immigraciones The main offices for any enquiries or renewals is on block 11 of 28 de Julio, at the Lima end of the Paseo de La Republica.

International telephones Calls can be made both nationally and internationally from Entelperu's offices in Colmena 878, just off the Plaza San Martin.

Krishna consciousness The headquarters for this movement, also known as the *Vedic Cultural Circle*, is at Jr. Junin 415.

Laundry Many hotels will do this quite cheaply, though there are also numerous *lavanderias* in most central and suburban areas.

Maps Ordnance survey type maps now available from the *Instituto Geografico Militar*'s shop on the Plaza San Martin (Av. Nicolas de Pierola 947).

Opticians Good shop on Schell in Miraflores, near the corner with Larco.

Phones All Lima call boxes are operated by *rins* which you can buy in many corner shops or on the street in Lima Centro. Most *bodegas* also have a phone for public use; this usually costs little more than the price of a rin.

Photography For gear, accessories or fast development there are only a few good places, all of them expensive: the co-op in Av. Galvez (off Av.

Grau, near the Sheraton); a small shop (one-hour rapid development service) on 28 de Julio, in Miraflores (near the corner with Larco); and *Hartmans* of Diagonal, Miraflores. Kodac's laboratories will develop Ektachrome though not Kodachrome (Av. Arriola, just off Javier Prado Este in La Victoria). *Camera repairs* are skilfully done by a little Japanese shop near the Cinés Romeo and Julietta in Miraflores.

Post restante   Letters are kept for up to three months in the Central Post Office (left side of the Government Palace on Plaza des Armas).

Railway tickets   From Desamparados station, to the back of the Government Palace, either the day before or just an hour prior to departure (opens 6am).

Tourist office   In a plush arcade at Belen 1066, near the Plaza San Martin (open Mon.-Sat. 9–7).

Travel agencies   Often combined as tour operators, most of these are in the centre. The best are probably *Lima Tours* (Belen 1040, near Plaza San Martin; tel. 276624) and *Explorama* (Camana 851; tel. 244764).

Trekking companies   Most reliable are *Explorandes* (Bolognesi 159, Miraflores), though there are plenty of others and some good local ones in Cuzco and Huaraz.

Turkish baths   These or saunas are available most days and evenings from: *Windsor*, Miguel Dasso 156, San Isidro; *Pizarro*, Jr. Union 284, Lima; and *Jose Pardo*, Av. Jose Pardo 182, Miraflores.

AROUND LIMA

THE LIMA BEACHES – AND PACHACAMAC

Most of the better **beaches** within easy reach of Lima are to the south – beginning about 30km out at the impressive pre-Inca ruins of Pachacamac, a sacred citadel which still dominates this stretch of coastline. The site, and a day at one or other of the beaches, can easily be combined – and it's little problem to get out there from the capital. A **microbus** (No. 120: blue and orange) leaves regularly for Pachacamac from Plaza Santa Catalina in Lima Centro, and there are also frequent departures, from the same square (red, blue and white **bus**) for the village-resort of PUCUSANA (65km from Lima), passing Pachacamac and three excellent beaches along the way.

   Closest of these – just a couple of kilometres outside Pachacamac – is **PLAYA SAN PEDRO**, a seemingly endless and usually deserted strip of

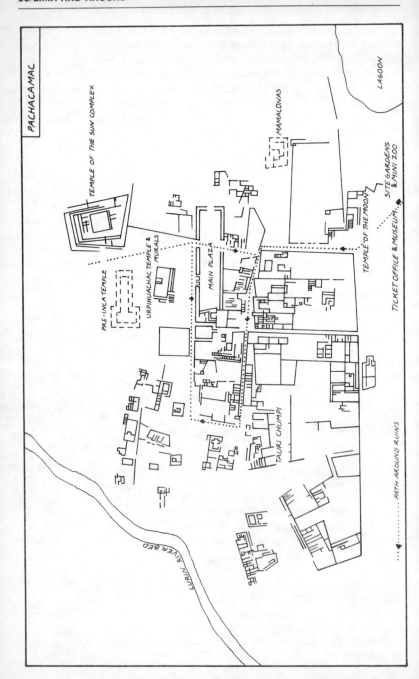

PACHACAMAC

TEMPLE OF THE SUN COMPLEX

LAGOON

MAMACONAS

PRE-INCA TEMPLE

URPIHUACHAC TEMPLE & MURALS

MAIN PLAZA

TEMPLE OF THE MOON

SITE GARDENS & MINI ZOO

TICKET OFFICE & MUSEUM

TAURI CHUMPI

PATH AROUND RUINS

LURIN RIVER BED

sand. Constantly pounded by rollers, however, it can be quite dangerous for swimming. Much more sheltered, and more popular, is the beautiful bay of **EL SILENCIO**, 6km to the south. This is in many ways the most tempting target. There are refreshments in hut-cafes at the back of the beach, some excellent seafood restaurants on the cliff above, and a couple of smaller, more secluded bays a short drive downcoast. At **PUNTA HERMOSA**, which is about 10 minutes on the bus beyond Silencio, you come to an attractive cliff-top settlement and, down below, what's becoming Lima's leading surf resort. And finally **PUCUSANA**: an old fishing village, gathered onto the side of a small hilly peninsula, which is now perhaps the most fashionable of the beaches, a holiday resort where the Limeños stay rather than drive out to swim. For the continuation of this road – the Pan American Highway – see p. 59.

Open daily from 9–5, **PACHACAMAC** is by far the most interesting of the Rimac's ancient sites – and a group of ruins you'll probably want to make time for even if you're about to head out to Cuzco and Machu Picchu. There's a small entry charge for the citadel, which includes admission to the site museum, well worth looking round on the way in. It takes a good 2 hours to wander round the whole extent of the ruins.

Pachacamac actually means something like 'the Earth's Creator'. It was certainly occupied by 500 AD and probably for a long time before that. At this stage, however, when other *huacas* were being constructed in the lower Rimac valley, Pachacamac was a temple-citadel, a centre for mass pilgrimages. Later it became one of the most famous shrines in the Inca Empire, with Pachacamac himself worshipped along with the sun. The Incas built their Sun Temple on the crest of the hill above Pachacamac's own sacred precinct. In 1533, Francisco Pizarro sent his brother Hernando to seize Pachacamac's treasure; it ended as a disappointing trip, with him finding only the incredible wooden idol on show today in the site museum.

Entering **the ruins**, after passing the restored sectors which include the **Temple of the Moon** and the **Convent of the Sun Virgins** (or *mamaconas*), you can see the **Sun Temple** directly ahead. Constructed on the top level of a series of 'pyramidical' platforms, it was built tightly onto the hill with plastered adobe bricks, all of the walls once painted in several bright colours. Below this is the **main Plaza**, originally covered with thatched roof supported on stilts and thought to have been the area where pilgrims assembled in adoration. The rest of the ruins, visible though barely distinguishable, were dwellings, store-houses, and palaces. From the very top of the Sun Temple there's a magnificent view out beyond the modern highway to the beach (Playa San Pedro) and across the sea to a sizeable, uplifted island. Standing in the ruins, this island – clearly geologically related to the Pachacamac mound – appears like a huge whale approaching shore.

ON THE CENTRAL HIGHWAY: PURUCHUCO AND CAJAMARQUILLA

Puruchuco and Cajarmarquilla, the most impressive sites around Lima after Pachacamac, are also quite easily reached. Both lie near the beginning of the 'Central Highway', the road which climbs up behind Lima towards CHOSICA, LA OROYA and the Andes. To get out to Puruchuco (signposted at km 11 of the highway) you can take bus 200, 202, or 204 from the Nicolas de Pierola terminal; Cajamarquilla, 6km further, is served by bus 202d, either from Pierola or by picking it up on the highway by Puruchuco. Both sites are open daily from 9–5.

An 800–year-old, pre-Inca settlement, PURUCHUCO comprises a labyrinth-like villa and a small site museum. The adobe structure was apparently rebuilt and adapted by the Incas shortly before the Spanish arrival. It's a fascinating 'ruin', superbly restored in a way which vividly captures what life was probably like before the Conquest. Very close by (ask the site guard for directions) in the Parque Fernando Carozi two other ruins – **Huaquerones** and **Catalina Huaca** – are being restored, and at **Chivateros** there's a quarry apparently dating back some 12,000 years.

The **CAJAMARQUILLA** bus – the 202d – actually goes to a refinery so ask the driver to drop you off shortly after leaving the main road, then ask for directions – the ruins are well hidden next to an old hacienda. First occupied in the Huari Era (AD 600–1000), Cajamarquilla flourished under the **Cuismancu culture**, a city-building State contemporary with the better known Chimu in northern Peru. It was an enclosed city containing thousands of small maze-like dwellings clustered around a higher section, probably nobles, quarters and relatively small plazas. Apparently abandoned before the Incas arrived in 1470, it may well have been devastated by an earthquake. Pottery found here in the 1960s by a group of Italian archaeologists suggests that the site was inhabited over 1,300 years ago.

THE PAN AMERICAN HIGHWAY: NORTH AND SOUTH OF LIMA

Stretching out along the coast in both directions, the **Pan American Highway** runs the entire 2,600 km length of Peru with Lima more or less exactly at its centre. Towns along the sometimes very arid coastline immediately north and south of the capital are only of minor interest to most travellers, though there are some glorious beaches (the closest ones covered on p. 57) and pretty much infinite potential for beach-camping.

North of Lima

After passing beyond the fashionable beach resort of ANCÓN, about 30km north of Lima, the Pan American passes over a high, often foggy, plateau from the Chillon to the **Chancay valley**. This fog zone, still covered by sparse vegetation, was a relatively fertile *lomas* (a place where plants grow from moisture in the air rather than rainwater or irrigation) area in Pre-Inca days. Evidence of winter camps from 5,000 years ago has been found here and it's an exciting spot to explore for anyone interested in a unique habitat. Beyond CHANCAY (by-passing the market town of HUARAL) the road continues through stark desert, broken only by more lomas at LACHAY (km 105). A little further, however, at km 133, a track turns off into a small peninsula making for the secluded bay of **EL PARAISO** – a magical beach perfect for camping, swimming and scuba.

Crossing more bleak sands, the Pan American comes next to **HUACHA**, an unusual place with some interesting colonial architecture and a ruined church in the upper part of town. From here to BARRANCA (see p. 158) only the town and port of SUPE break the monotonous beauty of desert and ocean.

Going south

A more appealing journey, and one which you may well decide to make for its own sake, is south as far as the **Pisco** or **Ica valleys**; comfortable, if old, **colectivos** make this 3 to 4-hour trip from Jr. Leticia, a few blocks from Parque Universitario ($6 single).

Beyond Pachacamac, Lima's weekend beaches and the peninsula of Pucusana, a newly opened road cruises south to Asia, passing the long beach and salt-pools of CHILCA, and the amazing lion-shaped rock of **Leon Dormido**. **ASIA**, a small town spread along the side of the road from km 95–103, is essentially an agricultural town, producing cotton, bananas and maize. Some interesting archaeological finds in local grave-yards reveal that this site was occupied by a pre-ceramic gardening society by around 2,500 BC associated also with the earliest examples of a trophy-head cult (many of the mummies were decapitated). The long **beach** at Asia is ideal for camping – particularly at the southern end.

Another 40km and you come to the larger settlement of CAÑETE, an attractive town with a colonial flavour and surrounded by marigolds and cotton fields, though not a place you'll probably want to stop in. If you feel like breaking the journey before Pisco, in fact, the only real candidate is **CHINCHA**, which appears after a stretch of almost Saharan landscape – and a mightily impressive sand dune – at the top of the coastal cliff. Quite a busy little town, selling wines and piscos, Chincha possesses several **hotels**. The flashiest, *El Sausal* (with pool) is on the right as you come into town; most of the cheaper ones are on the main street (left at the fork in the road) beyond the Ormeño bus depot. Although a strong centre of black culture, based originally around the slave plantations, Chincha is more often visited for its ruins. Numerous *huacas* lie scattered about this oasis, which was one of the richest prior to the Conquest. Dominated in pre-Inca days by the Cuismancu (or Chincha) State, most activity was focused around what were probably ceremonial pyramids. One of these, the **Huaca Centinela**, sits majestically in the valley below the Chincha table-land and the ocean – around 30 minutes walk from the turn-off by Hotel Sausal. Not far from Chincha, some 40km up the Castrovireyna road which leaves the Pan American at km 230, another impressive Cuismancu ruin, TAMBO COLORADO, lies within easy reach of either Chincha or Pisco (see p. 117).

INTO THE MOUNTAINS: EL TREN DE LA SIERRA

Difficult as it is to describe this **railway journey** up into the Andes from Lima, it's usually a momentous occasion – spectacular in itself (the construction of this line is hard to believe), and for many travellers their first sight of llamas, and of Peru's indigenous Indian mountain world. With the train climbing very slowly to a pass at some 4,800m above sea-level, however, it's also likely to be your first experience of altitude sickness, *soroche*, and you may well need to use the bags of air brought up and down the carriage at this point by the guard. If you're worried about altitude sickness, or can't face returning this way, the **colectivo** services between Lima and Huancayo (*Comite* No. 12 from Montivideo 733) or Tarma (*Comite* No. 1 from Renovacion 399) are a lot quicker. Otherwise, **the train** leaves the Desaparedos station (watch for pick-pockets here) every day except Sunday at around 7.40am, rolling into Huancayo around 5–9 pm; tickets are on sale from 6am but best bought the day before.

For President Balta of Peru and many of his contemporaries in 1868, the iron fingers of a railroad, 'if attached to the hand of Lima would instantly squeeze out all the wealth of the Andes, and the whistle of the locomotives would awaken the Indian race from its centuries-old lethargy'. Consequently, when the American railway entrepreneur, **Henry Meiggs** (aptly called 'Yankee Pizarro') arrived on the scene it was instantly decided that the coastal *guano* deposits would be sold off to finance a new railroad, one which faced technical problems (i.e. the Andes) never previously encountered by the engineers of iron-roads. With timber from Oregon and the labour of thousands of Chinese coolies (basis of Peru's present Chinese communities), Meiggs reached La Oroya alone via 61 bridges, 65 tunnels and, as mentioned, the startling 4,800m pass. A great accomplishment, it nevertheless tended to bind Peru to the New York and London banking worlds rather than to its own hinterland and peasant population.

It usually takes around 6 hours to reach LA OROYA, nearly all this time high in the Andes as the factories and cloudy Lima skies are swiftly left behind. At Oroya there's a connection – at 2.30pm – for CERRO DE PASCO, a possible approach to HUANUCO (see below), but most travellers stay on the tram for the ride to HUANCAYO. Passing through the astonishing **Javja valley**, this is the most beautiful scenery of the trip, striped by fabulous coloured furls of mountain. Even Paul Theroux, who didn't much care for Peru, and still less for this trip – 'no railway journey on earth can be so aptly described as going on *ad nauseam*' – was impressed. Arrival at HUANCAYO, however, is certainly a relief.

Going on from LA OROYA to HUANUCO your best bet is to move sharply and catch the bus connection at the end of the rail route at CERRO DE PASCO – it's only another 3–4 hours, which by this stage makes little difference. Neither **LA OROYA** nor **CERRO DE PASCO** are particularly inviting places, bleak little mining towns separated by 130km or so of rather desolate landscape, and fiercely cold at night. If you break the journey this way it is best do it in Cerro, which has a slightly wider selection of **hotels** – the *El Viajeno* by the plaza, *Los Angeles* in the market area, and *Gran Hotel Cerro de Pasco* on Av. Angamos in the suburb of San Juan. Trains **returning to Lima** from CERRO leave at 6am, a considerably quicker downhill trek.

HUANCAYO AND HUANCAVELICA

Although relatively close together, these two towns offer highly contrasting visions of life in the central Peruvian Andes. **Huancayo**, at 3,261m, is a large commercial city, thriving on agricultural produce, while **Huancavelica**, higher at 3,680m, is a remote colonial town with a sad history revolving around its mercury mines. Both fascinating in their own ways, and possessing a distinct culture represented in colourful rustic costumes and dances like the *Chunguinada* or *Huaylas*, these towns are also strategic points on the traditional (though no longer practicable) highland route to Cuzco. As well as the railway and colectivo **connections**, a bus service is run from Lima to Huancayo (*Etusca*, Prolongacion Huanuco 1439–1441, La Victoria). Trains leave Huancayo for Huancavelica daily at 7am (less than $2 first class, 4–6 hours).

Huancayo
HUANCAYO is now capital of the Junin Department, an important market centre dealing in vast quantities of wheat. It's a very old settlement, however, and the cereal and textile potential of the region has long been exploited. Back in the 1460s the native *Huanca* tribe was conquered by the Inca Pachacuti's forces during his period of Imperial expansion; occupied by the Spanish since 1537, it was on the map economically, though remaining little more than a pit-stop village; it was the railway, reaching Huancayo in 1909, which truly transformed it into a city. Being

relatively modern there's very little of architectural or historical merit in the town, though it's a lively place and it does have an extremely active market (best on Sundays), mostly for fruit and vegetables but also with a good selection of woollen jumpers and clothes – which, here, you'll be beginning to need.

There are several reasonable **hotels** in Huancayo, including the *Hotel Kiya* on the Plaza de Armas and the *Huancayo* or *Primavera* on Giraldez, just around the corner from the station. Excellent *bed and breakfast* is available at very low prices from Jr. Galena 169, in the district of Millotingo (tel. 233786). **Calle Real** is the main street, a wide commercial drag housing both the *Banco de la Nacion* and the tourist office. It's possible to eat and drink in a number of adequate **restaurants** around the Plaza de Armas. And although you should rest for a day or two if you've come straight up from the coast, there is plenty of **nightlife**. Local music and dance is performed most Sundays at the *Coliseo* (3pm) on Calle Real, and there are some good creole and folklore peñas – *Dale 'U'* (corner of Calle Ayacucho with Huancavelica), *Algarrobo* (13 de Noviembre, Libertad), and *Cajon* (Calle Real – open every night). Every year, in **May**, Huancayo erupts into the splendid *Fiesta de las Cruces*.

Using Huancayo as a base you can make a number of enjoyable **excursions into the Jauja valley**. The **Convent of Ocopa** (or Santa Rosa), about 40 minutes out of town, is easily reached by taking a micro from the Church of Immaculate Conception (or the Lima train – 7am daily, except Sundays) to CONVENCÍON, where another bus covers the last 5 or 6km to the monastery. Founded in 1724, and taking some 20 years to build, this was the centre for the Franciscan mission into the Amazon – until their work was halted by the Wars of Independence and their mission villages in the jungle disintegrated, most Indians returning to the forest. The *cloisters* are more interesting than the church, though both are set in a pleasant and peaceful environment; there's also an excellent *library* with chronicles from the sixteenth century onwards, plus a *Museum of Natural History and Ethnology* containing lots of stuffed animals and native artifacts from the jungle. A trip out here can be conveniently combined with a visit to the **Ingenio trout farm** or the villages of SAN JERONIMO and HUAYLAS, where **woollen goods** are cheaper than in town – buying directly from the maker. For the energetic, **bicycles** can be hired for this trip (or any other) from *Huancayo Tours* (Calle Real 543).

Two other worthwhile trips: 40km out is the old capital of the region, JAUJA, a little colonial town which was for a short while chosen as a possible capital of Peru – a past reflected in its architecture; buses from Huancayo market. And, near the pueblo of HUARI (again direct buses from the market) there are the **Huari-Huilca ruins**, the sacred complex of the Huanca tribe which dominated this region for over 200 years before the Incas. The distinct style they display went unrecognised before 1964 when local villagers rediscovered the site under their fields. At the site is a small museum showing collections of ceramic fragments, bones and stone weapons.

Huancavelica and beyond

After 3½ hours, and a beautiful uphill train ride, from Huancayo, **HUANCAVELICA** is a surprisingly pure Indian town – in spite of a long colonial history and a fairly impressive array of period architecture. The weight of its past, however, lies heavily on its shoulders. After mercury deposits were discovered here in 1563, the town began producing ore for the entire silver mines of Peru – replacing previous expensive Spanish imports. In just over 100 years so many Indian labourers had died of mercury poisoning that the pits could hardly keep going – so exorbitant were the salaries necessary to attract new workers after those locals bound to serve by the *mitayo* system had been literally used up and thrown away. Today the ore is taken by truck to Pisco on the coast, but many mines have been closed and people are somewhat discontented. On the borderline with the guerilla activities around Ayacucho and Huanta, they are sensitive to its influence.

If you do come here – and it's possible to complete a circuit down to the coast via Pisco, a spectacular 12-hour journey over amazingly high terrain – you'll probably not stay for long. The cheaper **hotels** are pretty nasty, though the *Turistas*, for once, is quite reasonable value. Around the main **Plaza de Armas** are the **cathedral** and a handful of **churches,** two of them – San Francisco and Santo Domingo – connected to it by an underground passage. These apart, there's not a lot of interest. If you're here on Sunday you'll hit the **market;** if you like walking at this altitude there are **thermal baths** on the hill north of the river, and a **weaving co-op** 4km out at TOTORAL. The **Pisco bus** is operated by *Oropesa* and leaves at 6am; make sure it's going the whole way though – sometimes it turns round midway at SANTA INES, a cold hamlet on top of the *Puna*. For Lima, via Huancayo, an *Empresa Huancavelica* bus leaves daily at 5pm.

The *Hidalgo* company, at the time of writing, continues to run a **bus to Cuzco** – a two-day journey via AYACUCHO, every Monday, Wednesday and Friday, leaving Huancayo at 7am. This is an incredible route – and a historically fascinating region – but for the moment the area between HUANCAVELICA and AYACUCHO is frankly too **dangerous** for gringos to enter with any degree of confidence. Accelerating guerilla activity makes it unsafe to pass through even on a bus. For the alternatives see p. 69.

TARMA AND THE HIGH JUNGLE

By far the nicest mountain town in this part of Peru, **TARMA** sits on the edge of the Andes almost within touching distance of the Amazon forest – a good alternative target from HUANCAYO, from which there are regular bus connections via LA ORAYA, allowing you to make a satisfying high jungle circuit via SATIPO. The region around Tarma is one of Peru's most beautiful corners, the mountains stretching down from high craggy limestone outcrops into steep canyons forged by *powerful* Amazon tributaries powering their way down to the Atlantic. And in Satipo and Pozuzo are two of the most accessible – and interesting – of Peruvian jungle towns.

Tarma itself is a pretty, colonial town, making a good living from flower growing and from its traditional textiles and leather goods. Its greatest claim to fame came during Juan Santos Atahualpa's rebellion in the 1740s and 1750s; taking refuge in the surrounding mountains he defied Spanish troops for more than a decade, though peace returned to the region in 1756 when Juan Santos and his allies mysteriously disappeared. Today it's a quiet little place – apart from the flow of trucks climbing up towards the jungle foothills, and the town's famous Easter Sunday procession from the main plaza, when the streets are covered in carpets of dazzling flowers. The *Hotel Turistas* (as you come into town from Lima) is reasonable at $10–15 single, but much more so are the *Hotel Galaxia*, on the plaza, and *Hostal America*, opposite the market.

A practical day's outing – though better appreciated if you camp overnight – takes you to the rural village of POLCAMAYO (1½ hours by bus). From here it's an hour's climb to the **Caves of Huagapo**, the country's deepest explored caves, and accessible for over 1km with flashlight and waterproofs. If you've a car or plenty of time at your disposal, the beautiful village of SAN PEDRO DE CAJAS, within hitching distance of the caves, produces superb quality weavings. Coincidentally, or not, it lies in a valley neatly divided into patchwork field-systems – an exact model of the local textile style. From here you can either take a bus or hitch back to Tarma.

SAN RAMON and **LA MERCED** (80–88 slow km from Tarma) mark the real beginning of the jungle. Both are well-connected by **buses** operated by *Etusca* and *Los Andes* – runs which continue on to SATIPO, or in the other direction back towards Lima. (Tarma is also connected to Lima by **colectivos**, which leave the capital at *Comité No. 1*, Renovacion 399, La Victoria.) Well-established settler towns, they are separated by only 8km of tarmac, some 2,500m below Tarma under the quiet strong sun of the high Jungle. Getting there the road winds down in ridiculously precipitous curves, keeping tight to the sides of the **Rio Palca canyon**, at present used for hydro-electric power generation. Originally a forest zone inhabited only by Campa-Ashaninka Indians, this century has seen much of the best land cleared by invading missionaries, lumber men, rubber collectors (mostly British firms and money) and, more recently, great waves of settlers from the Jauja valley.

The smaller of the two twin towns, SAN RAMON is probably the more pleasant place to break your journey. Its cheap **hotels**, *Chachapoyas* and *Selva*, are both reasonable, and if you're feeling extravagant or hurried there are 6 and 10 seater planes to Satipo and Puscillpa. LA MERCED (**hotels** *Christiana* and *Mercedes*), on the other hand, is quite a lot busier with a market and good plentiful restaurants thriving around the main plaza. Both places are on the river and surrounded by exciting hiking country and are linked with each other – and at least daily with Oxapampa/Pozuzo and Satipo – by a stream of trucks and buses.

Oxapampa and Pozuzo

Some 78km by bus from La Merced, **OXAPAMPA** is a small settlement dependent for its survival on lumber and coffee. Most of the forest immediately around the town has disappeared recently, giving way to pasture for cattle. The indigenous **Amuesha Indians**, disgruntled at being pushed off their land so that the trees could be taken away and cows put out to grass, are battling hard on local, national and international levels for their land-rights. Strongly influenced in architecture, blood and temperament by the nearby Germanic settlement of Pozuzo, this is actually quite a pleasant frontier town in its own way. There's a fair **hotel** – the *Bolivar*.

POZUZO, a weird combination of European rusticism and Peruvian culture, is all that's left of a unique eighteenth-century scheme to open up the Amazon using European peasants as settlers. Some 80km down the valley from Oxapampa, along a very rough road, its wooden chalets with tyrolean sloping roofs have been rebuilt ever since the first Austrian and German colonists arrived in the 1850s. The brainchild of President Ramon Castilla's economic adviser – a German aristocrat – 300 settlers left Europe in 1857; seven of them died at sea and six more were killed by an avalanche causing another 50 to turn back only 35km from here, but Pozuzo was eventually founded. Amazingly, many of the town's inhabitants still speak German, eat *schitellsuppe* and dance the polka. Well worth the ride, Pozuzo is an unusual and friendly place (try the *Hostal Tyrol* or *Hotel Maldonado*). **Trucks** for Pozuzo leave irregularly from opposite the Hotel Bolivar in Oxapampa.

Satipo

SATIPO is a real jungle town. Developing around rubber extraction some 80 years ago, it now serves as the economic and social centre for a widely scattered population of over 40,000 colonists – offering them tools, food supplies, medical facilities, banks and even a cinema. Above all else it's a town where settlers go to 'civilise' themselves, as they say. The **Campa-Ashaninka Indians**, indigenous to the area, have either taken up plots of land and begun to 'compete' with colonists, or moved into one of the ever-shrinking zones just out of permanent contact with the rest of Peru. Unmistakable in their reddish-brown or cream *cushma* robes as they walk through town, the more traditional natives are very proud of their culture.

An ideal town in which to get kitted out for a jungle expedition, or merely to sample the delights of the *selva* for a day or two, Satipo is about 8 hours drive down a bumpy road from La Merced (frequent buses and colectivos). It possesses an interesting **market**, an **airstrip** (two commercial airlines – *SASA* and *Aguila* – both flying to San Ramon, Pucallpa and Atalaya) and is in the middle of a beautiful landscape – a fascinating **walk** is to follow the path from the other side of the suspension bridge to one of the plantations left of town. Further afield, local colectivos go to the end of the *Caretera Marginal*, into relatively freshly settled areas. The *Hotel Majestic*, on the plaza, is the best **place to stay** in town (deliciously cool rooms), though the *Hostal* Palmero works out cheaper and there are others around the market area and along the airport road.

As an alternative to retracing your steps back via LA MERCED and SAN RAMON, there's a breathtaking **direct road to Huancayo** (*Los Andes* bus, 12 hours). For the really adventurous, a **flight to Atalaya** (see p. 251), a small settlement on the Ucayali river in deep jungle, could turn out to be an exciting excursion; it's sometimes quite simple to find a boat going downstream from here to PUCALLPA (two to five days; see p. 251).

TRAVEL DETAILS

Buses and colectivos

From Lima Regular connections to just about anywhere in Peru, including, among towns detailed in this chapter, Barranca (3–4hrs), Chincha (3–4hrs), Huancayo (10–12hrs) and Tarma (5–7 hrs). For frequency of service and journey times for other destinations in other chapters, see their respective listings and travel details.

From Huancayo Huancavelica (daily; 4–5hrs); Tarma (daily; 4hrs); Huanuco/Pucallpa (daily; 10–12hrs/ 20hrs or more); Cuzco (no longer practicable; see p. 69).

Huancavelica-Pisco (daily; 12hrs).

Tarma-La Merced (daily; 2–4hrs).

From La Merced Satipo (daily; 8hrs); Oxapampa/Pozuzo (more or less daily; 6hrs/14hrs).

Trains

From Lima La Oroya/Huancayo (daily except Sundays; 6hrs/9–14hrs).

Huancayo-Huancavelica (daily except Sundays; 6–8hrs).

La Oroya-Cerro de Pasco (daily connection with Lima train; 4½hrs).

Boats

Atalaya-Pucallpa (occasional boats; 2–5 days).

Flights

From Lima Numerous international connections (see p. 52 for location of airline offices). Domestic flights several times daily to Cuzco (1hr); twice daily to Arequipa (1¼hrs) and Tacna (2½hrs); daily to Juliaca (for Puno; 2hrs), Trujillo/Chiclayo (45mins/1hr40), Piura (1¼hrs), Iquitos (1½hrs), Pucallpa (1hr), Tingo Maria (40mins), and Huanuco (25mins); 5 a week to Yurimaguas (2hrs), and Rioja/Moyabamba (1½hrs); 4 a week to Tarapoto (1hr).

From San Ramon Satipo and Pucallpa (several times a week).

From Satipo Atalaya and Pucallpa (several times a week).

Chapter two
CUZCO AND THE SACRED VALLEY

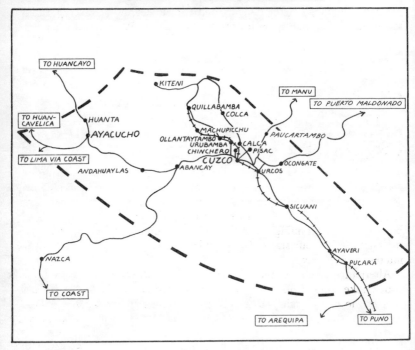

TO HUANCAYO

KITENI

TO MANU

TO PUERTO MALDONADO

QUILLABAMBA
COLCA

TO HUAN-
CAVELICA

HUANTA

MACHUPICCHU

PAUCARTAMBO

AYACUCHO

OLLANTAYTAMBO
URUBAMBA
CHINCHERO

CALCA
PISAC

TO LIMA VIA COAST

CUZCO

ANDAHUAYLAS

ABANCAY

OCONGATE

URCOS

SICUANI

AYAVERI

NAZCA

PUCARÁ

TO COAST

TO AREQUIPA

TO PUNO

Historically the most fascinating region of Peru, the mountain area encompassing Cuzco and the sacred **Urubamba valley** is the focus of interest for all travellers – South American and gringo alike. *Cuzco* itself is of course the prime target, a Spanish city built on sumptuous Inca foundations and as rich in human life and activity today as it can have been at the height of the Empire. Despite the floods of tourists it remains a welcoming place with a welcome dose of home comforts too, and a rare opportunity for close encounters with native Quechua Indians.

Once you've acclimatised – and the altitude here is something which does have to be treated with respect – there are dozens of enticing destinations within easy reach. For most people the **Sacred Valley** is the obvious first choice, with the magical site of **Machu Picchu** as its ultimate goal and hordes of other ruins – **Pisac** and **Ollantaytambo** in particular – amid glorious Andean panoramas on the way. To the south lie more

Inca and pre-Inca sites, at **Tipón** and **Pikillacta**, which are almost as spectacular and far less visited, while continuing beyond them the **rail journey to Puno** is as dramatic as any you could hope to find.

Around Cuzco, too, is some of the finest trekking country in Peru: not just the **Inca Trail** to Machu Picchu but hundreds of less known, unbeaten paths into the mountains. And heading further afield you can begin to penetrate the jungle, either staying on the train beyond the Sacred Valley to **Quillabamba**, or forging north-east by truck to **Paucartambo**.

CUZCO

GETTING THERE

Most people arrive in Cuzco either by air from Lima or by train via Arequipa and Puno. Unless you're really pushed for time there's little advantage in flying. The bus or colectivo ride down the south coast to AREQUIPA (18 hours), then by train to PUNO and Lake Titicaca (10–12 hours) before continuing north through the stunning Vilcanota valley for the final 10–12 hour stage, is a scintillating journey with a great deal of interest along the way.

Alternatively, and slightly faster, there are **direct buses** from Lima which take around 30–50 hours to reach Cuzco, either via Pisco and Ayachucho or through Nazca and Albancay. These are rough overland journeys passing through extravagantly steep mountain scenery and over extremely high passes: magnificent and often thrilling routes. But with the recent increase in guerilla activity in the area around AYACUCHO and, to some extent, ABANCAY (which both pass through), they are also potentially dangerous. Buses are occasionally stopped by 'terrorists' or more often hassled by police looking for guerillas and gun-runners.

The other traditional route, **by train from Lima to Huancayo** and across the Andes from there by bus or truck to Cuzco, is probably even more dangerous. It passes directly through the most terror-struck and politically explosive areas of Peru – especiaily around AYACUCHO – and although it used to be *the* route for the hardened traveller, few will attempt it now.

Ayacucho – a no-go zone
Once one of the most popular Andean cities in Peru – with over 30 colonial churches and a tradition for rumbustious fiestas – **AYACUCHO** is now effectively off the map for travellers. Foreigners can't even buy

seats on flights to the city. A radical University town, with a long tradition of fine craft works, Ayacucho today is more famous for its outbreaks of terrorism and police excesses. It cannot at present be recommended: a fuller account will be given when the area returns to some kind of status quo. If you do end up here in the meantime, *Alojamiento El Trocadero* is cheap and very near the main plaza, where *Savory Cafe* serves up excellent food. But remember, Ayacucho is in a state of military emergency and a curfew is rigidly enforced by trigger-happy police and soldiers.

ABANCAY, on the road between Ayacucho and Cuzco, is a large market town with little to offer the traveller apart from a roof for the night (try the *Gran Hotel*) and transport out by bus or truck. Between here and Cuzco, near the village of CARAHUASI, there's a beautifully carved ancient stone known as *Sahuite*. A graphic representation of an Inca village, it's worth a look if you're not too pressed for time.

CUZCO

'Navel of the world' for the Incas, **CUZCO** still captivates the hearts and imagination of all who pass through. A busy little city of nearly 250,000 inhabitants, it rests enclosed between high hills dominated by the imposing fortress of Sacsayhuaman and a more recent white-stone Christ figure, stretching his arms out across the town. At some 3 ½km above sea-level, Cuzco is a place to take in slowly, wandering about the surprisingly numerous sites and museums, sampling the active nightlife, and gradually absorbing its living history.

Since early Inca times Cuzco has been a major attraction for travellers and today hundreds – even thousands – of tourists arrive daily, often packing out every plane, bus and train. Not an expensive place by any standards, many of them end up staying quite some time, and although its often quoted role as the 'Katmandu of South America' is not entirely justified, the city remains an exciting centre of pilgrimage. For anyone planning to hang around here for a week or more, the most thorough guide to Cuzco and its surrounds is *Exploring Cuzco* by Peter Frost – on sale at most bookshops in town and some travel agencies.

According to legend, Cuzco was founded by Manco Capac and his sister Mama Occlo around AD 1200. Over the next 200 years the valley was home for the Inca tribe, one of many localised war-like groups then dominating the Peruvian sierra. A series of chiefs led the tribe after Manco Capac, the eighth one being Viracocha Inca. It wasn't until Viracocha's son Pachacuti assumed power in 1438 that Cuzco became the centre for an expanding empire. Pachacuti pushed outward the frontier of Inca territory at the same time as masterminding imperial Cuzco's design. He canalised the Saphi and the Tullumayo, two rivers which ran down the valley, and built the centre of the city between them: Cuzco's plan was conceived in the form of a puma – the fortress of Sacsayhuaman as the jagged tooth-packed head and Pumacchupan, the sacred cat's tail, at the point where the two rivers merge just below the sun temple of Koricancha.

It was a well-built city – walls and foundations of all important buildings were of hard volcanic rock, streets ran straight and narrow with stone channels to take away the heavy rains – but above all it was a sacred place whose heart, the heart of the puma, was *huacapata*, a ceremonial square approximating in both size and position to the modern Plaza de Armas. Four main roads radiated from the square, one to each corner of the empire. Pachacuti's palace was built on one corner of *huacapata* (you can still see the perfectly regular courses of andesite stone in the Restaurant Roma), while his grandson, Huayna Capac, sited his in the opposite corner next to the temple cloisters for the Virgins of the Sun. Overall, the achievement was remarkable, a planned city destined to be the centre of a huge empire.

By the time the Spanish arrived in Peru, Cuzco was a thriving capital. Nobles and conquered chieftains were allowed to live around the ruler in the body of the puma, servants and artisans on the outskirts, while subjects from all over the empire made regular official pilgrimages. Of all the Incas only Atahualpa, the last, never actually resided in Cuzco – he was on his way there to assume the imperial fringe when the Conquistadores captured him at Cajamarca. In his place, Pizarro eventually reached the native capital on November 15th 1533. The Spaniards were astonished – *huacapata*'s beauty surpassed anything they had seen before in the New World – but as usual they lost no time in discovering and plundering, its fantastic wealth of gold and booty.

DESIGNS ABSTRACTED FROM
AN INCA EMPEROR'S TUNIC

The Spanish city was officially founded in 1534, divided among 88 of Pizarro's men who chose to remain as settlers. Manco Inca was set up as a puppet Inca, ruling from a new palace on the hill just below Sacsayhuaman. But within a year power struggles between the younger Pizarro brothers and Almagro – an ally of Manco's – had reached the

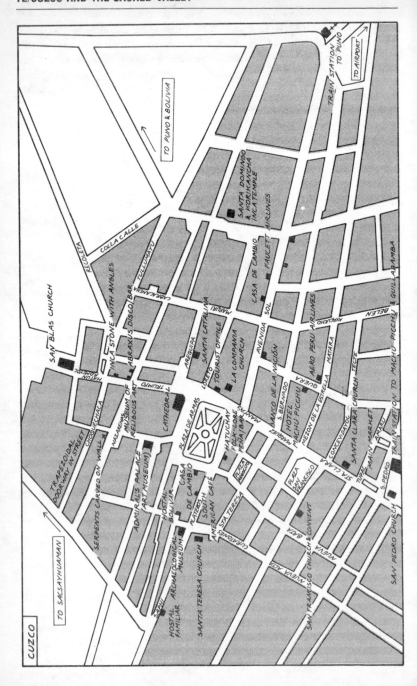

CUZCO

point of open violence – serious trouble only being averted by Almagro's departure at the head of an expedition to Chile. With him out of the way, Juan and Gonzalo Pizarro were free to abuse the Inca and his subjects – eventually provoking Manco to open resistance. In 1536 he fled to Yucay, in the Sacred Valley, to gather forces for the Great Rebellion.

Within days less than 200 Spanish defenders, with only 80 horses, were surrounded in Cuzco by over 100,000 rebel Inca warriors. On May 6th Manco's men attacked, setting fires among the dry thatched roofs and laying siege to the city for the following week. Finally, the Spaniards, still besieged in *Huacapata*, led a desperate attempt on horseback to break out. Riding up to Sacsayhuaman they counter-attacked the Inca base. Incredibly, the following day they defeated the native stronghold – putting some 1,500 warriors to the sword as they took the fortress.

Cuzco never again came under such serious native threat, but its battles were far from over. By the end of the rains the following year the small Spanish stronghold was still awaiting reinforcements: Hernando Pizarro's men were on their way up from the coast, while Almagro, returning from Chile, was at Urcos, only 35km to the south. Unsure of his loyalties and the cause of the Inca insurrection, Almagro tried to befriend Manco. The Emperor, however, wisely chose to retreat into a remote mountain refuge at Vilcabamba – unable to put his trust in any Spaniard. Almagro immediately seized Cuzco for himself and defeated the Pizarrist force arriving from Lima. For a few months the city became the centre of the Almagrist rebels until Pizarro himself arrived on the scene, defeated the rebel force on the edge of town and had Almagro garrotted in the main plaza.

The rebel Incas, meanwhile, held out in Vilcabamba until 1572, when the Viceroy, Toledo, captured Tupac Aymaru – one of Manco's sons who had succeeded as Emperor. Bringing him into Cuzco, Toledo had him beheaded in *huacapata*. From then on the city was left in relative peace, ravaged only by the great earthquake of 1650. Following this dramatic tremor, remarkably illustrated on a huge canvas in the Cathedral, Bishop Mollinedo (1673–99) was largely responsible for the reconstruction of the city – its architectural, artistic and cultural achievements. Mollinedo arrived in Peru with a superb personal collection of paintings – including two by El Greco – and his influence is closely associated with Cuzco's most creative years of art. The Cuzco school of painting, which emerges from his patronage, flourished for 200 years, much of its finer work is still exhibited in museums and churches around the city.

Today, more than anything else, Cuzco is geared towards tourism. A veritable haven for travellers in its wealth of reasonably priced hotels, relaxed cafes, fascinating little streets and hidden corners, it's the kind of town to savour during the last few weeks of a long trip, or to use as a base from which to explore Peru. Looking down on the red-tiled roofs from the amazing viewpoint of Sacsayhuaman, Cuzco can be held in perspective; a deceptively peaceful sight, snuggling in a valley on top of the world. Down below the streets constantly throng with townsfolk, tourists and Quechua Indians – the latter, more often than not, selling craft-goods in the Plaza de Armas or one of the many *artesania* markets. Only **one word of warning** – pick-pockets are numerous and extremely skilful. But don't let that put you off.

Getting around and finding a place to stay

Cuzco's ancient and modern centre, the **Plaza de Armas**, is the obvious place to get your initial bearings – facing uphill towards the ruined fortress of **Sacsayhuaman**, and with the **Cathedral** squat and unmistakable along one side. Behind is the **Church of La Compañia**, smaller than the Cathedral but with an equally impressive pair of belfries, and next door to it the glass-fronted **tourist office**. Wherever you are in Cuzco it's always possible to find your way back to the Plaza de Armas simply by locating the ruins of Sacsayhuaman or the often illuminated white **Christ figure** which stands beside it on the steep horizon.

Back on ground level there are a few other points of reference which ease orientation. From the bottom corner of the plaza, near La Compañia, two streets lead off at 90° to each other – **Mantas**, leading uphill to the **central market** and **San Pedro railway station** (for Machu Picchu and Quillabamba); and the wider **Avenida del Sol** going straight down towards **Koricancha**, the Puno railway station and airport. Both **railway stations**, and most of the **bus terminals** (scattered all over town, see p. 87), are within walking distance of the centre. From the **airport**, 6km out, you'll need to use a taxi or the very cheap local bus service.

Small enough not to get lost in, Cuzco is still sufficiently large to cater for all needs and keep you busy for as long as you like – most travellers stay at least a week. It's a good idea to check out a few **hostels** before deciding on the right one for you: if you're initially whacked by the altitude take the first you find, dump your gear and go out for a coca tea (*maté de coca*). You can always search out a better place later on.

Every regular visitor has their favourite hotel in Cuzco and mine is the *Hostal Familiar*. Only 2½ blocks uphill towards Sacsayhuaman from the Plaza de Armas, at Saphi 661, it is very reasonably priced, has private or communal showers, its own cafe with a noticeboard for travellers' information and messages, and a laundry service. There are many other slightly cheaper places between here and the plaza, particularly along Plateros and Procuradores. One of the very cheapest in town is the *Hostal Bolivar*; turn left at the top end of Procuradores and it's tucked away in a corner, behind the ancient walls of Pachacuti's palace. A typical gringo's basic hotel, it has earned a reputation for drugs and consequently gets raided, now and again, by the police.

Downhill from the Plaza de Armas there are plenty more, though they tend to be on the expensive side. The *Hostal Machu Picchu*, however, isn't overpriced and, set around a picturesque courtyard, is a pleasant place to stay (just off Avenida Sol at Quera 274). Over the road, at Quera 251, the plusher *Hostal del Inca* (tel. 2009) costs up to $5 per night in the high season (July and August), less at other times. Another option, surprisingly cheap and friendly, is the *Hostal Tipón*, slightly away from the town centre on Calle Tecte but handy for most bus and all train terminals.

Historic buildings and museums

To get into most of Cuzco's museums, churches and mansions – and many of the nearby sites in the Inca's Garden and Sacred Valley – you'll need a **general entrance ticket**: available from the tourist office on the Plaza de Armas at $10 (half-price for students). **Opening hours** for most of these buildings are daily from 9 until 5.30 (except Sundays), usually closing for lunch between 12 and 2.30. Notice, as you wander around Cuzco, how many of the important Spanish buildings have been constructed on the foundations of Inca palaces and temples. The closer you are to the Plaza de Armas, ancient *huacapata*, the more obvious this is.

Each of the zones outlined below is within easy walking distance of the plaza and can be covered in a couple of hours, allowing extra time for the real historical enthusiasts of if you want to browse in the bars and shops en route.

On the Plaza de Armas

The **Church of La Compañia**, erected after the earthquake of 1650, spreads its Latin Cross formation over the foundations of Huayna Capac's palace. Cool and dark, with a grand gold-leaf altarpiece, high vaulting and numerous paintings of the Cuzco School, it's most impressive in its external facade. To the right, the **Lourdes Chapel**, restored in 1894, is used mostly as an exhibition centre for local crafts, while the early Jesuit **University building** alongside often has traditional dance performances or film shows in the evening (check with the tourist office). On the other side of La Compañia, also covering the ancient space chosen by Huayna Capac, is the **House of the Inquisition**, a large hall today relatively harmlessly occupied by the **Tourist Office**.

Separating Huayna Capac's palace from the Acclahuasi, or Temple of the Sun Virgins, **Loreto Street** still displays the sturdily intricate walls of both. Today the Acclahuasi block is taken up by shops along the plaza, and the **Convent of Santa Catalina** down Arequipa Street. Santa Catalina has been closed for repairs over the last couple of years, but it should re-open soon, once again allowing the public to view its impressive Renaiss-

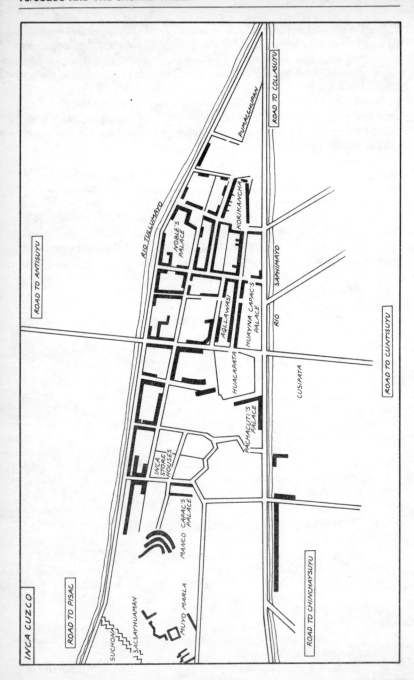

INCA CUZCO

ROAD TO ANTISUYU

ROAD TO PISAC

RIO TULLUMAYO

NOBLE'S PALACE

PUMACCHUPAN

ROAD TO COLLASUYU

KORIKAYCHA

AQLLAWASI

HUAYNA CAPAC'S PALACE

RIO SAPHIMAYO

HUACAPATA

CUSIPATA

ROAD TO CUNTISUYU

PACHACUTI'S PALACE

INCA STORE HOUSES

MANCO CAPAC'S PALACE

ROAD TO CHINCHAYSUYU

MUYO MARIA

SUCHUNA SACSAYHUAMAN

ance altarpiece, exceptional Cuzqueño paintings and unusual Moorish balconies.

The **Cathedral** sits squarely on the foundations of the Inca Viracocha's palace. Also constructed in the form of a Latin Cross, work began here as early as 1560. There are three naves – Triunfo Chapel as you enter, the main central aisle and the Chapel of Jesus, Joseph and Mary on the far side – all supported by only 14 pillars. Inside, the plateresque pulpit is exceptionally good, the main altar made entirely of fine silver, and there's a crucifixion attributed to Van Dyck; but the huge canvas depicting the terrible 1650 earthquake, high on the right as you enter Triunfo Chapel, is much the most fascinating of the Cathedral treasures. More than for anything you see, though, the temple's power lies in its mingling of history and legend. In the right-hand tower local myth claims an Indian chief lies imprisoned, awaiting the day when he can restore the glory of the Inca Empire. Here too hangs the huge and miraculous gold-and-bronze bell of Maria Angola, named for a freed African slave girl. And on the massive main doors of the Cathedral native craftsmen have left their own pagan adornment – the puma's head.

To the left of the Cathedral, and slightly uphill, Cuzco's most stunning colonial mansion, **the Admiral's Palace**, looks down onto the main square. Again, patently constructed on Inca foundations – this time the Waypar stronghold where the Spanish conquerors were besieged by Manco's forces in 1536 – it now houses the University's **Regional Historical Museum**. Particularly noteworthy for its simple but well-executed plateresque facade, surmounted by two imposing Spanish coats-of-arms, the museum itself is less spectacular. The main exhibition rooms, some done out in period furniture, face onto an aristocratic patio on two levels, and house a multitude of paintings from the Cuzco School. Mostly rather dull religious adorations, room 5 is worth checking out to see the rapid intrusion of canons, gunpowder and violence during the eighteenth century; while by room 10 the eighteenth- and nineteenth-century Cuzco-mestizo works display much bolder composition and use of colour. It deserves a quick visit, if only because it's included on the Cuzco entrance ticket.

The remaining two sides of the Plaza de Aramas are mostly taken up with shops and restaurants. Of these blocks, only one – Portal de Panes – had any significant Inca building before the Conquest. This was Pach-acuti's palace whose magnificent walls are now best appreciated from inside the **Restaurant Roma** on the corner.

Koricancha

The supreme example of Cuzco's combination of Inca stonework and colonial building is some way from the plaza (two blocks down Avenida del Sol), where the church of Santo Domingo rises from the walls of the ancient Sun Temple – **Koricancha**. The tightly interlocking blocks of polished andesite abut the street as straight and solid as ever – with the sixteenth-century church a poor contrast – but before the Conquistadores set their gold-hungry eyes on it the temple must have been a breathtaking sight indeed.

The complex consisted of four small sanctuaries and a larger temple set around a courtyard, the whole enclosed within a circular cornice of gold (*Koricancha* means 'golden enclosure'). Inner walls, too, were hung with sheets of beaten gold, and in the great Sun Temple stood a revered sun-disc – *Punchau* – of solid gold and far larger than a man. Ponchau had two companions in the temple, a golden image of *Viracocha* on the right and another representing *Illapa*, god of thunder, to the left. Below the temple, towards the tail of Cuzco's puma, was a garden in which everything was made from gold or silver and encrusted with precious jewels; from llamas and shepherds to the tiniest details of clumps of earth and weeds, even snails and butterflies. Not surprisingly, none of this survived the arrival of the Spanish.

Koricancha's position in the Cuzco valley was also carefully planned. Dozens of *ceques* (sacred lines, in many ways similar to ley-lines) radiate from the temple towards over 350 sacred *huacas*, in this case mostly special stones, springs, tombs and ancient quarries. Also, every June solstice, the sun's rays shine directly into a niche – the *tabernacle* – in which only the Inca was permitted to sit. Still prominent today, the tabernacle must have been incredible with the sun reflected off beaten plates of gold, studded with emeralds and turquoise.

Along with the main temple dedicated to the sun, there were others solely for the adoration of minor deities – the Moon, Venus, Thunder and Lightning, and the Rainbow. Some 200 *Mamaconas* (Sun Virgins) were attached to the divine household of Koricancha, their sole purpose to serve *Inti* – the Sun. They not only prepared his food and clothing, but were expected to ask favours from Inti on the emperor's behalf, and offer Him sexual satisfaction by sleeping on a stone bench next to his statue covered 'with blankets of iridescent feathers of rare Amazonian birds'. It was in Koricancha that the mummies of dead Incas were seated in niches at eye-level along the walls. The principal idols from every conquered province were also held 'hostage' here, and it was in Koricancha that every Emperor married his wives before acceding to the throne.

Plaza Regocijo and the Archaeological Museum

The **Plaza Regocijo**, today a pleasant garden square sheltering around a statue of Bolognesi, was originally the Inca *Cusipata*, an area cleared for dancing and festivities immediately beside the more ceremonious huacapata. Only a block from the Plaza de Armas, Regocijo is fronted by an attractively arched Municipal Building, the Hotel de Turistas and the **colonial mansion** which once belonged to the Inca Garcilaso. Although now housing the Departmental archives, it's possible to take a look around inside or merely to appreciate the impressive doorway – a neat mixture of Inca stonework with Spanish building from without. Garcilaso, half Inca and half Spanish, was a prolific post-Conquest writer – his most notable work being *The Royal Commentaries of The Incas*.

Leading off from the other side of Regocijo, along Santa Teresa Street, you pass the **House of the Pumas** (No 385). Not as grand as it sounds, this is now a small cafe: the six pumas above its entrance were carved into Inca blocks during the Spanish rebuilding of Cuzco. Turn right at the end of this street and you pass the **Church of Santa Teresa** (with an interesting collection of paintings on the life of the saint) before crossing Plateros to the Cuzco **Archaeological Museum** (Calle Tigre 165). Housed in a pleasant colonial mansion, it may not be the most impressive collection of pre-Columbian artifacts, but it is the best in town and worth checking out above all for some superb wooden *keros* – drinking vessels graphically painted with representations of the Inca and 'transitional' eras. The ceramics are generally of poor quality – you'll find better on the desks of executives in the National Institute of Culture – but there is a fascinating pottery monkey whose head was evidently filled with *chicha* beer so that it would 'urinate' into a long snaking channel, enabling initiated Inca priests to divine the future. The section on lithic art is also quite unusual, with many small carved stones and Inca architects' models such as the miniature prototypes of what look like Sacsayhuaman and Pisac; there's a collection of Inca weapons – essentially mace-heads and boleros – and upstairs lurks the inevitable mummy room including a number of trepanated skulls.

Plaza San Francisco and San Pedro

Ten minutes' walk below the Plaza de Armas, the area around Plaza San Francisco is a quietly interesting quarter. Opposite the Hotel de Turistas, where Mantas becomes Marquez, the graceful **Church and Convent of La Merced** sits peacefully amid the usual street bustle. A rich combination of baroque and Renaissance architecture, the church has a beautiful star-studded ceiling, a finely carved chair, and, like many Peruvian temples, a huge silver cross – an idol adored and kissed by a constantly shuffling crowd. Its real fame, though, comes from an incredible early eighteenth-century monstrance. This masterpiece of Cuzco craftmanship contains over 600 pearls, more than 1,500 diamonds and, being made of solid gold, weighs upwards of 22 kilos. The Convent also possesses a fine collection of paintings.

The **Plaza San Francisco** itself fronts the church and convent from which it takes its name, where two large cloisters boast some of the better colonial paintings by masters such as Diego Quispe Tito and Marcos Zapata. The square is best known though for its *papas rellenas*, delicious stuffed potatoes sold from stalls by Quechua women.

Passing under a crumbling archway from here you come to the **Church of Santa Clara**. Built around a single nave, its small inside, decorated with a gold-laminated altar and a few canvasses. The outside walls, however, show more interesting details: Inca blocks support the upper, cruder stonework, and four andesite columns, much cracked over the centuries, complete the doorway. So time-worn is the belfry that weeds and wild flowers have taken permanent root. Just up the street, in the busy market area next to the railway station for Machu Picchu, stands another colonial church – **San Pedro**, whose steps are normally crowded with colourful Quechua market traders. Relatively austere, with only a single nave, its main claim to fame is that somewhere among the stonework are ancient blocks dragged here from the small Inca fort of Picchu.

The Religious Art Museum and San Blas
The **Religious Art Museum**, one block uphill on the Triunfo side of the Cathedral, stands on the impressive foundations of the palace of the sixth emperor, Inca Roca. A superb mansion, once the Archbishop's residence, the museum now houses a valuable collection of paintings well displayed in period rooms. The most interesting exhibit – a large painting of the Last Supper – looks nothing special until you notice that Christ in partaking not of bread, but of the body of a guinea-pig. This unique work was painted in the seventeenth century by an anonymous artist who also appears to be responsible for several other canvasses; one of these, of San Sebastian, shows Inca nobles present at the saint's martyrdom.

Beside the museum, up the narrow Calle Hatun Romiyoc, every visitor to Cuzco seems to spend at least a few minutes trying to find the celebrated **Inca stone with 12 angles**; made even more famous by its popular representation on Cuzqueña beer bottles. One of the very best examples of Inca stonework, this 12 cornered block fits perfectly into the lower wall of Inca Roca's ancient residence. Indian women selling craft-goods usually place themselves strategically in front of it.

From here it's one-and-a-half blocks to the tiny **Chapel of San Blas**, with its unbelievably intricate pulpit. Carved from a solid block of cedar wood in a complicated churrigueresque style, it takes long, staring study to unravel the intricate detail: cherubim, a sun-disc, faces and bunches of grapes. Bishop Mollinedo donated the whole to the church in the late seventeenth century.

Returning to the main square via Plaza Nazarenas and you can pass by a couple more historic buildings. The sixteenth-century Seminary and Chapel of San Antonio Abad (closed for renovation into a hotel) was originally a religious school before becoming the **University of San Antonio Abad** in the seventeenth century. Virtually next door is the **Nazarenas Convent**, converted by OPESCO (the body responsible for restoring tourist sites) into their own offices. There were nuns here until the 1950 earthquake damaged it so badly that they had to leave. You can still look around, though, and its central courtyard has been sensitively rebuilt.

Sacsayhuaman and the Inca's Garden

The megalithic fortress of **Sacsayhuaman**, which overlooks the Plaza de Armas, is merely the closest, and most impressive, of several sites scattered around the sacred hills. Within easy walking distance beyond are the great *huaca* of **Kenko** and less visited **Salapunco** – the Cave of the Pumas. A few kilometres further, to what almost certainly formed the outer limits of the *Inca's Garden*, or estate, you come to the small castle of **Punca Pucara** and the stunning imperial baths of **Tambo Machay**. An ideal day's walking once you've acclimatised to the altitude, Sacsayhuaman and all other sites in the Inca's Garden can only be visited on a general **Cuzco tourist ticket**.

It's often a good idea to take Sacsayhuaman on in one day, leaving the other sites until just before you leave Cuzco, when you'll probably feel more energetic and adjusted to the rarefied air. If you would rather just walk downhill, it's always possible to take one of the regular Morales Moralitos buses going to Pisac (from Belen 451), or the more frequent mini-bus from the corner of Avenida Collasuyo and Calle Ejercito (just out of town along Recoleta), asking to be dropped off at Tambo Machay.

Sacsayhuaman

Although looking relatively close, it's quite a steep climb up to the ruins of Sacsayhuaman. The easiest route from the Plaza de Armas is along Calle Suecia, uphill from the Cathedral side, taking the first right (up a few steps) and turning almost immediately left up a narrow cobbled street, aptly named Resbalosa (slippery) to the Church of San Cristobal. This attractive adobe structure stands next to the even more impressive ruined walls of *Kolkampata* – palace of the expansionist Emperor, Manco Capac. From Kolkampata follow the road a few hundred yards to the point where it bends round on itself; here you'll find a well-worn path and crude stairway which takes you right up to the heart of the fortress. All in all it's about a 40–minute climb.

SACSAYHUAMAN, as the head of Cuzco's ethereal puma, points its fierce-looking teeth away from the city. Protected by such a steep approach from the town, the defensive walls were only needed on one side. Of megalithic proportions, the three walls zig-zag altogether for

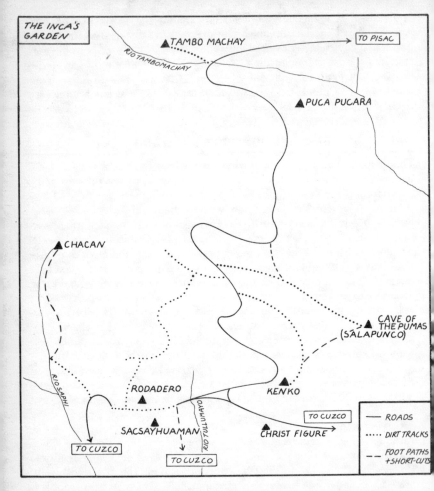

some 600m, enclosing what was originally a 'spiritual distillation' of the ancient city below, with many sectors being named after areas of imperial Cuzco. There's not much of the inner fortress left, but the enormous ramparts still stand 20m high, quite unperturbed by past battles, earthquakes or the passage of time. The quality of the massive polygonal stonework – one block alone weighs over 300 metric tons – is matched only by the brilliance of its design: the zig-zags, casting shadows in the afternoon sun, not only look like jagged cat's teeth, but also expose the flanks of any attackers trying to clamber up.

In Inca times, the inner fort was covered in buildings, a maze of tiny streets dominated by three major towers. Two of these – *Salla Marca* and *Pauca Marca* – had rectangular bases about 20m long; the other, **Muyu Marca**, whose foundations can still be clearly seen, was round with three concentric circles of wall, the outer one roughly 24m in diameter. Standing over 30m tall, Muyu Marca was an imperial residence with apparently lavish inner chambers and a constant supply of fresh water from subterranean channels. The other two towers were essentially warriors' barracks. All three were painted in vivid colours, had thatched roofs and were interconnected by underground passages: in its entirety the inner fortress could have housed some 10,000 people under siege. At the rear of this sector, looking directly down onto Cuzco and the valley, was a Temple of the Sun, reckoned by some to be *the* most important Inca shrine.

In front of the main defensive walls, a flat expanse of grassy ground – the esplanade – divides the fortress from a large outcrop of volcanic diorite. Intricately carved in places, and scarred with deep glacial striations, this rock, the **Rodadero** (or sliding place), was the site of an Inca throne. Originally there was a stone parapet surrounding this important *huaca*, and it's thought that here the emperor would have sat to oversee cermonial gatherings at fiesta times when there would be processions, wrestling matches and running competitions. On the far side was another cleared space, the sacred spring of **Calispucyo**, where ceremonies to initiate young boys into manhood were held.

It was the energetic Emperor Pachacuti who began work on Sacsayhuaman. The chronicler Cieza de León, writing in the 1550s, said that some 20,000 men helped in its construction: 4,000 cutting blocks from quarries; 6,000 dragging them on rollers to the site; and another 10,000 working on finishing and fitting them. Various types of rock were utilised in the fortress, including massive diorite blocks from nearby for the outer walls, Yucay limestone from over 15km away for the foundations, and dark andesite, some of it from over 35km distant, for the inner buildings and towers. With only fibre ropes, stone hammers, and bronze chisels, it must have been an enormous task. First, boulders were split by boring holes with stone or cane rods and wet sand; next, wooden wedges were inserted into these holes and saturated to crack the rocks into more manageable sizes; then, they were apparently shifted into place with levers. According to legend, some 3,000 lives were lost while dragging one huge stone! Despite the near century of creative work, though, it took only a few years for the Conquistadores to dismantle most of the inner structures, treating the place as a quarry for the building of Spanish Cuzco.

Little is known of the site's history apart from the fateful battle of 1536. Juan Pizarro, Francisco's younger brother, was killed as he charged the main gate in the desperate assault, and one of the leading Inca nobles, armed with a Spanish sword and shield, caused havoc by repulsing every enemy who tried to scale Muyu Marca, the last tower left in Inca hands. Sworn to fight to the death, he leapt from the top when defeat seemed inevitable, rather than accept humiliation and dishonour. Within hours the esplanade was covered in native corpses, food for vultures and inspiration for the Cuzco Coat of Arms which, since 1540, has had an orle of eight condors 'in memory of the fact that when the castle was taken these birds descended to eat the natives who had died in it'.

Today the only dramatic event which seems to take place at Sacsayhuaman is the colourful – if overcommercialised – **Inti Raymi festival** every June 24th. Generally packed by thousands of townsfolk and tourists, it is an attempt both to rekindle the vitality of Inca heritage and to make a few more bucks.

Kenko, Salapunco and Chacan

A gentle 20-minute walk from Sacsayhuaman brings you to the large limestone outcrop of **KENCO**, another important Inca *huaca*. This great stone, carved with a complex pattern of steps, seats, geometric reliefs and puma designs, illustrates the critical role of the **Rock Cult** in the realm of Inca cosmological beliefs. Worship in pre-Columbian Peru, from at least the Chavin Era (1000 BC), returned again and again to the reverence of large (and sometimes small) rocky outcrops, as if they possessed some hidden life-force; a power belonging to the spiritual dimension.

At the top end of the huaca, the Incas constructed a circulat amphitheatre containing 19 vaulted niches (probably seats) facing in towards the impressive limestone. Lama's blood or *chicha* beer may well have been poured in at the top of some of the prominent zig-zagging channels which run down the huaca – the speed and routes of the liquid, in conjunction with the patterns of the rock, giving the answers to the priests' supplications. Similar Inca models of divinatory channels can be seen in Cuzco's Museum of Archaeology and Anthropology, but only on site is it possible to appreciate fully the magnitude of this great oracle.

Another short stroll, slightly uphill and through a few fields from Kenco, leads to **SALAPUNCO**, the fascinating Cave of the Pumas. Essentially a small cavern where the rock has again been painstakingly carved, the main relief work at Salapunco seems to represent the puma motif, although some historians consider them monkeys rather than cats. Little is known about the Inca rituals associated with Salapunco but, without a doubt, it was another important sacred centre. Being off the main Pisac road, Salapunco is still rarely visited, yet this interesting site is set in inspiring countryside overlooking the Cuzco valley; what's more, coming this way cuts off long bends in the road between Kenco and Puca Pucara.

More important, though even less visited than Salapunco, is **CHACAN**, about 5km from Sacsayhuaman on the opposite side of the fortress to

Kenco. It's easily reached by following the Rio Saphi (in the gully on the western edge of Sacsayhuaman) uphill until a stream, Quespehuara, merges from the right: Trace the Quespehuara upstream for 2 or 3km to its source and you're at Chacan. A revered spring, there are still underground water channels emerging from the rock here, a fair amount of terracing, some carved rocks, and a few buildings. Like Tambo Machay just across the hills, Chacan represents the importance of water in Inca religion. On the one hand, as at Kenco, there was rock, the eternal; on the other, water, a less stable life-giving force. At Chacan the Incas concentrated their energies on the latter.

Puca Pucara and Tambo Machay

Although a relatively small fort, **PUCA PUCARA** is impressively situated: overlooking the Cuzco valley and on the road separating the ancient capital from the Sacred Valley. At most an hour's cross-country walk, uphill from Sacsayhuaman (or up to 2 hours keeping to the curvaceous main road), this zone of the Inca's Garden is dotted with cut rocks. Many were perhaps worked to obtain stones for building, but overall they must be seen as part of the carefully planned Emperor's estate. If Cuzco and its environs could be seen to be sacred ground, then the Inca's claim for ideological supremacy over neighbouring territories would be all the more valid.

Although in many ways reminiscent of a small European castle, it is generally thought that Puca Pucara (The Red Fort) was more a hunting lodge for the Emperor – on the outer edge of his gardens – than a genuine defensive position. Although well protected on three sides it could have contained only a relatively small garrison, and in any case Sacsayhuaman was far better equipped to secure Cuzco's rear. Puca Pucara may, however, have served also as a guard-post controlling the flow of people and produce between Cuzco and the Sacred Valley which lies just beyond the mountains to the north-east. Its semi-circle of protective wall is topped by a commanding esplanade, while on the lower levels there are a number of stone-walled chambers and you can still make out the ducts which distributed fresh water from a nearby spring.

TAMBO MACHAY, less than 15 minutes walk away, is one of the more impressive Inca baths. A sign-posted track leads off the main road just beyond Puca Pucara. Conveniently sited at a spring near the Inca's hunting lodge, its main construction lies in a sheltered, grotto-like gully where some superb Inca masonry revolves around the use and adoration of water. The ruins basically consist of three-tiered platforms: the top one holds four trapezoidal niches which were probably used as seats. On the next level, underground water emerges directly from a hole at the base of the stonework, and from here cascades down to the bottom platform, creating a cold shower just about the correct height for an Inca to bathe under. On this platform the spring water splits into two channels, both pouring the last metre down to ground level. Clearly a site for ritual bathing, the quality of the stonework suggests that its use was restricted to the higher nobility, and even by them it was perhaps used only on ceremonial occasions.

The spring itself is about 1km further up the gully; its water diverted through underground channels to the bathing area. Follow the *quebrada* up and you'll come to a cave (in Quechua, *Machay* means cave) where the stream emerges: here too there is quality stonework embellished with relief carving. Evidently an aqueduct once connected this water source with Puca Pucara, which can also be seen poking its head over the horizon from here. Not just important as a water supply for the Cuzco valley, Tambo Machay must have been a favourite site in the Inca's Garden – a place the Emperor could visit regularly to rest, bathe and worship.

Eating, drinking and other action

Generally speaking, **food** in Cuzco is very good, if not quite as interesting or varied as it is along the coast. Most of the more central cafes and restaurants cater for all tastes, offering anything from a toasted cheese sandwich or a hamburger to the best in creole dishes. Most places stay open from early in the morning until around midnight, when those hungry for other action disappear into one of the numerous late-night bars or night-clubs. No other Peruvian town has as varied a nightlife as Cuzco and, importantly, everywhere is within staggering distance of somewhere else. The most concentrated area for restaurants and bars is **Procuradores alley**, a true gringo dive leading off Portal de Panes on the Plaza de Armas. Down here, where you can get virtually anything at most times of day or night, there's a pizza-parlour, vegetarian food and several cheapish cocktail bars.

There are plenty of places for **breakfasts** and **day-time snacks**. Among these, *Le Paris* (on the corner of Calle Media and the Plaza de Armas) is cheap and friendly with background pop and rock; the *Allyu* cafe, beside the Cathedral, is a more tranquil place, a favourite meeting spot which plays perpetual classical music; there's also *Varayoc*, on Plaza Regocijo, which serves good coffee, has a noticeboard and offers an interesting magazine rack.

For **evening meals**, or simply more substantial food, the list could be almost infinite. There are several places – like the *Restaurant Roma, Chef Victor* and the *Chifa Los Angeles* – right on the Plaza de Armas. Better dishes, though, are generally available from the *South American Cafe* half a block up Plateros from the plaza; a gringo haven, very friendly, reasonably priced and jointly run by Peruvian and English partners.

For **vegetarians** there are a couple of excellent restaurants: *Govinda*, a Hindu place at Calle Espaderos 128, or, *Pura Vida*, attached to the 'Community of Sun – a universal fraternity', in the pleasant colonial courtyard of the Hostal Marqueses at Garcilaso 256.

If you're more into trying the **local food**, there are two obvious choices: you can eat from the stalls at the *central market* (near the Machu Picchu railway station) where there's an endless selection of good, very cheap meals; or you can try one of the many *Quintas*, which specialise in foods like chicharrones, guinea-pig and spicy creole dishes. Ordinarily, being open-air places, Quintas only serve at lunch-times – one favourite is the *Quinta Eulalia* (Choquechaca 384; tel. 2421), unusually central with a very keen atmosphere and a good juke-box well supplied with chicha music.

As far as **nightlife** goes, there are broadly three scenes: *peñas* for Peruvian music; discos for international jiving; and bars for heavy drinking. Of the peñas, *Q'Hatuchay* is the liveliest and most popular, on the Plaza de Armas at Portal Confituria 233. Just around the corner, *Ajha Wasi*, on Plaza Regocijo, has both music and food most evenings, while, *El Truco*, a creole peña on the same square caters for more upmarket clients. The best of Cuzco's discos is undoubtedly *Abraxus* (Herraje 171): although not very large, it has the advantage of a very long bar front and stays open till at least 3am every night. If you tire of this there are two other possibilities – *Studio 2000* (block 2 of Garcilaso) and the cave-like *El Muki* (Santa Catalina Angosta 114).

For **heavy drinking**, the traditional spit-and-sawdust spot is the *Bar Azul*, opposite the South American Cafe on Plateros. Most cafes serve drinks but only here does drinking go on until daybreak. On a less decadent level, and if you want to watch folk-dancing to mountain music, try the *Centro Quosqo* (Av. del Sol 604; tel. 3708) which has perform-ances most evenings between 6.30 and 8pm.

Some practical details

BOOKS The best bookshop for English books – new and second-hand – is *Libreria Studium*, on Meson de la Estrella 144.

BUSES Bus offices tend to be scattered around Cuzco, but here are a few of the main ones: *Ormeño* for Lima via Abancay (Portal de Carnes, on the north corner of the Plaza de Armas; tel. 228712); *Hidalgo* for Lima via Ayacucho and Pisco (Cuichipunco 299; tel. 232061); *Transturin* for Puno and La Paz (Portal de Panes 109 – over Rest. Roma; tel. 222332); *San Cristobal* for Juliaca, Arequipa and Lima (Av. Huascar 120; tel. 3184); *Morales Moralitos* for Lima via Nazca, and the Sacred Valley or Puno (Belen 451; tel. 5035).

CAMPING EQUIPMENT is generally quite easy to get hold of in Cuzco. Several adventure travel outfitters rent equipment, including *Sigui*

Tours (Portal de Panes 123), and a place on block 2 of Garcilaso: you'll need to leave a deposit (travellers' cheques will do) in either. Alternatively, travellers often advertise tent space for set hikes (like the Inca Trail) on noticeboards – try the *Hostal Familiar* on Saphi or the *South American Cafe* on Plateros.

CUZCO TOURIST TICKET The general entrance ticket – $10 from the Tourist Office and also available at some of the sites it covers – is a must, permitting access to most important sights in the town and many of the major attractions in the surrounding area.

DENTIST Teeth can play up at high altitudes, so if you've any sign of trouble it's well worth getting them seen to before going anywhere vaguely remote – try the little surgery at Quera 253.

FIESTA DATES Cuzco's principal annual fiestas usually begin in April with the traditional Holy Week processions, followed by those of Corpus Christi around June 14th. Between June 16th and 22nd there's an excellent folklore festival at Raqchi, south of Cuzco; and June 24th, at Sacsayhuaman, is the main day of *Inti Raymi*, now an internationally appreciated revival of the Inca Sun Festival. More exciting and less commercialised is the Virgin of Carmen fiesta at Paucartambo, on July 16th. Later in the year, All Saints' Day, November 1st, is celebrated with religious processions and music in the streets, as, of course, is Christmas, when the best day is December 24th.

FLIGHTS *AeroPeru* (office on Av. del Sol fly to Lima (8am and 11am – ($83 single), Puerto Maldonado (9am – $36 single) and Arequipa (11am $40 – single) every day if all goes well. *Faucett* (office at Av. del Sol 567; tel. 233451) has the same prices though a slightly sparser schedule – flying to Lima (8.20am and 10.20am), Puerto Maldonado on Tues., Thur. and Sat. (at 8.15am) and to Arequipa four days a week (also at 8.15am). It's vital to reconfirm any normal booking 24 hours before the flight. *Grupo Ocho* – the military airline – have one flight a week to Lima and Puerto Maldonado in a Buffalo aircraft. Their schedule is inevitably erratic and there's a long waiting list, but this is amply made up for by the prices (50 per cent of commercial airlines). The only Grupo Ocho office is at the airport.

HERBAL MEDICINES are available from Sr. Elaez, a practitioner who lives just below Koricancha in Calle Arrayan. You can also find herb stalls around the central market.

HOSPITAL Cuzco's Regional Hospital is in Avenida de la Cultura (tel. 223691, or 2486 for emergencies).

IMMIGRACIONES For any problems with passports/visas, the immigration offices are at Calle Santa Teresa 364.

MANU PARK OFFICE The Manu National Park, one of the Amazon's few protected areas, is also the closest jungle zone to Cuzco. Up to date information on access is available from the Park Office at Quera 235.

MAPS For maps of local hikes, particularly the Inca Trail, try *Sigui Tours* (Portal de Panes 123).

MEAT An excellent way of carrying your protein on treks is by taking along some dried meat (much tastier than it sounds). The Cusco meat co-op can be found at the side of the Cathedral (Triunfo 367).

MONEY CHANGING The *Banco de La Nacion* is on Av. del Sol (tel. 3488); *Casas de cambio* with more flexible hours can be found by the El Dorado Hotel on Av. del Sol and in the alley off the Plaza de Armas between Procuradores and Plateros.

POSTE RESTANTE The main post office in Cuzco, on block 8 of Av. del Sol, keeps mail for up to three months. You'll need your passport as I.D. when picking it up.

RAILWAYS For *Machu Picchu* the San Pedro railway station is at the top of Santa Clara Street, opposite the main market. Every day there are two local trains (6am and 12.25pm – both stopping at Ollantaytambo and going on to Quillabamba), one tourist train (7am), and a night train (10.15pm – also going to Quillabamba). Local trains have special ($1 flat rate extra), first and second class seats, while the tourist train is relatively plush throughout. You can get tickets either just before boarding or, to avoid hassles with your gear in crowds, the day before. Ticket office for the tourist train is open Mon to Fri. 6–12am 2–5pm; Sat., Sun. and holidays from 12 till 2.30pm: for the local train, Mon. to Fri. 5–6am, 11–2.30 and 4–5pm. For *Puno, Arequipa and the South*, the railway station is at the bottom of Av. del Sol. Trains leave every day except Sundays at 8am – arriving Puno around 6pm and Arequipa at 6am the following morning. Essentially first and second class ($4½ and $3½ to Puno, $8 or $6 to Arequipa) there's also a buffet wagon for an extra $1½. Again, you can buy tickets either just before leaving or in advance (ticket office open Mon. to Sat. 9.30–11am and 3–5pm; Sun. between 8 and 10am).

SAUNA A good sauna, spiced with pungent herbs, is open to the public in the *Hostal Colonial* (Av. Matara 288).

SHOPPING For *Ponchos and other artesania* try: the shop on the corner of Tupac Aymaru and Santa Clara; a small market on the corner of Quera and San Andres; another little market on block 5 of Av. del Sol; or the arcade at Triunfo 372. For *fresh foods* the central market is best, while for *tinned stuff* try the Chinese supermarket on first block of Av. del Sol.

TOURIST POLICE With their offices in Calle Espinar, the tourist police are helpful if you get ripped off or have any other problems – like being lost. Open 24 hours.

TREKKING There are several companies now running treks, white-water rafting expeditions, etc. *Explorandes* are probably the most helpful and reliable (office in Procuradores). *Mayuc Expediciones* (also in Procuradores) are good too. *Rio Bravo SA* specialise mostly in rafting (Portal Carnes 236); and Tom Hendrickson's *Peruvian Andean Treks* (Av. Pardo 575) are always fun, very reasonable and well-organised.

TRUCKS are the easiest, cheapest, and sometimes the only way to reach a lot of places around Cuzco. For Chinchero, Mollepata and Limatambo, trucks (and mini-buses) leave Calle Arcopata every morning until around 8am (till 10am for Chinchero's Sunday market). For Paucartambo, Tres Cruces or Shintuya, trucks leave Av. Huascar on Mon., Wed. and Fri., usually before lunch. For Ocongate, trucks leave daily from the small cobbled parking zone opposite Koricancha (any time of day).

THE SACRED VALLEY

The **Sacred Valley**, *Vilcamayo* to the Incas, traces its winding, astonishingly beautiful course to the north-west of Cuzco. Known today as the Urubamba river – Valley of the Spiders – it's still easy to see why the Incas considered this a special place. In the upper sector, the stupendous ruins of **Pisac** dominate the broad alluvial valley floor: less than an hour by bus from Cuzco, this is a site often compared to Machu Picchu in its towering elegance. Further downstream, beyond the ancient villages of CALCA, YUCAY and URUBAMBA, the road heads into the mountains at **Ollantaytambo**, a magnificent little town where a great temple-fortress clings to the sheer cliffs of the valley side. And eventually the valley twists below **Machu Picchu** itself, the most famous ruin in South America and a place which no matter how jaded you are, and however commercial it may at times seem, can never be a disappointment.

The classic way to arrive at Machu Picchu is from the three–five day hike over the stirring **Inca Trail**, but even if you're not into walking the **railway** trip from Cuzco or Ollantaytambo is a breathtaking experience in itself. Beyond Ollantaytambo the valley closes in around the tracks, the river begins to race, and the route becomes too tortuous for any road to follow.

If, after Machu Picchu, you're tempted to explore further afield, the evening train continues to **Chaullay** from where you can set out for the remote ruins of **Vilcabamba** – *Vitcos* and *Espiritu Pampa* – the refuge of the last rebel Incas, set in superb hiking country. Final destination of this train is the jungle town of **Quillabamba** (see p. 249), the only Amazon town reached by railway in Peru.

By road you can follow the Sacred Valley only as far as Ollantaytambo, from where a back route cuts across the hills (with frequent trucks and buses) to CHAULLAY and on to QUILLABAMBA. A slower route turns away from the valley at CALCA, crossing a high pass before tracing the river Yanatili down to KITENI, a small jungle village with access by road to Quillabamba and river routes deeper into the forest along the Urubamba, which here becomes navigable for the first time. A regular and very cheap **bus** service as far as Ollantaytambo is run by *Morales Moralitos* (Belen 451, Cuzco; tel. 5035) every 2 hours from 6am until 4pm. Still more frequent, slightly faster and perhaps more interesting, is the co-operative minibus service which picks passengers up from the corner of Av. Collasuyo and Calle Ejercito, some 24m down Recoleta from the heart of Cuzco.

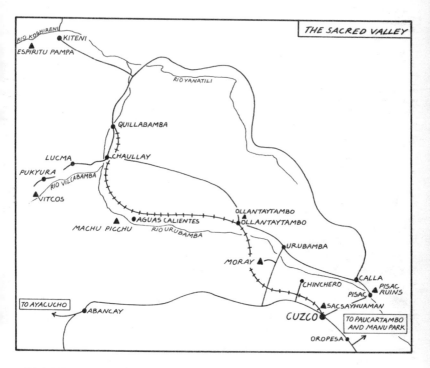

PISAC AND OLLANTAYTAMBO

Standing guard over the open end of the Sacred Valley, Pisac and Ollantaytambo are among the most powerful ruins in Peru. PISAC, only 30km from Cuzco, can be visited easily in a morning, maybe checking out the market on the main square (Thur. and Sun.) before taking a colectivo on to Ollantaytambo by lunchtime. OLLANTAYTAMBO itself is a charming place to spend some time, perhaps taking a tent and trekking off up one of the Urubamba's minor tributaries, or joining up with the Inca Trail for Machu Picchu. For either of the main sites here you'll need a general **Cuzco entrance ticket**, though this can be obtained at the sites themselves.

Pisac

A vital Inca road once snaked its way up the canyon which enters the Urubamba valley at **PISAC**. The ruins (open 9–5, daily), built at the entrance to this gorge, controlled a route which connected the Inca Empire with Paucartambo, on the borders of the 'savage' eastern jungles. Set high above a valley floor patchworked by patterned fields and rimmed by centuries of terracing amid giant landslides, the stonework and panoramas at Pisac's Inca citadel are magnificent. Terraces, water ducts and steps have been cut out of solid rock, and in the upper sector of the ruins, the main Sun Temple is easily the equal of anything at Machu Picchu.

It takes a good 1½ hours to climb directly to the ruins, heading up through the agricultural terraces still in use at the back of the village plaza. Alternatively you can walk along the new road (2–4 hours) to the right as you cross the bridge, or one of the locals might drive you up at a decent price.

Dozens of paths criss-cross their way through the citadel, and most of those ascending will eventually reach the **Temple of the Sun**, poised in a flattish saddle on a great spur protruding north-south into the Sacred Valley. Built around a natural outcrop of volcanic rock, its peak carved into a 'hitching post' for the sun, the temple more than repays the exertions of the steep climb. The 'hitching post' alone is intriguing: the angles of its base suggest that it may have been used for keeping track of important stars, perhaps after they had been lost on cloudy nights, or to calculate the changing seasons with the accuracy so critical to the smooth running of the Inca Empire. Way below the temple, on a large natural balcony, an almost semi-circular row of buildings is gracefully positioned under row upon row of fine stone terraces. The stonework of these huts doesn't compare with the temple masonry, but some of the walls contain striking trapezoidal niches. Above the temple lie still more ruins, mostly still unexcavated, and among the crevices and rocky overhangs even higher are crowds of ancient burial sites. One of the most amazing features of the citadel is that it must have channelled water from a much wider area of this upper mountain to irrigate so extensive a system of agriculture.

Back down in the village there are markets in the plaza on Thursday and Sunday mornings. Tourism notwithstanding, it's still possible to pick up the occasional bargain here and this is also the best place to buy some of the attractive, locally hand-painted ceramic beads. For lunch or a snack, try the excellent *Samana Wasi* restaurant on the corner of the square, with a pleasant little courtyard out the back. If you intend staying, there's the cheapish *Hotel Pisac* on the plaza, the *Hotel Roma* near the bridge, and a more expensive *Albergue Turistica* just out of town along the road towards the ruins. *Rooms* are often let out at ridiculously low prices by villagers, or you can *camp* almost anywhere if you ask permission first. The only month when it may be difficult to find accommodation is September when the village is generally full of pilgrims making their way to the nearby **Sanctuary of Huanca**.

Of the three towns between Pisac and Ollantaytambo, only Urubamba is really developed for tourism. CALCA, however, possesses popular thermal baths within an hour's walk of the modern settlement, and was a place favoured by the Incas for the fertility of its soil, sitting as it still does under the hanging glaciers of Mount Sahuasiray. YUCAY, a smaller village just before you get to Urubamba, is generally visited only briefly to appreciate the finely dressed stone walls of a ruined Inca palace, probably once the country home of Sayri Tupac – though also associated with an Inca princess or *Nosta*.

URUBAMBA itself, though well endowed with tourist comforts, has little in the way of historic interest. If you're after a hotel with swimming pool then try the expensive *Hotel de Turistas*. If, on the other hand, you simply want to use Urubamba as a base for visiting the site of Moray, or some fascinating, still functioning, Inca salt pans, the *Hotel Urubamba* works out a lot cheaper.

Moray, an amazing Inca farm, lies about 6km north of Maras village on the other side of the river, but within easy striking distance of Urubamba. The ruins, probably of an Inca agricultural experimental centre, are deep bowl-like depressions in the earth; the largest comprising seven circular stone terraces, facing inward and diminishing in radius like a multi-layered roulette wheel.

The **salt pans of Salinas**, operational now for over 400 years, are situated only a short distance from the village of Tarabamba, 6km along the road from Urubamba to Ollantaytambo. Cross the river by the footbridge in the village, turn left to follow a stream up beside the graveyard, and you'll soon stumble across these Inca salt-gathering terraces, set gracefully against an imposing mountain backdrop.

Ollantaytambo

Approaching **OLLANTAYTAMBO** from Urubamba, the river at first runs smoothly between a series of fine Inca terraces. Gradually, though, the potential land for cultivation diminishes and the slopes get steeper and more rocky until, just before the town, the railway appears and the road climbs a small hill into the ancient plaza. A very traditional little place – and one of the few surviving examples of an Inca grid system – it's an agreeable town to stay in for a few days, particularly during the

Ollantay Raymi Fiesta (generally on the Sunday after Cuzco's *Inti Raymi* – the last Sunday in June) or for Christmas when the locals wear flowers and decorative grasses in their traditional hats. There are several *hotels* to choose from, including an inexpensive rustic place set around a court-yard, 1½ blocks up the first street on the right as you enter the plaza arriving from Urubamba. Overnight lodging at reasonable rates is also available at the *Cafe Alcazar*, with the added advantage of varied food and good *pisco*. Down near the railway station, the *Albergue*, run by North Americans, is a beautiful old building, still without electricity but with a sauna and the chance to go on organised treks.

Ollantaytambo is an excellent spot to begin **trekking** into the hills, either following the Patacancha up to remote, very traditional villages, or by catching the train to km 88 for the start of the Inca Trail to Machu Picchu. Beyond here the Sacred Valley becomes a subtropical, raging river course, surrounded by towering mountains and dominated by the snow-capped peaks of *Salcantay* and *Veronica*.

In the immediate vicinity, though, the main attraction is the majestic fortress of **Ollantray**, just across the Rio Patacancha. As protection for the strategic entrance to the lower Urubamba valley, and an alternative gateway into the Amazon via the Pantiacalla pass, this was the only Inca stronghold ever to have resisted persistent Spanish attacks. Brought into the empire by Pachacuti after fierce battles with the locals, it remained a prize Inca possession until the rebel Inca Manco retreated to Vilcabamba in 1537.

Manco and his die-hard force had withdrawn to Ollantaytambo after the unsuccessful siege of Cuzco in 1536–7 with Hernando Pizarro in hot pursuit. Some 70 horsemen, 30 food-soldiers and a large contingent of native forces trooped down the Sacred Valley to approach the palatial fortress, stuck out on a river cliff at the lower edge of Patacancha canyon. But facing them were so many Inca warriors and archers contracted from jungle tribes that they supposedly overflowed the valley sides. So clearly impossible was it to proceed, particularly after the Incas had diverted the Patacancha stream to flood the Spanish camp and bog their horses' legs, that after several desperate attempts to storm the fortress Hernando Pizarro and his men slunk uncharacteristically away under cover of dark-ness, leaving much of their equipment behind.

Climbing up through the fortress today, the solid stone terraces, jammed tight against the natural contours of the cliff, remain frighten-ingly impressive. Above them, huge red granite blocks mark the unfinished sun-temple near the top, where, according to legend, the internal organs of mummified Incas were buried. From this upper level a dangerous path leads around the cliff towards a large sector of agricul-tural terracing which follows the Patacancha uphill, while at the bottom you can still make out the shape of a large Inca plaza through which stone aqueducts carried the ancient water supply.

THE INCA TRAIL

Although indisputably a very fine hike, the **INCA TRAIL** is just one of a multitude of paths across remote areas of the Andes. What it does offer, though, and what makes it so popular, is a fabulous treasure at the end – **Machu Picchu**

It's important to choose your season for hiking the Inca Trail. Between June and September it's usually a pretty cosmopolitan stretch of mountainside, with gringos from all over the globe converging on Machu Picchu the hard way. From October through till April, in the rainy season, it's much less crowded and there's a more abundant fresh water supply, but of course it can get very wet. That leaves May as the best month, with everything exceptionally verdant and vital after the downpours and fine weather to add a touch of springtime. According to local tradition, and it seems to work, around full moon is the perfect time to hike the Inca Trail.

As far as **preparations** go, the most important thing is to acclimatise, preferably allowing at least three days in Cuzco if you've flown straight up from the coast. Equipment, such as a tent, sleeping bag and rucksack can usually be hired in Cuzco (see p. 87), and adequate maps for the walk can be obtained from *Sigui Tours* (Portal de Panes 123), the Tourist Office, or the Explorers' Club in Lima (see p. 53). Porters for the Inca Trail, often an embarrassing luxury, charge less than $10 a day and can be arranged through most Tour Agencies in Cuzco.

If you can only allocate three days to the walk, you'll be pushing it the whole way. It's far more pleasant to spend five or six days, taking everything in as you go along. Those trekkers who mean to do it in two-and-a-half days should give themselves a head start by catching the afternoon train and striking up the Cusichaca valley as far as possible on the day before.

The hike begins at km 88, a barely noticeable stop announced almost clandestinely by the train guard. Have your gear ready to throw off the steps, since the train pulls up only for a few brief seconds and you'll have to fight your way past sacks of grain, flapping chickens, Indian men wearing woollen hats and ponchos, and women in voluminous skirts with babies wrapped tightly to their backs in multi-coloured shawls.

From the station a footbridge (which is where you pay the $6 fee – $3 for students – which includes entrance to Machu Picchu) leads across the Urobamba to a path beyond the Cusihaca Archaelogical Project – a British scheme which is expected to finish in 1985. Following the Cusichaca river it's a good 3–hour climb to HUAYLLABAMBA, the only inhabited village on route. This section of the valley is rich in Inca terracing among which rises an occasional ancient stone building with typical trapezoidal windows and niches.

The next 6 hours or so to **the first pass** (4,200m) is the hardest part

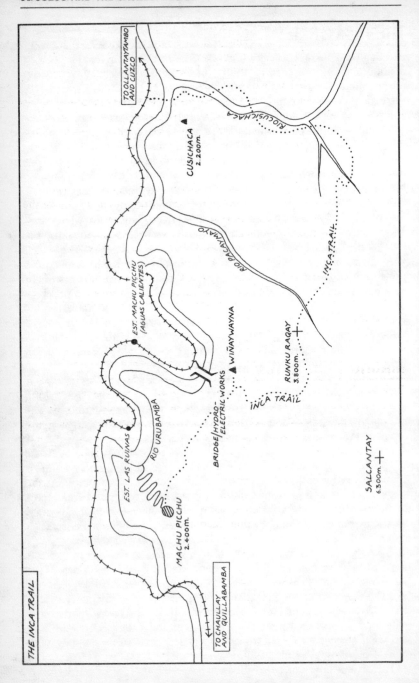

of the walk – leave this for the second day if you want to take it fairly easy. From here the trail continues through magnificent scenery on the slopes of snow-capped Mount Salcantay (6,264m) until, about an hour after **the second pass** (you'll probably be keeping to your own timetable by now), a flight of stone steps leads up to the Inca ruins of **SAYAC MARCA**. This is an impressive spot to *camp*, near the remains of a stone aqueduct which supplied water to the ancient settlement.

Continuing, you make your way down into increasingly dense cloud forest where delicate orchids and other exotic flora begin to appear among the trees. By **the third pass** you're following a fine, smoothly worn flagstone path where at one point an astonishing tunnel, carved through solid rock by the Incas, takes you beyond an otherwise impossible climb. The trail winds down to the ruin of **Puyo Patamarca** – 'Town Above the Clouds' – where there are five small stone baths and in the wet season constant *fresh running water*.

The next Inca site, a citadel almost as impressive as Machu Picchu, is **WIÑAY WAYNA** – 'Forever Young' – another place with *fresh water*. Taking a right fork after spending the night at this obvious spot, it's about 3 hours further, to INTIPUNKU, for your first sight of Machu Picchu; a mind-blowing moment however whacked you might be. Aim to arrive at Machu Picchu well before the 10.30am arrival of the tourist train, if possible making it to the 'hitching post' of the sun before dawn.

MACHU PICCHU (Open daily 6.30–5)

Perhaps the most dramatic and enchanting of Inca citadels, constructed from white granite in an extravagantly terraced saddle between two prominent peaks, **MACHU PICCHU** defies description. Set against a vast and scenic backdrop of dark green forested mountains spiking magnificently up around the Urubamba and its tributaries, the distant glacial summits are dwarfed only by a huge sky.

Virtually every tourist and traveller in South America seems to wind up here sometime, most of them on a **day trip** from Cuzco. This is easy enough to do, either taking the 6am train (arriving Machu Picchu at 9.35am) and returning at 3.50pm (getting back to Cuzco around 8pm), or on the tourist train which leaves daily at 7am (arriving 10.30am) and speeds back at 3.20pm (to arrive around 7pm). For about $40 most tour agencies will arrange such an excursion, with seats reserved on the train, lunch at the Machu Picchu *Hotel de Turistas*, and a guided walk around the ruins. But in no way is so much planning necessary, and the site is infinitely more stimulating for most people before the tourist train arrives in the morning, or after it has gone in the afternoon.

Better than rushing from Cuzco in a day, and certainly less strenuous than the Inca Trail, is to head for the tiny settlement of **AGUAS CALI-**

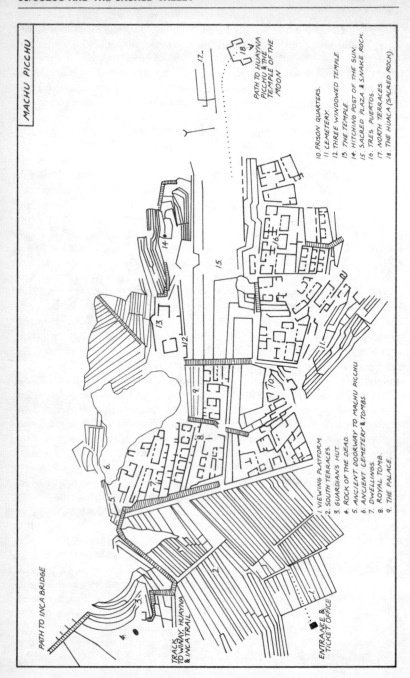

MACHU PICCHU

PATH TO INCA BRIDGE

TRACKS TO WIÑAY HUAYNA & INCA TRAIL

ENTRANCE & TICKET OFFICE

PATH TO HUAYNA PICCHU & THE TEMPLE OF THE MOON

1. VIEWING PLATFORM.
2. SOUTH TERRACES.
3. GUARDIAN'S HUT.
4. ROCK OF THE DEAD.
5. ANCIENT DOORWAY TO MACHU PICCHU.
6. ANCIENT CEMETERY & TOMBS.
7. DWELLINGS.
8. ROYAL TOMB.
9. THE PALACE.
10. PRISON QUARTERS.
11. CEMETERY.
12. THREE WINDOWED TEMPLE.
13. THE TEMPLE.
14. HITCHING POST OF THE SUN.
15. SACRED PLAZA & SNAKE ROCK.
16. TRES PUERTOS.
17. NORTH TERRACES.
18. THE HUACA (SACRED ROCK).

ENTES (now known as Machu Picchu railway station) where there are several places to stay overnight and a good selection of bars or restaurants. The *Hotel Machu Picchu* (beside the platform on the left-hand side of the train) is cheap and not a bad place to stay, or you could try the larger and slightly upmarket *Hostal Los Caminantes* over on the other side of the tracks. In peak season there can be a lot of competition for lodgings, with large groups of travellers turning up and taking over entire hotels: by arriving on an earlier train you'll leave yourself more choice. Wherever you stay, and particularly if you end up **camping**, you'll soon realise that you're now almost in the jungle. Flies and other buzzing insects are everywhere, the climate is distinctly muggy in comparison to Cuzco, and the vegetation is semi-tropical forest. At the back of the settlement there are some old **thermal baths** – *aguas calientes* – excellent revitalisation after a day's tramping around the ruins.

From Aguas Calientes it's about a half-hour walk down the track and through a tunnel to PUENTE RUINAS, the railway station for Machu Picchu itself. Here there's a small **site museum** (Tue.-Sun. 10.30–3.30) and **buses** heading on up the road over the Urubamba. These cost about $2 per person and run only at set times, basically to connect with the trains (uphill at 6, 8.30 and 10.20am). If you walk it'll take between 1½ and 3 hours depending on whether you take the very steep direct path or follow the tarmac. At the top, after an apparently infinite series of treacherous hairpins, you arrive at the *Hotel de Turistas* where there's a restaurant (even more expensive than the hotel itself), a left-luggage place, toilets, shop and the ticket office for the site.

The ruins are a little oversupervised these days. If you arrive from the Inca Trail with a heavy rucksack on your back, the guards – recognisable by their plastic miners' hats – will immediately order you to take your gear down to the ticket entrance below, when all you feel like doing is relaxing and absorbing the spell-binding atmosphere. Even the 'hitching post' of the sun has been roped off, and it's generally difficult to explore without a guard either blowing his whistle at you or shouting across the terraces if you deviate from one of the main pathways. Don't be put off, however: there's very little which could detract from so incredible an experience.

For years no-one knew exactly what to make of Machu Picchu. It lay forgotten except by local Indians and settlers until 1911, when it was 'discovered' by the North American explorer Hiram Bingham. Bingham's own enthusiasm proclaimed it to be Vilcabamba, the last refuge of the Incas where Tupac Aymaru lived in hiding until the Spanish captured him in the 1570s. By the eighteenth century the true history of Vilcabamba had been lost, and it was only in the 1790s that interest in finding this final Inca base began to develop. At this time most people agreed that the spectacular Inca ruin of *Choqquequirau*, on the Apurimac side of the

Vilcabamba mountain range, was the most likely candidate, but in 1909 the discovery of chronicles by Titu Cusi and Baltasar de Ocampo revealed that Choqqequirau was merely an outpost of Vilcabamba, with the true refuge lying somewhere near the village of Pukyura.

On July 24th 1911, Hiram Bingham, accompanied by a local settler who knew of some ruins, came upon Machu Picchu – a previously unheard of Inca citadel which was to become the most famous ruin in South America. Along with his subsequent discoveries (see Vilcabamba, p. 101) Machu Picchu fell into its place in Hiram Bingham's reconstruction of the Incas' past as the obvious site of the last refuge. Not until another American expedition surveyed the ruins around Machu Picchu in the 1940s did serious doubts begin to arise over this assignation. Machu Picchu began to be reconsidered as perhaps the best preserved of a whole series of agricultural centres which served Cuzco in its prime. With crop fertility, mountains and nature so sacred to the Incas, an important agricultural centre would easily have merited Machu Picchu's fine stonework and temple precincts. Between 1964 and 1965, another American explorer – Gene Savoy – went to *Espiritu Pampa* in the jungles to the east. Finding a much larger and obviously more important Inca city than Bingham had noticed here back in 1911, the new theories were proven. But even if Machu Picchu has lost its original claim to fame, none of its characteristic mystique has gone.

There's little point giving a zone by zone account of these incredible ruins; you simply have to wander around with a guide, a map or alone to absorb its provocative grandeur. The city was probably conceived and maybe even partly built by the Emperor Pachacuti, the first to expand the Empire beyond the Sacred Valley towards the forested gold-lands. More than 1,000m lower than Cuzco, Machu Picchu is constructed on the dizzy slopes overlooking a U-curve in the Urubamba river. Over 100 flights of steep stone steps interconnect its palaces, temples, storehouses and terraces, and the outstanding views command not only the valley below in both directions but also extend to the snowy peaks around *Salcantay*.

Perhaps the most enthralling sector of the ruins is that above the **Sacred Plaza** where you can find the Temple of the Sun, the Temple of the Three Windows and **Intihuatana**: the famous 'hitching post' of the Sun. An amazing carved rock in a tower-like position overlooking the Sacred Plaza, the Urubamba and the living huaca of *Huayna Picchu*, Intihuatana's base is said to have been cut to represent a map of the Inca Empire. Its main purpose, however, was as a clock for telling the time of year, indicating important celestial movements and predicting the solstices.

The prominent peak of **Huayna Picchu** – 'Young Height' – is easily scaled by anyone reasonably energetic (site record for this climb is apparently about 22 minutes). From the summit, whence there's an awe-inspiring panorama, another little trail leads down to a **Temple of the Moon** hidden in a grotto hanging magically above the Urubamba river.

Wherever you stand in the ruins spectacular terraces can be seen slicing across ridiculously steep cliffs, transforming mountain into suspended garden. Apparently the terracing was as much for landscape effect and to counter soil erosion as directly to help the production of food: a characteristic combination of aesthetics and practicality.

VILCABAMBA

Until recently **VILCABAMBA** was a relatively safe and accessible corner of the Peruvian wilderness; indeed the BBC were filming here as late as 1983. For the moment, however, it is a restricted zone and allegedly a hideout for *Sendero Luminoso* terrorists. With the army swooping the area in helicopters it's become very dangerous to wander around casually: nobody should enter the area without written permission from the National Institute of Culture (in San Bernando, two blocks from Cuzco's Plaza de Armas) – which is virtually impossible to obtain. Somehow this seems rather fitting; chosen by Manco Inca as the base for his rebel state in the sixteenth century, this has been a traditional area of guerilla activity: in 1963 Hugo Blanco launched an assault on the police barracks at Pukyura. Still, it's not the peaceful village it has been.

In 1911, after discovering Machu Picchu, Hiram Bingham set out down the Urubamba to CHAULLAY, then up the Vilcabamba valley to the village of Pukyura where evidence suggested he might find the Inca ruins of Vitcos. Stuck up on a high hill overlooking a major headwater of the Vilcabamba river, Bingham 'discovered' **Vitcos** – known locally as *Rosapata* – less than two weeks after finding Machu Picchu. It was a relatively small but clearly palatial ruin, based around a trapezoidal plaza spread across a flat-topped spur. Down below Rosapata, Bingham was shown a spring flowing from beneath a vast white granite boulder intricately carved in typical Inca style and surrounded by the remains of an impressive Inca temple. This white rock huaca – *Chuquipalta* – 15m long and 8m high, was proof that he really had found Vitcos. It was clearly the great Inca oracle where blood sacrifices and other 'pagan' rituals had, according to the chronicles, so infuriated two Spanish priests (guests at the rebel Incas' refuge) that they exorcised the rock and set light to its temple sanctuary.

Within another fortnight Bingham had followed a trail from Pukyura down into the jungle zone as far as the *Condevidayoc* plantation, near some more 'undiscovered' ruins at **Espiritu Pampa** – Plain of the Spirits. After briefly exploring some of the outer ruins at Espiritu Pampa, Bingham decided they must have been built by Manco Inca's followers, and were certainly post-Conquest Inca constructions since many roofs were Spanish tiled. Believing that he had already discovered the Inca's last refuge' in Machu Picchu, Bingham paid little attention to these later discoveries. Consequently, and in view of its being accessible only by mule trail, Espiritu Pampa remained covered in thick jungle vegetation.

Only in 1964 was serious exploration first undertaken by Grene Savoy: he found a massive ruined complex with over 60 main buildings and some 300 houses along with temples, plazas, wells and a main street. Clearly this was the largest Inca refuge in the Vilcabamba area, and Savoy rapidly became convinced of its identity as the true site of Vilcabamba. More conclusive evidence has since been provided by the historian John Hemming who, using the chronicles as evidence, was able, to match descriptions of Vilcabamba, its climate and altitude, precisely with those of Espiritu Pampa.

The sites of Vitcos and Espiritu Pampa, set in amazing and highly contrasted scenery, will hopefully soon re-open as superb hiking country for the outward-bound traveller. The village of PUKYURA, below Vitcos, is easily reached in 6 hours by truck from Chaullay station on the Cuzco-Quillabamba line. It used to be possible to camp at Pukyura and arrange for an *arriero* (muleteer) to take you over the two-or three-day trail to Espiritu Pampa for around $5 a mule per day. Given the circumstances as they stand, no-one is likely to get beyond the police control at Pukyura. If you're seriously interested in visiting this region you should check on the prevailing situation with the National Institute of Culture before attempting what may well prove a wasted journey.

AROUND CUZCO

Cuzco is easily the most exciting region in Peru, and all too many visitors overlook the less well-known attractions which surround it. Quite rightly, most people choose to spend at least three days in the immediate vicinity of the city, and nearly everyone visits Machu Picchu and the other sites in the Sacred Valley – at least another two or three days gone. But with more time there are an infinite number of villages and sites left to stimulate the energetic traveller.

Chinchero, an old colonial settlement resting on Inca foundations which boasts a spectacular market, is only a few hours west, overlooking the Sacred Valley. To the south are the superb ruins of Tipón, Pikillacta, Rumicolca and Raqchi, the rustic and legendary village of Urcos as well as an admirable trekking base at Sicuani. Towards the jungle is the fiesta village of Paucartambo, while nearby Tres Cruces offers perhaps the most incredible sunrise and maybe one of the greatest panoramas in the world – from the high Andes, east across the lowland Amazon basin. And even if you aren't bothered about seeing Lake Titicaca, the **rail journey to Puno** is one of the most soul-stirring train rides imaginable.

CHINCHERO

The best time to visit **CHINCHERO** (village of the Rainbow) is on September 8th for the lively traditional fiesta; failing that, on any Sunday morning you'll catch the **weekly market**, much less tourist orientated than the Thursday one at Pisac and with an interesting selection of local craft goods. **Trucks** leave Cuzco from Calle Arcopata every morning; until as late as 10am on Sundays. The 2-hour ride takes you up above the Cuzco valley to the *Pampa de Anta*, a huge lake during the Quaternary period which is now relatively dry pastureland, also crossed by the Cuzco-Machu Picchu-Quillabamba railway. Plans are afoot to build a new Cuzco airport here, one that will take international traffic and, no doubt, eventually cause vibration damage to many of the ruins within a wide radius of the city.

The village itself lies on a high *mesa* off to the right of the main road and railway tracks. From nearly 3,800m it overlooks the Sacred Valley of the Incas, with the *Cardillesa Vilcabamba*, and the snow-capped peak of *Salcantey* (over 6,000m), dominating the horizon in the other direction. It's a small, mud-built place where the women who crowd the plaza on Sunday mornings, still go about their business in traditional dress. You'll need a general **Cuzco tourist ticket** (which can be bought in the village) to gain access to the church and ruins around the plaza, and if you intend staying overnight there's a choice of only two places – the *Hotel Inca* or the *Albergue Chincheros* – though it is possible to *camp* beyond the village.

Raised above the square, an adobe colonial church has been built on top of the foundations of an Inca temple or palace, perhaps one belonging to the Emperor Tupac Yupanqui who particularly favoured Chinchero as an out-of-town resort. It was Tupac Yupanqui who had the stylish aqueducts and terraces around Chinchero built – some of them still in use today. One side of the plaza is bounded by a cyclopean wall, somewhat reminiscent of Sacsayhuaman's ramparts, though nowhere near as massive. Close to the village, too, is the quiet **Lake of Piuray**, although a more interesting walk of about 4 or 5 hours takes you down to the town and river of **Urubamba** – a good place to connect for Yucay or Ollantaytambo (see p. 93).

URCOS, SICUANI AND SITES IN THE HUATANAY/VILCANOTA VALLEYS

The first 150km of the road (and railway) south from Cuzco **towards Lake Titicaca** pass through the beautiful valleys of Huatanay and Vilcanota, whence the legendary founders of the Inca Empire are said to have emerged. A region outstanding for its natural beauty and rich in magnificent archaeological sites, it's easily accessible from Cuzco and offers endless possibilities for exploration or random wandering. With only one (slow) train a day in either direction it makes more sense to take one of the frequent buses or mini-buses along the route, stopping off when and where you like. *Transportes San Cristobal* (Av. Huascar 120; tel. 3184) run nine buses daily (between 6am and 5.30pm) all the way from Cuzco to Sicuani, while there's a faster and much more frequent mini-bus service along the road as far as Urcos which you can pick up from block 1 of Av. Huascar in Cuzco, or anywhere en route. Although an ideal area for camping and trekking, only Urcos and Sicuani are large enough to cater for overnight lodgings.

Leaving Cuzco by road, you pass through the little *pueblo* of SAN SEBASTIAN after about 5km. Originally a small discrete village, it's now become a virtual suburb of the city. Nevertheless, it has a tidy little church, well ornamented with baroque stonework, and apparently built on the site of a chapel erected by the Pizarros in memory of their victory over Almagro. The next village of any special interest is picturesque **OROPESA**, traditionally a town of bakers. Its church and plaza fit snugly on the hillside beneath recently planted eucalyptus groves, separated from the road and railway by the Rio Huatanay. The adobe church, with a uniquely attractive three-tiered belfry with cacti growing out of it, is also notable for an intricately carved pulpit. And although its only a small village, with no cafes as such, you can usually pick up some bread and a bottle of beer or coke from one of the tiny shops. Much more interesting than the town, though, is the ruined Inca citadel of **Tipón**, a stiff uphill walk from here.

Tipón

Both in setting and architectural design, **TIPÓN** is one of the most impressive Inca sites. Rarely visited, and with a site guard who seems to be permanently on holiday, it's essentially open all the time and free. From Oropesa, the simplest way to reach the ruins is by backtracking down the main Cuzco road some 2km to a sign-posted track. Following this up through a village, once based around the now crumbling and deserted *hacienda Quispicanchi*, you want to aim for the gully straight ahead. Once on the trail above the village, it's about an hour's climb to the first ruins. Well hidden in a natural shelf high above the Huatanay valley, this lower sector is a stunning sight: a series of neat agricultural terraces, watered by stone-lined channels, all astonishingly preserved and many still in use. Imposing order on nature's 'chaos', the superb stone terracing seems as much a symbol of the Incas' domination over a subservient labour pool as an attempt to increase crop yield.

At the back of the lower ruins water flows from a stone-faced 'mouth' around a spring – probably an aqueduct subterraneously diverted from above. The entire complex is designed around this 'spring' higher up, reached by a path from the last terrace, another sector of the ruins contains a reservoir and temple block centred around a large exploded volcanic rock – presumably some kind of *huaca*. Although the stonework in the temple seems cruder than that of the agricultural terracing, its location is amazing: by contrast the construction of the reservoir is of necessity very fine – originally built to hold 900 cubic metres of water which was gradually dispersed along stone channels to the Inca 'farm' directly below. Coming off the back of the reservoir, a large tapering stone aqueduct crosses a small gully before continuing uphill, about half-an-hour's walk, to a vast zone of unexcavated terraces and dwellings. Beyond these, over the lip of the hill, you come to another level of the upper valley literally covered in Inca terracing, dwellings and large stone store-houses. Equivalent in size to the lower ruins, these are still used by locals who've built their own houses among the ruins. So impressive is the terracing at Tipón that some archaeologists believe it was an Inca experimental agricultural centre, much like Moray (see p. 93), as well as a citadel.

With no village or habitation in sight, and fresh running water, it's a breathtaking place to camp and you feel you could explore for weeks. More ruins probably exist even higher up; though if you're only here for a day there's a splendid stroll back down to the main road following a path through the locals' huts in the upper sector (i.e. above the reservoir) over to the other side of the *quebrada* and following it down the hillside opposite Tipón. This route offers an excellent perspective on the ruins as well as vistas towards Cuzco in the north and over the Huatanay/Vilcabamba valleys to the south.

Pikillacta and Rumicolca

About 7km south of Oropesa, these two adjacent ruins can be seen alongside the road. After passing the Paucartambo turn-off, near the ruins of an ancient store-house and the small red-roofed pueblo of HUACARPAY, the road climbs to a ledge overlooking a wide alluvial plain and Lucre lake (now a weekend resort for Cuzco's workers). At this point the road traces the margin of a stone wall defending the rather special pre-Inca settlement of Pikillacta.

Spread over an area of at least 50 hectares, **PIKILLACTA** – the Place of the Flea – was built by the Huari culture around 800 AD, before the rise of the Incas. Its unique, geometrically designed terraces surround a group of bulky two-storied constructions: apparently these were entered by ladders reaching up to doorways set well off the ground in the first storey – very unusual in ancient Peru. The rest of the buildings are mainly barracks. When the Incas arrived they modified the site to suit their own purpose, possibly even building the aqueduct which once connected Pikillacta with the ruined gate-way which straddles a narrow pass by the road, just 15 minutes' walk further south.

This massive defensive passage, **RUMICOLCA**, was also initially constructed by the Huari people and served as a southern entrance and barrier to their Empire. Later it became an Inca checkpoint, regulating the flow of people and goods into the Cuzco valley: no-one was permitted to enter or leave Cuzco via Rumicolca between sunset and sunrise. The Incas improved on the rather crude Huari stonework of the original gate-way, using regular blocks of polished andesite from a local quarry. It still stands, rearing up to 12 solid metres above the ground, as one of the most impressive of all Inca constructions.

Andahuaylillas and Huaro

About halfway between Rumicolca and Urcos, the insignificant villages of Andahuaylillas and Huaro hide deceptively interesting colonial churches. In **ANDAHUAYLILLAS**, the adobe-towered church sits raised above an attractive plaza, just 10 minutes' walk from the road-side restaurant where buses and mini-buses stop to pick up passengers. Built in the early seventeeth century on the site of an Inca temple, it's a magnificent example of provincial colonial art. Huge Cuzqueño canvasses decorate the upper walls, while below are some unusual murals, slightly faded over the centuries: the ceiling, painted with Spanish flower designs, contrasts strikingly with a great baroque altar and an organ alive with cherubs and angels. The village itself is a tranquil and proudly preserved haven, its plaza fronted by colonial houses, one with an Inca doorway.

South, the road leaves the Huatanay river behind and enters the Vilcanota valley. **HUARO** is a very different place, crouched at the foot of a steep bend in the road, its much smaller church is characterised by an interior completely covered with colourful murals. Out in the fields beyond the village, climbing towards Urcos, you can see how boulders have been gathered together in mounds, keeping the earth free for the simple ox-ploughs which are still used here.

Urcos and Viracocha's huaca

Climbing over the hill from Huaro, the road descends to cruise past Lake **Urcos** before reaching the town which shares its name. According to legend the Inca Huascar threw his heavy gold chain into these waters after learning that strange bearded aliens – Pizarro and his motley crew – had arrived in Peru. Between lake and town, a simple chapel now stands poised at the top of a small hillock: if you find it open there are several excellent Cuzqueño paintings inside.

URCOS itself rests on the valley floor surrounded by weirdly sculpted hills. One of these, known locally as *Viracocha*, is said to have been climbed by the creator-god, Viracocha: from the summit he ordered beings to emerge from the hill, thus creating the town's first inhabitants. In tribute, ancient locals constructed an ornate *huaca* with a bench of gold to house a statue to the god. This local shrine probably stemmed from pre-Inca days, and it was here that the eighth Emperor received a divinatory vision in which Viracocha appeared to him to announce that 'great good fortune awaited him and his descendants'. In this way he obtained his imperial name, *Viracocha-Inca*, and supposedly the first inspiration to plan permanent take-overs of non-Inca territory, though it was his son, Pachacuti, who carried the Empire to its greatest heights.

Back in town, an inordinate amount of huge old trees give shade to the Indians selling bread, soups, oranges and vegetables around the plaza, which is particularly packed for the traditional Sunday market. On one side of the square there's an old church, on the other, low adobe buildings splattered with fervent graffiti supporting the United Left. It's not really a tourist town, but the occasional traveller is made welcome. In the back streets you can stop off at one of the *tiendas* for a glass of *chicha* beer (those selling chicha advertise by sticking out a pole with a blob of red plastic on the end) or a chat; and you can usually find **lodgings** either on the plaza (at F. Belaunde T. 150 – ask in the shop) or on the street coming into town (J. Arica 316). There are a couple of good **eating places** fronting the square, and this is also one of the few places in the world where you can buy good *quinoa soup* – supposed to be excellent for skin problems. Electricity lasts until midnight only – so take some candles and a torch if you're a late-nighter.

Raqchi Temple and Sicuani

Between Urcos and Sicuani the road passes CHECACUPE village, site of a church with a startling sixteenth-century mural and the turn-off for the textile-weaving centre of PIRUCARTI. About 30km before Sicuani, the imposing ruined **Temple of Raqchi** – once again dedicated to Viracocha – draws most passers-by to make another detour. Situated close to the village of SAN PEDRO DE CACHA (4km), the temple was evidently built to appease Viracocha after he had caused the nearby volcano of Quimsa Chata to spew out fiery boulders in a rage of anger. Even now massive volcanic boulders and ancient lava flows scar the landscape in constant reminder. With its adobe walls still standing over 12m high on top of polished stone foundations, and the site scattered with numerous other buildings and plazas, Raqchi strongly possesses the feel of a place of ritual. Barracks, cylindrical warehouses, palaces, baths and the usual aqueducts can also be identified, clearly showing that this was an important religious centre: probably it once housed a stone image of Viracocha. Today the only ritual left is the annual **Raqchi Festival** (normally June 16th–22nd), one of the most dramatic and least commercialised native fiestas in the Cuzco region.

SICUANI, nearly 150km from Cuzco, is quite a thriving agricultural and market town, not entirely typical of the settlements in the Vilcanota valley. Its busy Sunday market is renowned for cheap and excellent woollen artifacts, which you may also be offered on the train as it passes through between Puno and Cuzco. Perhaps more stimulating is a visit to the nearby thermal baths of **Uyumiri**. Although not a particularly exciting place in itself – daunting looking with too many tin roofs and an austere atmosphere – the people are surprisingly friendly and it's an excellent base for trekking into snowcapped mountain terrain, being close to the vast Nevado Vilcanota which separates the Titicaca Basin from the Cuzco valley. Camping is really the best way of seeing this part of Peru, but if you haven't got a tent there are several *hostals* in town, including the basic *Hotel Raqchi* and the plusher *Hotel de Turistas*.

SOUTH FROM CUZCO: THE RAILWAY

The railway journey from Cuzco south to Puno must be as enjoyable as any in the world. From the magnificent Vilcanota valley, it heads over La Raya pass at 4,313m, then gently rolls across a desolate pampa before reaching Lake Titicaca. There's no worry of *soroche* since you'll already have acclimatised to the altitude, and at Puno you can decide either to cross the lake by steamer (or go round it by road) and carry on to LA PAZ, or travel on down the track to Arequipa. **Trains run** every day of the week except Sunday, leaving Cuzco around 8am to arrive in Puno at about 6pm and Arequipa, after a cold dark night, at 6am the following morning: first class costs a mere $4½ or $8 respectively. Travelling to one of the intermediate stations – Urcos, Sicuani or Pucara – costs virtually nothing. However, it's best to buy your seats in advance – Mon. to Sat., 9.30–11am or 3–5pm; Sun., 8–10am. If you want to sit in the Buffet Wagon, with the relatively meaningless advantage of being near to the kitchen doors (it means that you finish your food first only to get battered by the waiters as they serve everyone else), it's an extra $1½. As with all train journeys in Peru, this is renowned for its thieving activities: keep anything valuable well hidden and a good eye on your gear as you board the carriage and find your seat. If you go all the way to Arequipa it may well end up a sleepless trip, paranoia understandably getting the better of you.

Most of the villages between Cuzco and Sicuani have already been dealt with, although it remains to be said that URCOS is about 1½ hours from Cuzco, CHECACUPE about 3 hours, SAN PEDRO (for Raqchi) some 3½ hours and SICUANI 4 hours.

Beyond Sicuani the Vilcanota valley begins to close in around the railway and for a while the essentially scarce population becomes slightly less sparse and the eucalyptus groves still scrubbier. For some 40 minutes the train climbs through the agricultural zone of MARANGANI to higher pampa around AGUAS CALIENTES, where it often stops long enough for you to jump off and dip your toes into the hot springs next to a cluster of huts beside the track. Next stop is **LA RAYA**, a scenic pass between the Vilcanota valley in the Amazon watershed, and the Titicaca Basin which flows down into the Pacific. Enclosed by towering mountains, some of them snowcapped, it's the sort of spot that makes you feel like leaving the train and everything else behind just to head for the horizon.

Passing beyond this magnificent glacial landscape, pastureland for llamas, and already over 6 hours out of Cuzco, the wagons pull up outside AYAVIRI station (3,903m). Once a great Inca centre with a palace, sun temple and well-stocked storehouses, it's now a market town, notable for the women's weird hats. You can see an interesting old church from the train – low but with two stone towers and a cupola. This is a good place to buy meat, even through the carriage window, and a perfect base for trekking if the urge has grabbed you after the previous panoramas. If it hasn't, then maybe it will at PUCARA, a fair-sized town some 30 minutes further on. Selling ceramic china bulls and other typical local ware, it's an area relying mainly on subsistence farming with some grazing land for sheep, alpacas and cattle.

JULIACA (see p. 148) is only an hour away from here, across a grassy pampa where it's easy to imagine a straggling column of Spanish horse– and footmen followed by a thousand Inca warriors – Almagro's fated expedition to Chile in the 1530s. Today, much as it always was, the plain is scattered with tiny isolated communities, many of them with conical adobe kilns, self-subsistent even down to kitchenware. Another 60 minutes and the train rolls into PUNO – the passengers file furiously off into a milling crowd of hotel owners and small-time tour operators all scrambling for clients. Like the beginning of the journey, the end contrasts miserably with the beauty in between. It's a time to hold on to your passport, money and baggage, while you head for a hotel as fast as possible.

PAUCARTAMBO – ITS JULY FIESTA – AND TRES CRUCES

North-east of Cuzco, **PAUCARTAMBO** – the village of the Flowers – guards a major entrance to the jungle zone of Manu. Trucks – leaving Cuzco on Mondays, Wednesdays and Fridays only from Av. Huascar – take around 4 hours to get there. Beyond, following the Kosnipata valley, the road continues through cloudy tropical mountain regions to the mission of SHINTUYA on the edge of the Manu National Park (see p. 247). *Kosnipata* – its name means 'Valley of Smoke' – allegedly enchants anyone who drinks from its waters at Paucartambo, drawing them to return again and again. But even without such magic Paucartambo regularly attracts visitors by the thousand during the month of July, when it's transformed from a peaceful colonial village into one huge mass of frenzied costumed dancing.

Eternally spring-like because of its proximity to the tropical forest, Paucartambo spends the first six months of every year preparing for the **Fiesta de la Virgen de Carmen**. Usually taking place in mid-July (actual dates from Tourist Office in Cuzco), this energetic, almost hypnotic ritual continues for three full days. Many themes recur during the dances, but particularly memorable is one in which the dancers, wearing weird, brightly coloured costumes with grotesque blue-eyed masks, act out a parody of white man's powers. Malaria tends to be a central theme, being basically a post-Conquest problem: the participants portray an old man suffering its terrible agonies until a Western medic appears on the scene, with the inevitable hypodermic in his hand. When he manages to save the old man – a rare occurrence – it is usually due to an obvious and dramatic muddling of the prescriptions by his dancing medical assistants; cured by Andean fate rather than medical science. Anyone who gets it together to go to Paucartambo for the fiesta will have a fascinating few days. If you can't make this, there are some ruined chullpa burial towers at Machu Cruz, only one hour's walk away. At any time it's best to take a tent with you to Paucartambo where lodgings are difficult, though not impossible, to find.

Sunrise at **TRES CRUCES**, particularly in the months of May and June, is in its own way as magnificent a spectacle as the Paucartambo festival. A site of pilgrimage since pre-Inca days, Tres Cruces is situated on the last mountain ridge before the eastern edge of the immense Amazon forest: at any time the view down (at night an enormous star-studded jewel, by day a twisting jungle river system) is a marvel. Yet when the sun rises it's a spectacle beyond words. Some 25km down the road towards Shintuya, then left for another 20km, transport to Tres Cruces is rarely a problem. Cars and truck-loads of people frequently leave Paucartambo just to see this phenomenal drawn-out dawn, which can last as much as 3 or 4 hours.

TRAVEL DETAILS

Buses

From Cuzco Several departures a day for Lima (via Nazca or Pisco; 30–50hrs), Arequipa (20hrs), Juliaca (10hrs) and Puno (11hrs), Abancay (10hrs) and Ayacucho (24hrs). To La Paz every Sunday (24hrs – S70). Trucks to Puerto Maldonado leave every other day (48–60hrs). **Local routes** are all detailed in the text.

Trains

Cuzco-Juliaca/Puno and Arequipa daily except Sundays (10/11 and 22hrs) **Cuzco-Machu Picchu and Quillabamba** 4 times a day (4 and 7½hrs).

Flights

At least one plane a day **from Cuzco** to Lima, Arequipa and Puerto Maldonado. To La Paz every Tue. and Sat. with Lloyd Aereo Boliviano (Av. Sol 348; tel. 222990).

Chapter three
THE SOUTH

Although **the south** has been populated as long as anywhere in Peru –
for at least 9,000 years in some regions – it was the north coast and
Andes which dominated the country's archaeology until the beginning of
this century. A dry, arid zone, nobody expected the southern coast to
have maintained a large enough population for any significant culture to
emerge. In 1901, however, brilliant pre-Inca ceramics were unearthed at
Nazca, and in 1927 an even more important find at Paracas revealed,
intact, dozens of huge funerary textiles – highly sophisticated in their
design and exhibiting an intense interest in the aesthetics of living and
dying long in advance of Inca times. With the subsequent discovery of
pre-Incaic sites throughout the coastal zone, it now seems clear that this
was home to at least three major **cultures:** the **Paracas** (from around 500
BC–AD 400), the influential **Nazca** (AD 500–800) and finally, contemporaneous with the Chimu of Northern Peru and the Cuismancu around
Lima, the **Ica Culture**, or **Chincha Empire**, overrun and absorbed into
Pachacutec's mushrooming Inca Empire around the beginning of the
fifteenth century.

Pisco, Ica and **Nazca** each preserve important and intriguing sites from
the three cultures: most excitingly at Nazca, where an amazing network
of lines and figures remains etched over almost 500 square km of bleak
pampa – one of Peru's most enduring archaeological enigmas. All of them
are worth time on a journey most travellers make in a couple of fast
steps down the Pan American from Lima to Arequipa. And if you've any
interest in wildlife, Pisco and Nazca offer three of the most outstanding
reserves in the country – the **Ballestas Islands** and **Paracas National Park**
(outside Pisco), and the rare Vicuña reserve of *Pampa Galeras* (off the
Nazca-Cuzco road).

Arequipa, second city of Peru, reflects a different and altogether more
dramatic environment, poised at the edge of the Andes against an extraordinary backdrop of volcanic peaks. The major centre of the south, it's
an enjoyable place to rest up for a while before going on to Chile and
across the high Andean pass to Titicaca, distinguished in its architecture
(including the magnificent **Santa Catalina Monastery**) and in some spectacular, if hard-going, excursions.

Lake Titicaca, and its main town and port of **Puno**, is a region where
you'll probably want to spend less time – a sad, austere place with a cold
climate and incredibly rarefied air. It is impressive in its own way, though:
quite unique to South America and an interesting route to travel, allowing
you to make the circuit round from Arequipa to Cuzco or on into Bolivia.

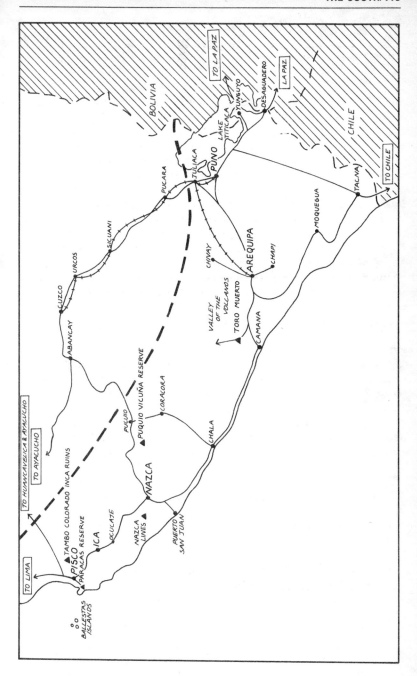

PISCO AND THE PARACAS PENINSULA

Only 3 hours by bus from Lima, **PISCO** is an obvious and rewarding stop en route south to Nazca and Arequipa. If of sparse interest in itself, it is a pleasant base – and provides access to the Paracas National Reserve, the wildlife of the Ballestas Islands, and the well-preserved Inca coastal outpost of Tambo Colorado. Just off the Pan American Highway, it is also a crossroads for going up into the Andes: you can take roads from here to Huancavelica and Huancayo, as well as to Ayachuco and Cuzco.

Presumably for this reason, the Spanish considered making Pisco their coastal capital before they eventually decided on Lima. The town still possesses a few fine colonial showpieces, clustered about the **Plaza de Armas** with its statue of San Martin poised in the shade of ancient ficus trees. The **mansion** where the liberator actually stayed on his arrival in Peru is still to be seen – a block out towards the **bus station** and now adapted as the local Social Club. Another impressive building, unusual in its Moorish style, is the **Municipal Palace**, and if you're wandering about there are a couple of elegant churches too, among them the heavy baroque **Compañia** with its superb carved pulpit.

The focus of activity is around the **plaza** and adjoining **Jiron Commercio**; every evening the square is crowded with people walking and talking, stopping to buy *tejas* (small sweets made from pecan nuts and manjar blanco) from street vendors. **Hotels** are all good value, even the plush-looking *Hotel Embassy* on Jiron Commercio; *Hostal Pisco* on the plaza is more basic, though very friendly, and with its own restaurant; *Hostal Callao* (Callao 163), cheaper still but very rudimentary. **Nightlife** really revolves around relaxing in the plaza or eating and drinking in one of the many restaurants and bars. On the main square an excellent corner *chifa* serves good *pisco* (local grape brandy), while on the same side as Hostal Pisco *Las Vegas* offers traditional dishes. Going down towards the Hotel Embassy, another cafe, *Restaurant Flamengo*, prepares very fresh fish and chips. The town **disco** is on block 2 of Callao. Plenty of hotels and boat-trip companies change cash dollars but only the **Banco de la Nacion** (on the main street towards San Andres) takes cheques.

Colectivos to Lima, Cuzco and most other destinations leave from the Plaza de Armas. For Lima (3–4 hours), Nazca (3–4 hours), Arequipa (14 hours) or Ayacucho (12 hours) the best **bus** company is undoubtedly *Ormeño* (one block east of the plaza); while for Huancavelica (14 hours) it's *Oropesa* on Calle Commercial. If you're heading for the Paracas reserve the best way is to catch a bus from the market to the sea-front at San Andres, then hitch a lift on from there.

The Ballestas Islands

Guano islands, the very rocks of the Ballestas seem to be alive: every inch covered in bird droppings, and moving with a mass of flapping, noisy pelicans, penguins, terns, boobies and cormorants. Offshore, too, their nature-life is dense – the waters sometimes almost black with the shiny dark bodies of seals and sea-lions.

If you want to make a circuit of the isles, two companies in Pisco run combined bus and boat tours – each similarly priced (around $5–6), leaving early in the morning and returning towards midday. Tickets are best bought the day before – from the *Hotel Pisco* or the office at *Jr. Commercio 128* – and you'll be picked up around 6.30am, usually from the plaza in front of the Hotel Pisco.

The buses run south along the shoreline past the old fishing port of SAN ANDRES, where you can watch the fishermen bringing in their catch, and on the way back stop and eat fresh *ceviche* or local turtle steaks. Turtles are a favourite local food and are known as the meat with seven flavours – some parts of the creature taste of fish, others of chicken, another of beef and so on. Warm turtle blood, too, is still occasionally drunk here, reputedly a fool-proof cure for bronchial problems.

At the far end of San Andres the road passes by the big Pisco air-force base before reaching EL BALNEARIO (14km), a resort for wealthy Limenians, whose large bungalows line the beach. If you want to stay out here it is possible to camp on the sand, though the Paracas Reserve is really a much nicer place to be: the *Hostal* is currently closed and serves as a base for the Ballestas boat-trip people, though there is an expensive *Hotel de Turistas*. From El Balneario you climb off a small jetty surrounded by pelicans into a wooden launch and chug out across the sea for the next 3½ or so hours, circling one or two of the *islas* and returning past the famous 'Paracas trident' – a huge cactus-shaped figure drawn in the sand-stone cliffs (see below).

Getting back to land at El Balneario, you have two or three alternatives. You can go back in the bus to Pisco; get the driver to drop you off for lunch in San Andres; or more exciting, hitch a few kilometres further south along the bay road, well beyond the fish-processing factories and the obelisk commemorating San Martin's landing, into the Paracas Nature Reserve.

Paracas National Park

A peninsula of equal nature interest to the Ballestas, Paracas has added attractions in superb and quite deserted beaches where you can camp for days without seeing anything except the lizards and birdlife, and maybe a couple of fishing boats. It really is a magical sort of place, devoid of vegetation yet full of energy and life. Schools of dolphins often play in the waves off-shore, condors frequently scour the peninsula for potential food and lizards scrabble across the hot sands. If you go, plan to stay a few days, and take food, water and a sunhat – facilities are few.

The entrance to the reserve is marked these days by a barrier-gate where the wardens collect a small fee from visitors, a charge which allows you to stay in the park for up to a week. Not far from the barrier is a small archaeological museum, and the **park office** where maps are sometimes available. The **museum**, the first landmark as you make your way up a gentle slope into the very bleak and arid peninsular zone, is well worth a look. Restored in 1983, its exhibits include a wide range of Paracas culture artifacts – mummies, ceramics, funerary cloths and reconstructed dwellings. Right next door is the oldest discovered site in the region, the **Necropolis of Cabeza Largas**, dating back over 5,000 years and once containing as many as sixty mummies in one of its graves. Most were wrapped in vicuna skins or rush matting, and buried along with personal objects like shell beads, bone-necklaces, lances, net-bags and cactus-spine needles. A little further on, near the beach (where you can often see dozens of tall, pink and graceful flamingos) are more remains – the Disco Verde, a Chavin-related settlement.

PARACAS FLYING FIGURE

Another 2km or so on from the museum you come to a fork in the main road: the tarmac carries straight on, parallel to the shore, while a dusty sand-trail goes off to the left towards the tiny fishing port of likeable LAGUNILLAS some 6km away. The tarmacked road eventually terminates at PUNTA PEJERREY, the modern port for Pisco, full of fish-conserve factories. There's nothing of interest here – but shortly before the port a sandy side-road leads away from the sea and around the hills on the outer edge of the peninsula. This trail, just about suitable for a car, takes you to **the Trident** looking out over the Pacific. Vaguely sign-posted, a 13km walk across the hot desert (if you're on foot best be prepared to camp), this massive candelabra or cactus-shaped symbol stands over 100m high and more than 20m wide in places. No-one knows its function or who built it. The writer Eric Von Daniken reckoned it was a sign for extra-terrestrial space-craft, pointing the way (inaccurately as it happens) towards the mysterious Nazca lines that are inland to the south east; others suggest it was constructed as a navigational aid for eighteenth-century pirates. Somehow it seems more likely that it was a kind of ritual object, perhaps representing a pre-Incaic cactus or tree of life. High Priests during the Paracas or Nazca eras perhaps worshipped the setting sun from this spot.

LAGUNILLAS, a fishing hamlet with a few huts serving *conchitas* (scallops) and other seafood, is really the point on Paracas to make for – a strange, very beautiful part of the peninsula, so flat that if the sea rose just another metre the whole place would disappear. Pelicans and sea-lions hang around the bobbing boats waiting for a fisherman to accidently drop a slippery fish and little trucks regularly arrive to carry the catch back into Pisco.

From Lagunillas the rest of the Paracas Reserve is at your disposal. Nearby are the glorious **beaches of La Mina and Yumajque**, where you can often stay for days without seeing anyone. Further afield a track goes off 5km north to a longer sandy beach, **Arquillo;** on the cliffs beyond there's a viewing platform (*Mirador de los Lobos*) above a large colony of sea-lions. Another path leads north from here, straight across the peninsula to the Trident and on to Punta Pejerrey (20km).

South around the bay from Lagunillas, turning right across the sandy hills rather than heading back to the museum, it's about 4km to the spectacular **cathedral cave** (*La Catedral*) down on a pebbly beach. Bats line its high vaulted ceilings and huge waves pound the rocky inner walls. This trail continues to the fishing village of **Laguna Grande**, from where it's possible to track back inland to Ocucaje on the Pan American Highway between Ica and Nazca: there's usually enough traffic to hitch a lift.

Tambo Colorado

Some 48km from Pisco, the Inca ruins of **TAMBO COLORADO** are easily enough reached: the road to Huancavelica runs straight through the site, and you can take the Oropesa bus which leaves from Calle Commercio at 10 each morning. The ruins are around 20 minutes beyond the village of HUMAY.

Originally a fortified administrative centre, Tambo Colorado was probably built by the Chincha before its adaptation and used as an Inca coastal outpost. Its position at the base of steep foothills in the Rio Pisco valley was perfect for controlling the flow of people and produce along the ancient road down from the Andes. You can still see dwellings, offices, store-houses, row upon row of barracks and outer walls, some of them retaining traces of coloured paints. The rains have taken their toll, but even so this is reckoned to be one of the best preserved adobe ruins in Peru – roofless, but otherwise virtually intact. In some ways reminiscent of a fort from some low-budget western, it is a classic example of a custom-built, pre-planned adobe complex; everything in its place and nothing out of order – autocratic by intention, oppressive in function and rather stiff in style.

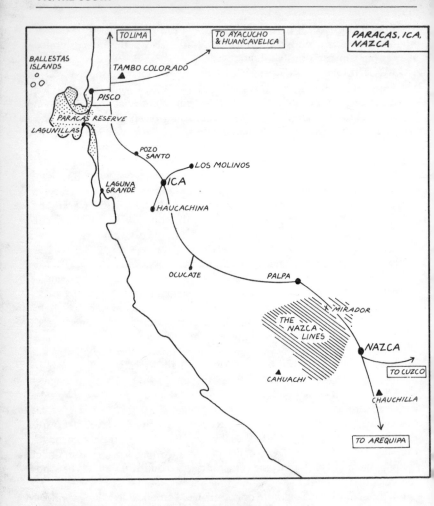

SOUTH FROM PISCO: TOWARDS THE ICA OASIS

South of Pisco, the Pan American Highway sweeps some 70km inland to reach the fertile wine-producing lea valley, a virtual oasis in this stretch of bleak desert. **POZO SANTO**, the only real landmark en route is distinguished by a small towered and white-washed chapel, built on the site of an underground well. Legend has it that on this spot *Padre Guatemala*, the friar Ramon Rojas, died, water miraculously beginning to flow from the sands as he passed away. There's a restaurant here now where colectivo drivers sometimes stop for a snack, though little else.

Beyond, the road crosses the **Pampa de Villacuri**. An hour's hike to its north along a track from km 280 are the ruins of an ancient defensive **camp** constructed from adobe. You can see dwellings, plazas, a 40m-long outer wall and ancient man-made wells – still used by local peasants to irrigate their maize-plots. Sea-shells and brightly coloured plumes from the tropical forest found in the graves here suggest that there was an important trade-link between the ancients on this southern coast and the tribes from the eastern jungles beyond the formidable Andean mountain range.

Further down the Pan American, the pretty roadside village of **GUAD-ALUPE** (km 293) signals the beginning of the Ica oasis. To the right there's a large, dark, conical-shaped hill, *Cerro Prieto*, behind which, in amongst the shifting sand-dunes, are more *ruins*, dating from 500 BC. Just a few kilometres on, beyond a string of wine *bodegas* and shanty-town suburbs, you reach the centre of **ICA** itself.

ICA

An attractive old colonial city, **ICA** is famous throughout Peru for its wine and pisco production. Its very foundation (in 1563) went hand in hand with the introduction of grape-vines to South America, and for most Peruvian visitors it is the *bodegas* which are the town's biggest pull. For travellers they're likely to be at least equalled by the *Museo Regional*, whose superb collections of pre-Colombian ceramics and Paracas, Ica and Nazca culture artifacts would alone be worth an excursion.

The town's colonial heart – the inevitable **Plaza de Armas** – remains its modern centre, adapted with the intrusion of an obelisk and fountains. Within a few blocks are most of the important churches, rarely of great architectural merit but considerably revered in this region. The **Cathedral**, just off the plaza, contains Padre Guatemala's tomb – said to give immense good fortune if touched at the New Year. On the main street around the corner, **Calle Municipalidad**, is the perhaps grander **San Fran-cisco**, whose stained-glass windows dazzle against the strong Ican sunlight; whilst to the south of the plaza (down Calle Lima, then left along Ayabaca) is a third major church, **El Sanctuario de Luren**. This, housing the *Imagen del Señor*, patron saint of the town, is something of a national shrine, and the centre of pilgrimage on the third Sundays of March and October.

The **Museo Regional** (open Mon.-Sat. 8–6, Sun. 8–12) is a little further from the centre on the Prolongacion Ayabaca. To get there take bus No. 17 from the plaza, or walk six blocks down Avenida San Martin from the church to San Franciso, then another six blocks right along Ayabaca; either way you'll see the concrete museum stuck out on its own in the middle of barren desert parkland.

Certainly the most striking and possibly the most important of the museum's collections is its display of **Paracas textiles**, the majority of them discovered at Cerro Colorado in the Paracas Peninsula by Julio Tello in 1927. Enigmatic in their apparent coding of colours and patterns, these funeral cloths (exhibit 217 is an outstanding example) consist of blank rectangles alternating with elaborately woven ones – repetitious and identical except in their multidirectional shifts of colour and position. They are displayed in the first room to the right, from where you pass into the main lobby and its collections of *mummies, trepanated skulls, grave artifacts* and *trophy heads*. It seems very likely that the taking of trophy heads in this region was related to specific religious beliefs – as it was until quite recently among the head-hunting Jivaro of the Amazon Basin. The earliest of these skulls, presumably hunted and collected by the victor in battle, come from the Asia Valley (north of Ica) and date from around 2000 BC.

The museum's main room is almost entirely devoted to pre-Columbian **ceramics**, possibly the finest collection outside of Lima. On the left as you enter are spectacular Paracas urns – one particularly outstanding with an owl and serpent design painted on one side, a human face with arms, legs and a navel on the other. There is some exquisite Nazca pottery, too, undoubtedly the most colourful and abstractly imaginative designs found on any ancient Peruvian ceramics. The last wall is devoted mainly to artifacts from the Ica-Chincha culture (see p. 267), which seems to have been specifically marked by a decline in importance of the feline god, and in a move towards urbanisation. My favourite example is the beautiful feather cape, its multi-coloured plumes in almost perfect condition.

Displayed also in the main room are several *quipus*, the pre-Incaic (and Inca) method of accounting using bundles of knotted strings as mnemonic devices. According to the historian Alden Mason these numerical records followed a decimal system very much like our own – a simple knot representing 'one', digits from two to nine denoted by longer knots in which the cord was wound or looped a given number of times before it was pulled tight. The concept of zero was apparently understood and shown by the absence of any knot in the expected position while place value is indicated by any particular knot's distance from the main cord. Census records of population and produce were of considerable import-ance to the Inca Empire, leading to the development of a *quipumayoc* accountant elite. Quipu's were also mnemonic aids for the recitation of ancient legends, genealogies and ballads. They have survived better here on the coast than in the mountains and the Ica collection is one of the best in the country.

Another smaller archaeological museum, the **Museo de Prospero Belli** needs an appointment to visit (tel. Campo 2293), but if you've still energy and enthusiasm there's a rather bizarre and controversial third museum back on the Plaza de Armas. This, **el Museo de Piedra**, consists of the private collection of Javier Cabrera's engraved stones – which, so he claims, are several thousand years old. Despite him being a well-respected member of the community and descendant of Ica's heroic founder, however, few share this belief. Some of the stones depict patently modern surgical techniques and, perhaps more critically, you can watch craftsmen turning out remarkably similar designs over on the pampa at Nazca. Nevertheless, the stones are remarkable modern pieces of art and an enthusiastic local guidebook claims that 'dinosaur hunts are portrayed, suggesting that Ica may have supported the first culture on earth'! The museum, at Bolivar 174, is open daily 9–1 and 4–9.

About the best imaginable way of escaping Ica's hot desert afternoons, however, is to wander about the cool chambers and vaults, and sample the wines, at one or other of the town's **bodegas**. The most accessible – and very good too – is *Vista Allegre* (open daily, 9–5; tel. 231432). It's easily reached by walking down Avenida Grau from the main plaza, crossing over the Rio Ica bridge then turning left. Follow this road for about 20 minutes till you come to a huge yellow colonial gateway on your right (or take the orange microbus from town – No. 8); the arch leads via an avenue of tall eucalyptus trees to the bodega itself, an old *hacienda* still chugging happily along in a forgotten world of its own. There's usually a guide who'll show you around free of charge, then arrange for a wine and pisco tasting session at the hacienda's shop. You don't have to buy anything but you're quietly expected to tip.

If you follow the road up beyond Vista Allegre for another 6km you'll come to **Bodega Tacama**, a larger and slightly more important wine producer with the same basic procedure regarding guided tour and opening times. An interesting aspect of Tacama is that their vineyards are still irrigated by the **Achirana** canal which was built by the Inca Pachacutec (or his brother Capac Yupanqui) as a gift to Princess Tate, daughter of a subjugated local chieftain. According to Inca legend it took 40,000 men only ten days to complete this astonishing canal which brings cold pure water down from some 4,000m in the Andes to transform what was once an arid desert into a startlingly fertile oasis. Clearly a romantic at heart, Pachacutec is supposed to have personally named it *Achirana* – 'that which flows cleanly toward that which is beautiful'.

Sleeping, eating and some practical details
There are plenty of **hotels** in Ica, though they can get full over fiesta weekends; even so it's usually possible to find some kind of room here, or alternatively at nearby Huacachina (see the following section). In Ica the *Hotel Colon* on the main Plaza de Armas is one of the best – if not quite as comfortable as it should be for the price (about $2 single); its restaurant, looking out onto the plaza, offers cheap and varied set meals.

The less pricey *Hostal del Valle* (San Martin 159 – around the corner from Iglesia San Francisco) is a quiet place with a pretty courtyard, garden-aviary and its own basic restaurant.

Not surprisingly, Ica wines are very much a part of the town's life and it's quite customary here for passers-by to pop into a *bodega* and knock back a quick glass of neat pisco before carrying on about their daily business. Probably the best places to do likewise are *La Vina*, on the Plaza de Armas, or a cheaper shop on the left half a block along Calle Lima from the square. Another place where you can sometimes get a drink, and meriting a visit anyway by virtue of the fascinating artesania that it sells, is the *Feria de Ponchos* on Avenida Municipalidad 344. Among **restaurants** my own favourite is the *Mogambo* (just off the plaza, up Tacna) where they dish up an exquisite *aji de gallina* and sometimes the local speciality *la carapulchra*. The Mogambo has a strong Iqueñan atmosphere and frequently adds spice to appetite by blasting out invigorating salsa music as you eat. On Sunday lunch-times it's also worth checking out the restaurant in the *Hotel de Turistas* (Avenida Los Maestros; near the stadium, en route to Huacachina) where they lay out an amazing 'eat as much as you can' spread for a few dollars per person. Or at any time you can get fresh *empañadas* from the bakery on the Plaza de Armas – ideal for a snack lunch.

Free maps of Ica and the region are usually available at the **tourist information office**, near the main square of Jiron Cajamarca 179 (tel. 2173). The **post office** is on Calle Callao, two blocks north of the plaza, beside the Hotel Colon, and there's a Casa de Cambio (9–6 daily) on Avenida Municipalidad (263) less than a block from the square, much faster than the Banco de La Nacion, and often with a better rate of exchange. The **Banco de La Nacion** itself is opposite the tall mushroom-shaped tower on Av. Matias Manzanilla, some eight blocks west of the plaza towards the Picasso Stadium and Hotel de Turistas.

There are several important **fiestas** during the Ica year. Probably the most enjoyable period is in March, after the grape harvest has been brought in, when there are open-air concerts, fairs, artesan markets, cock-fighting and *caballo de paso* meetings. Over the *Semana de Ica* (mid-June, climaxing on the 17th) there are more festivities, and again in September for the *Semana Turistica*. As at Lima, October is the main month for religious ceremonies, processions and pomp.

Colectivos for Lima, Pisco and Nazca leave from the Plaza de Armas all day long. **Buses** to Lima, Nazca, Arequipa and Cuzco also run at least daily, operated by four different companies – *Ormeño* (the best – on Lambayeque, three blocks from the plaza), *Roggero, Morales* and *Tepsa*.

Huacachina

Only 5 or 6km outside Ica, **HUACACHINA** was one of Peru's most elegant and exclusive resorts in its 1940s heyday – an old world lagoon surrounded by palm trees, sand-dunes and waters long famous for their curative powers. Since those times the lagoon's subterranean source has grown erratic and its waters are perhaps less inviting. At best they look a murky green, and when really low can become a positively thick, viscous syrup – red in colour and apparently radioactive. However, though visitors these days are few, it's a place which retains considerable mystique, and is a delightfully quiet, secluded spot if you want to rest up. On my last visit freak weather conditions had actually raised the level of the waters and people were bathing again to test its powers.

There are two old-established **hotels**. The most stylish, the *Mossone*, was once the haunt of politicians and diplomats, entertained by concerts on the colonial-style verandah overlooking the lagoon; rooms here go for around $9 single and $11 double. Alongside is the *Salvatierra*, cheaper at only $4 for a single room with shower, but becoming a little decrepit. In the last (or first) resort it's also possible to **camp** in the sand-dunes around the lagoon – very rarely is it cold enough to need more than a blanket and you may even get a cure into the bargain.

To come out to Huacachina jump on the **red bus** in Ica, either from its starting point outside the Sanctuario de Luren or as it passes through the Plaza de Armas; it runs about every 15 minutes.

THE NAZCA LINES

One of the great mysteries of Peru – indeed of South America – the 'Nazca Lines' cover an area of some 500 square kilometres. They are drawn across the bleak stony Pampa de San José, a series of animal figures and geometric shapes, none of them repeated, and some up to 200m in length. Each one, even sophisticated motifs like *the spider monkey* or *the hummingbird*, is executed in a single, continuous line, most often created by clearance of the hard stones of the plain to reveal the fine dust beneath, but occasionally stretching up into the quebradas heading for the Andes. They were evidently a kind of agricultural calendar to help regulate the planting and harvesting of crops, while perhaps at the same time some of the straight lines served as ancient sacred paths connecting *huacas*, or power spots. But whichever theory you end up favouring, they are among the strangest and most memorable sights in the country.

Getting to the lines

To reach the Pampa de San José, the Pan American Highway cuts south from Ica, quickly leaving behind the oasis fields for a long stretch of bleak wilderness. Amidst this the one settlement breaking out from the barren life is OCUJAJE, an ex-*hacienda* and another of Peru's finest wine and pisco producers. Shortly afterwards you pass the village of SANTA CRUZ, where a bad track leads up into the hills to reach **TIBILLO** (68km), a small place surrounded by minor sites from the Nazca culture. At 2,000m, it was apparently the highest region these people lived in. If you make it up here there's good scope for camping, but it's fairly isolated and you'll need to take most of your own food and water.

THE LINES begin on the tableland above PALPA, where there's a small *hostal* amid the orange groves. You probably won't want to stay here, however, since it's a further 20km until you can make them out. This, to be exact, happens at km 420, where a tall metal framed **mirador** has been built above the plain. Unless you plan to go on a flight above them from Nazca, it's the nearest and best view you'll get, even better if you've time to climb up onto one of the hills behind. Buses will let you off here, but they won't hang around, so if you're stopping en route you may have to hitch the remaining 20km to Nazca. Alternatively, you can come back out by taxi from the town.

If you've the cash, three companies in Nazca operate **flights** over the lines – they range from $25–45 a person and from 10 minutes to an hour in length so ask around carefully before settling. The main private companies are *Aeroica* (Tacna 476, off the Plaza de Armas; tel. 64) and *Aerocondor* (office at the airport; tel. 134); or you can take the new plane run by the *Hotel Montecarlo* – whose English-speaking pilot has some interesting tales to tell and has probably photographed the lines more than anyone else. Getting a flight place is no problem but it's best to book an early morning trip since it gets hazier as the sun rises higher. The airport is about 3km down the main road south of Nazca.

Some theories

The greatest expert on the lines is undoubtedly **Maria Reiche**, who has worked at Nazca almost continuously since 1946, and now believes that the lines and cleared areas were linked to the rising and setting points of celestial bodies on the east and west horizons. She considers the lines and cleared areas to be the most important features; next the animals and lastly the spirals. The whole complex, according to her theories, is an agricultural calendar to help organise planting and harvesting around the seasonal changes rather than the fickle shifts of weather. In most developed Central and South American cultures there was a strong emphasis on knowledge of the heavens, and in a desert area like Nazca where the coastal fog never reaches up as high as the pampa this must have been highly advanced.

In the late 1960s an American, **Gerald Hawkins**, computed that two mounds on the pampa were aligned with the Pleiades in the era between AD 600 and AD 700 – during the Nazca period. The Incas revered the Pleiades, calling them *Quolqua* (or granary) because they believed them to watch over and protect the seeds during germination. This kind of information, if it wasn't common knowledge anyway in ancient Peru, might have been adopted by the Incas from the Nazca culture when it was drawn into the Empire in the fifteenth century. Hawkins's computer also suggested, however, that sun, moon and star alignments of the lines are frequently accurate enough to raise themselves just slightly above the level of chance.

In many cases the lines connect with low hills on the plain or the foothills of the Andes along its edge. Fragments of Nazca pottery found around these hills suggest that they may have been sacred sites, perhaps as important ritually as the celestial movements. Recent theories on the lines take this as evidence that at least some of them were *ceques*, or sacred pathways, between *huacas*. In Inca Cuzco, ceques radiated from the Sun Temple, Koricancha, to surrounding huacas, many of these being hills on the distant horizon. Each of the ceques was under the protection of a particular *allyu* or kin group. This theory is all the more feasible since if the lines were purely for astronomical observations they wouldn't need to be so long. **Tony Morrisson**, one of the proponents of this idea, discovered many similar ceques in the sierra between Cuzco and La Paz. They were related to huacas and still owned by specific local kin groups. Morrisson concludes that the various stone piles often found at the end of lines at Nazca were ancient *huacas;* and the lines are paths between sacred places. They were in a straight line, he says, because this is the shortest distance between any two huacas. It follows that the cleared areas were ceremonial sites for larger allyu gatherings. The animal figures might be explained by them pre-dating the lines; this would fit into the early and late pottery phases (the former being most closely associated with animalistic motifs).

Maria Reiche's theory isn't necessarily contradictory. Many of her alignments were confirmed by Hawkins's computer (particularly those for the solar solstices and the Pleiades) and even if the lines and animal designs were separated over time, conclusions draw a connection: designs like the spider and the monkey might be representations of the constellations of Orion and Ursa Major. It's difficult for a Western mind to visualise the constellations except through the stereotyped images we've reflected into them. The Nazca on the other hand were free to impose their own ideas and there are remarkable similarities between the motifs on the pampa and some of the major constellations.

On a slightly less esoteric level it's interesting to note how many of the extended lines are amazingly straight. One theory claims that they were made using three cane poles and a rope, in much the same manner as a surveyor uses ranging sticks and a theodolite; when Maria Reiche first came to Nazca some of the locals could indeed remember wooden poles at the end of certain lines – perhaps sighting posts for the stars. How long they took to construct is a last, inevitable question – and since none of them can be properly seen from the ground it is tempting to believe they must have been the skilled product of numerous generations. In strictly physical terms this isn't necessarily so. A few years back a local school project tried building its own line and calculated that a thousand patient and inspired workers could have made the lot inside a month!

NAZCA

Some 20km south of the mirador, **NAZCA** spreads along the margin of a small coastal valley. Although the river is invariably dry Nazca's valley remains green and fertile through the continued application of an Incaic subterranean aqueduct. It's a small town – slightly at odds with its appearance on the maps – but an interesting and enjoyable place to stay. There are adobe ruins only a couple of kilometres outside, an excellent local museum, and two important *Nazca culture* sites within an easy day's range.

Coming into town, **Bolognesi**, the main street, leads straight into the **Plaza de Armas**. In the most impressive building here you'll find the

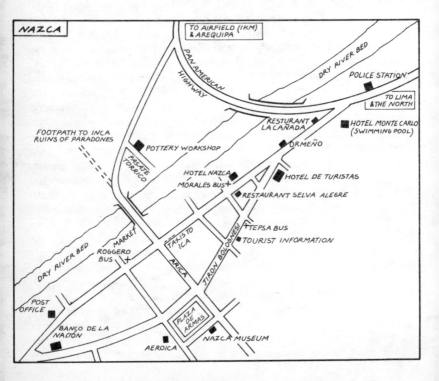

Municipalidad and the **Archaeological Museum** (open daily; 10–12, 2–6), its steps beautifully tiled with Nazca-style ceramic bird designs. The exhibits, crowded as they are into one small room, include Nazca pottery, lengths of hair up to 2m long found in the graveyards, and large maps showing the layout of the Nazca lines. One magnificent bulb-shaped pot, about half a metre tall, is stood upsidedown to display two beautifully stylised monkeys. Each one is visibly attached to the other by a fish-bone or serpent motif stretching around the pot. Something like a tongue of fire comes from the upper monkey into the top of the other's head. The bottom monkey has two tongues coming out of its mouth to encircle the pot at its widest point, finishing on one side with a condor motif and on the other as a vampire bat.

Almost as amazing as the original ceramics in the museum are those produced today by a pair of brothers at the **Taller Artesania** in Barrio San Carlos. This is only a short walk south of the plaza along Calle Arica and across the bridge; from here curve right with the road – the ceramics are at Pasaje Torrico 240, about 200m down on the right. Even if you don't plan to buy anything the *Taller* is worth a visit; if a few people turn up they'll demonstrate the whole craft process from moulding to polishing.

The **tourist information office** on Bolognesi has free maps of the town – and sells interesting pamphlets on the local archaeology – but it's not a difficult place to find your way around and **hotels** are simple enough to find. Most desirable, and cheap for what it offers, is the *Hotel Montecarlo* (Jiron Callao; tel. 100) with a swimming pool and occasional disco. More expensive but with a good restaurant is the *Hotel de Turistas* on Bolognesi (tel. 60); most people only make it as far as the bar here to have a drink and to meet Maria Reiche who appears to get free board and lodging in return for being nice to passers-by. Cheapest of the good places is the *Hotel Nazca* (Jiron Lima 438; tel. 85), run by a friendly woman who seems to have a finger in most pies. She changes dollars (cash and cheques) and has contacts with the taxi drivers who specialise in taking people (at quite reasonable prices) to the sites around Nazca; if you give her a ring or speak to her one afternoon she can usually set things up for the following morning.

There are two really **good places to eat**: the ramshackle *Selva Allegre* (opposite the Hotel Nazca) and La Cañada (near the Hotel Montecarlo). At Selva Allegre the cook will fix you up with roast *cuy* (guinea-pig) as soon as wink; La Cañada, on the other hand, is one of those criolla places – laid back and tropical with loud salsa music and spicy seafood or the traditional *rocoto relleno*.

There are several **bus services** to Lima, Cuzco or Arequipa, once again operated by several companies: *Ormeño* (offices near the Hotel Montecarlo – the best company), *Morales Moralitos* (Near the Hotel Nazca),

Roggero and Tepsa. **Colectivos** for up or down the coast generally wait in Jiron Lima, not far from the Hotel Nazca.

Paradones, the graveyard and the Inca canal

The most impressive archaeological sites around Nazca are some distance out – dealt with in the following section and best reached by taking on one of the taxi-guides. If you've an afternoon to spare, though, or just feel like a walk, there are a few interesting targets you could take in. The route covered below will take only a leisurely 3 or 4 hours on foot if you don't end up staying through the day at the Cantay swimming pool midway round.

Los Paradones was an Inca trade centre where wool from the mountains was exchanged for cotton growing along the coast, and a modern road, following more or less the same trail as the ancient route from Nazca to Cuzco, passes just below the ruins. Follow Calle Arica from the Plaza de Armas, cross the bridge and carry straight on (off the main road which curves to the right). The ruins are about a kilometre directly ahead of you at the foot of the sandy valley mouth, underneath a political slogan – APRA – etched onto the hillside.

The buildings, made from adobe with stone foundations, are in a bad state of repair and the site dotted with huaquero's pits, but if you follow the path to the prominent central sector you can get a good idea of what it must have been like. Overlooking the valley and roads, it's in a commanding position – a fact recognised and utilised by local cultures long before the Incas arrived.

Another 2km up the Puquio road is a **Nazca graveyard**, its pits open and remains spread around. Though much less extensive than the cemetery at Chauchilla (see the following section), it is still of interest – with subterranean galleries to explore if you can find them.

Across the valley from here is the former *hacienda* of **Cantay**, now a model co-operative. A short walk through the cotton fields and along a track will bring you to its central plaza and swimming pool – one of the previous owner's more luxurious hand-downs. Just a little further up above the co-operative settlement, you can make out a series of inverted conical dips, like swallow-holes in the fields. These are the air vents for a vast underground canal system which syphons desperately needed water from the Bisambra reservoir; designed and constructed by the Incas, it is possibly even more essential today. If you want, you can get right down into the openings and poke your head or feet into the canals – they usually give off a pleasant warm breeze, and you can see small fishes swimming in the flowing water. The canals are well-built of cut stones, usually about 90cm by 60cm, just large enough for a person to climb in when it needs cleaning or fixing; they run underground in a gentle zig-zag fashion, slowing down the flow and avoiding rapid silting.

SITES AROUND NAZCA

Chauchilla and Cahuachi, the most important sites associated with the Nazca culture, are each difficult to reach by public transport, and unless your energy and interest are pretty unlimited you'll want to arrange a local *guide cum taxi-driver* in Nazca. This is easily enough done since they generally advertise themselves by loud tuneful horn-hooting. If you need to search one out ask the woman who runs the Hotel Nazca, or look up Maria Raul Pino Etchebarne (Jiron Los Espinales 101, Nazca). He's a good driver and a reliable guide to the lines, Chauchilla cemetery, Cahuachi or the nearer (walkable) ruins detailed above.

Chauchilla
Roughly 30km south along the Pan American, then out along a dirt-track beside the Poroma river-bed, **CHAUCHILLA CEMETERY** is a site which needs a certain commitment to visit. Once you reach it though, it is an atmospheric place which makes you realise how the riverbanks must have maintained a considerable civilisation in the time of Nazcan culture. Scattered about the dusty ground are literally thousands of graves (mostly opened), skeletons, broken pieces of pottery, skulls, shroud fabrics and lengths of plaited hair, strangely unbleached by the desert sun. Further up the track, near Trancus, there's a small ceremonial temple – Huaca del Loreto; and beyond this at Los Incas you can find Quemazon petro-glyphs. The guide will want more than the standard $5 a person fare to take you to these last two, but if you bargain with him when you get to Chauchilla he may prove willing.

Cahuachi
The ancient centre of Nazca culture, **CAHUACHI** lies to the west of the Lines; only 17km from modern Nazca, but a good 4–hour round trip ($7 a person by taxi).

The site consists of a religious citadel split in half by the river, with its main temple (one in a set of six) constructed around a small natural hillock. Adobe platforms step the sides of this 20m mound and although they're weathered today, you can still make out the general form. Attached to each of the six pyramids a separate courtyard can be distinguished – but exactly what their use was we'll probably never know.

Quite close to the main complex is a weird temple construction known as *El Estaqueria*, 'the Place of the Stakes', and still retaining a dozen rows of huarango log pillars. *Huarango* trees (known in the north of Peru as *algarrobo*) are the most common form of desert vegetation, their wood, baked by the sun, as hard as any. They have been much reduced by locals who use them for fuel.

Cahuachi is typical of Nazca ceremonial centres in its exploitation of natural features to form an integral part of the chief structures. The places where they lived showed no such architectural pretensions – indeed there are no major towns associated with the Nazcas, who tended to live in small clusters of adobe huts; villages at best. One of the largest of these, the walled village of **Tambo de Perro**, is to be found in Acari, the next dry valley. Stretching for over a mile, and situated next to an extensive Nazca graveyard, it was apparently one of their most important dwelling sites.

Until 1901, when Max Uhle discovered the **Nazca culture**, a group of beautiful ceramics had been hanging around in Peru's museums unidentified and unclassifiable. With Uhle's work all that changed rapidly (though not quickly enough to prevent most of the sites being ransacked by *huaqueros* before proper excavations could be undertaken) and the importance of Nazca pottery came to be understood. Many of the best pieces were found here in Cahuachi.

Unlike contemporaneous Mochica Ware, Nazca **ceramics** rarely attempt any realistic reproduction of images. The majority – painted in three or four earthy colours before a surface polish with resin – are relatively stylised or even completely abstract. Nevertheless, two main categories of subject matter recur: naturalistic designs of bird, animal and plant life; and mythological motifs of monsters and bizarre deities. In later works it became common to mould effigies onto the pots, and in Nazca's declining phases, under Huari-Tihuanuco cultural influence, workmanship and design became less inspired.

The style and content of the early pottery phases, however, shows remarkable similarities to the symbols depicted in the Nazca lines, and although not enough is known about this culture to be certain, it seems reasonable to assume that the early Nazcas were also responsible for those mysterious drawings on the Pampa de San José. With most of the evidence coming from their graveyards, though, and that so highly abstract, there is little to characterise the Nazca and little known of them beyond the fact that they were into collecting heads as trophies, that they built a ceremonial complex here in the desert at Cahuachi, and that they eked a living from the Nazca, Ica and Pisco valleys from around AD 200 to AD 600.

THE PAMPA GALERAS VICUÑA RESERVE AND PARINACOCHAS CIRCUIT

PAMPA GALERAS is one of the best and most accessible places in Peru to see the **vicuña**, the finest-woolled member of the cameloid family. Here, in a reserve where they have lived for centuries and which is now maintained as their natural habitat, there are over 5,000 of the creatures.

Well-signposted at km 89 of the NAZCA-PUQUIO/CUZCO road, the reserve is easily reached by hopping off one of the buses. If you want to stay at the *Park Camp* it's advisable to have written permission from the Ministry of Agriculture and Fauna in Lima as they have few beds; if you're happy to camp you'll probably be allowed in without a permit.

The vicuña themselves are not easy to spot. When you do see a herd, if you catch its attention you'll see it move as if it were actually one organism. They flock together and move swiftly in a tight wave, each bounding gracefully across the hills. The males are strictly territorial, protecting their patches of scrubby grass by day, then returning to the rockier heights as darkness falls.

Going on from the reserve another 55km or so you reach **PUQUIO**. Entering over a metal bridge you immediately feel this place is different to the hot desert town of Nazca. Puquio was an isolated community until 1926 when the townspeople built their own road link between the coast and the sierra. There are three *hostals* in the town, none of them particularly enticing; however, this is a potential journey breaker and a good place to stock up or have a hot meal.

The road divides at Puquio with the main track continuing over the Andes to CUZCO via ABANCAY while a side-road goes south along the mountains about 140km to PARINACOCHAS (*Lake of Flamingos*) before curving down another 130km to the coast at CHALA. Although frequently destroyed by huaycos in the rainy season, local trucks always seem to travel this road and they'll usually take passengers for a small price.

Fifty km before you get to Parinacochas, the road passes the small administrative capital of this remote province – **CORACORA**, a quiet little town with only one hotel. Around the plaza there are some reasonable restaurants but there's little here to interest most travellers. Far better to continue the 16km to **CHUMPI**, an ideal place to camp amid stunning sierra scenery. Nearby are the thermal waters of **Bella Vista**; and the amazingly beautiful lake of **Parinacochas**, probably one of the best unofficial nature reserves in Peru, is within a few hours' walk.

From Chumpi you can either back-track to PUQUIO and then on to CUZCO or NAZCA, or go on down the road, passing the lake and within a day's easy ride reach CHALA back on the desert coast.

SOUTH TO AREQUIPA

There is little in the 170km of desert between NAZCA and CHALA, and what there is can be avoided without regret – PUERTO SAN JUAN, the one place of any size, is a modern industrial port for the local iron-ore and copper mines.

The first break in this stark area, known for its winds and sandstorms, are the olive groves of the Yauca valley as you approach Chala. Just beyond this, at km 595, is a strange uplifted zone, a natural moisture-gathering oasis in the desert with its own micro-climate stretching for about 20km. It's a weird but fascinating place to spend some time camping and exploring; there are Inca and pre-Inca ruins hidden in the Lomas, but today the area is virtually uninhabited.

CHALA, the main port for CUZCO until the building of the Cuzco-Arequipa railway, is now an agreeable little fishing town. If you want to stop over a while there's a 2-star hotel, a couple more rather basic ones and as much fresh seafood as you could want. Continuing to AREQUIPA the road keeps tightly to the ocean wherever physically possible, passing through a few small fishing villages and over monotonous arid plains to turn eventually inland for the final uphill stretch into the land of volcanoes and Peru's second largest city. At km 916 a road leads off into the Majes canyon towards the Toro Muerto petroglyphs and the valley of the volcanoes (see p. 142) – a good place to hitch inland from, but a very remote spot.

AREQUIPA AND AROUND

AREQUIPA

It's not certain – but it seems probable – that the name AREQUIPA is derived from the Quechua phrase 'Are quepay', meaning 'Okay, let's stop here'. Sited well above the coastal fog-bank, at the foot of an ice-capped volcano (*El Misti*), this place has long been renowned for having one of the most pleasant climates in Peru.

Not only the Incas found Arequipa to their liking. When Pizarro offici-ally refounded the city in 1540 he was moved enough to call it *Villa Hermosa*, 'Beautiful Town', and despite a disastrous earthquake in 1687 it was endowed with some of the country's finest colonial churches and mansions. These, for the most part, it retains, and with the area's often startling countryside, they constitute the main appeal to travellers.

For Peruvians, Arequipa has somewhat different historical conno-tations. Developing late as a provincial capital, and until 1870 connected only by mule track with the rest of Peru, it has the century's reputation as *the* centre of right-wing power. Whilst popular movements tend to have emerged around Trujillo in the north, Arequipa has traditionally represented the solid interests of the oligarchy. Sanchez Cerro and Odria both began their coups here, in 1930 and 1948 respectively, and Belaunde himself sprung into *politicas* from one of the wealthy Arequipa families.

In recent years, at least among the local students, things seem to be changing – and in 1983 demonstrations against police harassment brought the city to a standstill. Nonetheless, most Arequipans continue to feel themselves distinct, if not culturally superior to the rest of the country, and resent the idea of the nation revolving around Lima.

The town, its mansions and churches

Although an active city, with a population approaching half a million, Arequipa does maintain a very individual feel. The most striking, visible feature is that so many of its buildings are constructed from the white volcanic *sillar*, cut from the slopes of the mountain and often flecked with black ash. With El Misti poised above like a melting ice-cream zone, this gives the place a rather legendary sort of appearance. As if to confirm such ideas **El Misti** and **Chachan**, the smaller extinct volcano to its left, are known collectively as 'the Protectors of the White City'.

Among the huge number of churches spread about the old colonial centre there is one, the **Monastery of Santa Catalina**, of outstanding beauty and interest. The finest and most prestigious establishment in Peru, it is covered individually in the following section (p. 136). Within a few blocks of the Plaza de Armas, though, there are half a dozen churches well deserving a brief visit, and a couple of superb old mansions.

The **Plaza de Armas** is itself a particularly striking array of colonial architecture, dotted with palms and flanked by arcades and by the Cathedral – which actually manages to draw your sight away from El Misti towering away behind. Inside, though, it is disappointing, having been gutted by fire in 1844. Much more exciting is the elaborate **Compañia** (open 9–1 and 3–8), just off the opposite side of the plaza, with its extraordinary zig-zagging sillar-stone doorway. Built over the last decades of the seventeenth century, this is magnificently sculpted with a very local inspiration of baroque relief – curiously two-dimensional, using shadow only to outline the figures of the frieze. Next door to the church are fine Jesuit Cloisters (open 8am–10pm; Sun. noon–8pm), again superbly carved.

Less spectacular, but nevertheless elegantly designed, is the **Iglesia San Augustin** (open 8–12) on Calle San Augustin, one block west of the plaza; its old convent cloisters are now attached to the University, while inside only the unique octagonal sacristy survived a quake in 1868. **Santa Domingo** (open 7–11 and 3–6; free), two blocks east of La Compañia, was again badly damaged by quakes – but more recently, in 1958 and 1960. It has been well restored, however, and on its main door you can make out another interesting example of Arequipa's *mestizo* craftsmanship – an Indian face carved amidst a bunch of grapes.

Over the Chili River, the large Franciscan **Monastery of La Recoleta** stands conspicuously on its own (open 9–1pm; small charge). Founded

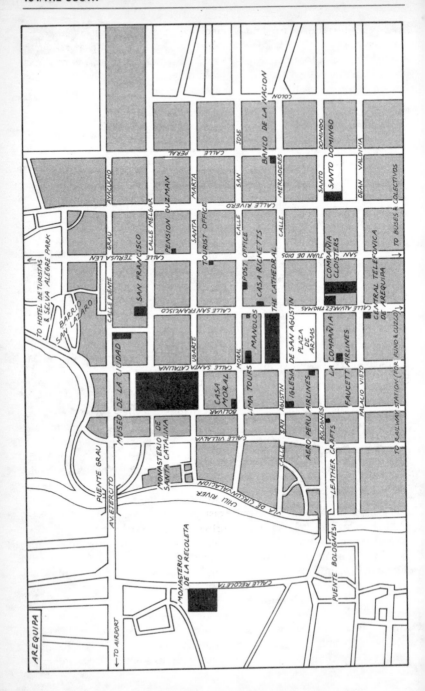

AREQUIPA

TO AIRPORT

MONASTERIO DE LA RECOLETA

CALLE RECOLETA

PUENTE GRAU

AV. EJERCITO

MONASTERIO DE SANTA CATALINA

CHILI RIVER

VIA DE CIRCUNVALACION

PUENTE BOLOGNESI

LEATHER CRAFTS

TO RAILWAY STATION (FOR PUNO & CUZCO)

MUSEO DE LA CIUDAD

CALLE PUENTE

BARRIO SAN LAZARO

TO HOTEL DE TURISTAS & SELVA ALEGRE PARK

GRAU

AYACUCHO

TERUSA LEN

USARTE

SAN FRANCISCO

CALLE MELGAR

PENSION GUZMAN

SANTA MARTA

SAN

CALLE

PERAL

CALLE

JOSE

COLON

BANCO DE LA NACION

SANTO DOMINGO

DEAN VALDIVIA

MERCADERES

TO BUSES & COLECTIVOS

CALLE RIVERO

TOURIST OFFICE

POST OFFICE

CASA RICKETTS

THE CATHEDRAL

SAN JUAN DE DIOS

SANTO DOMINGO

CALLE ALVAREZ THOMAS

COMPANIA CLOISTERS

CENTRAL TELEFONICA DE AREQUIPA

CALLE SAN FRANCISCO

MANOLOS

MORAL

PLAZA DE ARMAS

LA COMPANIA

FAUCETT AIRLINES

PALACIO VIEJO

CALLE SANTA CATALINA

CASA MORAL

BOLIVAR

LIMA TOURS

SAN AGUSTIN

IGLESIA DE SAN AGUSTIN

AERO PERU AIRLINES

BOLOGNESI

CALLE VILLALVA

CALLE SAN

in 1648, not one brick of the original building is left, but around the Mission Cloisters is a fascinating *Amazon Museum*, dedicated to the Franciscans' long-running missionary activity in the Peruvian tropical forest regions and displaying artifacts collected over the years from jungle Indian tribes and examples of forest wildlife.

Situated around the small plaza off Calle Melgar, just one block east of Santa Catalina, you can find another striking Franciscan complex – dominated by the sixteenth-century church of **San Francisco** (open 6–11 and 3.30–7). This, too, has suffered heavily from various quakes but it retains its most impressive feature – a pure silver altar. Adjoining the church are rather austere cloisters and the very simple *Chapel of the Third Order* (open 8–11 and 3–5), its entrance decorated with modest mestizo carvings of St Francis and St Clare, founders of the First and Second orders.

Of the town's many colonial **mansions**, two of excellence are open to the public. **La Casa del Moral**, lies just one block down from the walls of Santa Catalina. An eighteenth-century building, restored and refurbished with period pieces, its most engaging feature is a superbly worked sillar stone gateway carved with motifs very similar to those shown on Nazca ceramics. Puma heads with snakes growing from their mouths curiously surround a Spanish coat-of-arms. The mansion's name – nothing to do with ethics – comes from an old mora tree, still thriving in the central patio. The other mansion that's open, **La Casa Ricketts**, stands opposite the north-east corner of the Cathedral. Built in 1738 this has one of the finest facades in Peru – much more intricate and harmonised than the Moral, if in its content (a Jesuit monogram) less inspired. Owned by the Banco Continental – banks are major arts patrons throughout Peru – it houses a small museum and art gallery (open Mon.-Fri. 9–3 and 5–8).

The city museum, the **Museo de La Ciudad**, devotes itself principally to Arequipa's local heroes – army chiefs, revolutionary leaders, presidents and poets (including the renowned Mariano Melgar). Open Mon.-Fri. 8.30–1 and 4–6.30, it's just above Santa Catalina on the Plazuela de San Francisco. More interesting to most tastes are the universities' **archaeological museums**, located in the suburbs on either side of the city. *San Augustin* is the largest, with good collections of everything from mummies and replicas of Chavin artwork to colonial paintings and furniture. Stuck out in the campus along Avenida Independencia (by the corner with Victor Morales) it's not very far from the road to Paucarpata and the exit route across the mountains for Puno and Cuzco; opening hours are officially 8.30–12.30 and 3–5 but it's best to telephone for an appointment in advance (Arequipa 29719). The other museum belongs to the *Catholic University of Santa Maria* (open Mon.-Fri. 8–12) and concentrates on items from Pre-Conquest cultures such as the Huari, Tiahuanuco, Chancay and Inca. It is a little difficult to find: out across the Puente Bolivar (south of the Bolognesi), and amid the university buildings a few hundred metres to the right.

The oldest quarter of Arequipa – and the first place where Spaniards settled in this valley – is the **Barrio San Lazaro**, an uncharacteristic zone of tiny, curving streets stretching around the hillside at the top end of Calle Jerusalen. If you feel like a walk, and some good views of El Misti, you can follow the stream-bed from here to Puente Grau – a superb vantage point. From here, a longer stroll takes you across to the west bank of the Chili, along Avenida Ejercito and out to the suburbs of **Cayma** and **Yanahuara**, quite distinct villages until the railway boom of the late nineteenth century which brought the first wave of peasant-migrants from as far afield as Cuzco. Built up now, they still command stunning views across the valley, above all from their churches; at Cayma you can climb up to the rooftop (9–4pm), while Yanahuara's possesses the famous mirador from which all the classic postcard views of Arequipa seem to be captured.

Santa Catalina Monastery (open daily 9–5; last entrance at 4pm)
Just two blocks north of the Plaza de Armas, **Santa Catalina's** vast protective walls maintained up to 500 nuns in seclusion until it was opened to the public in 1970. Architecturally the most important and impressive religious building anywhere in Peru, it takes a good hour or two to wander around the enormous complex of rooms, cloisters and tiny plazas – an extraordinary and haunting micro-world. Nuns do remain here today, but they're restricted to the quarter bordered by Calles Bolivar and Zela, worshipping in the main chapel only outside of opening hours.

The most striking general feature of the monastery's architecture is its prominent 'Mudejar' style, adapted by the Spanish from the Moors but rarely found in their colonies. This is pointed and beautifully harmonised by an incredible interplay between the strong sunlight, white stone and brilliant colours – both in the ceilings and in the deep blue sky above the maze of little streets. You notice this at once, as you enter, filing left along the first corridor to a high vaulted room with a ceiling of opaque Huamanga stones imported from the Ayacucho valley. Beside here are the **locutorios** – little cells where on holy days the nuns could talk, unseen, to visitors.

The **Novices Cloisters**, beyond, are built in solid sillar-block columns, their antique wall paintings depicting the various qualities to which their occupants were expected to aspire. Off to the right, surrounding the **Orange Tree Cloister** (5 on the key) a series of paintings show the soul evolving from a state of sin through to the achievement of God's grace – perhaps not certain to aid spiritual enlightenment but at least a constant

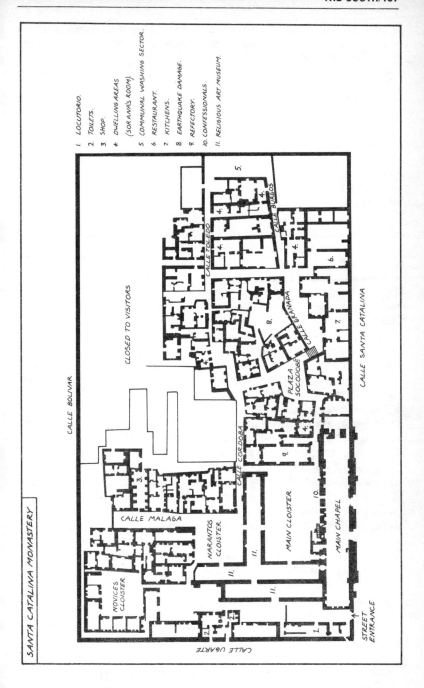

SANTA CATALINA MONASTERY

1. LOCUTORIO.
2. TOILETS.
3. SHOP.
4. DWELLING AREAS (SOR ANA'S ROOM).
5. COMMUNAL WASHING SECTOR.
6. RESTAURANT.
7. KITCHENS.
8. EARTHQUAKE DAMAGE.
9. REFECTORY.
10. CONFESSIONALS.
11. RELIGIOUS ART MUSEUM.

CALLE BOLIVAR

CLOSED TO VISITORS

CALLE TOLEDO

CALLE BURGOS

CALLE GRANADA

CALLE SANTA CATALINA

PLAZA SOCODOBE

CALLE CORDOBA

CALLE MALAGA

NARANTOS CLOISTER

NOVICES CLOISTER

MAIN CLOISTER

MAIN CHAPEL

CALLE UGARTE

STREET ENTRANCE

reminder of ITS permanent existence. In one of the rooms off here dead nuns were mourned before burial always within the monastic confines.

Along **Calle Malaga** (beyond the doorway marked 'M. Dolores Llamosa') there's an interesting old mud-brick oven; opposite, in the **Sala Zurbaran** you can find original robes, Cuzco paintings and some fine crockery displaying luxurious scenes from the grandeur of early colonial days.

Calle Toledo, a long street brought to life with permanently flowering geraniums, connects the main dwelling areas with the lavanderia, or communal washing sector. There are several rooms worth exploring off here, including small chapels, prayer rooms and a kitchen. The **lavanderia** itself, perhaps more than any other area, offers a captivating insight into what life must have been like for the closeted nuns – open to the skies and city sounds yet bounded by high walls. In a garden behind here there's an old fig tree, a species unique to Arequipa.

If you're feeling a bit thirsty by this stage, there's a little **restaurant** just off to the left along the broad Calle Granada. Straight on is the **Plaza Socodobe**, a fountain courtyard to the side of which is the **bañera** where the nuns used to bath. Around the corner, down the next little street, is **Sor Ana's room**. Dying at the age of 90, in 1686, Sor Ana was something of a phenomenon, leaving behind her a trail of prophecies and cures. Her own destiny in Santa Catalina, like many of her sisters, was to castigate herself in order to offer up her torments for the salvation of other souls – wealthy Arequipan patrons who paid for exactly this privilege. Sor Ana is currently being considered in Rome, and is said to be 'well on her way to becoming a saint'.

The **refectory**, immediately before the main cloisters, is deceptively plain – its exceptional star-shaped stained-glass shedding dapples of sunlight through empty space. Nearby, confessional windows look into the **main Chapel**, but the best view of its majestic cupola is from the top of a staircase beside the Cloisters. An interesting little room underneath these stairs has an intricately painted wall-niche with a centrepiece of a heart pierced by a sword. The ceiling is also curious, painted with three dice, a crown of thorns and other less recognisable items. The Cloisters themselves are covered with murals following the life of Jesus and the Virgin Mary.

Leaving this area and entering the **lower Choir Room** you can see the **tomb of Sor Ana** and the full interior of the grand, lavishly decorated Chapel. Beyond the last sector of the monastery is a rather dark museum full of obscure seventeenth-, eighteenth-, and nineteenth-century paintings. The best of these are in the final outer chamber, lined mainly with works from the super-religious Cuzco school of *mestizo* art. One eyecatching canvas, the first on the left as you enter this room, is of Mary Magdelen by a nineteenth-century Arequipan, remarkably modern in its treatment of the flesh of Mary and the near cubism of rocky background.

El Misti and Paucarpata

If **El Misti** exercises a compulsion on you to climb it, bear in mind that it's considerably further and taller (5,821m) than it looks. It is a perfectly feasible hike, but you will need a full two days for the ascent and another day to get back down.

If you're just entertaining the idea of an afternoon's escape into the countryside, **Paucarpata** is perhaps the best target. About 9km out of Arequipa (2 hours walk/local bus), it's a large village surrounded by farmland based on perfectly regular pre-Inca terraces – *paucarpata*, the Quechua word from which it takes its name. Set against the backdrop of El Misti, this is a fine place to while away an afternoon with some wine and snacks. Or, if you've cash to spare, there's a very upmarket restaurant, **Sabandia**, just a stone's throw away, with its own swimming pool.

Hotels, restaurants and practical details

Finding a **place to stay** in Arequipa is rarely a problem and for most travellers there's just one natural choice – the *Pension Guzman* at Calle Jerusalen 408 (tel. 237142). Within four block of the plaza, most of its rooms (some communal) are set around a pretty colonial courtyard where you can arrange breakfast for even the most unreasonable hours; there's often hot water, they'll do your washing quite cheaply and you can ask them to buy your train tickets. A slightly cheaper place, friendly but nothing very special, is the *Hotel Mercaderes* – just off the plaza. The *Hotel de Turistas* is in a beautiful setting on the spur above the San Lazaro barrio, surrounded by the eucalyptus trees of Selva Alegre park where young couples and families take a stroll in the afternoons and on Sundays, but, as usual, it's on the expensive side.

Arequipa is particularly famous for a dish called *ocopa*, a cold starter with potatoes, eggs, olives and a spicy yellow chili sauce (not too hot), but there are all sorts of **restaurants** dotted about the town supplying a wide variety of foods. For traditional dishes and pancakes try *Bonanza* on block one of Jerusalen (open until late), or the picanteria *Sol de Mayo* (Jerusalen 107, Yanahuara, off Avenida Ejercito, about 15 minutes stroll from the plaza). More central are the slightly crummy, very small joint, *La Esquina* (corner of block two of San Juan de Dios) and, on Calle San Franciso, *Manolo's*. There's also a specifically *vegetarian* place on block four of Jerusalen, or for a quiet snack the *Salon de Te* on block three.

OTHER THINGS

AIRPORT Daily flights to Lima and Cuzco; a long way out, you'll need a taxi.

BANKS/MONEY EXCHANGE The *Banco de La Nacion* is on Mercaderes 127, but it's not the only place that will change money; guys in suits carrying briefcases generally pace up and down the street between the restaurant La Esquina and the Plaza de Armas – offering much better rates.

BOOKS If you've run out of English books to read, the *ABC* bookshop in Calle Santa Catalina usually stocks a few and there's an excellent English library in the *Instituto Cultural Peruano-NorteAmericano*, Calle Melgar 109.

BUSES AND COLECTIVOS mostly leave from Calle San Juan de Dios, the main exception being the *Juliaca Express* to Puno and Cuzco which is based at Av. Salaverri 111 (tel. 27893). It's a long haul of some 700km to Cuzco and most people prefer to go by train (see below), even though it's a notorious journey for being ripped off by thieves (again see below!).

CAMERA REPAIRS *Fernando Delange* (303 at Zela) near the northside of Santa Catalina is supposed to be best and fastest around.

FIESTAS If you can arrange exactly when you'll be in Arequipa, the best times are over the last two weeks in February (for the carnival) or for August 15th when the town has a major firework display in the Plaza de Armas.

FILMS The *Instituto Cultural Peruano-Aleman*, San Juan de Dios 202, shows good films and sometimes performs children's theatre.

HIKING EQUIPMENT *Turandes* in the first block of Calle Mercaderes (tel. 22962) offer a service of guides, camping equipment and maps.

HOSPITAL/DENTIST Dr Jaraffe (tel. 215115 from 3–7pm) speaks English, or you can try the *General Hospital* (tel. 231818). Although the altitude in Arequipa isn't particularly high there is still a slim chance that some people will have trouble with their teeth; Dr Morales (Santa Catalina 115; 3rd floor) is a *dentist* who comes well-recommended.

INFORMATION The Guardia Civil on block three of Jerusalen are pretty helpful. They have information, sometimes free maps and will be able to help out if you get ripped off (see THIEVES below).

MARKET For shopping or merely to wander around in an interesting, lively atmosphere there's nowhere better than the **central market**, a couple of blocks down from Iglesia Santa Domingo. One of the largest in Peru, with all sorts of foods, leather work, musical instruments, hats, herbal stalls, cheap shoe repairs (up on the balcony at the bottom end) – I've even seen llama and alpaca meat on sale. Even with police surveillance in the market, however, this is the most likely spot in Arequipa for gringos to get ripped off. Keep everything valuable in money belts, out of sight and covered with as many layers of clothing as possible! All the same, the atmosphere here is a good one. Some of the old quechua ladies serve excellent fruit juices and special mixtures including eggs and stout beer.

NIGHTLIFE A strong tradition of folk-singing and poetry are reflected in several *peñas*. The *El Romé* (opposite the Plazuela de San Francisco) starts around 8pm and warms up a few hours later with good food and music (liveliest at weekends); another with a good atmosphere and strong *pisco sours* is opposite Santa Catalina in Calle Santa Catalina. For less traditional stuff there's also the town disco – *Carnaby Club*, on block one of Jerusalen.

POST OFFICE   The central post office is on Calle San Jose 1½ blocks up from the plaza. **Telephones** for long-distance calls are in the Entel Peru offices on Alvarez Thomas, 1½ blocks straight downhill from the square.

THIEVES   If no-one's told you on the way, be warned that Arequipa is one of the worst places for thieving in Peru – a distinction it shares with Cuzco and Lima. Working in pairs the pick-pockets have become very skilful in recent years – one distracting your attention while the other does the job. Wherever you go, and above all in the market or railway station, keep anything you don't fancy giving away well hidden. See *information*, above, for the address of the Guardia Civil police.

TRAINS   Dangerous though it is in terms of rip-offs, the Arequipa-Puno railway is a journey most people are going to want to make. The *train station* is on Avenida Tacna y Arica, seven blocks south of the Plaza de Armas, and is always packed first thing in the morning on Monday, Wednesday and Friday when the train leaves (at around 8am) for the 10-hour trip to Puno. It's best to buy tickets in advance whenever possible and to be at the station an hour before departure to be at the front of the queue when the rush to get on begins – a particularly vulnerable time. The night-train to Puno, which leaves around 9.30pm, is best avoided. Whenever you go, stock up on glucose tablets – at altitudes of up to 4,476m you might need them.

WATER   Arequipa's tapwater is supposed to be safe for drinking, but locally bottled springwater (and *Arequipeña beer*) taste a lot better.

THE COLCA CANYON, TORO MUERTO, THE VALLEY OF THE VOLCANOES AND OTHER TRIPS AROUND AREQUIPA

Arequipa is one of those towns where it's all too easy to pass the time away – and the only view many travellers get of the spectacular country-side around is from the train east to Puno. If you've a couple of days or more to spare try to do otherwise, for there are some particularly exciting and adventurous possibilities around. The **Colca Canyon** – nearly twice the size of Colorado's Grand Canyon – is one of the most extraordinary; or, more arduously, you can explore the amazing petroglyphs – engraved stones – of **Toro Muerto**, perhaps continuing to hike amid the 86 cones of the **Valley of the Volcanoes**!

If time is limited or you're lacking the energy to fit in with the sparse transport and few facilities around any of these places, you might want to consider the unlikely titled *Holley's Unusual Excursions*, run by landrover from Arequipa by an extremely knowledgeable and devoted Englishman. These are all more than reasonable in price, and range from morning trips to the Inca terraces and sillar quarries around rural Arequipa, to long day excursions out to Toro Muerto or the flamingo-packed Salinas Lake in the shadow of Mount Ubinas – Peru's most active volcano. To get in touch with Anthony Holley you can either find him and his landrover parked outside the Santa Catalina monastery or you can phone him on Arequipa 224452. All passengers are insured and oxygen is available. The only condition is that a minimum of six people (maximum 12) get together for any one trip.

Chivay and the Colca Canyon, and Chapi

Reputedly the deepest canyon in the world, Colca is about 150km from Arequipa – a vast and incomparable place where you can sometimes see condors diving down into the gorge.

Using local transport you have a choice of taking a bus to CHIVAY or to CABANACONDE, 50km further on; both leave Arequipa daily from the terminal on Calle Antiquilla. **CABANACONDE** is the better option if you just want to take a look over the canyon – it's positioned right on the cliff-top above. You can camp there or stay in the small *pension*. **CHIVAY**, in the upper Colca valley, is, however, in the finer hiking country, surrounded by some of the most impressive and intensive ancient terracing in South America. There's a *hostal* here too and you can pick any direction, set off, and come upon some fantastic spot with views across the mountains.

A shorter trip by bus from Arequipa – and manageable as a day's excursion – is to **CHAPI**, 45km south-east. Though less dramatic, the landscape here is still magnificent. Chapi itself is famous for its white church, the Sanctuary of the Virgin, set high above the village at the foot of a valley which itself is the fountain of a miraculous natural spring. Thousands of pilgrims come here annually on May 1st to revere the image of the Virgin, a marvellous burst of processions and fiesta fever. There's no hotel, so if you intend to stay overnight you'll need a tent. Buses leave Arequipa from the *Empresa Zevallos* terminal at San Juan de Dios 621.

Toro Muerto and the Valley of the Volcanoes

Even if most archaeological sites or geological phenomena leave you unmoved, it's difficult not to be overwhelmed by the sheer size and isolation of **Toro Muerto** and the **Valley of the Volcanoes** – and though it's a long and exhausting trip out from Arequipa it has to be one of the most exciting in Southern Peru. To combine both sites you'll need at least six days: leaving Arequipa on the afternoon **bus** (3.30pm every Sunday, Wednesday and Friday), wandering around the petroglyphs on days two and three, and catching the next bus on to the Valley for another couple of days camping and hiking before returning to Arequipa on a Monday, Thursday or Saturday. You could theoretically cut down on this by hitching one or more of these stages, but don't depend on it. Holley takes groups out as far as Toro Muerto on day trips but rarely ventures as far as the Valley.

The **Andagua-Oropampa bus** operated by the *Delgado* bus company covers the whole of this route in what makes quite a gruelling overnight journey. Leaving Arequipa it follows the Lima road to SIGUAS, a small oasis town where you can see the drainage channels cut into the hillside waiting for water to irrigate the desert pampa north of the town. At present the fertile strip of Siguas is very narrow – little more than 200m in width by 1983 – but recently sprinklers have begun to water the sandy plain above and small patches of alfalfa have been planted with a view to producing a humus-rich soil. This is the first stage of the vast $650 million **Majes Project** which plans to irrigate 60,000 hectares in the dry pampas of Majes and Siguas, build two hydro-electric power stations and develop four large and 20 small centres for some 200,000 people. With costs escalating to some $20,000 a hectare, it is reckoned by many people to be a complete waste of time. Yet it seems slightly strange that so much effort, worry and controversy should surround plans very similar in theory to successful Inca irrigation schemes such as the Achirana aqueduct which still maintains the Ica oasis after 500 years.

Just beyond the sprinklers, a few km north of Siguas, the bus turns off the Pan American to head across stony desert. After around 20km you find yourself driving along the top of an incredible cliff, a sheer drop of almost 1,000m separating the road from the Majes valley below. This amazing contortion was created by a fault line running down the earthquake belt which stretches all the way from Ayacucho. Descending along winding tarmac, you can soon see right across the well-irrigated valley floor, the cultivated fields creating a green patchwork against the stark dusty yellow moonscape. At the bottom, a steel-webbed bridge takes the road across the river to the small village of PUNTA COLORADO, dwarfed below a towering and colourful cliff – an ancient river bluff.

For the Toro Muerto petroglyphs you'll have to hop off the bus a few kilometres down the wide dirt track which continues from Punta Colorado towards CORIRE and APLAO (and on into the hills for the Valley of the Volcanoes). The driver should know the best spot to drop you but even so the petroglyphs are difficult to find and since it's usually dark by the time the bus arrives you are probably better off stopping the night at **PUNTA COLORADO**. You can camp here, stock up with water and supplies and walk on in the morning. There's a further lure in the fresh crayfish caught locally and served up at a restaurant called *Condesuyos*, on the left just after the bridge.

When I first visited **Toro Muerto** I was expecting to see a few indecipherable etchings on an outcrop of rock. Much to my amazement the site is strewn over a kilometre or two of hot desert and more than a thousand boulders have been crudely yet very skilfully engraved with a wide variety of distinct representations. No archaeological remains have been directly associated with these pictures but they apparently date from between 1,000 and 1,500 years ago. The engravings include representations of humans, snakes, llamas, deer, parrots, sun-discs and simple geometric motifs. Some of the figures appear to be dancing, their shapes almost moving as you watch; others look like spacemen with large round helmets – obvious potential for Von Daniken, particularly in view of the high incidence of UFO sightings in this region. Curiously, and perhaps the main clue to their origin, there are no symbols or pictures relating to coastal life – not one seabird or fish. One possibility is that they were a kind of communal drawing session during a tribe's migration from the mountains towards the coast. Some of the more abstract geometric designs are very similar to those of the Huari culture who may well have sent an expeditionary force in this direction, across the Andes from their home in the Ayacucho basin, around AD 800. To be certain, however, archaeological traces would have to be found along the route, and no such work has been undertaken. They are not among Peru's most well-known or visited sites.

Probably the best way of discovering the exact locality of the petroglyphs is in relation to the mountains on this side of the valley. The site is a good hour's walk from the 'main road' and at least 500m above it. What you're looking for is a vast row of white rocks, which were presumably scattered across the sandy desert slopes by some mammoth prehistoric volcano. After crossing through maize, bean and alfalfa fields on the valley floor, there's a sandy track running parallel to the road along the foot of the hills. Follow this to the right until you find another track heading up into a large gully towards the mountains. After about a kilometre – always bearing right on the numerous criss-crossing paths and trying to follow the most well-worn trail – you should be able to see the line of white boulders: over 3,000 of them in all. The natural setting is almost as magnificent as the glyphs themselves and even if you were to camp here for a couple of weeks it would be difficult to examine every engraved boulder.

Unless you try hitching you'll have to flag down the bus on to the Valley of the Volcanoes on a Sunday, Wednesday or Friday evening, or on a Monday, Thursday or Saturday if you want to go straight *back to Arequipa*. Check the exact times with the driver on the way out since they tend to vary.

Going **on to the Valley of the Volcanoes**, the bus winds endlessly uphill through the darkness for at least another 10 hours. After tracing around Mount Coropuna, the second highest Peruvian peak at 6,450m, the little town of ANDAGUA (337km from Arequipa) appears at the foot of the valley. This is the normal alighting point although the bus also goes on a little beyond to ORCOPAMPA, a good starting place if you've the energy to walk the whole way down the valley. The Mayor of Andagua offers a roof and meals to travellers when he's in town, but there are no hotels as such. However, all the local people are generally very hospitable, often inviting strangers they find camping in their fields to sleep in their houses. As a rarely visited region where most of the locals are pretty well self-sufficient, there are only the most basic of shops – set up by some of the more entrepreneurial folk in their houses.

A pleasant enough Andean valley in conventional human terms, the *Valle de Los Volcanos* is one of the weirdest geological formations you're ever likely to see, its surface scored with extinct craters varying in size and height from 2–300m yet perfectly merged with the environment.

The main section is about 65km long; to explore it in any detail you'll need to get **maps** (two adjacent ones are required) from the *Explorers Club* or the *Instituto Geografico* in Lima, or from the *Instituto de Cultura* in Arequipa. The best overall view can be had from Anaro mountain (4,800m), looking south-east towards the Chipchane and Puca Maura cones.

Camping here, or at the petroglyphs, you won't really need a tent – a sheet of plastic and a good sleeping bag will do – but you will need good supplies and a sunhat; the sun beating down on the black ash can get unbelievably hot at midday.

If you don't fancy returning to Arequipa by the route just followed it's occasionally possible to catch a truck from Andagua on its way across the often unpassable trail to CAILLOMA, from where there's a bus service to CHIVAY (and Arequipa). This is a long shot, though, and entirely dependent on what you might be told in Andagua – there are rarely more than three trucks this way in any month.

TOWARDS PUNO: YURA AND SUMBAY

Two trips beyond the immediate environs of Arequipa, but which are easily made on your own, are to Yura and Sumbay – both of them on the **Arequipa to Puno railway line**.

YURA, only 30km up the tracks, is perched right on the side of Mount Chachani, and although marred by modern cement works it offers a really stupendous view. There are fairly well maintained **thermal baths** here, as well as a *Hotel de Turistas* and a more basic *hostal*, but it's not a very inviting place to stay and there are regular buses back into Arequipa if you're not going on.

SUMBAY, which the train reaches after a continuous 3–4–hour ascent, is more basic and much less visited. If you stay here you'll be camping, which is really the best way to see the place – waking up to the morning sun on this high pampa is always exhilarating. Close to Sumbay are a series of 8,000-year-old rock paintings, mostly found in small caves, representing people, pumas and cameloids; but the surrounding country-side is amazing enough in itself. Herds of alpacas roam gracefully around the plain looking for itchu grass to munch; vast plasticine-looking rock strata of varying colours mix smoothly together with crudely hewn gullies as reminders of their primeval formation through immense heat and constant shattering blasts.

For the main part of this route – and for practical details – see THE ROUTE FROM AREQUIPA (p. 147).

SOUTH FROM AREQUIPA: TACNA AND THE CHILEAN FRONTIER

Most people arrive on this corner of Perus by bus from Lima (24 hours) or Arequipa (7 hours) with only one intent – to cross into Chile. The border crossing is a relatively simple affair, involving no more than a bus or colectivo from Peruvian Tacna to a customs control where virtually all nationalities (except the Communist Bloc) are given a routine 90-day tourist card.

The road from Arequipa meets the Pan American Highway at the small control town of REPARTICION, continuing south about 200km to MOQUEGUA – once a quiet colonial town, now dominated by copper mines.

TACNA, 150km on across desert landscape, is a notoriously expensive place, renowned among travellers for its pick-pockets and offering little incentive to hang about before getting a shuttle-bus to the frontier. If you do, the main focus of activity in this sprawling city is around the Plaza de Armas and along the tree-lined Avenida Bolognesi. Fronting the square is a *Cathedral* designed by Eiffel in 1870 (though not completed until 1955), and around the corner a *Casa de Cultura* where, if you've an hour to spare, they have pre-Conquest artifacts and exhibitions related to the wars with Chile. The cheap and reasonable *Hotel International* is just off the plaza, while the *Comedor* in the market is the best place to get a decent meal at the right price. *Tourist information* is available from the office at Avenida Bolognesi 2088, and scores of money changers hang around this same street. It's better to change your *soles* into *pesos* here rather than across the border, and if you're coming into Peru from Chile these guys usually offer a better rate of exchange than in Santiago or Arica.

The frontier (open 7am–11pm)

The **frontier** is about 40km across the desert from Tacna. There are regular buses and colectivos to ARICA (20km beyond the border) and two trains a day (8.30am and at 2.30pm). At around $2 the train is the cheapest option but it's slow and you have to sort out your passports before leaving Tacna with the PIP (on the plaza) and the Chilean Consulate (five long blocks from the plaza, just off Coronel Albarracin). *Colectivos* (normally $8 – leaving from the Avenida Bolognesi) are slightly more expensive than the bus but the odd couple of dollars are well worth it since the cars will stop (reliably) at the border controls while you get a Peruvian exit stamp and Chilean tourist card. They are also a lot quicker.

ARICA is often described as a fun town, and being a free port (and gambling resort) with no taxes on booze it's admittedly a good place to get acquainted with the excellent Chilean wines. **Coming into Peru** from Arica is equally simple. Colectivos run all day long and the train leaves at the same times as the one from Tacna. Night travellers, however, might be required to have a *salvoconducto militar* (safe-conduct card), particularly in times of tension between the two countries. If you intend travelling at night, check first with the tourist office in Arica (Calle Prat 375, on the second floor).

PUNO AND LAKE TITICACA

THE ROUTE FROM AREQUIPA

By train

It's a 10–hour trip from **Arequipa to Puno** – which means that if you take the (officially 8am) morning train you'll arrive sometime in the evening. It's a rare event if the train actually leaves Arequipa much before 9 or 10am. Tickets are all cheap and you've a choice of three classes: buffet (around $18), first ($12), and second ($6). Second class is alright if you don't mind chickens scrambling over your feet all day but it's quite a battle getting on since seats are unnumbered and unreserved.

Beyond YURA (1 hour, see p. 145) you're into an almost continual ascent for the next 4–5 hours, a strange process which never really gives you the feeling of entering the mountains. Instead you edge slowly through a series of deceptively small-looking hills and across apparently flat pampa. Around 2½–3 hours out of Arequipa the vegetation has, however, changed completely. The tufted grass looks like electrified sea urchins, powerful sprays extend towards the sun, and you can get occasional glimpses of vicuña herds, darting away as one when they spot the train's approach. There are llamas, too, along with alpacas, sheep and cows, tended by the occasional herder – sitting here on top of the world.

At CANAGUAS (4,078m) the first indication that you're bound for Titicaca is the sudden sight of hundreds of bowler hats, worn by the majority of local peasants. Shortly after, the weird rock formations of SUMBAY (3½ hours from Arequipa: see p. 146) appear, and in another couple of hours you reach CRUCERO ALTO, the highest point on the track at 4,476m. At this altitude many people are feeling pretty terrible – see Paul Theroux's account for the full horrors! – and the only thing for it is a cup of *maté de coca*, served on the train, and a packet of glucose tablets. If you can take it, food is also served around this point.

After crossing an even sparser stretch of pampa, covered in vast volcanic boulders, the train stops at IMATA – a largish settlement based on the railway, and surviving on sheep and alpaca wool spinning. From here on it's all downhill into the lakeland region of the Titicaca Basin: another shift to a landscape which, if it weren't for the flamingos, would resemble nothing so much as the Scottish highlands.

SANTA LUCIA (7½ hours from Arequipa) is a lively tin-roofed town with another small hotel, closely followed by the old colonial buildings of CABANILLOS. It's under 100km from here to Puno, but at 3,885m the air is still intense. At JULIACA, a while further on and the junction for Cuzco, there's often a long wait as scores of Indian women pile onto the train to peddle their ponchos, scarves, sweaters and socks. Initial prices are reasonable, but they get better as the train begins to pull out for the last section of the journey. Unless you're waiting for a connection there's no particular reason to stop here, though the Monday market is one of the cheapest around for woollen goods, and the daily market around the station sells everything down to stuffed iguanas. If you get stranded (trains can leave without warning) try the *Hostal Peru* on the central plaza – cheap, comfortable and one of the safest.

By bus
The road between Arequipa and Puno runs parallel but mostly to the south of the railway – crossing the pampa at TOROYA (4,693m). **Buses** are much less comfortable than the train, and usually take a bit longer, but they do go past the spectacular Lake of Salinas, in the shadow of the active Ubinas Volcano and normally covered with thousands of deep-pink flamingos.

Services from Arequipa are operated by *Morales Moralitos* at Nicolas de Pierola. Or, alternatively, you could hitch this route quite easily, starting at the police control point on the outskirts of Arequipa.

PUNO

The first Spanish settlement at **PUNO** sprang up around a silver mine discovered by the infamous Salcedo brothers in 1657: a camp which forged such a wild and violent reputation that the Lima viceroy moved in with a force of soldiers to crush and finally execute the Salcedos before things got too out of hand. At the same time – in 1668 – he created Puno as the capital of the region and from then on it developed as the main port of Lake Titicaca and an important town on the silver trail from Potosi. The arrival of the railways, late in the nineteenth century, brought another boost, but today it's a relatively poor, rather grubby sort of town, even by Peruvian standards, and a place which has suffered badly from recent drought and an inability to manage its water resources.

With a dry, cold climate – frequently falling below freezing in the winter nights of July and August – Puno represents no more than a crossroads to most travellers, en route from Cuzco to Bolivia or Arequipa and maybe Chile. In some ways this is fair. It's a breathless place, well graced with pick-pockets (beware the bus and train terminals), and not well-known for its ancient past. Yet the town has its own traditions and a couple of unusual attractions. It's famed as the folklore capital of Peru, has its own *folk-music co-operative* (just off the main plaza), and most nights you can find a group of musicians playing somewhere. And on the edge of the town is the vast lake of Titicaca – enclosed by white peaks and specked by the somewhat weird floating islands. Densely populated since well before the Incas, the Titicaca region is also dotted with Chullpa Tombs, often battlement-like rings of burial towers.

The town

There are three points of reference in Puno: the central plaza with the **Cathedral;** the **railway station;** and the **port.** It all looks an impressive sight from a distance but in fact the only real attractions, beyond the basics of sleeping, eating and drinking, are contained within or about these limits.

The **Cathedral,** built with an exquisite baroque facade, is slightly unusual for Peru: very simple and humble inside, in line with the local Aymara Indians' austere attitude to religion. Opposite its north face, at Conde de Lemos 284, is the **Museo Municipal** (open Mon.-Fri. 7–2.45) with an interesting collection including grave goods from the *chullpas.* An **artesania shop** between here and the large Prefectura building sells good craft items, but the **market** (between the railway and the port) has wider and cheaper range.

A common sight around Puno – and if you're struggling to find a hotel room, a welcome one – are **bicycle carts**. For a small fee the cart-boys will carry your gear anywhere in town. Most of the cheaper **hotels** are strung out between the railway station and main plaza on Calles Deustua and Moquegua. For around $5 you can get a good double room at the *Hotel Nesther* (in Deustua), complete with private bathroom – although, as with all hotels in Puno, water is often available for only 2 hours a day. More basic are the *Hostal Roma* (below the Restaurant International on Calle Libertad) and the *Hotel Torino* (further down Libertad, on the other side of the street). Others include the *Hotel Extra* (Calle Moquegua 124), its communal dormitory rooms (under $1 a bed) grouped around an attractive colonial patio, or the *Hotel Samaray* at Jiron Deustua 323 which has its own snack bar and laundry service (about $3 for a double). The *very cheapest hotels*, not exactly recommended, are along Avenida Tacna.

Strangely enough, the four most popular **restaurants** in Puno face each other at the crossing of Moquegua and Libertad – between the plaza and the railway station. Best for breakfast is the *Bar-Cafe Delta;* restaurants *International* and *Sillustani* have much the same kind of food and quality; the other, *Club 31*, has rather less to offer. Next door to the Restaurant Sillustani, the *Cafe Misky* opens for breakfast around 5.30am on most mornings – very handy if you're catching the train. The *Restaurant Ferrocarril* (by the railway station) serves excellent evening meals.

Folk-music concerts are always being advertised at various venues around Puno. The most regular seem to revolve around *Club Samana* (Jiron Puno 334; just down from the main plaza) where there's music from the *altiplano* – incorporating drums, pan-pipes, flutes, churrangos and occasional dancers – more or less every evening from around 9pm.

The **tourist office** (Calle Cajamarca 527) usually has information on concerts as well as maps and details on travel in the region and local fiestas. The town's own main **festival**, the *Fiesta de la Virgen de la Candelaria*, takes place during the first two weeks of February, climaxing on the second Sunday. For further information, especially about **tours** to Sillustani or the floating islands, try *Tranextur* at Jiron Puno 525 (off the Plaza de Armas).

The **Banco de la Nacion** is on block 5 of Tacna; a casa de cambio (open until 7pm for cheques as well as cash) is at Jiron Puno 280. Mail seems to take ages to get anywhere from Puno, and the **post office** (on Moquegua, between Libertad and Deustua) rarely has change for large bills. For more immediate communications, the **telephone and telegram offices** are on Calle Ayacucho, off block 4 of Libertad (near the sauna).

On from Puno: some travel details

Puno is one of the few towns in Peru where you have any real choice about where or how to move on. To **Arequipa or Cuzco**, the day train is the obvious choice – both roads are rough and you can always see much more from the train windows. The train *to Arequipa* leaves on Tuesdays and Thursdays at 6.55am, on Saturdays at 9.20am, or there's a night-train daily at 8.30pm. To Cuzco, departures are Monday to Friday at 6.55am (arriving around 5.30pm), Saturdays 9.20am. Tickets can be bought either in the hour before the train leaves or, more securely, the evening before (after the Arequipa night-train has left).

Heading **south to Bolivia** there are two options. A *boat* leaves every Wednesday night across Titicaca to GUAQUI (13 hours), from where a train takes you on to La Paz, or you can go any day of the week *by road* via either DESAGUADERO or YUNGUYO. This is a much more interesting route and is detailed on p. 154; and if you don't want to miss out on the lake you could always take a trip out to one of the islands, or cross the Straits from Yunguyo. **Tickets** for the steamer and train to La Paz can be bought from the jetty in Puno only 2 hours before embarkation ($10–25 depending on class). Unfortunately, almost the entire journey in either direction is made in darkness; the boat returns to Puno from GUAQUI every Friday night.

LAKE TITICACA: THE FLOATING ISLANDS AND CHULLPA TOMBS

The highest navigable lake in the world, **TITICACA** is also one of the biggest – some fifteen times the size of Lake Geneva, with a surface area of over 8,000 square km. Around its sides the villages depend mainly on grazing, the altitutde limiting the potential for maize cultivation. But for all travellers the lake's great fascination is inevitably its man-made **floating islands**, inhabited for centuries since their construction by retreating Uros Indians. They are, quite literally, floating platforms – built from layer upon layer of *tortora* reeds, the same organic material used for the island huts and local fishing rafts.

There are over 40 tortora islands, but most trips from Puno limit themselves to the largest one, **Huacavacani**, where several Indian families live, rather bizarrely, alongside a floating 7th Day Adventist mission school. Short 3–4-hour trips can be arranged either through a tour agency, or directly with the skipper of one of the many launches which leave about every half hour from the jetty. To get there walk down Avenida Titicaca, a continuation of Deustua from the Plaza de Armas.

There are only about 300–400 Indians living on the islands these days, most of them a mixture of the original Uros and the larger Aymara tribe. When the Incas controlled Collao, they considered the Uros so poor – almost sub-human – that only a section of hollow cane filled with lice was required from them as a monthly tribute. Life here has certainly

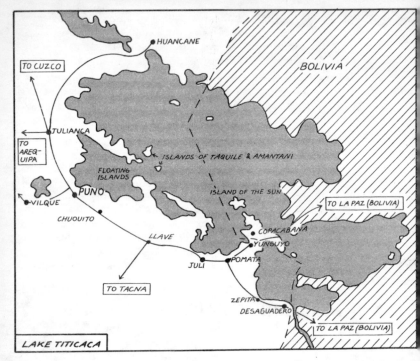

LAKE TITICACA

never been easy. The inhabitants have to go at least 2km to find fresh water, and the bottoms of the reed islands rot rapidly, needing fresh matting to be constantly added above. Struggling on amid this vegetable decay, over half the islanders are now Catholic and the largest community is very much dominated by its evangelical school.

Visiting the islands, particularly Huacavacani, leaves an ambivalent aftertaste. On the one hand, the Indians have been turned into a human zoo (with no escape) and have learnt to squeeze as much from visitors as possible (they appreciate money and fresh fruit); on the other, you do get a glimpse of another viable form of human existence and the opportunity to ride on a tortora reed raft. The islanders generally sit in lines selling tons of craft-work and woollen goods – most of it cheaper in Juliaca or Puno, although the children's drawings and the brilliant stylised tapestries are unique.

Taquile and Amantini
Two genuine – *non-floating* – islands in Titicaca can also be visited. **Taquile** and **Amantini**, peaceful places which see fewer gringos, are both around 25km across the water from Puno on the outer edge of the Gulf of Chucuito.

Boats for these islands leave early every morning, around 6–9am; a 5–hour trip which costs $5 or $6. The sun's rays reflected off the lake can burn even accustomed skins so it's a good idea to protect your head and shoulders during this voyage. The boats return after lunch the same day, and since this doesn't give you enough time to look around, most people prefer to stay a night or two in (very cheap) bed and breakfast accommodation. Sleeping bags are recommended for the cold night air; fresh fruit and vegetables are warmly appreciated by the host-islanders.

Both islands have managed to maintain a degree of cultural isolation and the women dress in fine colourful cloths, very distinctly woven. The ancient agricultural terraces are maintained in excellent condition and traditional crafts of stone masonry are still practised. Taquile, which is where most of the boats go, also has a few scattered pre-Inca and Incaic ruins.

The **Island of the Sun**, largest and most sacred of all the islands, lies to the south-east in Bolivian waters and can best be visited from Copacabana, just over the border from Yunguyo. Boats from there take some 6 hours and work out about $3–$6 per person.

The Chullpa tombs of Sillustani

Chullpas, built by the Collao tribe who dominated this region before the Incas arrived, are scattered all around Titicaca. Some of these ancient funeral towers stand 10m in height – the largest built in white stone for local chieftains.

Those at **Sillustani**, set on a little peninsula in Lake Umayo, overlooking Titicaca, are the most spectacular. A battlement-like ring, they have guarded this land of the dead for over 500 years – some occasionally tumbled by earthquakes or, more recently, by *huaqueros* intent on repossessing the rich grave goods (ceramics, jewellry and a few weapons) buried with important mummies. Two main styles predominate at this site: the honeycomb chullpas and the Inca stone-work types. The former are set aside from the rest and characterised by large stone slabs around a central core; some of them are carved though most are simply plastered with white mud and small stones. The Inca-type stone-work is more complicated and in some cases you can see the elaborate corner jointing more typical of Cuzco masonry.

You can get to the site by local bus from Puno, but a more efficient service is offered as an afternoon trip by **minibus** ($4); this can be booked from one of the agencies or most hotels. If you want to camp overnight at Sillustani (remembering how cold it can be) the site guard will show you where to pitch your tent. It's a magnificent place to wake, with the morning sun rising over the snow-capped Cordillera Real on the Bolivian side of Titicaca.

ROUTES TO BOLIVIA: DESAGUADEROS AND YUNGUYO

You can (see p. 151) travel directly to Bolivia by boat – across Titicaca to GUAQUI. Much the most interesting routes, however, involve at least some overland travel, crossing the frontier at either **Yunguyo** or at the river border of **Desaguaderos**. En route to either you'll pass by some of Titicaca's more interesting colonial settlements, each attractively individual in their architecture. Several of the Puno **bus companies** cover these routes – two of them, *4 de Noviembre* and *Cruz del Sur*, taking in the detour to YUNGUYO from where a minibus (tickets from most agencies, including *Turisloop* at Jiron Libertad 115) continues to COPA-CABANA. If you're in a hurry you'll want to go via Desaguaderos, and two companies (*Morales Moralitos* buses and *Juliaca Express* colectivos) run right through to La Paz. All of these leave from blocks 2 and 3 of Avenida Tacna.

CHUCUITO, 20km out of Puno, is dwarfed by its intensive hillside terracing and by huge igneous boulders poised behind the brick and adobe houses. Early in the morning, small blotchy-cheeked Aymara children clamber onto the stone walls around their homesteads to bask in the sun's first warming rays. Chucuito was once a colonial town and its main plaza retains the *picota* (pillory) where the severed heads of executed criminals were displayed. From here the road cuts 60km across the plain to JULI, a larger town nestling between gigantic round-topped and terraced hills. There are a few *hostals* here (a basic one on the main plaza), a *Hotel de Turistas* and a very expensive (up to $80), somewhat out of place, **hovercraft service** to Copacabana. The Jesuits chose Juli as the site for their novel training centre preparing missionaries bound for the remoter regions of Bolivia and Paraguay. The concept they developed, a form of community evangelisation, was at least partly inspired by the Inca organisational system and extremely influential through the seventeenth and eighteenth centuries. Fronting the large open plaza are the parish church of San Pedro and the amazing-looking **Casa Zavala** (House of the Inquisition) with thatched roof and fantastically carved double doors. Juli's other churches are worth a look too, if you're breaking the journey here – each having served its own quarter of the town for some three centuries. So too is **POMATA**'s pink granite *iglesia*, 20km on, where you may want to make the connection to YUNGUYO.

The **YUNGUYO-COPACABANA** crossing is much the most enjoyable route into Bolivia, though unless you intend staying overnight in Copacabana (or taking the 3-hour Puno-Copacabana minibus) you'll need to set out quite early from Puno. The actual **border** (open 8am–6pm) is 2km walk out of Yunguyo; the Bolivian control, where there's usually a bus for the 10km or so to Copacabana, a few hundred metres on. Only enough money to carry you to LA PAZ should be changed at the stalls in Yunguyo's plaza; the cheap afternoon service from Copacabana takes you through some of the most exciting scenery of the Titicaca basin. At TIQUINA you leave the bus briefly to take a passenger ferry across the narrowest point of the lake, the bus rejoining you on the other side from its own individual ferry. Officially all travellers have to report to the Bolivian Naval Office – this is one of the few countries in the world which has a navy but no ocean – beside the passenger ferry terminal before crossing the Straits; but in practice there are often too many people and there's a very real danger of missing the bus (and your luggage) on the other side by hanging around in a hopeless queue. Once over the Straits it's a 4–5-hour haul on to La Paz.

Allowing you to get from Puno to LA PAZ inside 12 hours with a minimum of hold-ups and changing (as opposed to the more complicated Copacabana route), the **DESAGUADEROS CROSSING** sees most of the traffic across the Peru-Bolivia border. If you're on one of the *Morales Moralitos* buses (Sun., Tues. and Thurs.; $20 to La Paz) or *Juliaca Express colectivos* (daily but slightly more expensive) all you'll need to do is get a stamp in your passport; the Peruvian control is by the market, the Bolivian just across the bridge. If you arrive here by local bus – or by one of the new minibuses from Puno – it's a short walk between the two and you can pick up an *Ingravi* bus to La Paz (more or less hourly). Money can be changed on the bridge approach but the rates are poor, so buy only as much as you'll need to get you to La Paz.

For anyone **coming into Peru from Bolivia** by either route the procedure is just as straightforward, only reversed. One real difference worth noting is that when leaving COPACABANA there is a customs and passport check for all those going into Peru. This takes place in two little huts on the left just before the exit barrier. Now and again Bolivian customs officials take a heavy line (probably when they're hard up for cash) and thoroughly search all items of luggage. In come cases completely unnecessary bribery has to be resorted to, simply to avoid undue hassle or delay. If you get stranded crossing the border there are some basic **hostals**: the *Hotel Amazonas* in YUNGUYO; the sordid *Alojamiento Internacional* at DESAGUADEROS, or several places in COPACABANA.

TRAVEL DETAILS

Buses and colectivos

From Pisco Several daily to Lima (3hrs) and on to Ica and Nazca (1–3hrs). Ayacucho (1 daily; 14hrs) and Huancavelica (1; 14hrs).

From Nazca To Arequipa (nightly; 12hrs) and Cuzco (every other day; 35hrs).

From Arequipa To Tacna (several daily; 5hrs), Puno (daily; 12hrs) and Cuzco (daily; 20hrs).

From Puno To Cuzco (1–2 daily; 12–15hrs) and La Paz (several daily; 12hrs upwards).

Trains

Arequipa-Puno Leaves Mon., Wed. and Fri. at 08.10 (officially), arriving at Yuma (1hr), Sumbay (3½hrs), Santa Lucia (7½hrs), Juliaca (9hrs; connection to Cuzco, 9hrs on) and Puno (10hrs). Also, not recommended, a *night-train* leaving Arequipa every evening at 21.30.

Puno-Arequipa Leaves Tue. and Thurs. at 6.55, Sat. at 9.20, or, again not recommended, the *night-train* at 20.30.

Puno-Cuzco Leaves Mon.-Fri. 6.55, arriving 17.35, Sat. at 9.20 arriving around 19.50 – via Juliaca (1½hrs) and Sicuani (6½hrs).

Boat train

Puno-La Paz Leaves every Wednesday evening (17hrs).

Flights

From Arequipa Daily with both Faucett and AeroPeru to Lima and Cuzco; AeroPeru only daily to Puno.

From Puno (Juliaca airport) Daily to Lima with AeroPeru.

Chapter four
ANCASH
AND HUANUCO

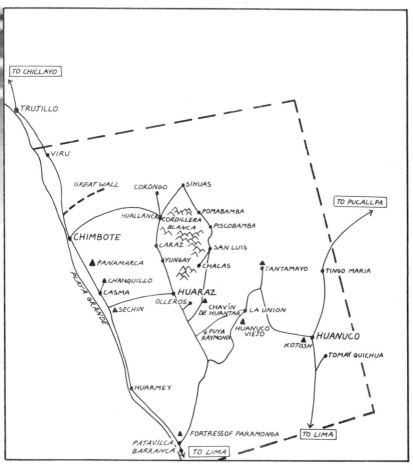

Dividing Lima from the coastal attractions around Trujillo and the central jungle zone of Pucallpa, the departmentos of Ancash and Huanuco are remarkably little visited. Yet there's a great deal of interest here, and above all some of the finest mountain hiking in South America.

Ancash stretches itself along an immense desert coastline, where pyramids and ancient fortresses are scattered in easy reach of several small resorts which are, in turn, close to vast and perfectly empty Pacific beaches. Behind range the barren heights of the Cordillera Negra, and beyond that the spectacular tropical backdrop of the snow-capped Cordillera Blanca. **Huaraz**, in the valley between the two, is the vital centre of this inland region. A magnificent **hiking** base, it's also the place from which to explore several important ruins including **Chavin de Huantar**, heart of one of the earliest and most influential of Peru's civilisations.

Land-locked **Huanuco** is, if anything, still less known. From the capital – the thriving market city of **Huanuco** – you can again visit a series of fascinating archaeological sites, above all the huge and puzzling complex at **Tantamayo**, and **Huanuco Viejo**, a remarkably preserved Inca regional capital. In the mountains round about are any number of welcoming traditional villages, and from here too it's just a short trip down to **Tingo Maria**, and the luxuriant forested regions where the eastern slopes of the Andes merge into the jungle of the Amazon Basin.

Connected by road from Huaraz via La Union to Huanuco, and each easily accessible from Lima, they're two genuinely stimulating and extremely beautiful states which even several weeks' exploration will only begin to reveal.

THE ANCASH COAST

Despite its easy access, the Ancash coast is not well known: most people travel the whole distance between LIMA and TRUJILLO in a single 9-hour bus journey. If you're short of time you'll probably want to do the same, but it's worth at least considering a stop at either **Barranca**, **Casma** or **Chimbote**. Each of them offers the advantage of nearby archaeological sites and alternative routes up into the **Callejon de Huaylas**.

BARRANCA AND PARAMONGA

North of Lima, **PARAMONGA** is the first site of real interest, the best preserved of all Peru's coastal fortresses, built originally to guard the southern limit of the powerful Chimu Empire. To explore the ruins, the easiest plan is to get off the bus at **BARRANCA**, where there's a wide choice of hotels and restaurants, or even the chance to rent a beach-villa (sometimes advertised in local hotels and papers). *Hotel Chavin* is cheap and good, and there's an excellent *chifa* restaurant on the main street. Buses and colectivos on their way between Lima and Trujillo or Huaraz will nearly all stop at Barranca. For Paramonga, or the smaller town of Patavilca (5km north), there is an efficient local bus service. **PATAVILCA**, the village where Bolivar planned his campaign to liberate Peru, is also a possible alternative base with a cafe, small museum and the rudimentary *Hostal del Sol.*

Less than a kilometre from the ocean, the **Fortress of Paramonga** looks in many ways like a feudal castle. Constructed entirely from adobe, its walls within walls run around the contours of a natural hillock – similar in style and situation to the Sun Temple of Pachacamac, near Lima. There are differences of opinion as to whether the fort had a military function or was purely a ritual centre. Bearing in mind the tendency most pre-Conquest cultures had of worshipping while utilising the natural personality of the landscape and environment (rocks, water, geomorphic oddities, etc.) it seems likely that the Chimu built it on a more ancient *huaca*, both as a well-protected and fortified ritual shrine and to delimit the southern boundary of their empire. It was conquered by the Incas in the late fifteenth century, the new overlords maintaining a road down from the Callejon de Huaylas and another which ran along the sands below the fortress.

Hernando Pizarro was the first Spaniard to see Paramonga in 1533 during his exploratory journey from Cajamarca to Pachacamac. He described it as 'a strong fort with seven encircling walls painted with many forms both inside and outside, with portals well built like those of Spain and two tigers painted at the principal doorways'. There are still red and yellow based geometric murals visible on some of the walls in the upper sector, as well as chess-board patterns.

As you climb up from the road, by the small site **museum** (open 8–5 daily) and ticket office, the main entrance is to the right. Heading into the maze-like **ruins**, the rooms and sections get smaller and narrower the closer you get to the top – the original palace-temple. From here there were once commanding views across the desert coast in either direction; today, looking south, you see vast sugar-cane fields, now farmed by a co-operative, which used to belong to the US Grace Corporation when they controlled nearly a third of Peru's sugar production. In contrast to the verdant green of these fields, irrigated by the Rio Fortaleza, the fortress stands out in the landscape like a huge, dusty, yellow pyramid. If you're travelling straight through, you can't miss it from the passing bus; it's best seen from the right-hand windows.

CASMA, SECHIN AND CHANQUILLO

Just 3km south of Paramonga (at km 207), a road to HUARAZ turns off and uphill from the main Pan American Highway. North, sand-dunes encroach on the main coastal road as it continues past Paramonga to

HUARMEY (km 293). As well as exhilarating, usually deserted, beaches (La Honda, El Balneario and Tuquillo), you'll find the *Hotel Venus* here and a 24-hour restaurant, *El Piloto*, geared towards serving truckers.

Leaving Huarmey the road closely follows the shore-line, passing by the magnificent **PLAYA GRANDE**, a seemingly endless beach with powerful rolling surf – often a luminous green at night due to microscopic plankton being tossed around in the white water crests – and a perfect spot for getting off the bus to camp. The road, straight as far as the eye can see, seems to have a life and tempo of its own; for the bus, truck and colectivo drivers it is where they have spent and will spend most of their lives, winking and waving as they hurtle towards each other at combined speeds of 200km per hour. Some of the desert you pass through has no plant life at all beyond the burnt-out tumbleweed which roams around the humps and ridge-backed undulations fringed with curvy lines of rock strata – intrusions of volcanic power from the ancestral age. In places huge hills crouch like sand-covered jelly-fish squatting on some vast beach.

CASMA, the next town from Huarmey, marks the mouth of the well-irrigated Rio Sechin valley. Surrounded by maize and cotton fields this small place is peculiar in that most of its buildings are just one storey tall yet all of them are modern. For a long time the port for the Callejon de Huaylas, it was razed to the ground by the 1970 earthquake. There's not a lot of interest here except the temple complex of SECHIN, 5km south-east of the town, and the PAÑAMARCA PYRAMID over 20km north. With a few road-side cafes and a couple of **hotels** (*El Farol* or the more basic *Hotel Central*) this is another potential journey-breaker. **Buses** run to Lima, Huaraz (a scenic but dusty trail over the Cordillera Negra via the Callan Pass), Chimbote and Trujillo.

SECHIN (8–5 daily, the same entrance ticket can be used for Panamarca) is a long hour's walk from Casma, south along the Pan American for a couple of kilometres then up the side-road to Huaraz for about the same distance. The main section of **the site**, unusually stuck at the bottom of a hill, consists of an outer wall clad with around 90 tall monolithic slabs engraved with eerie, sometimes monstrous, representations of belli-cose warriors with trophy-heads, and mutilated sacrificial victims or prisoners of war. Some of these stones, dated to about 750 BC, stand 4m high. The carvings have a very characteristic style, curvier than the complicated Chavin designs found in the sierra, and a little frightening. Although they have no feline features and are not really similar to the contemporaneous Chavinoid engravings, some small objects discovered on the coast do bear designs which link the two styles. Little, however, is known about the symbolism involved or the militaristic (perhaps sadistic) cult which surely must have built Sechin. Behind the standing stones an interesting-looking inner sanctuary lies hidden; a rectangular building consisting of a series of superimposed platforms with a central stairway on either side. The sanctuary has been closed to the public for some time and you get the impression that the restoration of this site bears little relation to how it originally looked.

Out in the Sechin Valley there is a maze of ancient sandy roadways, and it seems that this area was an important pre-Incaic junction where a coastal road merged with one from the sierra. Several other lesser known sites dot the region. A huge complex of dwellings can be found on the **Pampa de Llamas**; there's a terraced, stone-faced pyramid with stone stairs, feline and snake designs at **Mojeque**; and some 12km from Casma, is the ruined, possibly pre-Mochica, fort of **Chanquillo**. To the latter there are trucks every morning at around 9 from the *Petro Peru* garage in Casma – ask the driver to drop you off for *El Castillo* (half-an-hour's walk uphill). It's an amazing ruin set in a commanding position on a barren hill with four concentric ring-walls and watch-towers in the middle keeping an eye over the desert below.

CHIMBOTE AND 'THE GREAT WALL OF PERU'

Going north towards CHIMBOTE from CASMA, the next major landmark is the Nepeña valley. At km 395 on the Pan American Highway there is a turn-off which leads 11km to the ruined adobe pyramid structures of **PAÑAMARCA**. Three large painted panels were found here and on another wall a long procession of warriors was depicted – but both have been badly damaged by rain. Although an impressive monument to the Mochica culture (AD 500) it is not an easy site to visit; you'll have to make it a day trip from either CASMA or CHIMBOTE and rely on your hitching skills or try to wave down one of the passing long-distance buses.

From here **CHIMBOTE** is only another 25km to the north, a modern city and the site of the country's most spectacular urban growth outside of Lima. A quiet fishing port and favourite honeymoon spot until the early part of this century, its ugly, sprawling development – which reeks of fish-processing and canning factories – was stimulated by the Chimbote to Huallanca railway (1922), the hydro-electric plant in the Cañon del Pato, and by government planning for an anticipated boom in the anchovy and tuna fishing industry. The population rose rapidly from 5,000 in 1940 to 60,000 in 1961 (swollen by squatter settlers from the mountains) and an incredible 159,000 by 1972 – making it Peru's fifth city. In 1970 nearly every building in Chimbote was levelled by the earthquake whose epicentre was not far off-shore.

Chimbote's fish-conserve factories, over 30 of them, utilise some of the world's most modern canning equipment, one of the nation's pride and joys. Unfortunately the fishing industry has been undergoing a crisis since the early 1970s: overfishing and *El Niño* have necessitated the imposition of bans and catch-limits for the fishermen. Yet over 75 per cent of Peru's fishing-related activities continue here.

It smells too awful to stay very long in Chimbote and most travellers remain overnight at most, continuing as soon as possible to Lima, Huaraz (via the stupendous Cañon del Pato) or north to Trujillo. The *Hotel Venus* on Av. Prado (the main street) is bearable and not too expensive, or there's the noisy *Hostal Los Angeles* near the market half a block from Prado (on Galvez). **Cars** to Trujillo (only 2 or 3 hours) leave regularly from opposite the Hostal Los Angeles (slightly up towards the market) – the drivers make themselves known by shouting out their destinations. **Buses** for Trujillo leave from just outside the Hostal, while for Caraz and Huaraz they leave from the corner of Galvez over the other side of Prado and on block 7 of Bolognesi. Colectivos to Lima hang around on Manual Ruiz, one block towards the sea off Avenida Prado.

Leaving Chimbote north-bound, the coast road crosses a rocky outcrop into the Santa Valley, where stands the **GREAT WALL OF PERU** – a stone and adobe structure more than 50km long. This region was occupied by the Mochicas towards the end of their history (AD 600–700) and later by the Chimu. The enormous wall was first noticed in 1931 by the Shippee-Johnson Aerial Photographic Expedition. Julio Tello thought it was pre-Chimu since it seems unlikely that the Chimu would have built such a lengthy defensive wall so far inside the limits of their Empire. It may, however, have been constructed prior to a second phase of military expansion or, as the chronicler Garcilaso de la Vega believed, the Spaniards might have placed it here against the ever-increasing threat of Inca invasion either from the coast or down from the Callejon de Huaylas.

In its entirety **the wall** stretches from Tambo Real near the Santa's estuary up to Chuqucara where there are scattered remains of pyramids, fortresses, temples and stone houses. The best surviving section lies just to the west of the Hacienda Tanguche, where the piled stone is cemented with mud to more than 4m high in places. Higher up the valley lies a double-walled construction with outer turrets, discovered by Gene Savoy's aerial expedition in the late 1950s. Savoy noted 42 stone-built strongholds in the higher Santa Valley in only two days' flying, evidence which supports the chronicles' claim that this was the most populated valley on the coast prior to the Spanish Conquest of Peru. Hard to believe today, it seems more probable if you bear in mind that the zone is still fed by the largest and most reliable of the coastal rivers. In 1962 Savoy led an expedition into the area on foot, finding that most of these parapeted defensive structures were well hidden from the valley floor. Once you climb up to them, however, you can see the towering peaks of the Cordillera Blanca to the east and the Pacific Ocean in the west.

The bridge over the river Santa is about 20km from Chimbote: simply head upstream to find the ruins. It's an interesting desert region which offers the opportunity to spot wild-life – the desert fox, a condor or two if you're lucky – while exploring the valley for pre-Columbian sites. The climate is hot but ideal for sleeping rough, and the only things you'll need to carry are your own food and preferably bottled drinking water. **Maps** of the region are available in Lima from the *Instituto Geografico Militar* (see BASICS).

Continuing north, the road cuts up the normally dry river-bed of Chau, a straggling, scrubby green trail through absolutely barren desert. The next town is **VIRU** (km 515), a small place along the roadside, with a bridge over the river bed which in the dry season looks as though it has never seen rain. An impressive cultural centre around AD 300 when it was occupied by the Gallinazo or Viru people, the town today offers very little. Nearby, however, there are abundant **archaeological remains**.

In the Gallinazo period the **Viru valley** saw great developments: dwelling sites became real villages (basically large groups of adjacent rooms and stone pyramids); improved irrigation produced a great population increase; and a society with a stronger tendency towards control of labour and distribution began to arise. The Gallinazo started to build defensive walls just prior to being invaded by the Mochicas (around AD 500) on their military conquests south as far as the Santa and Nepeña valleys. Later on, during the Chimu era, the population was dramatically reduced again, perhaps through migration north to Chan Chan, capital of this highly centralised pre-Incaic state.

There are two main sites within easy reach of Viru. Closest to the road is **CERRO PRIETO** near the fishing village of Guanape – a short walk from the northern side of the bridge towards the mouth of the Rio Viru. This ancient rubbish tip was the site of an agricultural settlement around 1200 BC and some of the earliest ceramics on the coast were found here. A more interesting and visual ruin is the **GRUPO GALLINAZO** near Tomabal, 24km to the east of Viru up a side-road just north of the bridge. Here you can see the dwellings, murals and pyramids of a significant religious and administrative centre, its internal architectural structure derived from kinship networks. It's built entirely of adobe, with separate cultivation plots irrigated by an intricate canal system.

From VIRU the Pan American cuts across a desert plain, close to the sea. Before reaching Trujillo there is a huge multi-crescent dune to the left, sheltering a chicken battery farm on the sands below. The road then runs down into the expansive plains of the Moche valley with the great Mochica temples of the Sun and Moon (see p. 200) a couple of kilometres to the right under Cerro Blanco, and the likeable city of TRUJILLO (km 561) spread out in front.

HUARAZ AND THE CORDILLERA BLANCA

Huaraz – the centre of inland Ancash – is hardly one of Peru's most interesting towns, but it's a lively place and the centre for exploring a tremendous region dominated by the **Cordillera Blanca,** the highest tropical mountain range in the world. Only 8 hours by bus from Lima, 9 or 10 from Trujillo, it's one of *the* places to base yourself if you've any interest at all in South American hiking. There are spectacular ruins such as **Chavin de Huantar,** natural thermal baths, and immense glacial lakes. Throughout the whole region, too, you come upon traditional mountain villages, unusual and exotic flora like the weird *Puya Raymondi* cactus, and unwritten legends encapsulated only in the ancient carved stones.

HUARAZ AND AROUND

Less than a century ago **HUARAZ** was still a fairly isolated community, barricaded to the east by the dazzling snow-capped peaks of the *Cordillera Blanca* and separated from the coast by the dry, dark *Cordillera Negra*. Between these two mountain chains is a single corridor, the **Callejon de Huaylas** – fountainhead of the largest river in Peru, and a region with strong traditions of local independence. In 1885 the people of the Callejon waged a guerilla war against the Lima authorities which saw the whole valley in rebel hands for several months: a revolt which was sparked off when a native leader, the charismatic Pedro Pablo Atusparia, and 13 other village mayors protested over taxation and labour abuses. Sent straight to prison and humiliated by having their braided hair (a traditional sign of status) cut off, the local peasants reacted by overrunning Huaraz, freeing their natural chieftains and expelling all officials before looting the mansions of wealthy landlords and merchants (many of them expatriate Englishmen who had been here since the Wars of Independence). The rebellion was eventually quashed by an army battalion from the coast which recaptured Huaraz while the Indians were celebrating their annual fiesta – but even today, Atusparia's memory survives close to local hearts, and village peasants remain distinctly unimpressed by the claims of central government.

The town itself, however, has become almost cosmopolitan – developing commercially since completion of the highway through the river basin from Paramonga. Virtually the entire city was levelled by the 1970 earthquake, but the old houses have been replaced with onestoreyed modern structures topped with gleaming tin roofs. Surrounded by eucalyptus groves and fields, it must have been really beautiful before

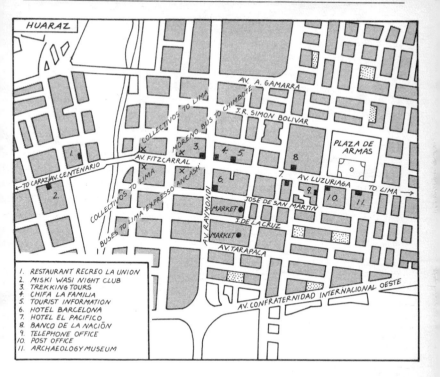

HUARAZ

AV. A. GAMARRA

J.R. SIMON BOLIVAR

COLLECTIVOS TO LIMA

MORENO BUS TO CHIMBOTE

PLAZA DE ARMAS

AV. FITZCARRAL

←TO CARAZ AV. CENTENARIO

COLLECTIVOS TO LIMA

BUSES TO LIMA Y EXPRESSO ANCASH

AV. LUZURIAGA

TO LIMA →

AV. RAYMONDI

JOSE DE SAN MARTIN

MARKET

J.DE LA CRUZ

MARKET

AV. TARAPACA

AV. CONFRATERNIDAD INTERNACIONAL OESTE

1. RESTAURANT RECREO LA UNION
2. MISKI WASI NIGHT CLUB
3. TREKKING TOURS
4. CHIFA LA FAMILIA
5. TOURIST INFORMATION
6. HOTEL BARCELONA
7. HOTEL EL PACIFICO
8. BANCO DE LA NACIÓN
9. TELEPHONE OFFICE
10. POST OFFICE
11. ARCHAEOLOGY MUSEUM

– and is still a fine place in which to rest up after the rigours of hard travel. There are any number of easy trails just outside of town, and if you fancy nothing more than an afternoon's stroll you can simply walk out to the eastern edge and follow one of the paths or streams uphill. In town, the only place really worth checking out is the **Regional Museum** (open daily, 10–6) beside the modern Plaza de Armas. Apart from a superb collection of ceramics (including many from the little-known Recuay culture) it has gardens and an abundance of the finely chiselled stone monoliths typical of this mountain region, most of them products of the incredible Chavin culture.

Practical details

Around the centre of town, from the Plaza de Armas along Luzuriaga, there are countless **hostals** and many smaller places seeking pin-money; outside of high season (July and August) it is often possible to bargain for a room, especially if there are a few of you to share it. Without a doubt the most popular place with travellers is the *Hotel Barcelona* (Av. Raymondi 612; tel. 2179), cheap and very friendly; there's no hot water but *Baños Raymondi*, nearby, offers good public showers. On the top floor of the Barcelona you'll find *Pepe's Palace* where you can share floor-space with backpackers and sell, swop, buy or rent all sorts of camping gear. An alternative hotel is *El Pacifico* (on Av. Centenario) which does offer hot water and is still quite reasonable. For a little luxury, though not as dauntingly plush as it looks at first glance, try the *Hotel Monterrey*, about 7km further down the valley with regular bus connections (No. 1) to Huaraz centre; this has a swimming pool and even thermal baths and, if you can afford it, makes a perfect base for trekking.

There's no shortage of **restaurants** in Huaraz, though they do vary considerably in value and quality. I've always found the *Chifa Familiar* (on the corner of Raymondi and Luzuriaga) better than most; while for local fare an excellent spot is *El Recreo Union* in Manco Capac. There are several **discos** scattered about the centre, but more interesting is the *Miki Wasi Taberna* (Av. Centenario 203, from 11pm) with dancing, music and an occasional live band.

If you intend **to hike** at all it's essential to spend at least a couple of days acclimatising to the altitude beforehand. Huaraz is only 3,100m above sea level but most of the Cordillera's more impressive peaks are over 6,000m. A number of places give free **information**, including the shops at Luzuriaga 459 (tel. 2394), Fitzcarral 458 and Pomabamba 415, the Municipal Building on the plaza and *Ancash Tours* on Jr. Francisco de Zela 210 (tel. 2310). In 1984 there were also three or four places selling and renting **camping equipment** – notably *Pepe's Palace* (Hotel Barcelona) and the shop at Fitzcarral 458. If you are keen to trek in the Huascaran National Park (which encompasses virtually the whole Cordillera Blanca) you should register beforehand with the **Park Office** at the top end of Raymondi where you can also get information and friendly advice. Ideally you should have detailed maps and one or other of the excellent *Backpacking and Trekking in Peru and Bolivia* or *Trails of the Cordillera Blanca and Huayhuash* (see pp. 286–7). These aren't currently available in Huaraz, though you should be able to get them in Lima at the South American Explorers' Club on Av. Portugal 146.

Huaraz is a noted **crafts** centre, too, producing such things as tooled leather goods (customised if you've got a few days to wait around) very cheaply. Other quality bargains include woollen articles, embroidered blankets, delicious local honey, *manjar blanco* and, if you've got the room, interesting replicas of the Chavin stone carvings.

The **Banco de la Nacion** is on Luzuriaga (half a block north of the plaza); the **post office** is next to the Municipal Building (on the plaza), and the **telephone office** is just off Luzuriaga (slightly downhill and opposite the side of the post office).

Buses going north down the Santa valley to Yungay and Caraz leave more or less hourly from the market area and Av. Fitzcarral, and buses or trucks bound for Recuay and Catac can be picked up at the southern exit to town where Luzuriaga merges with the Av. Confraternidad Inter-nacional Oeste. Two other bus companies which might come in useful are: Empressa Soledad (to Casma), Raymondi 336; and Moreno (to Chimbote), Av. Fitzcarral.

The best **time of year** to be in Huaraz is between May and October; it rains frequently through the summer months, with the Lima road often impassable. **Fiestas** occur all year round in the local villages and hamlets. They are always particularly bright, energetic occasions in this region, with chicha and aguardiente flowing freely, roast pigs, bullfights and rigorous communal dancing with the peasants dressed in outrageous masks and costumes. The main festival for Huaraz is usually in the first week of February, but September seems to be a lively month for the rural get-togethers which you'll often come across en route to the various sites and ruins in the Callejon de Huaylas.

Around Huaraz
There are a number of fascinating sites within a day's easy reach of Huaraz. Only 7km away is the dramatic **Wilkawain temple**, its inner labyrinths open for exploration. On the other side of the valley, just half-an-hour by bus, is **Punta Callan**, the ideal locale for magnificent views across the Cordillera Blanca. To the north are the alluring thermal baths of **Chancos** and to the south the weirdly intriguing **Puya Raymondi** cactus reserve.

WILKAWAIN can be reached from the centre of Huaraz by following Av. Centenario downhill from Fitzcarral, then turning right up a track (just about suitable for cars) a few hundred metres beyond the Hotel de Turistas. From here it's about an hour's stroll, winding slowly up past several small hamlets, to the sign-posted ruins. If there are four or five of you, a taxi there and back shouldn't work out more than about $3 each.

The temple, with a few small ancient houses round about, is set against the edge of a great bluff. With a flashlight you can wander around some of its inner chambers, checking them out along with ramps, ventilation shafts and the famous masonry (stone) nails. Most of the rooms, however, are still unentered – filled with the rubble and debris of at least a thousand years. The temple base is only about 11m by 16m, sloping up to large slanted roof slabs which create a gable-type protection, long since covered with earth and rocks to form an irregular domed top. In short, the construction is unmistakably a small replica of the Castillo at Chavin de Huantar – with four superimposed platforms, stairways, a projecting course of stones near the apex and a recessed one below it. There was once a row of cats' heads tenoned in beneath this, typical of classic Huari-Tiahuanucu culture masonry: a cultural influence evidently spread up here from the coast some time between AD 600 and 1000.

PUNTA CALLAN is reached by a short bus ride from Raymondi 336 – ask the driver to drop you off at CALLAN, shortly before the village of Pira along the road to Casma. There's no other spot which can quite match the scintillating views of the Cordillera Blanca from here, so save it for a really clear afternoon when the opportunities for capturing Huascaran's towering ice-cap on celluloid are at their best. From Punta Callan you can sense how the snowy range across the valley is dependent on the Cordillera Negra for protection against the drier coastal climate. Around Callan and Pira is grazing land as pleasant as you could find for a picnic and it's a relatively easy walk of a few hours back down the road to Huaraz. Passing trucks or buses will usually pick up anyone who waves them down along the way.

For **CHANCOS** take any of the frequent valley buses heading towards Yungay or Caraz from the market area or along Fitzcarral. Get off at MACARA and follow the track uphill, passing small peasant settlements beside the stream for about 4km, until you reach the **Baños de Chancos** situated in a beautiful *quebrada* below the village of Vicos. Above, the Nevado Copa glacier looms another 3,000m over these thermal waters. The baths at Chancos, known traditionally as 'the Fountain of Youth', claim to be excellent for respiratory problems, but with natural saunas and great pools gushing hot water you don't have to be ill to enjoy them. The valley bus service is good enough to get back to Huaraz within an hour or so, but if you want to camp, that's OK, and there are a couple of basic restaurants on hand.

From Chancos a small track leads off to the hamlet of ULLMEY, following the contours of the Legiamayo stream to the upper limit of cultivation and beyond into the barren puna zone directly below the glaciers. Keeping about 500m to the right of the stream, it takes 1½–2 hours to reach **Laguna Legia Cocha**, a lake hung between two vast glaciers, receiving their icy meltwater at 4,706m above sea-level. It's an exhilarating spot, with the added bonus of amazing views across the Santa Valley – to Carhuaz in the north, Huaraz in the south and Chancos directly below. If you leave Huaraz early one morning, this is the ideal place to stop for lunch, leaving time to get down to Chancos for a stimulating bath before going on to Macara to catch the bus back into town.

A lengthier excursion is to visit the pride and glory of the **Huascaran National Reserve** – the *Puya Raymondi* cactus. With an early start from Huaraz you could get there and back in a day; or you can camp on the site, either returning the next day or continuing to La Union (and Huanuco). The cheapest access from Huaraz is to hitch or catch the local bus (along the Lima road) as far as CATAC (45km), where you can get the *San Cristobal* bus down the La Union road; or carry on from Catac another 5km to PACHACOTO (where there are a couple of *cafes* often used as pit-stops by truck drivers) and hitch from here along the dirt track which turns off the main road across the barren grasslands of the low puna. This road is fairly well travelled by lorries on their way to the mining settlement of Huansalla, before it turns south to Huallanca and La Union.

About 30km down the track – roughly an hour's drive – you're surrounded by gigantic cacti, some of them reaching 12m into the rarefied air. This incredible plant, called *cuncush* or *cunco* by the locals (and *Pourretia gigantea* by botanists) only grows between altitudes of 3,700m and 4,200m and is unique to this region. May is the best month to see the Puya Raymondi, which is usually in full bloom by then – averaging an unbelievable 8,000 flowers and 6 million seeds per plant. There's not a lot more one can say about the cactus except perhaps that you have to see it to believe it. In many ways they look like upside-down trees, the bushy part for a base and a phallic flowering stem pointing to the sky. Dotted about the area like candles on an altar, each one has a life-span of around 40 years, and there's nothing else in sight bar grasses, rocks, lakes, snowy mountain crests, llamas and the occasional hummingbird. Isolated as they are, it's a good idea to take along something warm, something waterproof and something to eat. For a leisurely look at this marvellous countryside, very different to the Santa valley, you'll need to take a tent and stay a day or two. Returning, you should be able to hitch back to the main road at Huaraz – or alternatively go on to La Union – without undue problems. Rather than having to rely on buses and trucks, though, it might be worth going along to *Ancash Tours* (Jr. Francisco de Zela 210, Huaraz) where $10 could save a lot of hassle. Outside of late April, May and early June, the cacti can prove disappointing, often becoming burnt-out stumps after dropping their flowers and seeds, but the surrounding scenery remains sensational.

YUNGAY, CARAZ AND THE CORDILLERA BLANCA

Yungay and **Caraz**, although not very far down the Santa valley from Huaraz, are quite distinct little settlements – visible contrasts to the larger market town and each a popular base from which to begin treks into the Cordillera Blanca. Physically they have little in common – Yungay the sad site of several catastrophic natural disasters, Caraz surviving the centuries as one of Peru's prettiest little towns – but to understand either properly they have to be considered in relation to the overwhelming mountain range which divides them from the Amazon Basin.

The **CORDILLERA BLANCA** – the highest range of hills in the tropical world – consists of some 35 peaks poking their snowy heads over the 6,000m mark. Until 1918 it was possible to see this white crest from the Pacific, but since then the glaciers have receded, leaving *cochas* which feed the Rio Santa with meltwater all year round. Of the many mountain lakes, Lago Paron, poised dangerously above Caraz, is renowned as the most beautiful. Recent fears have begun to spread about Paron's dam of ice and moraine collapsing, leaving the waters free to gush down the hills and engulf Caraz, but the chances of this happening while any particular traveller spends a few days here are patently very remote. Above Yungay, and against the sensational backdrop of Peru's highest peak (Huascaran, 6,768m), are what many people consider to be the equally magnificent Llanganuco lakes. More often than not an emerald green, their waters change colour according to the time of year and the sun's daily movements.

Fortunately, most of the Cordillera Blanca falls under the auspices of the **Huascaran National Park;** as such the habitat has been left relatively unspoilt. Among the more exotic **wild-life** which hikers can hope to come across are such creatures as the viscacha, vicuña, grey deer, pumas, foxes, the rarer spectacled bear (Paddington's relative!) and several species of hummingbirds. All of these animals are shy, so you'll need a good pair of binoculars and a fountain of patience to get at all close to any of them.

The number of **possible hikes** into the Cordillera is virtually infinite, depending more than anything else on your own initiative and resourcefulness. Maps of the area, published by the *Instituto Geografico Militar*, are good enough to allow you to plot your own routes confidently if you wish, or you can follow one of the more standard paths outlined by the expert trekkers – Hilary and George Bradt or Jim Bartle (see pp. 286–7). I don't intend to do any more than outline a couple of possible treks, including what is probably the most popular one – the *Llanganuco to Santa Cruz Loop* – which begins at Yungay and terminates at Caraz.

Yungay and the Llanganuco to Santa Cruz loop

YUNGAY was a mere 58km down the Santa valley from Huaraz until 1970, when it was obliterated in seconds during Peru's last major earthquake. Long before the final destruction the 'Pearl of the Huaylas Corridor' had shown itself to be most unwisely situated: in 1872 it was almost completely wiped out by avalanche, and on a fiesta day in 1962 another avalanche buried the tiny neighbouring village of Ranrahirca. The merciless 1970 quake also arrived in the midst of a festival, and although casualties proved impossible to calculate with any real accuracy, it's thought that at least 70,000 died – locals, their friends, relatives and visitors.

The new town, an ugly conglomeration of modern buildings including some 90 cabins sent as relief aid from Russia and a concrete Plaza de Armas, lies a little further north, still cowering beneath the threat of Huascaran but hopefully sheltered from further dangers. Just before you reach it there's a car park and memorial monument to the dead, while in a rather morbid way the buried **old town** has developed into one of the region's major tourist attractions. Its site is covered with a grey flow of mud and moraine, now dry and solid, with a few stunted palm trees to mark where the Plaza de Armas once stood. Local guidebooks show before and after photos of the scene, but it doesn't take a lot of imagination to reconstruct the horror. I, for one, quickly made my way to the rebuilt town which is surprisingly (and somewhat optimistically) alive.

Modern Yungay has a helpful tourist information office (open Mon.–Sat. 9–5) on the Plaza de Armas, where you can get free **maps and information** on the area. Nearby, and also on the plaza, is a reasonable cafe – *El Palmero* – which usually has a few rooms available. The only reason to stay here, though, is to make the trip up to Lagos Llanganuco and Huascaran; trucks leave most mornings from outside El Palmero.

The lakes, only 26km away, take a good hour-and-a-half to reach, the road crawling up beside the canyon created by thousands of years of Huascaran's meltwater and a long history of avalanches. On the way you get a dramatic view across the valley and can clearly make out the path of the 1970 devastation. The last part of the drive slices through rocky crevices and snakes around breathtaking precipices, not much fun for anyone suffering from even the faintest trace of vertigo. Eventually reaching **Chinan Cocha**, the first of the two Llanganuco lakes, the track continues around its left bank and onto the second – **Orcon Cocha** – where the road ends and a footpath begins.

Immediately to the south of the lakes is the unmistakable sight of the massive **Huascaran ice-cap**, teasingly tempting yet a very difficult 3,000m climb to the top. This imposing peak is much higher than Mount McKinley in North America and an explicit display of the fact that the Andean crests are second only to Himalayan peaks. Surrounding Huascaran are scores of lesser glaciated mountains stretching almost 200km and dividing the Amazon Basin from the Pacific watershed. Although there are some 300 glacial lakes in the Cordillera Blanca, those of Llanganuco are the most accessible, the deadliest and in my opinion the most majestic of them all.

To have a crack at the **LLANGANUCO TO SANTA CRUZ LOOP** you simply follow the clear trail which leads off from the end of the road along the left bank of Orcon Cocha. The entire trek shouldn't take more than about five days for a healthy (and acclimatised) back-packer. It is, however, essential to carry all your food, camping equipment and ideally a medical kit and emergency survival bag. Throughout the trail there are hundreds of potential camping sites, each one as enchanting as the next. It's a perfect hike to take at your own pace: some will probably manage it in three days at a push, others will prefer to take a whole week, savouring every moment. The best time to attempt this trek is between April and October, in the dry season, unless you enjoy getting stuck in mud and spending several days soaked to the skin.

From Orcon Cocha the main path climbs the **Portachuelo de Llan-**

ganuco pass (4,767m) before dropping to the enchanting beauty of the **Quebrada Morococha**, through the tiny settlement of VAQUERIA. From here you can go on to Colcabamba and Pomabamba (in the Callejon de Conchucos – not advisable in the rainy season when you may well find yourself stranded) rather than continuing back to the Callejon de Huaylas via Santa Cruz. The Loop Trail heads north from Vaqueria up the **Quebrada Huaripampa** and around the ice-cap of **Chacraraju** (6,000m), a stupendous rocky canyon with a marshy bottom, snowy mountain peaks to the west and Cerro Mellairca to the east. Following the stream uphill, keeping the lakes of Morococha and Huiscash to your left, you pass down (via Punta Union, 4,750m) into the Pacific watershed along the **Quebrada Santa Cruz**. Emerging eventually beside the calm waters of **Laguna Grande**, you go around the left bank and continue down this perfect glacial valley about another 8 hours' walk to the settlements and cultivated lands of **Cuncash** and **Santa Cruz**. From here it's but a short step (about 2km) to the by now extremely inviting thermal baths of **Shangol**, while from Santa Cruz or Shangol there's a road to Caraz or a more direct 3-hour trail across the low hills to the south.

Around Caraz

The town of **Caraz**, a little less than 75km down the Santa valley from Huaraz, sits quietly below the enormous Huandoy glacier. Palm trees and flowers adorn a classic colonial Plaza de Armas and the small market is normally vibrant with gentle activity. Close to the main square stands the attractive old *Hotel La Suiza Peruana*, cheap and basic but with an excellent restaurant, while on the other side of the plaza the cafe *El Paris* serves good sandwiches and other snacks. Most of the bus companies have offices on the main square too, but for the *Banco de la Nacion* you have to head ten blocks north, then two blocks right and it's opposite the track to the lake.

Unless you've travelled miles for the delicious honey produced in this little town, you're probably here to visit **Lago Paron**, the deep-blue lake sunk resplendently into a gigantic glacial cwm and hemmed in on three sides by some of the Cordillera Blanca's highest ice-caps. The lake is only accessible by climbing straight up the Rio Paron gorge from town. Taxis and colectivos (working out about $6 per person when full) leave daily or you can walk it: the best part of a day's hike. You'll need to take food and a tent since the purpose-built *tourist lodge*, a cabin with views across the lake, is often closed.

Just across the Rio Santa from Caraz, set on the lower slopes of the Cordillera Negra, is the small settlement of HUATA, a typical rural village with regular truck connections to Caraz and the rest of the Callejon de Huaylas. From here there are a number of easy-going walks, such as the 8km stroll up to the unassuming lakes of **Yanacocha** and **Huaytacocha** or, perhaps more interesting, north about 5km along a path up Cerro Muchanacoc to the small Inca **ruins of Cantu.**

Another short trip from Caraz is to the village of SANTA CRUZ (buses around midday from Huaraz market) where you can sample the **hot springs** at nearby Shangol and try out your legs on pleasant country paths. If you fancy camping in glorious glacial scenery without doing a major hike, it's only an easy day's stroll up the Quebrada Santa Cruz to **Laguna Grande**, a perfect spot to pitch a tent and soak in the clear mountain air. Back down in Santa Cruz there is basic accommodation available for those who want it, although unless you've got a tent, Caraz is a much more comfortable place to stay.

North of Caraz the first major settlement is **HUALLANCA**, where the road to CHIMBOTE (another 140km) begins. The main attraction of the entire Caraz-Chimbote route is this first 40km stretch, squeezing through the spectacular **Cañon del Pato** (*Duck's Canyon*). An enormous rocky gorge, cut out of solid rock by the Rio Santa's struggle to get to the Pacific, it curves around the Cordillera Negra for most of the way between Caraz and Huallanca. Sheer cliff faces rise thousands of metres on either side while the road passes through some 39 tunnels – an average of nearly one every kilometre. Situated within the canyon is one of Peru's most important hydro-electric power plants; the heart of these works, invisible from the road, is buried 600m deep in the cliff wall. The road is undoubtedly one of Peru's most exciting journeys, and although severely damaged by the 1970 earthquake, the tunnels and road surface are in fairly good condition. Even if you don't intend going all the way to Chimbote it makes a good day-trip from Caraz and can also be taken en route to CORONGO and the Callejon de Conchucos.

CHAVIN DE HUANTAR (Temple Ruins open 8–4 daily)

Only 5–6 hours by bus south-east of Huaraz are the village and ruins of **CHAVIN DE HUANTAR**, the most important site associated with the Chavin Cult, a culture active for close on a millennium between 1,200 and 300 BC. Although partially destroyed by earthquakes, floods and erosion from the Mosna river, enough of the ruins survive to make them a fascinating must for anyone even vaguely interested in Peruvian archaeology. The religious cult which inspired Chavin's construction also influenced subsequent cultures and cultural development throughout Peru right up until the Spanish Conquest some 2,500 years later, and the temple complex of Chavin de Huantar is equal in importance, if not grandeur, to most of the sites around Cuzco.

From Huaraz, the road to Chavin leaves the main highway at CATAC before heading through the Cordillera Blanca via the impressive Cahuish tunnel, 4,178m above sea-level. **Buses** leave Huaraz every morning around 10am (*Empresa Condor de Chavin*, Tarapaca 312; tel. 2039; or *Empresa Huascaran*, Tarapaca 133; tel. 2208), or **colectivos** (Comite 11, Fitzcarral 212; tel. 2091) and *Ancash Tours* do a faster, though more expensive, run.

A more adventurous way to reach Chavin is by following the two- or three-day **trail over the hills** from OLLEROS. Trucks leave Huaraz market every day for this small village (2 hours) and the hike from there is fairly simple, clearly marked all the way. It follows the Rio Nearo up to Punta Yanashallash (at 4,680m), cuts down into the Marañon watershed, and from there traces the stream to the ruins another 1,500m below. Hilary and George Bradt give a good account of this walk in *Backpacking and Trekking in Peru and Bolivia* and the South American Explorers' Club in Lima will be happy to give advice and information on it.

CHAVIN DE HUANTAR itself is a pretty little village only a couple of hundred metres from the ancient remains. Hidden behind its whitewashed walls and traditional tiled roofs is a deceptively good supply of amenities for the traveller: the *Hotel Monte Carlo* is clean and quite cheap, there's a neat and pleasant little albergue just an hour or so's walk along the road to Huari, and you can camp by the thermal springs some 20 minutes' stroll from the village. For food the best bet is to try the *Cooperativa* behind the main church, but there are several other places to choose from if this is full or closed.

The **main temple** at Chavin shows several stages of rebuilding between about 1000 and 200 BC, although the complex has always maintained its roughly east-west orientation. Julio Tello first looked at the site in 1919 when the temple was still buried under cultivated fields; during 1945 a vast flood reburied most of it and the place was damaged again by the 1970 earthquake and the rains of 1983. Undaunted, it remains a palatial ruin.

The main construction consists of a central rectangular block with two wings projecting out to the east. The larger, southern wing, known as the **Castillo**, is the most conspicuous feature of the site: enlarged three times it now stands some 10m high. Massive, almost pyramid-shaped, the platform is built of dressed stone with gargoyles (nearly all now removed) tenoned in. Throughout the buildings are inner chambers on various levels connected by ramps and steps: in the seven major subterranean rooms you'll need a flashlight to get a decent look at the carvings (even when the electric lighting is switched on) while all around you can hear the sound of water dripping, a chilling sensation which modern travellers can share with the ancient pilgrims. Still in its original underground site, too, is the awesome *Lanzon*, a prism-shaped block of carved white granite which tapers nearly 4m down from a broad feline head to a point stuck in the ground.

Some way in front of the Castillo, down three main flights of steps, is the **Plaza Hundida**, or sunken plaza, covering about 250 square metres with a rectangular, stepped platform away to either side. Here, almost certainly, the thousands of pilgrims thought to have worshipped together at Chavin would gather during the appropriate calendrical *fiestas*. And it was here that the famous Tello Obelisk (now in the Archaeology Museum in Lima) was found, next to an altar shaped to represent a jaguar and bedecked with seven cavities forming a pattern very close to that of the Orion constellation.

THE FANGED DEITY
(CHAVIN RAYMONDI STONE)

Another large stone slab discovered at Chavin in 1873 – the *Estela Raymondi* (also now in the Lima Museum – was the first of all the impressive carved stones to be found. This too seems to represent a monstrous feline deity, the same one which recurs with awesome frequency both in human form with snake appendages and as a bird figure, sometimes both at the same time. The most vivid of the carvings remaining at the site are the gargoyles (known as *Cabeza Clavos*), guardians of the temple which again display feline and birdlike characteristics. From this **stone iconography**, all of it very intricately executed, distinctive in style and highly abstract, it appears that the Chavin people, whoever they were, worshipped three major gods: the Moon (represented by a fish), the Sun (depicted as an eagle or a hawk), and an overlord, or creator divinity, normally shown as a fanged cat, possibly a jaguar. It seems very likely that each god was linked with a distinct level of the Chavin cosmos: the fish with the underworld, the eagle with the celestial forces, and the feline with earthly power. This is only a calculated guess but ethnographic evidence from the contemporary Amazon Basin suggests that each of these main gods may have also been associated with a different moiety (or sub-group) within the Chavin tribe, or priesthood, as a whole.

The **Chavin Cult** had a strong impact on the Paracas culture, and later on the Nazca and Mochica civilisations. Theories as to the origin of its religious inspiration range from extra-terrestrial intervention to the more likely infiltration of ideas and maybe individuals or entire tribes from Central America. There is an extraordinary affinity between the ceramics found at Chavin and those of a similar date from Tlatilco in Mexico, yet there are no comparable Mexican stone constructions as ancient as these Peruvian wonders. More probable, and the theory expounded by Julio Tello, is that the cult initially came up into the Andes (then down to the coast) from the Amazon Basin via the Marañon valley. The inspiration for the beliefs themselves may well have come from visionary experiences sparked off by the ingestion of hallucinogens: one of the stone reliefs at Chavin portrays a feline deity or fanged warrior holding a section of the psychotropic mescalin cactus – *San Pedro* – still used by curanderos today for the invocation of the spirit world. This would make sense in terms of an Amazonian link since many of the tribes living in the forest also traditionally use hallucinogens (*Ayahuasca* and *Datura*) to contact the spirits – their ancestors.

Chavin itself may not have been the centre of the movement, but it was obviously an outstanding ceremonial focus: the name Chavin comes from the Quechua *Chaupin*, meaning navel or focal point. As such it might have been a sacred shrine where natives flocked in pilgrimage during festivals, much as they do today, visiting important *huacas* in the sierra at specific times in the annual agricultural cycle. The appearance of the Orion constellation on Chavin carvings fits with this since it never fails to appear on the night-time skyline just prior to the traditional harvest time in the Peruvian mountains. During these pilgrimages the people would also have brought food and artifacts for sale or barter, and this may have been the moment, too, for marriage rituals and even inter-group truces. In order to have organised the building of the centre there must have been a high-priesthood wielding an enormous secular power and presumably controlling the labour of thousands of pilgrims – the local population was far too small to have done it alone.

THE CALLEJON DE CONCHUCOS

To the east of the Cordillera Blanca, roughly parallel to the Santa valley, runs another long natural corridor, the **callejon de conchucos**. Virtually inaccessible in the wet season and off the beaten track even for the most hardened of back-packers, it's nevertheless a challenging target, with the town of Pomabamba in the north and Chavin de Huantar just beyond its southern limit. This is also one of the few regions of Peru where the bus drivers sometimes allow passengers to lounge around on the roof as they career along ludicrous mountain roads, bowing their heads and crossing themselves before plummeting into each steep drop of the dusty track: an electrifying experience with the added bonus of 360° vision.

Until the Conquest, this zone was also the centre of one of the most notoriously fierce of the ancient tribes — the Conchucos — who surged down the Santa valley and besieged the Spanish city of Trujillo as late as 1536. By the end of the sixteenth century, however, even the fearless Conchuco warriors had been reduced by the colonial *encomendero* system to virtual slavery: besides a vast array of agricultural and craft produce, the area's annual levy demanded the provision of 80 people to serve as labourers, herders and servants in the distant town of Huanuco. In his excellent book *The Conquest of the Incas*, John Hemmings gives a succinct account of exactly what the natives could expect in return for their tribute: the encomendero was charged 'to instruct the said natives in the tenets of our Holy Catholic Church'. Wary of strangers and reluctant to be pushed around, the people of the Callejon de Conchucos nevertheless remain manifestly proud of their heritage.

Most days a bus leaves the main plaza in CARAZ at around 5.30am for CORONGO via the Cañon del Pato; from here there are fairly regular trucks (at least between April and October) on to POMABAMBA. Alternatively, Pomabamba can be reached from HUARAZ via CHAVIN, where a bus coming all the way from Lima goes north up the Callejon de Conchucos more or less every other day.

POMABAMBA itself is a small town, 3,000m up in dauntingly hilly countryside, surrounded by little-known archaeological remains which show common roots with Chavin de Huantar. Its very name — originally *Puma Bamba* — means the Valley or Plain of the Pumas, and may reveal direct links with the ancient Chavin cult of the feline deity. Today the town is a valuable trekking base, though one that's seldom used by travellers. From here you can connect with the **Llanganuco to Santa Cruz Loop** (see p. 171) by following trails south-west to either COLCABAMBA or PUNTA UNION. Or, a hard day's hike above Pomabamba, are the unstudied stone remains of **YAINO**; an immense fortress of megalithic rock, its buildings locked into labyrinthine formations. On a clear day you can just about make out this site from the Plaza de Armas, appearing as a tiny rocky outcrop high on the distant horizon. The climb takes longer than you might imagine, but locals will point out short-cuts along the way.

There are a couple of small **hostals** in Pomabamba, one of them just off the main square, the other on the edge of town; and there are good thermal baths as well. As with the rest of Ancash and Huanuco, though, you'll undoubtedly have a better time, and enjoy greater flexibility, if you take a tent and ask the locals for good camping spots.

Between Pomabamba and the exceptional attractions of Chavin de Huantar, there's little specific to detain you. The village of **PISCOBAMBA** (Valley or Plain of the Birds) doesn't have a great deal to offer and nor does **HUARI**, though you might want to stop and eat here because it's a long haul (141km) over barren mountains between the two. From Huari, Chavin is only another 30km.

HUANUCO

From Lima, **Huanuco** is usually reached via the Central Highway, or train, to La Oroya, then north through the Cerro de Pasco. However, for anyone already in and around Huaraz, or those willing to risk possible delays in return for magnificent scenery, there is a direct route over the Cordillera Blanca which takes you to **La Union** and the magnificently preserved Inca ruins of **Huanuco Viejo** before continuing to the modern city. Round about are several more fascinating excursions, while heading inland beyond Huanuco you can begin to penetrate the jungle regions of the Amazon basin.

HUARAZ TO LA UNION: HUANUCO VIEJO

The dusty minor road from HUARAZ to LA UNION sets off along the same path as that to the Puya Raymondi cacti (for details see p. 168). From here it's a matter of hitching a ride in a truck on to the mining settlement of HUANSALLA (another hour or two) then walking, or busing it, 10km further to HUALLANCA where there are frequent trucks all the way to La Union. More complicated than it sounds, this whole journey can be completed in about 6 hours and is only some 120km in all. In LA UNION there are a couple of hotels (try the *Dos de Mayo*) and several reasonable restaurants (*El Danubo*, near the market, is central and quite good) but it's not the nicest of towns. You should keep a watchful eye on your gear and make the 2- or 3-hour hike to the ruined city of **Huanuco Viejo** as soon as possible. There's a nightly bus on to HUANUCO (the modern town), or you can ride on top of a truck (11 hours) which leaves La Union market most mornings.

Situated well above La Union, the superb Inca stonework of **HUANUCO VIEJO**, virtually untouched by the Spanish Conquistadores and without any later occupation, lies on the edge of a desolate pampa. The grey stone houses and platform temples are set out in a roughly circular pattern radiating from a gigantic *unsu* (Inca throne) in the middle of the plaza. To the north are the military barracks and beyond that the remains of suburban dwellings. Directly east of the plaza is the palace and temple known as *Incahuasi*, and next to this the *Acllahuasi*, a separate enclosure devoted to the Chosen Women or Virgins of the Sun. Behind this and running straight through the Incahuasi is a man-made water channel diverted from the small Rio Huachac. On the opposite side of the plaza you can make out the extensive administrative quarters.

Without a doubt one of the most complete existing examples of an Inca provincial capital and administrative centre, there's a powerful impression of a once-thriving city – you can almost sense the activity after 400 years as a ghost town. Poised on the southern hillside above the main complex are over 500 store-houses which, in daily use, must have catered for a rapid turn-over in all sorts of produce and treasure – tribute for the Emperor and sacrifices to the sun. Well away from the damp of the valley floor, and each separated by a few metres to minimise the risk of fire, they also command impressive views across the plain.

Arriving here in 1539, the Spanish very soon abandoned the site to build their own colonial administrative centre – Leon de Huanuco – at a much lower altitude, more suitable for their unacclimatised lungs and with slightly easier access to Cuzco and Lima. **Spanish Huanuco**, built along the standard city plans specified by Royal Decree, grew into a thoroughly rich *encomienda:* nevertheless, the colonists always regarded it as one of those remote outposts (like Chile) where Spanish or mestizo criminals, or anyone unpopular with officialdom, would be sent into lengthy exile.

The region remained a centre of native dissent too – in the early years Illa Tupac, a relative of the rebel Inca, Manco, and one of the unsung heroes of the Indian resistance, maintained clandestine Inca rule around Huanuco Veijo until at least 1545. And as late as 1777 the royal officials were thrown out of the area in a major – albeit shortlived – insurrection.

HUANUCO

The charming modern city of **HUANUCO**, more than 100km east of the deserted Inca town, is relatively peaceful nowadays – depending for its livelihood on timber, tea and coca, along with a little low-key tourism.

Its old narrow streets ramble across a handful of small plazas, a pleasant environment where travellers often spend a couple of days roaming the bars and cafes, an endless source of trail tales.

There are no outstanding attractions in the town, but a couple of old churches, convents with airy cloisters, a small **natural history museum** and a **Cathedral** whose altar-pieces have the saints counterposed by Inca deities of the Sun and Moon, do offer some focus for activity. The church of **San Cristobal** is actually built on the foundations of the site where the *Curaca de los Chupacos* once lived and where the Portuguese Pablo Coimbra celebrated the first Mass. **San Francisco**, meanwhile, shows a strong indigenous influence, its altars richly carved with native fruits – avocados, papayas and pomegranates. The church also boasts a small collection of sixteenth-century paintings.

Of the **hotels**, the *Hostal Confort* (Jr. Huanuco 608; tel. 2404) isn't bad, or you could try the more basic *Bella Durmiente* (opposite the market on Jr. Arequipa) and *Hotel Astoria* just two blocks from the plaza (General Prado 988; tel. 2310). If you prefer to **camp**, this is permitted down by the Rio Huallaga near the stadium, but you'll have to cope with the midges which sometimes overrun the site. *El Cafe* is a good **restaurant** on the main square or *Bar Venecia* (on Dos de Mayo) offers a more entertaining atmosphere in the evenings. *Huanuco Tours*, near the Hostal Confort, offer **tourist information** and **dollar exchange**: the **post office** and **telephones** are alongside each other, two blocks up Jr. Castillo from the plaza. **Huanuco carnival week** begins around August 15th when the town's normal tranquillity explodes into a wild fiesta binge. Peruvian Independence Day (July 28th) is also a good time to be here, with performances of traditional dances like the Chunco, and at Christmas the children put on their own public displays. If you've come directly up from Lima via La Oroya and want to visit Huanuco Viejo, **buses** leave for La Union every morning at 8 from the lively market area – 9 or 10 hours' drive if there are no hold-ups.

The Temple of Kotosh and Tomay Qichua

Only 8km along the road to La Union, the fascinating, though poorly maintained, **Temple of Kotosh** lies in ruins on the banks of the Rio Tingo. At over 4,000 years old, this site pre-dates the Chavin era by more than a thousand years. Between 1960 and 1962 a team of Japanese archaeologists excavated the large mound which had been created by the fallen debris of the original temple: its occupation proved to span six phases, the first two of which fall into the Early Agricultural Period when the ceramic arts were beginning to develop rapidly. Potsherds found here bear clear similarities to works from the lower jungle areas. The first evidence of massive stone constructions (from about 2000 BC) suggests that complicated building work began here many centuries before it

started anywhere else on the American continent, and more or less permanent settlement continued through the Chavin era (though without the
monumental masonry and sculpture of that period) and with Inca occupation right up to the Conquest. One unique feature of the Kotosh
complex is the Crossed-Hands symbol carved prominently in stone –
the gracefully executed insignia of a very early culture about which
archaeologists know next to nothing.

An equally easy trip from Huanuco – less than 30km south, just off
the road to La Oroya – is the village of **TOMAY QICHUA**, birthplace
of Santa Rosa's grandmother and of the infamous *La Perricholi*, mestizo
actress and seductress. Legend has it that in a valley not far from Tomay
Qichua the Indians cultivate a secret medicine which magically cures all
ills – its Quechua name means 'this plant is more powerful than God'!

Tantamayo

About 150km north of Huanuco, poised in the mountainous region above
the higher reaches of the Marañon river, the small village and extensive
ruins of **TANTAMAYO** make a rather longer excursion. Nevertheless,
a regular bus service from Huanuco makes it easy enough to do – some
14 hours' travel over poor roads. In the village local guides are available
for the 2- or 3-hour hike to the scattered site, and excellent accommodation is offered at the Swiss-style **tourist lodge** for anyone without a
tent.

The precise age of this remote pre-Columbian complex is unknown.
Its buildings appear to fit into the later Tiahuanuco-Huari phase, which
would make them some 1,200 years old, but physically they form no
part of this widespread cultural movement and the site is considered to
have developed separately, probably originating among tribes migrating
to the Andes from the Selva and adapting to a new environment over a
long period.

At Tantamayo the architectural development of some four centuries
can be clearly seen – growing from the simplest of structures to really
complex edifices. Tall buildings dot the entire area – some clearly watch-
towers overlooking the Marañon, others with less obvious functions,
built for religious reasons as temple-palaces, perhaps, or as store-houses
and fortresses. One of the major constructions, just across the Tantamayo
stream on a hill facing the village, was named *Pirira* by the Incas who
conquered the area in the fifteenth century. At its heart there are concentric circles of carved stone, while the walls and houses around are all
grouped in a circular formation – clearly this was once an important
centre for religious ritual. The main building rises some 10m on three
levels, its bluff façade broken only by large window niches, changes in
the course of the stone slabs, and by centuries of weathering.

A detailed archaeological survey of the ruins may well reveal links with

Chavin and Kotosh. In the meantime, more than 30 separate, massive constructions make up an impressive scene, offset by the cloud-forest and jungle which begin to flourish along the banks of the Marañon just a little further to the north.

TINGO MARIA AND THE ROAD TO PUCALLPA

The ramshackle town of **TINGO MARIA** lies at the foot of the mountain where, according to legend, the lovesick Princess Nunash awaits the waking kiss of Kunyaq, the sorcerer. It's a strikingly well-favoured setting – 670m above sea-level on the forested eastern slopes of the Andes, amid the fecund tropical climate of the ceja de selva – and Tingo Maria was once known as the Garden City. Today, though, the ravishes of Western civilisation have made their mark. Dominated by sawmills and plywood factories financed by external subsidy, and with a booming trade in stolen goods and cocaine, Tingo Maria displays all the symbols of relative affluence; but the tin roofs below the forest of TV aerials spattered across the township only serve to belie the poverty of the majority.

The spiralling descent **from Huanuco** is a stunner, with views across the jungle as thrilling as those from a small plane and a highlight in the **Pass of Padre Abad** with its glorious waterfalls. By the time the bus reaches Tingo Maria (4–5 hours) the Huallaga has become a broad tropical river, navigable downstream in small canoes or by balsa raft. And the tropical atmosphere, in the shadow of the forested ridges and limestone crags of the *Bella Durmiente* (Sleeping Beauty) mountain, is delightful. Nevertheless, as anything more than an overnight stop to break the journey from Lima (or Huanuco) to PUCALLPA, the town has nothing much to recommend it.

For sightseeing there's little beyond the rather sorry zoo and botanical gardens attached to the University or – about 14km out of town – the **Cueva de las Lechuzas** (Owls' Cave); vast, picturesque and dark (you'll need a flashlight). **Bed and breakfast** are available at Av. Benavides 263, or the *Hotel Viena* (Tulumayo 245; tel. 2194) which is reasonably priced, as are *La Cabaña* (Av. Raymondi 342; tel. 2146) and the *Hotel Royal* (Av. Benavides 206; tel. 2166). For Western eating it's hard to beat the *Cafe Rex* (Raymondi 500), while *La Cabaña* also serves up tasty food. The last week in July is Tingo Maria's major **fiesta** period, but on no account leave your gear unattended at this time.

PUCALLPA, second largest town in the Peruvian Amazon region, is a further 8 to 10 hours on the bus – 260km directly north-east through virgin forest (much of which is in the process of being cleared). Since 1980, and months of local protests and strikes against paying taxes to Iquitos, it has been capital of the newly created Departmento of Ucayali. Quite apart from any intrinsic interest (see full details on p. 252), this is the ideal point from which to find embarkation up the Ucayali to IQUITOS and from there on to Brazil, or to set off on expeditions deeper into the seemingly limitless wilderness of tropical forest.

It's often difficult to get seats on the **buses** from Tingo Maria to Pucallpa since nearly all of them arrive full on their way from Lima via Huanuco. However, if you book in advance at one of the offices in town and you're pushy enough as you struggle into the bus, you should be able to secure a seat or two. If you do get stuck you can always fly there (see travel details below) or go back to Huanuco (or Lima!) and start again.

TRAVEL DETAILS

Buses and/or colectivos
From Barranca Lima (several daily; 3hrs); Casma/Chimbote (several daily; 2hrs/3hrs); Huaraz (several daily; 4hrs).
From Chimbote Trujillo (several daily; 3hrs); Lima (several daily; 6hrs); Huaraz (1 or 2 daily; 7hrs).
From Huaraz Lima (several daily; 7hrs); Casma (daily; 7hrs); La Union for Huanuco (see text above).

From Huanuco Lima (daily; 12hrs); Tingo Maria/Pucallpa (several daily; 4hrs/12hrs); Tantamayo (more or less daily; 14hrs).

Flights
From Chimbote Daily to Lima.
From Huanuco Daily to Lima
From Tingo Maria Daily to Lima.

Chapter five
TRUJILLO AND THE NORTHERN CIRCUIT

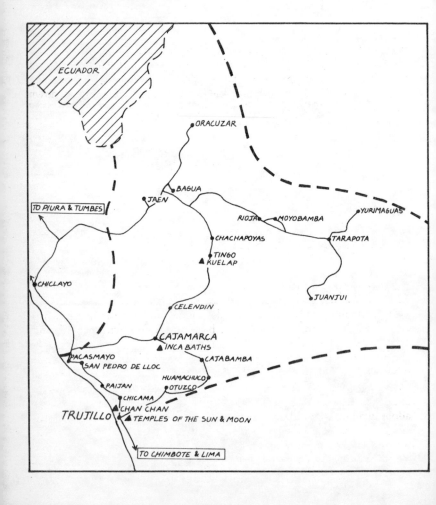

ECUADOR

ORACUZAR

BAGUA

JAEN

TO PIURA & TUMBES

RIOJA

MOYOBAMBA

YURIMAGUAS

CHACHAPOYAS

TARAPOTA

TINGO

▲ KUELAP

CHICLAYO

JUANJUI

CELENDIN

CAJAMARCA

▲ INCA BATHS

PACASMAYO

CAJABAMBA

SAN PEDRO DE LLOC

PAIJAN

HUAMACHUCO

OTUZCO

CHICAMA

TRUJILLO

▲CHAN CHAN

▲ TEMPLES OF THE SUN & MOON

TO CHIMBOTE & LIMA

Though far less known than the Cuzco region, Trujillo, and the northern circuits to Cajamarca and beyond, stand good comparison. **Trujillo** itself, one of the friendliest and most interesting towns in the country, is something of a northern capital. Few people seem to have heard of it before they arrive, but almost everyone seems to spend more time here than planned. The attractions are partly in nearby ruins – including the immense city and temple-citadel of **Chan Chan** – partly in the city life and beaches, some of the best around. **Huanchaco**, 12km from Trujillo and an alternative base, is a good case in point, still essentially a fishing village, and an enormously likeable travellers' resort.

'**The Northern Circuit**' is actually a variety of possible routes, all of them taking in **Cajamarca** as the main focus. It was here that Pizarro first met up with the Emperor Atahualpa in 1532, and around the modern city are a number of fascinating pre-Inca sites (many linked with water and ritualised baths), and a couple of fine, reasonably easy hikes. Cajamarca is also the springboard for the smaller town of **Chachapoyas** and the ruined city complex of **Kuelap** – perhaps the most overwhelming prehistoric site in Peru. Beyond, there are two possible routes down Amazon headwaters to the jungle town of **Iquitos** – both long and arduous, but well worth while if you have the time and enthusiasm. Alternatively, you can just loop back down to the coast, either via **Jaen** and **Olmos**, or back to Trujillo along the **Huamachuco** route and its remote and newly discovered ruins of **Gran Pajaten**.

TRUJILLO AND AROUND

TRUJILLO

Though small by European standards, **TRUJILLO** has the real feel of a city – very lively and cosmopolitan, but friendly too, with people often asking you back to their homes for a meal, and constantly into bars. The climate here is probably the most pleasant on the whole Peruvian coast, warm and dry without the fogs you get around Lima, and not as hot as in the northern deserts. Most people come to visit the ruins scattered about the Moche valley. With their pyramids and endless stretches of adobe walling, these deserted cities held populations a thousand years ago as great as any in the region today. Allow yourself a full week if you want to explore them in any depth.

Pizarro, on his second voyage to Peru in 1528, sailed by the site of ancient *Chan Chan*, then still a major city throbbing with life as an important regional centre of Inca rule. Little could he have imagined that within eight years he would be founding a new Spanish town in the same valley and naming it after his birthplace in Estremadura. In 1536, a year after *Trujillo* was settled, the town was besieged by the Inca Manco's forces during his second rebellion against the Conquistadores. Many thousands of Indian tribes – like the fearless Conchucos – swarmed down to Trujillo, killing Spaniards and collaborators on the way and sacrificing their victims to Catequil, the tribal deity. But, surviving this attack, Trujillo grew to become the capital of the north; the Spanish treasure fleets wining and dining themselves here on their way from Lima to Panama.

Ever since declaring Independence from Spain in 1820, long before the Liberators ever arrived, Trujillo has been a centre for popular rebellion. The enigmatic *APRA* (American Popular Revolutionary Alliance) leader, Haya de la Torre, was born here in 1895, standing, after years of struggle, in the elections of 1931. The dictator, Sanchez Cerro, however, counted the votes and declared himself the winner. *APRA* was outlawed and Haya de la Torre imprisoned, provoking the Trujillo middle classes to stage an uprising. Over 1,000 deaths resulted, many of them *Apristas* taken out to the fields of Chan Chan by the truck-load to be shot.

It was the Revolutionary Military government though, in 1969, which eventually unshackled this region from the strangle-hold of a few large sugar-barons – families who owned the enormous *haciendas* in the Chicama valley. Their land was given over to worker co-operatives – the *Casa Grande* a showcase example, and now one of the most profitable and well-organised agricultural ventures in Peru. Even so, the 1932 massacre still leaves a permanent rift between the people of Trujillo, particularly the old *APRA* members, and the army; walking around the town you often see urban areas declaring their allegiance in graffiti – *Las Delicias es APRISTA!*

The town

Radiating from its colonial heart, Trujillo's old grid system gives way to commercial buildings, light industry and shanty-type suburbs, before thinning out into rich sugar-cane fields stretching far into the neighbouring Chicama valley. It seems hard to credit a city of 3–4 million inhabitants – walk a couple of kilometres in any direction and you're out in the *campo*, open fields hedged by flowering shrubs. At its centre – a dominating force – is the University, founded by Bolivar in 1824. Around it spread rather elegant, Spanish-style streets, lined with ancient green ficus trees and overhung by long wooden-railed balconies. Most of the older *calles* are named after famous men, liberators and heroes in the Trujillo fashion. **Gammarra** is the main commercial drag, with ugly, modern, brick and glass buildings, shops, hotels, a pin-ball arcade and restaurants (one claims to be open 24 hours a day). And life still revolves within the limits of the old town – falling roughly between San Martin, Ayacucho, Almagro and Colon.

Trujillo's **Plaza de Armas** is a modern square, packed with sharp-witted boot-shine boys playing around the central statue – the *Heroes of the Wars of Independence*, created by a German sculptor. Although fairly recent, this statue, along with the plaza's foundations, is apparently sinking noticeably year by year. Subsidence, however, doesn't seem to have affected the colonial mansions which front the square, two of which, tastefully restored by banks, now host small museums (open Mon.-Fri. mornings). Also on the Plaza de Armas is the city's **Cathedral**, built in the mid seventeenth century and again the following century after earthquake damage. It seems almost plain by Peruvian standards, but houses some colourful baroque sculptures and a handful of paintings by the Quiteña School. Perhaps more impressive are the big, white outside walls – splashed with political graffiti in huge red-painted letters. Though you can't visit it – and though it has also been extensively rebuilt (this time after flood damage) – the most interesting architecturally of the city's churches is the **Monastery of Santa Clara**. This is a 5-minute stroll away, to the north, and really stands out as something special within the confines of the old city.

More than for its churches, though, Trujillo is renowned for **colonial houses**, most of which have been kept in good repair and are still in use today. Between the Plaza de Armas and the central market, at Calle Orbegozo 553, there is the old **mansion of Marshal Don Luis José de Orbegozo**. Born into one of the city's wealthiest founding families, Orbegozo fought for Independence and became President of the Republic in 1833 with the support of the liberal faction. He was probably the most ineffectual of all Peruvian leaders, resented for his aristocratic mould by the mestizo generals, and from 1833–9, although still officially President, lost control over the whole country – first in civil war, then to the invited Bolivian army, and finally to a combined rebel and Chilean force. Orbegozo's rule marked a nadir in the history of his *patria* and so he disappeared from the political scene to return to his mansion in Trujillo. Today even his family home has been invaded. Although it's still in perfect condition, the main rooms around the courtyard have been converted into offices for lawyers and the *Colonial Rent-a-Car* company. Still, if you want to sit and read a while, or get your bearings away from the turmoil of the city, the courtyard is as pleasant a spot as any.

The **Palacio Iturregui**, an incredible mid-nineteenth-century mansion on Pizarro (two blocks west of the Plaza de Armas) has held rather more of its splendour. Painted a horrific blue on the outside, it has a very striking, almost surreal courtyard – in pseudo-classical style, tall columns are topped by an open roof and under the blue desert sky one gets the

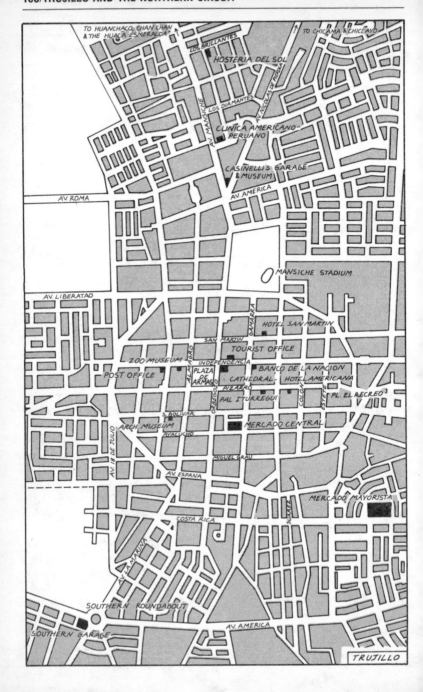

TO HUANCHACO, CHAN CHAN & THE HUACA ESMERALDA

TO CHICAMA & CHICLAYO

LOS BRILLANTES

HOSTERIA DEL SOL

LOS DIAMANTES

AV. MANSICHE

AV. NICOLAS DE PIEROLA

CLINICA AMERICANO-PERUANO

CASINELLI'S GARAGE & MUSEUM

AV. AMERICA

AV. ROMA

MANSICHE STADIUM

AV. LIBERATAD

GAMARRA

HOTEL SAN MARTIN

SAN MARTIN

TOURIST OFFICE

ZOO MUSEUM

ALMAGRO

INDEPENDENCIA

BANCO DE LA NACION

POST OFFICE

PLAZA DE ARMAS

CATHEDRAL

HOTEL AMERICANA

OREGO

BIZARRO

COLON

ESTETE

PL. EL RECREO

PAL ITURREGUI

S. BOLIVAR

ARCH. MUSEUM

AYACUCHO

MERCADO CENTRAL

AV. 18 DE JULIO

MIGUEL GRAU

AV. ESPANA

MERCADO MAYORISTA

SUAREZ

COSTA RICA

AV. LA MARINA

SOUTHERN ROUNDABOUT

SOUTHERN GARAGE

AV. AMERICA

TRUJILLO

impression of being on Mount Olympus rather than in Trujillo. It was built, as most of the city's mansions, by an army general with a long name – in this case the nineteenth-century Don Juan Manuel de Iturregui y Aguilarte. Today the palace is used by the *Club Central* who allow you to visit some of the interior rooms in the mornings (Mon.-Fri. only); the courtyard can be seen though, just by popping your head inside. Also worth a look – at Pizarro 4461 – is a last mansion, **La Casa Urquiaga**, back by the Plaza de Armas. This is said to be the house where Bolivar stayed when visiting Trujillo. Inside it is decorated and restored throughout, with period pieces to set it off and collections of pre-Columbian ceramics (free admission, Mon.-Fri.).

A few minutes' walk further out along Pizarro is the diminutive old square of **Plazuela El Recreo**, where huge trees are always full of chirping birds; just off here is the *Tepsa* bus office where you can buy tickets going north or south. Another three blocks to the south and you come to the limit of the old town and a piece of the original **city wall** to prove it. The wall used to surround the city in a more or less circular route but today the crumbling ruins are a sorry sight, a last-minute attempt at conservation and patchy restoration stuck in the middle of a busy ring-road.

Probably the best, and without a doubt the most curious, museum in Trujillo is underneath José Casinelli's *Petro Peru* garage. Set right in the middle of the road just north of the large Mansiche sports stadium, it's impossible to miss. Stuffed with ceramics collected over many years from local *huaqueros*, **Casinelli's museum** (open Mon.-Fri. 8.30–11.30 and 2–6; small fee) houses pottery and artifacts spanning literally thousands of years. The Salinar, Viru, Mochica, Chimu, Nazca, Huari, Recuay and Inca cultures are all represented. My particular favourites are the *Mochica pots* with their graphic images of daily life, people, animals and anthropomorphic deities; there are two very Chinese-looking ceramic men, one with a fine beard, the other with a moustache and sitting in a lotus position. On another shelf Casinelli (who often shows his visitors around personally) has displayed a range of *Chimu silver objects* including a tiny set of pan-pipes. Also of note are the owl figures, symbols for magic and witchcraft, and the perfectly represented *Salinar houses* which show how the culture used to live far better than any site restoration.

The **University** also runs two free museums for the public, both somewhat more central than Casinelli's. Their **Archaeological Museum** (open weekdays 8–12 and 3–6, Jan.-March 8–1 only) is on block 4 of Bolivar and specialises in ceramics, early metallurgy, textiles and coral. The other building, just behind the Plaza de Armas on block 3 of San Martin, is a fascinating **Zoological collection** (same hours), full of dozens of stuffed animals I never even knew existed.

There are two large **markets** in Trujillo, the *Mercado Central*, in the block which corners Ayacucho and Gammarra, and the busier *Mercado Mayorista* in the southern sector of town. The central market, more convenient, sells most essentials (juices, food, clothing, etc.) and has an interesting line in herbal stalls around it, not to mention unionized shoe-cleaners!

Haciendas and festivals

Until recent years Trujillo still possessed a British-owned and operated railroad connecting it with the sugar-growing **haciendas**, whose lumbering old wagons used to rumble down from the plantations full of molasses and return loaded with crude oil; they were, incidentally, never washed between loads. Things have changed in the last 20 years, with Trujillo now specialising in wheat, rice and mechanical engineering as well as producing nearly half of Peru's sugar. And the old haciendas, *Casa Grande*, *Cartavio* and *Laredo*, are all viable collectives – converted in 1969 into CAPs (*Co-operativas Agrarias de Produccion*). If you feel like taking a look at one there are regular colectivos from the Av. de España.

The region around **Paijan**, in the Chicama valley, is the heart of this vast sugar-cane zone – and also a special place for the breeding of *Caballos de Paso* – horses reared in the colonial tradition for competing in who-can-trot-the-nicest contests. This long-established sport is still popular with high society here and around Lima. Most of the Caballos de Paso meetings are held during Trujillo's **spring festivals** – when teams of horses are trotted around paddocks looking as if their feet never actually touch the ground. The **September fiestas** are also celebrated with a number of regional dances – particularly notorious being the *Marinera*, named in honour of the Navy by Gammarra in 1880. A combination of Andalucian, African and aboriginal music, its dancers hold kerchiefs above their heads and skilfully prance around each other; energetic and very sexual, the Marinera is performed in *peñas* all over the country but rarely with the same spirit and conviction as here.

Trujillo's beaches: Buenos Aires and Las Delicias

Perhaps more tempting as a quick escape from the city are Trujillo's excellent **beaches** – the best and most easy going of which, HUAN-CHACO (12km out), is covered in the following section.

Closer to the centre of town, however, is the sea-front *barrio* of **Buenos Aires**, 5km of sand just north of Trujillo – very popular locally and constantly pounded by a not very pacific surf. Like all other coastal resorts around, its seafood restaurants are a big attraction.

To the south, after crossing the Rio Moche's estuary, you come to the settlements of MOCHE and **Las Delicias**, another fine beach – though little more than that, and a handful of restaurants. The famous healing wizard *El Tuno* lives in Las Delicias; his house, which also serves as a restaurant and 'alternative' surgery, is right on the beach, its walls painted with Mochica designs. Going to El Tuno's a year or so back I witnessed a diagnostic session while eating a ceviche. The curer first rubbed a live guinea-pig over the patient's body, then split the animal open – removing its innards for inspection while the heart was still pumping. It didn't do much for my appetite but seemed to reveal the patient's problems and he was prescribed and sent away with a mix of pre-treatment herbs.

Hotels, action and practical details

Generally speaking the majority of Trujillo's **hotels** are within a few blocks of the central market: most of them to the south but a number of reasonable ones, too, along Pizarro, Independencia and San Martin. My favourites are the very central and stylish 1-star *Hotel Americana*, a grand, former colonial mansion on block 7 of Pizarro; the modern *San Martin* (on block 7 of San Martin); and the *Hosteria del Sol*, a little out of town towards Chan Chan at Calle Los Brillantes 224 (tel. 231933). The latter has upped its prices recently but, prominently styled after a Bavarian castle, it does offer bizarre and wonderful views over town from the top of fortified turrets and some of the cleanest rooms in Peru. It also runs a bus to an annexe some 140km away into the mountains (the village of COINA – at 1,500m) where in a dry subtropical micro-climate, you can visit thermal waters, a trout farm and several pre-Incaic ruins.

There's no shortage either of **bars** or **restaurants** – some of the liveliest on streets like Independencia, Pizarro, Bolivar and Ayacucho, to the east of the market area. Seafood is good and quite reasonably priced at the *Costa Azul* restaurant (on the little plaza between Orbegozo's house and the central market), although it is probably better prepared by the sea at Huanchaco, Moche and Buenos Aires. Some tasty **vegetarian** dishes are offered all day long by a small restaurant on the 7th block of Bolivar; there's also a **pool hall** just around the corner from here on Colon.

In addition to the bars there are several **discos** in town. *Billy Bobs*, small, friendly and one of the longest running, stays open late (Av. Nicolas de Pierola 716). *Nancy's* is more central at Av. España 303. Out at Huanchaco there are also *Charly's* and a folklore *peña* (held in the French restaurant on Friday and Saturday nights).

More than any other town in Peru, Trujillo seems to be a **cinema-going** one. There are several venues, clustered within a radius of a few blocks from the central market, which show all sorts of films from great classics to US comedies, Italian soft-porn and Bruce Lee specials. Audience participation is the most enjoyable thing about going to the cinema here. Way back in the 1950s, the writer George Woodcock noted from a few days in town that the uninhibited and infectious response of Trujillo's cinema audiences 'made one realise how much the use of sound in films had turned audiences into silent spectators instead of vociferous participants'.

It's the same today: however boring the film, you always leave with a feeling you've shared a performance and perhaps rattled a few barriers with laughter.

Trujillo's main **fiestas** tend to turn the town into even more of a relaxed playground than it normally seems. September is the main month for festivities with the *International Spring Fair* being held from the 29th until the 3rd of October. The main religious fiestas are in October and December. The 17th of October is generally set aside for the procession of *El Señor de Los Milagros;* while in Huanchaco, the first two weeks of December are devoted to their patron saint – another good excuse for wild parties.

The **banks** are all within a couple of blocks off the Plaza de Armas but just on the square you'll find a **casa de cambio** (cash only changed). The **post office** is on the corner of Independencia with Bolognesi, 1½ blocks from the plaza. **Tourist information** is officially available from an office at Independencia 509, but although they do sometimes have free maps of the town it's actually more of a tour agency. If you need **medical attention** the best place is the *Clinica Peruana-Americana* (block 8 of Mansiche, on the right just beyond Casinelli's garage); if you don't get any joy at reception, go to the emergency door where they'll usually see to you straightaway if they've nothing more serious to deal with.

Hitching isn't all that difficult in these parts. Going north, two good places to start are beside the stalls near the Mansiche Stadium, or from Casinelli's garage one block further and the start of the Pan American. Going south there is another big garage at the roundabout before the Pan American leaves towards Moche and Chimbote. Most of the **buses** have terminals either in the centre of town on streets like Colon (blocks 4 and 5), Pizarro (block 7) and Ayacucho (block 8), or they stop over a while at the stalls near the Mansiche stadium. **Colectivos** mostly leave from Avenida España.

HUANCHACO

HUANCHACO, only 20 minutes by bus from Trujillo, is an alternative choice to staying in the city, and an equally good base for visiting many of the sites around the region – it in fact lies just beyond the ruins of Chan Chan. There is an organised campsite here and three small, fairly cheap **hostals** which despite growing popularity should have room to stay.

Only eight years ago Huanchaco was a tiny fishing village, quiet and hardly ever seeing tourists. Today it is one of the fastest growing settlements in Peru, with land being sold off for the construction of weekend beach houses, and hotels and restaurants continually growing. This, however, hasn't yet diminished the intrinsic fishing village appeal. There is a long jetty where fishermen are usually jostling for the best positions, and stacked along the back of the main beach are rows of *caballitos del mar* – the ancient sea-going rafts used by the Mochicas and still used by locals today. They are basically constructed from four cigar-shaped bundles of tortora reeds, tied together into an arc tapering at each end. The fishermen kneel or sit at the stern and paddle, using the surf for occasional bursts of motion. The local boat-builders here are the last people left who know the craft of making *caballitos* along the design of the Mochica prototype.

There are seafood **restaurants** all along the front, a few of them with verandas actually extending to the beach. Crab seems to be a local speciality and you can often see groups of women and children up to their waists in the ocean picking them and other shell-fish with one hand, while holding baskets, alive with claws, in the other.

The very best time to visit Huanchaco is during its **June fiesta** week or the first fortnight in December, but it's always alive in a quiet way with people on the beach, others fishing and usually a few travellers hanging around the restaurants. As far as nightlife goes, there's *Charly's* nightly disco and a new weekend follore *peña* at the French restaurant. I met one traveller who had been stuck in Huanchaco for two years he liked the place so much.

Huanchaco is connected to Trujillo by an unusually frequent and very regular orange and yellow **microbus**. On the way out to Huanchaco the bus travels the whole length of Calle Estete (returning via Colon); to get back into town there's normally a queue of micros picking up passengers on the sea-front.

CHAN CHAN AND THE SITES AROUND TRUJILLO

Trujillo's most interesting attractions are without a doubt the numerous **archaeological sites** dotted around the **Moche and Chicama valleys.** Although in many ways comparable to the ruins around Cuzco – and generally more ancient – apart from Chan Chan these sites have been strangely underplayed within the scheme of Peruvian tourism. There are three main zones of interest within easy reach of Trujillo, first and foremost being the massive adobe city of **Chan Chan** on the northern edge of the modern town. To the south, standing alone under Cerro Blanco you can find the largest mud-brick pyramids in the Americas – the **Temples of the Sun and Moon.** While further away to the north of Trujillo, by crossing into the **Chicama valley,** the incredible remnants of vast pre-Inca irrigation canals, temples and early settlement sites stand in stark contrast to the massive green sugar-cane haciendas. **Buses** and **colectivos** connect the centre of town with the Chan Chan complex and the Temples of the Sun and Moon, though to move about in the Chicama valley things are a little more complicated (see p. 202).

The Chan Chan complex

The ruined city of **CHAN CHAN** stretches across a large sector of the Moche valley, beginning almost as soon as you leave Trujillo on the road to Huanchaco. A huge complex, it needs only a little imagination to raise the weathered mud walls to their original grandeur; in fact, I've always thought of the city much like one from an Edgar Rice-Burroughs' story – highly civilised, rule-bound, slaves carrying produce back and forth while artisans and courtiers walk the streets slowly, stopping only to give orders or chat with people of similar status. On certain preordained days there were known to have been great processions through the streets, the priesthood setting the pace, loaded down with gold, silver jewelry, and flowing, brightly coloured feather cloaks as they all made their way to one of the principal temples along roads between 10m-tall adobe walls.

Chan Chan was the capital city for the **Chimu Empire**, an urban-minded civilisation which appeared suddenly on the Peruvian coast around AD 1100. The Chimu built both cities and smaller towns throughout the region, stretching from Tumbes in the north to as far south as Paramonga. Their cities were always extremely elaborate with large, flat-topped buildings for the elite nobility and intricately decorated adobe pyramids serving as temples. Tending to develop methods of social control rather than new technologies, their artwork, particularly ceramics, became essentially a mass production with quantity being much more important than quality. Food was rationally distributed amongst the population which grew it, while nobles involved themselves in politics, religion and the high art of commerce – bringing treasures such as skins, gold, silver, gems and plumes into the heart of the empire.

Recognised as the best goldsmiths by the Incas, the Chimu used to panel their temples with gold and 'cultivate' palace gardens where the plants and animals were made from precious metals. Even the city walls were brightly painted. The style of architecture and relief decoration is sometimes ascribed to either the Mochica or Chimu having migrated from Central America into this area, bringing with them knowledge and ideas from an advanced civilisation like the Maya. But although this is a possibility, it's not really necessary to look beyond Peru for inspiration and ingenuity. The Chimu must have inherited ideas and techniques from a host of previous cultures along the coast and, most importantly, stood on the shoulders of many generations of trial and experiment in irrigating the Moche valley. In the desert, organisation and access to a regular water supply were critical in the development of an urban civilisation like that of Chan Chan, whose very existence depended on extracting water not only from the Moche river but also, via a complicated system of canals and aqueducts, from the neighbouring Chicama valley.

Without written records, the **origin of Chan Chan** and the orders for its construction are mere conjecture, but there are two traditional local legends. According to one, the city was founded by a certain Naymlap, who arrived by boat with his royal fleet; after establishing an empire, leaving his son, Si-Um, he disappeared into the western horizon. The other reckons that Chan Chan was inspired by an original creator deity of the same name, a dragon who made the sun and the moon and whose earthly manifestation is a rainbow – sign of life and energy, evidence of the serpent's body. Whatever the impulse behind Chan Chan, it remains one of the world's marvels and, in its heyday, was one of the largest pre-Columbian cities in the Americas.

FISH IN A WAVE (ADOBE RELIEF AT CHAN CHAN)

Of the three **main sectors** specifically opened up for tourism, the Tschudi temple-citadel is the largest and most frequently visited. Not far from Tschudi, the Huaca Esmeralda displays completely different features, being a ceremonial or ritual pyramid rather than a citadel. The third sector, the Huaca Arco Iris across on the other side of this enormous city, although similar in function to Esmeralda has an entirely unique design which has been restored with relish if not historical perfection. One **ticket**, bought at any of these three sites, covers the entrance to each of them; all are open daily from 8.30am–4pm. **Guided tours** are easily arranged (guides often hang around at Tschudi but are willing to tour the others) for a few dollars – well worth the money if you can afford it.

The Tschudi temple-citadel

No where better than at **TSCHUDI** can you see or feel what Chan Chan must have been like – stuck out in the desert amongst a myriad of high ruined walls, dusty streets, gateways, decrepid dwellings and open graves. Only a few hundred metres from the Pacific Ocean, and bordered by maize fields, this was once the heart of the capital, the power-base from which the Chimu elite ruled their massive empire. To reach the main section of the ruins take the orange and yellow **microbus** from Calle Estete in town, getting off at the concrete Tschudi/Chan Chan signpost about 2km beyond the outer suburbs. From here you just follow the track to the left of the road in a straight line until you see the ticket office (on the left) beside the huge defensive walls around the inner temple-citadel.

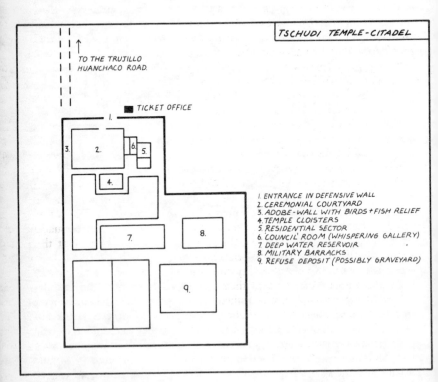

TSCHUDI TEMPLE-CITADEL

TO THE TRUJILLO HUANCHACO ROAD.

TICKET OFFICE

1. ENTRANCE IN DEFENSIVE WALL
2. CEREMONIAL COURTYARD
3. ADOBE-WALL WITH BIRDS + FISH RELIEF
4. TEMPLE CLOISTERS
5. RESIDENTIAL SECTOR
6. 'COUNCIL' ROOM (WHISPERING GALLERY)
7. DEEP WATER RESERVOIR
8. MILITARY BARRACKS
9. REFUSE DEPOSIT (POSSIBLY GRAVEYARD)

All the inner courtyards and passages of the **citadel** are laid out according to some well-ordered and preordained plan – now carefully restored and enclosed. This area of the ruins is located only 10 or 15 minutes' walk off the main road between Trujillo and Huanchaco;

beyond it extend acres of ruins, untended and, according to the locals, **dangerous** for gringos – some certainly have been robbed after wandering off alone. This is frustrating, since Tschudi is thought to have been the central citadel among a major group of at least ten complexes, each divided by wide streets and clearly forming separate wards or sacred urbanisations. Like Tschudi, each distinct sector was designed along typical Chimu lines – with a rectangular layout and divided by enormous trapezoidal walls. As you walk from the road towards Tschudi, although it's difficult to make out at all clearly, you are actually passing at least four of the other citadels: **Bandelier** and **Uhle** to the left, **Velarde** and **Laberinto** on the right. Each of these individual complexes was most likely based around a royal clan of its own with their retinues.

Very little is actually known about the history or even the daily life of those who lived in Tschudi; unfortunately, the Chimu didn't leave us such a graphic record as the earlier Mochica culture who built their temples on the other side of the Moche valley. But, following the **indicated route around the citadel** through a maze of corridors, chambers, and amazingly large plazas, you will undoubtedly begin to form your own picture of this ancient civilisation. Eventually finding yourself in a court-yard with some 24 seats set into niches at regular spacings along the walls you can actually participate in a technology probably designed for major clan-heads to meet and thrash out important issues. By sitting in one niche and whispering to someone in another you'll find that this simply designed **council room** cleverly amplifies all sounds; the niches appear to be connected by adobe intercoms.

One thing we do know for sure about the Chimu is that in the 1470s Tupac Yupanqui led the Inca armies down from the mountains in the east to cut off the aqueducts supplying Chan Chan with its vital water supply. After lengthy discussions, the Chimu council managed to persuade its leader against going out to fight the Incas. You could say that the Chimu succumbed to the Inca deterrent – they knew full well how the Incas met resistance with brutality and surrender with peaceful takeover. They were quickly deprived of their chieftains, many of them taken to Cuzco (along with the highly skilled metallurgists) to be indoctrinated into Inca ways. These turbaned aliens from the coast must have formed a strange sight there – strutting around its cold stone streets with huge golden nose ornaments dangling over their chins. Sixty years later when the first Spaniards rode through Chan Chan they found only a ghost town full of dust and legend.

La Huaca Esmeralda

One of the most beautiful, and possibly the most venerated, of Chimu temples, the ruins of **LA HUACA ESMERALDA** lie a couple of kilometres before Tschudi, just off the main Huanchaco road from Trujillo. Unlike

Tschudi, the Huaca is actually on the very edge of town, stuck between the outer suburbs and the first maize fields. Getting off the orange and yellow **microbus** (again, catch this from Calle Estete) where the road begins to narrow, only a block or so beyond the *Hosteria del Sol*, the first thing you can see, set back to the left away from the traffic, is the old church of **San Salvador de Mansiche** – a good example of early colonial religious building. From here, follow the path along the right-hand side of this chapel for some three small blocks (through the modern *barrio* of *Mansiche*) and you come to the temple.

La Huaca Esmeralda – the Emerald Temple – was built in the twelfth or early thirteenth century – at about the same time as the Tschudi complex and is one of the most important *huacas* scattered around Trujillo. Unusually, most of its relief motifs are concerned solely with the ocean – marine life, related human activities and wave formations. It was only uncovered in 1923 but its exterior walls were severely damaged in the El Niño rains of 1925. While the guardian of the ruins and his dog, Lilly, showed me around this site, telling me about the freak rains and pointing out where the adobe had been washed away, I suddenly realised the full meaning of the name. *El Niño*, the warm water current which causes the periodic freak weather is also the term applied to the bad weather itself. Simply translated it means 'the Boy' and, strangely enough, people see it just like that – a frustrated kid who pushes his warm waters south every now and again, merely out of curiosity, but a dire nuisance whenever it happens.

Today, because of the rains, you can only just make out what must have been an impressive polychrome **façade**. All of the **relief work** on the adobe walls, however, is original, showing friezes of fish-nets containing swimming fishes, waves, a flying pelican, and frequent repetitive patterns or geometrical arabesques. The *huaca* has an unusually complex **structure**, with two main platforms, a number of surrounding walls and several sloping pathways giving access to each section. From the top platform you can see across the valley to the graveyards of Chan Chan, out to sea, over the cultivated fields around the site and into the primitive brickworks next door. Standing there it seems obvious that the site was a place for adoration, possibly serving also as a royal tomb. Only some shells and *chaquiras* (stone and coral necklaces) were found when the *huaca* was officially dug out some 60 years ago – but that was after centuries of *huaqueros* (treasure hunters) had exhausted it.

The locals living in the barrio of MANSICHE, next to the site, are apparently direct descendants of the Chan Chan people. In many ways you can see it in their faces and by the way they walk. Mansiche, now with strange street names like Liverpool Street, was the nearest settlement to Chan Chan when the Spaniards arrived in the Trujillo area. Whenever I've been to the Huaca Esmeralda, local boys have asked me if I want to buy strings of *chaquira* which they sift out of the sand from remote graves in the Chan Chan complex. Some of these are in perfect condition and they're generally cheaper here than at Huanchaco or in Trujillo. In law it's illegal to take pre-Columbian artifacts out of Peru, but a stone or coral necklace seems to be generally acceptable.

La Huaca Arco Iris

LA HUACA ARCO IRIS – the Rainbow Temple – is the most fully restored ruin of the Chan Chan complex. Its site is just to the left of the Pan American Highway about 3 or 4km north of Trujillo in the middle of the urban district of LA ESPERANZA. There's a regular bus service (red and blue **microbus**, Comite 19) which you can catch either from the centre of Trujillo or over the road from Casinelli's garage. The ruins are indicated by a blue concrete sign at the side of the main road. Get off the bus here and you'll see the *huaca* set back behind some sandy waste ground and surrounded by a tall wall.

The *huaca*, or temple, flourished under the Chimu between the twelfth and fourteenth centuries. No one knows exactly what to call it although several interpretations have been made of the central motif, which is endlessly repeated throughout the pyramid. It has been called a dragon, a centipede and, more recently, a rainbow. In fact, the dragon and the rainbow need not exclude one another – both possibly representing the creator divinity. The centipede, however, is a fairly widespread motif (notably on the Nazca ceramics) whose original meaning seems to have been lost. Large poisonous centipedes, up to 20cm long, actually do live in the Andes. They're still looked on with some awe because of the way they move and control their myriad legs; people are very careful not to tread on them.

Most of the main **temple walls** have been restored, and they are covered with the recreated 'rainbow' design. Originally, the outer walls were decorated in the same way with identical elaborate friezes cut into the adobe. This design looks like a multi-legged serpent arching over two lizard-type beings. Each of the serpents' heads, one at either end of the arc, seems to be biting the cap (or tip of the head) off a humanoid figure.

There are two tiers to the temple, the **first platform** consisting of 14 rectangular chambers, possibly used for storing maize and precious metals for ritual purposes. A path slopes up to the **second tier**, a flat-topped platform – the ceremonial area where sacrifices were held and the gods spoke. From here there is a wide view over the valley, towards the ocean, the city, other huacas and the city of Chan Chan.

Down below you can visit the small **site museum**, built while the Huaca was being restored in 1964 and housing a minor selection of ceramics from the site itself and some interesting wooden idols found in a tomb here. The ticket man also sells good prints of Chimu and Mochica designs.

Fifteen minutes' walk down the main road, back towards Trujillo, brings you to the **Pedro Puerta gallery** where you can usually find English-speaking **guides** to any of the Trujillo ruins; the gallery, however, was closed on my last visit – and may still be so (ask at the museum).

La Huaca del Sol and La Huaca de la Luna

Set on the south bank of the Moche river in a barren desert landscape, these two temples are really stunning. The **Huaca del Sol** (Temple of the Sun) is in fact the largest adobe structure in the Americas – and easily the most impressive of the many pyramids on the Peruvian coast. Its twin temple, **Huaca de la Luna** (Temple of the Moon) is smaller, but more complex and brilliantly frescoed.

To reach these sites – **entrance** to which is currently unrestricted – take one of the direct minibus **colectivos** from the first block of Suarez in Trujillo; these leave all through the day. Or, alternatively, catch the yellow and green **microbus** (marked *Salaverry* or *Moche*) which leaves town by the southern roundabout: about 1km beyond the bridge over the Moche a sandy track turns off the main Pan American Highway to the left – you can already see the Huaca del Sol to the left of a conical white hill (Cerro Blanco), just follow the track through maize fields and small-holdings for about half an hour until you reach the foot of the pyramid.

LA HUACA DEL SOL was built as a temple by the Mochica around AD 500 and, although very weathered, its pyramid edges still slope at 77° to the horizon. The larger part of the structure, which you come to first, is made up of a lower level base-platform. On top of this is the demolished stump of a four-sided, stepped pyramid surmounted about 50m above the surrounding desert, by a ceremonial platform. On the other side of this platform is another, larger one leading off down to a causeway at the end and from the top you can see how the river Moche was diverted by the Spanish, way back in 1602 in order to erode the Huaca and find treasure. They were quite successful at washing away a large section but little except adobe bricks were uncovered. The first real archaeological work here was done by Max Uhle in the early 1900s; he discovered over 3,400 objects and ceramics, most of which were removed to the University of Berkeley museum in California.

Estimates of the pyramid's **brickwork** vary – but it must contain somewhere between 50 and 140 million adobe blocks. Each brick, made of pure sand and water, was marked in any one of 93 different ways – probably the makers' distinguishing signs – and used in the counting of tribute. It must have needed a massively well-organised labour supply to put together, though Calancha, one of the chroniclers, tells us that it was built in three days by 200,000 Indians! Three days might actually mean

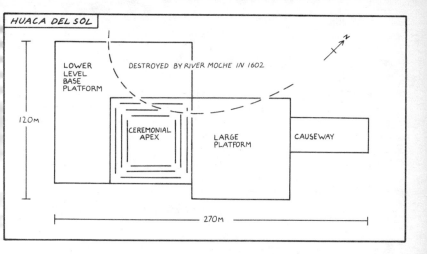

HUACA DEL SOL

LOWER LEVEL BASE PLATFORM

DESTROYED BY RIVER MOCHE IN 1602

120M

CEREMONIAL APEX

LARGE PLATFORM

CAUSEWAY

270M

three stages but even so someone must have been working on those bricks for a long time. It would be interesting to know exactly how the Mochica priests and architects decided on the shape. If you look at the form of the Huaca against the silhouette of Cerro Blanco from the main road there is a remarkable similarity; and if you look at the Huaca side-on from the vantage point of the Huaca de La Luna, it has the same general outline as the hills behind.

Clinging to the bottom of Cerro Blanco, just 500m from the Sun Temple is another Mochica edifice – **LA HUACA DE LA LUNA**. Again, this was probably a sacred building, separate in its own right from the Huaca del Sol though constructed in the same era. It may even have been an administrative centre when the Priest-Lord was in residence. The Temple of the Moon is only the visible part of an older complex of interior rooms; ceramics dug up from the vast graveyard which extends between the two Huacas and around the base of Cerro Blanco suggest that this might have been the site for a cult of the dead. Some frescoed rooms were discovered behind the Moon Temple by a *huaquero* in 1910 and more were found in 1925, displaying murals with up to seven colours (mostly reds and blues). The most famous of these paintings has been called *The rebellion of the artifacts* because, as you find on some Mochica ceramics, all sorts of objects are depicted attacking human beings, getting their revenge, or rebelling: there are war clubs with faces and helmets with human legs chasing after people.

You can still scramble about on the Huaca de La Luna but you'll need a torch to find your way around the rooms and cave-niches inside. The interior rooms are in a bad state: in one you can just see the top of a mural poking above a pile of rubble. I get the impression that it will stay this way until the National Institute of Culture can find the money to clean it up, put a glass panel over the murals and employ a permanent guard for the site.

With the Huacas being so close to the coastal villages of MOCHE and LAS DELICIAS, it's a good idea to combine a visit to the ruins with one of the local *picanterias*. Walking back from the Huaca del Sol to the Pan American, you can pick up the yellow and green **microbus** and get into MOCHE without problem, a small settlement with lots of big restaurants, all serving freshly prepared seafood. There are a couple more restaurants on the beach in the next settlement, **LAS DELICIAS**, one of them (see p. 190) that's run by the famous Trujillan *curandero* El Tuno.

LITTER BEARERS (DESIGN FROM MOCHICA CERAMIC)

The Chicama valley

Chicama is the first valley north of the Moche 35km from Trujillo, the heart of its fertile plain. In the Mochica and Chimu eras the Chicama river was connected to the fields of Chan Chan by a vast system of canals and aqueducts over 90km long, and remains of this **irrigation system**, fortresses and evidence from over 6,000 years of residence can still be seen around the valley. Today, however, the region is most striking in its appearance as a single enormous sugar-cane field, although in fact it's divided up between a number of large sugar-producing co-operatives, again originally family-owned *haciendas* which were redistributed during the Military Government's agrarian reforms in 1969. The sugar-cane was first brought to Peru from India by the Spaniards and quickly took root as the region's main crop.

Three important ancient sites – **La Huaca Prieta, Chiquitoy** and **Ascope** – and the isolated seaside village of **Puerto Chicama** make a trip out here worth while. For the villages of CHICAMA, PAIJAN or ASCOPE you can pick up **buses** in Trujillo over the road from Casinelli's garage, or from around the main market (where most of them start). **Colectivos** to CARTAVIO leave from the Av. Espana – and are best if you want to start off at *Chiquitoy* or the *Huaca Prieta*. The whole valley is also served by local colectivos so it's quite easy to get from one centre to another, although there is always a little walking to do; from Cartavio to the Huaca Prieta, for instance, it's 7km, about half-an-hour's stroll. **Taxis** to anywhere in the Chicama valley can be found in CHOCOPE.

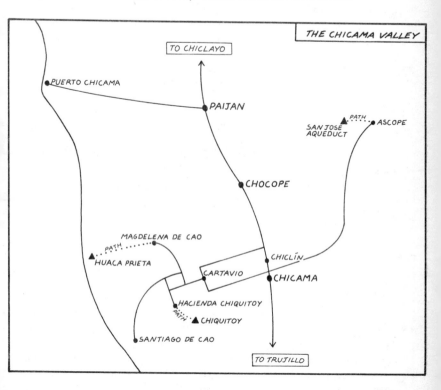

La Huaca Prieta

This, quite literally, is a heap of rubbish – right next to the *Playa El Brujo* at the edge of the ocean. But it's a garbage tip redeemed, in that it has been accumulating for some 6,500 years, crowded with evidence and clues about the evolution of culture and human activity on the coast.

The normal route to get here is by *colectivo* to CARTAVIO, then walk via the hacienda/co-op of MAGDELENA DE CAO. **Prieta** is a small dark hill about 12m high – its coloration due to thousands of years of decomposing organic remains. On the top part there are signs of subterranean dwellings, long since excavated by Larco Hoyle and Junius Bird.

Like the Moche, the Chicama valley is full of huacas and the locals have a long tradition as *huaqueros*. Rumours abound about vile deaths from asphyxiation, a slow process sometimes lasting days, for anyone who ventures into a tomb. '*Le llamó la huaca*' they say – the huaca called him!

Chiquitoy

The well-preserved ruins of **CHIQUITOY** are rarely visited – stuck out as they are on an empty desert plain unconnected by road. To reach the site you'll need to take a *colectivo* to CARTAVIO then walk to the HACIENDA CHIQUITOY. There you should be able to find someone to put you on the right track, which leads off into the desert; follow this across the flat pampa for about 5 or 6km (45 minutes' walk) and you can't miss the ruins. These comprise a temple complex with a three-tiered pyramid – very Mayan like – in front of a walled, rectangular sector. There is evidence of some dwellings and a large courtyard, too, though little is known of Chiquitoy's history.

If only because of its location and the good condition of the pyramid, Chiquitoy's well worth the walk, or alternatively you can normally find **taxis** in Chocope or Chicama who'll take you to this site for a few dollars per person; the more people the cheaper.

Ascope and Puerto Chicama

The two other places of interest around the Chicama valley are Ascope and Puerto Chicama. Near to **ASCOPE**, just a couple of kilometres out of the settlement, is a great earthen **aqueduct**, standing 15m high, which used to carry water across the mouth of this dry valley. Still an impressive site after about 1,400 years, it was functioning until damaged by the heavy rains of 1925. The *San Jose*, as it's called, was one of a series of canal bridges which traversed ravines along the La Cumbre irrigation system which joined the Moche and Chicama valleys during the Mochica and Chimu periods. Again, there are regular **buses** to Ascope; you can pick them up either over the road from Casinelli's garage or in the first two blocks of Mansiche by the sports stadium.

PUERTO CHICAMA is a small fishing village which used to serve as a port to the sugar haciendas. These days it tends to be a meeting place for young surfers; there is a **campsite**, the chance to rent a **beach hut** and some of the best **surfing rollers** on the Pacific coastline. To reach Puerto Chicama take the **bus** from Trujillo to PAIJAN (where, if you've got time you can inspect some *caballo de paso* stables or stud farms) and wait for a connecting bus or *colectivo* going down to the coast.

THE NORTHERN CIRCUIT

Even if you're not planning to venture out east, **Cajamarca** is worth considering – a *sierra* town, it is second only to Cuzco in the grace of its architecture and impressiveness of mountain scenery. From TRUJILLO there are two main routes, each exciting and spectacular, and many travellers choose to make a circuit, going up by one and returning by the other. The speediest is **via Pacasmayo** along a relatively new paved road which follows the Jequetepeque river, passing small settlements and families at work in terraced fields along precipitous valley walls. There are *colectivos* this way from both TRUJILLO (about 8 hours) and CHICLAYO. Alternatively, it's possible to hop buses from town to town **via Huamachuco and Cajabamba** – around 22 hours' travelling in all. This latter route is best done in two or three stages. First is a 12–hour bus ride from Trujillo to HUAMACHUCO where there is a reasonable hotel, *La Libertad*. From here, too, you can make a 2-hour walk to the pre-Inca fort of *Marca Huamachuco*, or prepare for a major expedition to the remote, relatively recently discovered ruins of *Gran Pajaten* (for anyone seriously interested in visiting these incredible ruins of a sacred city, information and advice can be found from the universities and the *Instituto de Cultura* in either Trujillo or Cajamarca). On from Huamachuco it's another 3-hour bus trip to CAJABAMBA (*Hotel Florez* on the main plaza) and finally 8 more hours on a different bus to CAJAMARCA. All of these small towns are interconnected by a regular, very cheap, local service.

CAJAMARCA

Almost European in appearance, **CAJAMARCA** squats placidly below a high mountain in a neatly organised valley. The stone-based architecture of the town seems to reflect the cold nights up here, over 2,700m above the Pacific Ocean. Charming as it all is – elaborate stone filigree mansions and churches and old baroque façades wherever you look – most buildings are actually quite austere in appearance.

The narrow streets, usually thronging with peasants on their way to market, are fixed on a grid system based around the **Plaza de Armas**. This square is on the same site as – though smaller than – the original triangular Inca courtyard where Pizarro captured Atahualpa on that fateful day in 1532 (see the section immediately following for the history of this). Four centuries on, the battle scene looks rather different – and sad. On one side of the plaza is a late seventeenth-century **Cathedral**, its walls incorporating various pieces of Inca masonry, its internal atmosphere lifted only by a splendid churrigueresque altar created by Spanish craftsmen. On the other is the strange-looking San Francisco, in whose sanctuary are thought to be the bones of Atahualpa – originally buried in the church's cemetery. One of the Cajamarca's unique features was that, until relatively recently, none of the churches had towers – a concerted effort to avoid the colonial tax rigidly imposed on 'completed' religious buildings. The eighteenth-century chapel of La Dolorosa next to San Francisco, followed this pattern; inside, however, are some of Cajamarca's finest examples of stone filigree, both outside and in. The church of Belen, just around the corner on Calle Belen, also boasts a lavish interior.

More stylish than the churches, though, and a superb example of colonial stonecraft is the Palace of Condes de Ucedo on Calle Apurimac – one block from the plaza; a splendid colonial mansion, this has been taken over and conserved by the Banco de Credito. Not far away in the University Museum (Jiron Arequipa, 1½ blocks from the plaza, by the central market; open Mon.-Sat. 8–12 and 2–5) particularly interesting for the breadth of its collections of ceramics, textiles and other objects, spanning some 3,000 years of culture in the Cajamarca basin. If the director, Rodolfo Ravines, is around he is always very keen to chat about archaeology and local sites, something he probably knows more about than anyone else alive. San Francisco convent, by the plaza, has a separate museum devoted to religious art, not as good as the one in Cuzco but an insight, nevertheless, into the colonial mind.

The most famous site in town, however, is the so-called Ransom Room, El Cuarto del Rescate, the only Inca construction still standing in Cajamarca. For a long while this claimed to be the room which Atahualpa, as Pizarro's prisoner, promised to fill with gold in return for his freedom. Although fitting the dimensions described in detail by the chroniclers (not surprisingly, considering the symmetry and repetitiveness of Inca design), historians now agree that this was in fact Atahualpa's cell. Its bare Inca masonry is notably poorer than you find around Cuzco, and the trapezoidal doorway a post-Conquest construction (probably Spanish rather than native).

With places of interest being so centralised in Cajamarca, the best hotels are those on the main square. This is one of the few places where the State-run Turistas hotel is quite reasonably priced (and with good hot baths). The Gran Hotel Plaza, too, is stylish and cheap with hot showers. You can get free maps and information from the Conjunto de Belen, just around the corner from the plaza on Calle Belen. Cajamarca Tours (2 de Mayo 323) are also very helpful and can advise on arranging trips to most of the nearby sites. Within a stone's throw of the Cathedral are several good restaurants, the most popular, and excellent value, is La Taverna. The Banco de La Nacion is at Jiron Tarapaca 647 and the post office nearby, on block 4 of Calle Lima. National and international **phone calls** can be made from *Entel-Peru*'s offices at Jiron San Martin 363. The **central market**, a flurry of activity in the mornings, is on the corner of Apurimac and Amazonas, within 3 minutes' walk of the Plaza de Armas.

If you can arrange it, the best time to visit Cajamarca is during the months of May or June (depending on the religious annual calendar) for the **Festival of Corpus Christi**. Until 80 years ago this was the country's main fiesta procession, explicitly coinciding with the traditional Inca sun festival, and led by the elders of the Canachin family who were directly descended from local pre-Inca chieftains. The procession still brings in Indians from all around, though one gets the impression that increasing commercialism has eaten away at the traditional roots. Notwithstanding this there are plenty of parties, bullfights, *Caballo de Paso* meetings and an interesting trade fair.

Some history – Atahualpa and Pizarro

The fertile Cajamarca basin was domesticated long before the cows arrived to graze its pastures, or the white fences parcelled up the flat valley floor. As early as 1000 BC it was occupied by well-organised tribal cultures – the earliest sign of Chavinoid influence in the northern mountains. The existing sites, scattered all about this region, evidence advanced civilisations capable of producing elaborate stone constructions without hard metal tools, and reveal permanent settlement from the **Chavin era** right through until the conquering **Inca** army arrived in the 1460s. Then, and over the next 70 years, it developed into an important provincial garrison town, evidently much favoured as a pit-stop by the Inca Emperors on their way along the Royal Highway between Cuzco and Quito. With its thermal waters it proved, too, a convenient spot for resting up and licking wounds after the frequent Inca battles with 'barbarians' in the eastern forests. The city was endowed with sun temples and sumptuous palaces, and their presence must have been felt even when the supreme Lord was over 1,000km away to the south, paying homage to the ancestors in the capital of his empire.

Atahualpa, the last Inca Lord, was in Cajamarca in late 1532, taking it easy camped beside the thermal baths when news came of **Pizarro** – breathlessly dragging his 62 horsemen and 106 foot soldiers up into mountains higher than most Europeans even realised existed. Atahualpa's spies and runners kept him well informed of the Spaniards' movements and he could quite easily have destroyed the small band of weary aliens in one of the rocky passes to the west of Cajamarca. Instead he waited patiently until Friday the 15th of November when a dishevelled group entered the silent streets of the deserted Inca city. For the first time, Pizarro saw Atahualpa's camp, its cotton tents 'extending for a league, with Atahualpa's own in the middle. All his men were standing outside the tents and their arms, which were spears as long as pikes, were stuck in the earth'. Estimates varied, but there were something between 30 and 80,000 effective Inca warriors – outnumbering the Spaniards by at least 150, and possibly by 400, to one.

Pizarro sent his hot-headed brother Hernando and one Captain de Soto to visit the Inca camp, with the idea of inviting Atahualpa to come and meet the Spaniards on 'peaceful' terms. Soto arrived first but the Lord Inca kept his gaze fixed at the ground and refused to respond or acknowledge him. An interpreter informed the Spaniard that Atahualpa was on the last day of a ceremonial fast. When Hernando arrived and delivered a speech inviting the Emperor down into the city, he looked up from the floor and scolded the Spaniards for their ill-treatment of his coastal subjects. But after a brief conversation, Atahualpa promised to visit the next day.

Pizarro meanwhile was planning his coup along the same lines which had been so successful for Cortes in Mexico: he would capture Atahualpa and use him to control the realm. The square in Cajamarca was perfect for the following day's operation: 'Long low buildings occupied three sides of it, each some 200 yards long. Pizarro stationed the cavalry in two of these, in three contingents of 15 to 20.'

The next morning nothing happened. Pizarro became anxious; his plans could easily be foiled. In the afternoon, however, Atahualpa's army began to move in a ceremonial procession, slowly making their way across the plain towards the city of Cajamarca. Tension mounted in the Spanish camp. As the Indians came closer they could be heard singing a graceful lament and their dazzling regalia could be made out. 'All the Indians wore large gold and silver discs like crowns on their heads. . . . In front was a squadron of Indians wearing a livery of chequered colours, like a chessboard.'

Leaving most of his troops outside on the plain, Atahualpa entered with some 5,000 men, unarmed except for small battle axes, slings and pebble pouches. He was being carried in a litter by 80 nobles – its wooden poles covered in silver, the floor and walls with gold and brilliantly coloured parrot feathers. The Lord himself was poised on a small stool, dressed richly with a crown placed on his head and a thick string of magnificent emeralds around his aristocratic neck. Understandably bewildered to see no bearded men and not one horse in sight, he shouted – 'Where are they?' A moment later, the Dominican friar, Vicente de Valverde, came out into the plaza; with a cross in one hand and his holy book in the other, he made his pompous way through the Inca army to Atahualpa's side. Here, with the minimum of reverence to one he considered a heathen in league with the devil, he invited Atahualpa to dine at Pizarro's table. The Lord Inca declined the offer, saying that he wouldn't move until the Spanish returned all the objects they had already stolen from his people. The friar handed Atahualpa his bible and began a Christian discourse which no-one within earshot could understand. After examining this 'strange' object Atahualpa threw it on the floor, visibly angered, probably more at the friar's spoutings than at the holy book. Vicente de Valverde, horrified at such a sacrilege, hurried back to shelter screaming – 'Come out! Come out, Christians! Come at these enemy dogs who reject the things of God.'

Two canons signalled the start of what became a massacre. The Spanish horsemen flew at the 5,000 Indians, hacking their way through flesh to overturn the litter and capture the Emperor. Knocking down a 2m thick wall, many of the Inca troops fled out onto the surrounding plain with the cavalry at their heels. The foot soldiers set about those left in the square with such speed and ferocity that in a short time 'most of them were put to the sword'. Not one Indian raised a weapon against the Spaniards.

To the vain Spanish, it was patently obvious why Atahualpa, an experienced battle-leader, had led his men into such an obvious trap. He had underestimated his opponents, their crazy ambitions and their technological superiority – steel swords, muskets, canons and horse power. On the other hand, perhaps the Inca Lord knew that the inevitable was about to happen – the oracles had warned him. He could kill Pizarro but there were doubtless others, maybe even more ruthless, where these strange foreigners on four-legged monsters had come from. Whatever the explanation for what must surely be one of the world's biggest ever massacres of indigenous people, it was a bloody beginning to Cajamarca's colonial history. (Quotes here are from John Hemming's translations of the original Chronicles in *The Conquest of the Incas*.)

Inca ruins – and some local hikes
A short stroll from Cajamarca's central plaza, two blocks along 2 de Mayo, brings you to the path up the **Cerra Santa Apolonia**, the grassy hill which overlooks the town and which offers by far the best view across the valley. Originally a sacred spot, on top you'll find what is thought to have been a sacrificial stone used by the ancients around 1000 BC. It is popularly called the 'Inca's Throne', and if you sit in it for a while you'll see why.

Just 2km to the south-west of this hill, along the road towards Cumbemayo, are a group of other ruins – prominent among them a rambling old pyramid. Little is known about this, the Spanish used to call it a temple of the sun but the locals today use the name *Agua Tapada*, 'covered water'. Quite possibly, there is a subterranean well below the site – they're not uncommon around here and it might initially have been a temple related to some form of water cult.

Many of the ruins around Cajamarca are in fact related to water, in a way that seems both to adore it in a religious sense and to use it in a practical manner. Only 5km away from the city are the **Inca Baths** where Atahualpa was camped when Pizarro arrived, and from where the Inca army marched, or paraded, to their doom. You can take a taxi or *colectivo* out here very cheaply; or you can walk, which is probably a better way to appreciate the thermal waters when you arrive. To reach the baths follow Amazonas east from the market five blocks until you reach the corner with Cinco Esquinas; turn up here, then immediately make a right into Calle El Inca – this is laid on the foundations of the old Inca road and will take you all the way up in about an hour-and-a-half. For a small fee you can still use the baths – which are of pure thermal waters (hot, cold or a mixture) as they bubble straight out of the mountain. The adjoining *Hotel Chavez* seems to have something of a monopoly over the springs but this doesn't spoil either the beneficial effect or the pleasure of using them.

An enjoyable 2-hour walk from the Inca Baths, following the Rio Chonta gently uphill to its source, brings you to another important site – the **Ventanillas de Otuzco**. The *Ventanillas* (or windows) are a huge pre-Incaic necropolis where the dead chieftains of the Cajamarca culture were once buried in deep niches cut by hand, sometimes metres deep, into the volcanic rock. If you want to go directly back into town from here, a road goes all the way (about 12km), becoming the Avenida Aviacion and coming out on Arequipa, four blocks north of the Plaza de Armas.

Further afield: Cumbemayo and Kuntur Huasi

About 20km by road north-west of Cajamarca is **CUMBEMAYO**, an ancient canal stretching for over a kilometre in an isolated highland dale. There are no buses here from Cajamarca and only infrequent trucks, but you can walk/hitchhike in around 3–4 hours, depending on how many short cuts you find across the bends in the road – starting from the back of Cerro Santa Apolonia on the south-west side of town. Alternatively, if you don't fancy a walk, and there are four or five of you, it's not difficult to find a taxi willing to do the trip for around $3 per person (*Cajamarca Tours* run trips which cost $5 a piece).

Just before you reach Cumbemayo there is a weird natural rock formation, the **Bosque de Piedras** ('Forest of Stones'), where clumps of eroded limestone outcrops taper into thin figure-like shapes – known locally as *los fraillones* ('the friars'). A little further on is the well-preserved and incredibly well-made water channel, **El Cumbemayo**, built perhaps 1,200 years before the Incas even arrived here. The amount of effort and precision which must have gone into constructing this, cut as it is from solid rock with perfect right angles and superb geometric lines, suggests that it was more for a ritual or religious function than to irrigate the land. Water was certainly a very important, probably sacred substance for the Incas; there are many examples of whole citadels designed by them around natural springs. Sites like Cumbemayo and Tipón (near Cuzco) illustrate how it is sometimes fruitless to try to differentiate between the practical use and religious adoration of natural phenomena in attempting to understand non-industrial cultures. In some places along **the canal** there are rocks cut into what look like seats and sacrificial tables – in fact forms left by the quarrying of stones during the building of the canal. Cumbemayo originally transferred water between the Pacific and the Atlantic watershed via a complex system of canals and tunnels, which are still visible and in some cases operational. Perhaps an extravagant project, the waterway displays an inspiring knowledge of surveying and engineering.

To the right-hand side of the aqueduct (with your back to Cajamarca) there is a large face-like rock on the hillside, with a man-made **cave** cut into it. This contains some interesting 3,000-year-old petroglyphs etched in typical Chavin style (you'll need a flashlight) and dominated by the omnipresent feline features.

It is possible to walk from Cumbemayo to another pre-Incaic site – **KUNTUR HUASI** – in the upper part of the Jequtepeque river valley, to the east of the Cajamarca Basin. This, however, takes three or four days so you'll need a tent and food. Hilary and George Bradt's *Backpacking and Trekking in Peru and Bolivia* has a good detailed description and sketch map of the trail: you'll need this, or at least a survey map of the area since neither site is marked. An easier way of getting there, though much less spectacular, is to take a bus from Cajamarca to CHILETE, a small mining town about 50km along the paved road to Pacasmayo. At Chilete you can connect with a bus to the village of SAN PABLO (two **hotels**) which is just a short uphill walk from the ruins.

Although Kuntur Huasi has lost what must once have been a magnificent temple, you can still make out a variation on Chavin designs carved onto its four stone monoliths. Outside of Chavin itself this is the most important site in the Northern Sierra related to the feline cult. Golden ornaments and turquoise were found in graves here but so far not enough work has been done to date the site. The anthropomorphic carvings, being variations on the Chavin theme, indicate differences in time – perhaps Kuntur Huasi belonged to the late Chavin era, placing it around 400 BC. Whatever its age, the pyramid is an imposing ruin amidst quite exhilarating countryside.

CHACHAPOYAS

CHACHAPOYAS, the unlikely capital of *El Departmento de Amazonas*, is poised on an exposed plateau between two river gorges, over 2,300m above sea-level. In the Aymaru mountain Indian language, Chachapoyas evidently means 'the cloud people': a description, perhaps, of the fair-skinned tribes who used to dominate this region, living in at least seven major city complexes, each one located high up above the Utcubamba valley on prominent, very dramatic peaks and ridges. The town today, surrounded by wooded hills, is of no particular interest to the traveller except as a base from which to explore the area's wealth of archaeological remains, above all the ruins of **Kuelap**. Other – apparently spectacular – monuments also exist in this area but they're yet to be surveyed. If the pioneering spirit takes you, the local inhabitants – many of them blonde and remarkably pale faced to this day – are (and will probably for many years remain) the best source of information about the ruins.

There are two **land routes** up to Chachapoyas from the coast, both of them arduous, bumpy and meandering. By far the easiest is from CHICLAYO **via Olmos and Jaen;** there are daily buses this way (15 hours in the dry season – 20 or so from November through March due to frequent *huaycos*, landslides, along the road). This route, though less spectacular than the Cajamarca approach, involves less climbs and crosses the Andes by the Porculla Pass, the lowest possible track across the Peruvian Andes, obviously a better alternative for those travellers worried by *soroche* (mountain sickness). The **road from Cajamarca,** however, is certainly memorable – crossing into the Marañon valley beyond LEIM-ABAMBA along winding mountain roads and nearly achieving 4,000m before descending to the town of CELEDIN. The rugged road continues from here through the *Cordillera de Mishacocha* onto level plains around Cajamarca. The whole trip lasts a minimum of 20 hours (8 hours more from Trujillo and the coast) and there are only two buses a week. Trucks are more frequent though also slower and less reliable; however, you can break the journey up by stopping off at CELEDIN (*Hotel Amazonas* near the plaza) which does have a daily bus service connecting it to Cajamarca. If you're more bothered about retreading old ground than *soroche* there is no need to choose between these routes – you can reach Chachapoyas from the coast via one and return by the other.

Once a rich colonial possession with gold and silver mines as well as extremely fertile alluvial soil, Chachapoyas fell into decline during the Republican era. Recently, however, with the building of the Cajamarca road (in 1961) and the opening up of air-communications, it has developed into a thriving, if small, market town with a population of some 7,000. As the centre of a military zone, the town has a **PIP** (*Policia de Investigaciones*) office – where all travellers are obliged to register their passports. This is close by the **main plaza,** where you'll also find some pretty good, if limited, **restaurants** and, fronting the square, the *Hotel Amazonas,* cheap, usually very friendly, and the only place in town to **stay**. As a gringo you're likely to attract lively curiosity from the local folk; travellers are still a rare sight in Chachapoyas.

KUELAP AND PURUNLLACTA

Even with no attempt at restoration the ruined city complex of **KUELAP** is among the most overwhelming prehistoric sites in Peru. Only 40km south of Chachapoyas (along the Cajamarca road) it sits above the tiny village of TINGO in the verdant Utcubamba valley, remote and only rediscovered in 1843. To reach the village (where there is a small *pension*) take one of the trucks which cruise around the main square in Chachapoyas around 9 every morning, picking up passengers for the long journey along the road to Celedin; ask someone to give you a nudge when you get to Tingo (it's easily missed). A road giving access to the scattered community, collectively known as *Kuelap*, was under construction until 1981 when the project was (for good or bad) abandoned. Consequently, the actual **site** is reached only by a hard 1,500m climb (around 4 hours) from the west bank of the Utcubamba river.

The fortress is situated on a ridge, commanding terrific views of the surrounding landscape, but it is the structure itself which immediately arrests your attention. It really is enormous, with walls towering to 20m in height. Some are constructed with gigantic limestone slabs arranged into geometric patterns; other sectors are faced with rectangular granite blocks over 40 courses high. Going inside the ruins you come across hundreds of round stone houses decorated with a distinctive zig-zag pattern (like the local modern ceramics), small carved animal heads, condor designs and intricate serpent figures. There are also various enclosures and large crumbling watch-towers partly covered in wild subtropical vegetation, shrubs and even trees. One of these towers is an inverted, truncated cone containing a large bottle-shaped cavity, probably an ancient reservoir. It has been calculated that some 40 million cubic feet of building material was used at Kuelap, three times the volume needed to construct the Great Pyramid of Egypt. It is the strongest, most easily defended of all Peruvian fortress-cities and, occupied from about AD 1000 by the Chachapoyas tribe, is thought to be the site which the rebel Inca, Manco, considered using for his last-ditch stand against the Conquistadores in the late 1530s. He never made it here, ending up instead in the equally breathtaking Vilcabamba area, just north of Cuzco.

The only residents in the ruins today are two rather lonely guardians, José and Domingo, always delighted to receive visitors. José provides hot food and they have recently finished building a small *albergue* to accommodate anyone who would prefer to sleep in the ruins than back down in Tingo. You can also camp, but either way you'll be best off with your own sleeping bag. The guardians are familiar with other, smaller ruins in the immediate vicinity (such as **Revash**, near the village of SANTO TOMAS) and will also direct those prepared for larger expeditions to the village of CHOTAMAL, where guides and mules are available to still more remote, largely unexplored sites, or to LEVANTO (a few hours' walk from here) with its beautiful ruins of **Yalap**.

The most impressive of the charted ruins in the Utcubamba valley, however, are those of the archaic metropolis of **PURUNLLACTA**. This can be reached fairly easily from Chachapoyas by taking the daily bus to PIPOS on the MENDOZA road; getting off here you can walk to the village of CHETO, from where it's a short climb to the ruined city. The return trip is possible in a day – though it's more enjoyable to camp at the site. Purunllacta is considered to have been the capital and one of the seven major cities of the Chachapoyas culture, all of which were eventually conquered by the Inca Tupac Yupanqui in the 1470s. The 'site' consists of numerous groups of buildings scattered around the hilltops, all interconnected by ancient roads and each one surrounded by elegant agricultural terraces. At the centre of the ruined city you can clearly make out rectangular stone buildings, plazas, stairways and platforms. The most striking are still two storeys high, constructed in carved limestone blocks. The explorer Gene Savoy estimated that the entire complex covered about 150 square km – and even if only one-third of this calculation, it is an astonishing accomplishment.

Characteristic of this region are **necropoli** with elaborately moulded anthropomorphic sarcophagi, often stuck inaccessibly into horizontal crevices high up along cliff faces and painted in vivid colours. A fine example – and a third rewarding excursion from Chachapoyas – is the **PUEBLO DE LOS MUERTOS** ('City of the Dead') some 30km to the north. This is positioned a short way above the **Lake of Tingobamba**, easily enough reached by taking the CHICLAYO bus to PUENTE TINGOBAMBA or by hitching on one of the many trucks along this road. The **sarcophagi** are about 3 hours' hike from Puente (ask directions there), up to 2m high, carved with human faces, and staring blankly across the valley from a natural fault in the rock face. Each one has been carefully moulded into an elongated egg-like shape from a mixture of mud and vegetable fibres, then painted purple and white with geometric zig-zags and other superimposed designs. Savoy described them aptly as 'standing like ten pins in a bowling alley', and most of them are still intact. If you get close in, though, you can see that the casings are hollow, some containing mummies wrapped in funerary shrouds, others just filled with sun-bleached bones. Protected as they are from the weather by an overhang, these ancestors of the Chachapoyas race may well be watching over their land for at least another thousand years.

INTO THE JUNGLE: TWO RIVER TRIPS TO IQUITOS

Two rough, very adventurous **journeys by land and river** will take you on from CHACHAPOYAS to the Peruvian jungle capital of **IQUITOS** not far from the Brazilian border on the Rio Amazonas. It's difficult to estimate the length of each trip – there are always inevitable waiting periods for connections and embarkations – though you'd be unlikely to do either in less than a week's hard travelling. Unless, of course, you take the easy way out: at Moyabamba and Yurimaguas there are a number of airstrips with scheduled internal flights.

The Moyabamba–Yurimaguas route

The main overland route to Iquitos, this involves one of the best of Peru's Amazon river trips – not as long as most, and reasonably straightforward. You begin, however, by taking a series of trucks and *colectivos*: first (by truck) from CHACHAPOYAS along the Mayo river valley to RIOJA/MOYABAMBA, then (by *colectivo*) to TARAPOTO, and finally north (by truck) to the end of the road at YURIMAGUAS. It takes about 12 hours in the dry season to reach **RIOJA/MOYABAMBA**, twin towns set just above the Rio Mayo in a hot, humid, tropical forest environment. Moyabamba is the older of the two, founded in 1539 by Don Alonso de Alvarado on one of his earliest explorations into the Amazon jungle. Although a small town, like Chachapoyas it is the capital of a large – though for the most part sparsely populated – *departmento*. During the colonial period it was a camp for pioneers, missionaries and explorers – like Pedro de Urzúa who used it as a base on his search for the 'Land of Cinnamon', one of the mythical carrots cleverly used by Pizarro to keep his men happy and busy. Having noticed Indians using dry buds which tasted of cinnamon in cooking, Urzúa conceived a goal almost as alluring and potentially as lucrative as El Dorado's gold. If he had been successful in finding cinnamon plantations in the jungles where the Indians traded for it, then the Portuguese monopoly with the Spice Islands could have been challenged, Columbus's original aspirations fulfilled and Moyabamba might have become a rich city. As you can see today, Urzúa failed in his attempt, and Moyabamba is much the same as any other jungle town – hot, muddy and laid back, with a Cathedral and a cheap **hotel** (the *Monterrey*) on the Plaza de Armas.

From Moyabamba there are regular **colectivos** to **TARAPOTO** (4–5 hours), a larger town with a *Turistas hotel* (complete with swimming pool) and a military airbase connecting the Iquitos Amazon with the coast. The town is located only 420m above sea-level yet the Huallaga river flows on from here, via the Amazon, until it finally empties into the Atlantic Ocean. A strange sort of place, Tarapoto has a large prison and a big drug-smuggling problem, with people flying out coca paste from here to Colombia, where it is processed into cocaine for the US market. There are a few **hotels** – the *Hotel Gran* on the main plaza is reasonable – but, transit aside, the town doesn't have a lot of interest for travellers. You could, however, make a trip to the nearby village of **LAMAS**, about 30km up into the forested hills. This is a small, exotic, native settlement whose inhabitants are reputed to be direct descendants of the Chanca tribe who escaped from the Andes to this region in the fifteenth century, fleeing from the clutches of the conquering Inca army. The people still keep themselves very much to themselves, carrying on a highly distinctive life-style which displays an unusual combination of jungle and mountain Indian cultures – the women wearing long blue skirts and colourfully embroidered blouses (more typical of the Ecuadorian Sierra), the men adorning themselves on ceremonial occasions with strings of brightly plumed, stuffed macaws. Everyone goes barefoot and speaks a curious dialect, a mixture of *Quechua* and *Cahuapana* (a forest Indian tongue), and the town is traditionally renowned for its *brujos* (wizards) who use a potent hallucinogen, *Ayahuasca*, for their night-time divinatory and healing sessions. The best month to visit is August when the village's **festival** is in full swing, the days are spent dancing and drinking and most of the tribe's weddings occur. There isn't a htoel here, but if you ask nicely someone may let you camp in their garden, or alternatively you can easily make it there and back from Tarapoto in a day. The *Lamas* are renowned all over Peru as the best jungle porters – being able to carry large loads quickly over vast distances, never using river transport if it can be avoided.

From Tarapoto it's another 140km by rugged road to **YURIMAGUAS**. In the dry season you can make this by truck in about 6 hours, but from November till March it's more likely to take between 10 and 15. There are **hotels** in Yurimaguas (the *Estrella* is best) but I would recommend going straight to the port to look for **boats downstream to Iquitos**. These leave regularly though not at any set times; it's simply a matter of finding a reliable Captain (preferably the one with the biggest, newest or fastest looking boat) and arranging details with him; the normal price is about $15 – which isn't bad for a four-day trip inclusive of food. All you actually need to take is a hammock and sun hat, but some extra biscuits, bottles of drink and tinned fish – and if you want to try fishing yourself, a line and hooks (sold in the town's *fereterias*) – will make this magnificent, but tiring, river journey all the more enjoyable. The scenery en route is electric: the river gets steadily wider and slower, and the vegetation on the river banks more and more dense. Remember, though that during the day time the sun beats down with incredible force and wearing a sunhat is essential to avoid 'river fever' – sweats and the trots caused by the constant strong light reflected off the water.

An alternative – via Oracuzar

A more sensational route to Iquitos, but really only for the seasoned outward-bound traveller, is **from Chachapoyas via Oracuzar**. The first stage here is relatively simple – you take the daily **Chiclayo bus** to BAGUA GRANDE or JAEN and then pick up a truck bound for ORACUZAR.

Shortly before arriving at Oracuzar you pass through **PUERTO DELPHUS** (250km from Chachapoyas). At this small port (ask in the restaurants if you need a *pension*) you can find **boats going down the Marañon river**. Only a few launches will be going all the way to Iquitos, so you'll have to decide on the spot whether to risk attempting the journey in stages (which can involve many days of waiting in river settlements) or to stick it out in Puerto Delphus until someone offers to take you the whole way. This river trip never fails to be an experience including shooting rapids in the first couple of days, before the Marañon smooths out into a pacific snake of water, gliding slowly on towards Iquitos, Brazil and the Atlantic. The whole expedition should take around six days on the river, more if you choose to do it in stages with smaller craft. You'll need all the things that were required for the Yurimaguas–Iquitos journey, but it is advisable to take enough **food** for at least ten days (and lots of **mosquito repellent**) just in case you get stuck (as I have) for a week on the riverbank literally in the middle of nowhere. Only one thing is certain about this route – when you arrive in Iquitos it'll appear to be the biggest, best stocked city you've ever come across, after a week or so of eating only fish, yucca and bananas.

TRAVEL DETAILS

Buses and/or colectivos

From Trujillo Lima (several daily; 9 hrs); Chiclayo/Piura (several daily; 3hrs/7hrs); Cajamarca (several daily; 8hrs).

From Cajamarca Lima (several daily; 17hrs); Celedin (daily; 5hrs); Chachapoyas (Every Tue. and Sun; 20hrs); Chiclayo (daily; 7hrs).

From Chachapoyas Chiclayo (daily via Jaen; 17hrs); Rioja/Moyabamba (irregular trucks; 12hrs; thence on to Tarapoto and Iquitos – see text above).

Flights

From Trujillo Daily to Lima; Mon., Wed. and Fri. to Trujillo. From Cajamarca Mon., Wed. and Fri. to Trujillo and Lima.

From Rioja/Moyabamba Daily to Lima (except Thurs. and Sat.); Tue. and Sat. to Chiclayo.

From Tarapoto Daily to Lima; Wed. and Fri. to Trujillo; Tue., Thurs., Fri. and Sat. to Iquitos.

From Yurimaguas Daily to Lima (except Thurs. and Sat.); Tue. and Sun. to Iquitos.

Chapter six
THE NORTHERN DESERT

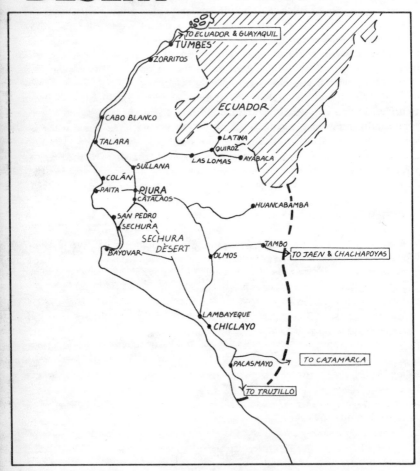

One of the most travelled but least visited parts of Peru, the **Northern Desert** has a distinct and complex identity. Its popular image is of a desolate zone of scattered rural communities – a myth which belies both past and present. Before Pizarro arrived here in the sixteenth century, to begin the Conquest, it had formed part of both Inca and Chimu Empires and hosted a number of local pre-Columbian cultures. Today, its main cities of **Chiclayo** and **Piura** are each important and lively commercial centres – serving not only the desert coast but large areas of the Andes as well.

In comparison to the region around Trujillo, or to southern Peru, it's not an area of great or spectacular interest. There are, however, a number of worthwhile lesser **sites** around both Chiclayo and Piura, a couple of adventurous **routes into the Andes** (to **Huancabamba** and **Ayabaca**), and a series of smaller **coastal resorts** – the only ones on the Peruvian coast where the sea is ever really warm. If, like so many travellers, you decide to bus through from Trujillo to Tumbes (or vice versa) in a single journey you'll be missing out on all of this – and also the region's strong sense of history. It was at Tumbes that Pizarro's Andalucian sea-pilot Bartholomew Ruiz discovered the first evidence of civilisation – a large balsa sail-raft – beyond the known world south of the Equator in 1527. And here too, five years on, the Conquistadores set anchor before the northern city outposts of the Inca kingdom.

With the Andes rising over 6,000m to the east, this northern coastal strip of Peru has always been slightly isolated. Coast-mountain access even today is restricted to just three **roads**, only two of them straggling over and down to navigable sites along the jungle rivers. And, worse perhaps than the rugged terrain, the region is subject to extremely heavy rainfall. In 1983 rains devastated even the normally arid coast around Tumbes and Piura, destroying the year's crops, carrying away bridges and washing away most of the few existing roads.

THE PAN AMERICAN FROM TRUJILLO TO CHICLAYO

The **Pan American**, mainstay of the north's transport system, offers a fast approach from TRUJILLO to CHICLAYO. An impressively stark and barren landscape, it is broken by few villages – though the valleys here have yielded notable finds from the 'Early Formative' cultures.

SAN PEDRO DE LLOC, the first settlement of any real size, puntuates the countryside for miles around with its tall white-washed Republican buildings, its old town wall and railway station (now inactive but a National Monument). A quiet little village, San Pedro has one small hotel and a reputation for its local delicacy of stuffed lizards – something I've yet to find on any menu. If you're around here in late June it may be worth some planning to coincide with the town *Fiesta*, held on the 29th amid colourful religious processions.

Ten km to the north a huge cement works heralds the approach of **PACASMAYO**, a growing port and town with a rather grim roadside appearance. Despite this it's not unattractive, particularly if you've time to wander down to the old jetty, and a useful point to get trucks up to

CAJARMACA (though buses are easier from Trujillo or Chiclayo). If you need to stay overnight there a few small hotels, though it's unlikely that you'll get stranded.

The one site along this stretch of road is only a few kilometres beyond, just before you reach the village of GUADALUPE. At the beginning of a large curve in the route a track leads off left towards the coast. This runs down to the well-preserved ruins of **PACATNAMÚ** – the *City of Sanctuaries* – overlooking the mouth of the Jecetepeque river. Ubbelohde-Döering excavated these remains in 1938 and 1953 showing them to be a great complex of pyramids, palaces, store-houses and dwellings. Digging up the forecourts in front of the pyramids and some nearby graves he discovered that the place was first occupied during the Gallinazo period (around 350 AD). It was subsequently conquered by the Mochica and Chimu cultures. Being off the main road and not too close to any towns, Pacatnamú has survived relatively untouched by archaeologists, treasure hunters or curious browsers – a very abandoned city. If you can get here by colectivo or bus fairly early one morning it is possible to check out the ruins and hitch on or back to Trujillo or Chiclayo without much problem. The road is busy with plenty of trucks, some half empty colectivos, buses and private cars – but it gets very hot without shade around midday and if you're going to linger you should take your own food and drink.

There are more ruins, probably of similar age, at ZAÑA – right beside the small town of MOCUPE (several kilometres before Chiclayo) – but effectively destroyed by floods in the eighteenth century, they present only an eerie half-outline.

CHICLAYO AND LAMBAYEQUE

Unusual among Peruvian towns, **CHICLAYO** is an active commercial centre through its strategic position, rather than any industrial development. Originally it was just a small annex to the old colonial town of **Lambayeque**, 12km north, but things have swung the other way over this century with all the vibrancy and energy concentrated here.

As ever the heart of the town is the **Plaza de Armas**, where you'll find the Cathedral and municipal buildings. The main focus of activity is along the main **Avenida Jose Balta**, between the plaza and the town's fascinating **mercado central**. Packed daily with food vendors at the centre, and other stalls around the outside, this is one of the best markets I've come upon in the north – and a revelation if you've just arrived in the country. A kind of rayfish known as *la guitarra* is hung up to dry in the sun before being sold to make one of the favourite local specialities – *pescado seco*. There's a whole section of live animals, including wild fox cubs, canaries, and even the occasional condor chick. One famous baby condor was bought here several years ago and has been reared to work in an amazing circus act, terrifying the spectators as it swoops down from a trapeze with its 3m wing-span fully spread. But probably the most compelling displays are the herbalists' shops, selling everything from herbs and charms to whale-bones and hallucinogenic cacti. The Chiclayo area, and more specifically Lambayeque, is a centre for wizard healers and traditional folk-medicine in general.

At weekends in Chiclayo, families crowd out to the **beaches** of SANTA ROSA and LA PIMENTEL – each well served by buses from the market area. Santa Rosa is the main fishing village on the Chiclayo coast and scores of big colourful boats go out early every morning – along with the occasional *caballito de tortora*, reed canoes used by people here for almost two millennia. If you ask local permission it's usually OK to camp out at either beach, or there's a cheapish hotel at Santa Rosa. At weekends, too, the *Chiclayanos* congregate for the Sunday afternoon **horse races** at the town's *Santa Victoria Hipodromo*, 2km south of the Plaza de Armas (just off the Avenida Roosevelt).

Most of the good, reasonably priced **hotels** in Chiclayo are around the Plaza de Armas or along José Balta, the street leading towards the market; the *Mediterranea*, on the latter, is reccommended. If you need it, **tourist information** is available from two offices: one on Las Acacias 305 (tel 4409); and the other in the street behind the Cathederal, Sáenz Peña 838. The **Correo** is seven blocks west of the plaza, just before the *Hotel de Turistas* on the Avenida Felipe Santiago Salaverry (a continuation of Elias Aguirre); whilst money can be changed in most of the **banks** near the plaza or (all day long) in the travel agents next to the Hotel Royal. Most of the **buses**, and some **colectivos**, leave from the market area; the main exception are *colectivos* to Trujillo which run from the Plaza de Armas.

Lambayeque

Only a short *colectivo* ride – from Chiclayo market – **LAMBAYEQUE** is a rather forlorn old colonial town, quite a grand place in the seventeenth century but fallen well into decay for most of the years since. Its main pull, beyond a handful of fine old mansions, is the unexpectedly modern and extremely well-stocked **Brunning Museum** (open daily 9–12 and 3–5; closed Sun. pms). Named after its founder, a successful businessman and expert in the ancient Mochica language and culture, the museum boasts superb collections of early ceramics and metal work. The Lambayeque valley is long renowned for turning up pre-Columbian metallurgy – particularly gold pieces from the neighbouring hill graveyard of *Zacame* – and local *huaqueros* (site treasure hunters) have sometimes gone so far as using bulldozers to dig them out.

On an incidental and somewhat more prosaic note, Lambayeque is also known for its sweet pastry cakes – filled with manjar blanca and touted under the unlikely name of *king-kongs!* Between here and Lima, travelling on the buses or walking the streets of any town, you're bound to be bombarded with *ambulantes* (street vendors) pushing out piles of the cake, shouting 'King-Kong! King-Kong!'

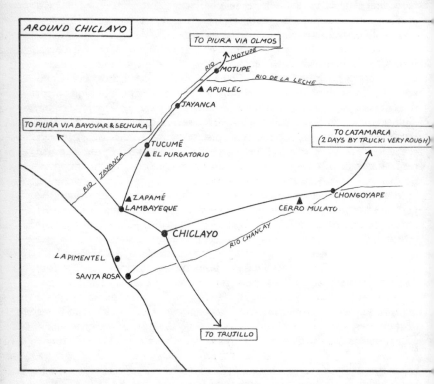

AROUND CHICLAYO

TO PIURA VIA OLMOS
RIO MOTUPE
RIO MOTUPE
MOTUPE
RIO DE LA LECHE
APURLEC
JAYANCA
TO PIURA VIA BAYOVAR & SECHURA
TUCUMÉ
EL PURGATORIO
RIO JAYANCA
TO CAJAMARCA
(2 DAYS BY TRUCK; VERY ROUGH)
ZAPAMÉ
LAMBAYEQUE
CERRO MULATO
CHONGOYAPE
CHICLAYO
RIO CHANCAY
LA PIMENTEL
SANTA ROSA
TO TRUJILLO

SITES AROUND CHICLAYO: CERRO MULATO, EL PURGATORIO AND APURLEC

A northern heartland of successive ancient cultures, it was in the Chiclayo area that Pizarro and his mob actually turned inland in search of the city of Cajamarca, the Inca overlord Atahualpa and the legendary treasures. There is some dispute among historians as to which route they in fact took into the mountains but it's generally accepted to have been along the course of either the Chancay or Saña rivers – both just south of modern Chiclayo.

A similar route today to CAJAMARCA (see p. 205) takes the best part of two days by local trucks, a rough and hardgoing journey. You can get an initial sense of it, however, just by travelling up to **CHONGOYAPE**

– an attractive journey which follows the climb of the Chancay valley. The road at this stage, 80km out of Chiclayo is tarmacked and there's a regular service by bus or *colectivo*. A bright little hill town, Chongoyape lies close to the site of **Cerro Mulato**, where you can see some impressive Chavin petroglyphs (engraved stones). Around the region, too, archaeologists have uncovered a number of graves, their finds indicating that the Chavin feline cult survived well into the fifth century BC, the latest yet recorded.

You could camp at Chongoyape if you're waiting for trucks on to Cajamarca, or at nearby **TINAJONES**, site of a massive new irrigation project, there's a new **tourist centre** offering swimming, sailing and water-skiing facilities.

For most travellers, though, the **Chimu culture ruins** en route to Piura are likely to prove more immediate and accessible targets. Both of these sites – *El Purgatorio* and *Apurlec* – can be visited within a day's trip from Chiclayo (*colectivos* from Pedro Ruiz between the plaza and market, or local bus to Olmos), or starting early in the day you could just about take them in and continue on to Piura. Whichever way you decide on, take some drink and a sunhat: neither site has any shade and for the return journey you'll probably have to hang around waiting to wave down a bus or truck.

CHAUVRNOID DESIGN (FROM A VASE DISCOVERED AT CHONGOYAPE)

EL PURGATORIO, just outside TUCUME (20km north of Lambayeque), was a major Chimu city – second in size and spendour only to the great capital of Chan Chan (see p. 194). Spread on and around the base of a hill it remains an extensive site, the ruins of adobe pyramids, raised platforms, walls and courtyards all quite visible. It has apparently yielded few archaeological remains and virtually no treasure – nothing like the riches found at the hill-grave of Zapame by Lambayeque – but it's a place with a reputation of great local power. *Curanderos*, healing wizards, still perform their magical rites here. Near the site is the **Huaca Pintada**, an adobe temple, also of Chimu construction, which was covered with beautiful coloured murals when it was unearthed in 1916.

El Purgatorio was part of an enormous Chimu irrigation complex which took water from the rivers Chancay and Leche to sustain the cultivated areas essential for a developing urban population. **APURLEC**, another vast adobe city a little further north, was another link in the chain. First occupied in the eighth century BC it seems to have still been flourishing 500 years later under the great Chimu planners and architects. There are remains here, scattered over a huge area, of pyramids, forts and palaces, temples and store-houses, and long city streets. Built throughout from adobe, mud-bricks raised from the dust, its walls have been eroded by heavy rains but are again quite recognisable.

Heading on in either direction from APURLEC you'll do well to hitch any truck going any way. At **MOTUPE** there are *colectivos* back to CHICLAYO, or buses on to the small town of **OLMOS** where the track off to JAEN and CHACHAPOYAS (see p. 211) leaves the main trail. Around Olmos another new irrigation project is in the process of construction, allowing water to be pumped down through tunnels from the Amazonian watershed. Beyond, the old route of the Pan American Highway extends on through the arid sands into the Piura valley and to the city itself. There are fairly regular buses at each stage of the way.

NORTH TO PIURA: THROUGH THE SECHURA DESERT

Buses and *colectivos* between CHICLAYO and PIURA can take any of three different routes: that via OLMOS outlined above; the new *Expresso* section of the Pan American – right through the middle of the Sechura desert; or around its edge – down to the sea near the oil refineries of BAYOVAR and on along the coast past a series of small fishing hamlets to the town of SECHURA. If you particularly want to take one or other of these routes you'll have to check with the buses beforehand. They vary between around 4–6 hours and each, though impressive in its desert scenery, is a journey where you'll want to keep some reading to hand.

The route via Sechura is a slightly strange one. The buses run quickly towards the turning to **BAYOVAR** (which is itself a forbidden zone) and then switch up to the coast at a vast obelisk and roundabout right in the middle of nowhere. To the south, accessible only on foot, are the **Sechura hills** – an isolated and unofficial wildlife reserve of wild goats and foxes, and the occasional condor come to feast on washed-up, rotting carcasses of whales and sea-lions. There is no water in the region, and it's a good three days' walk from the road to the beach; maps are available in Lima, however, if you're interested in a serious exploration.

North of the roundabout there is little more – just a handful of hermit goat-herders and two or three scattered groups of roadside restaurants until you approach the edge of the desert and the town of SECHURA.

As you do, there are a few tiny hamlets – basically clusters of huts on the beach – often inhabited by the same fishing families since no-one knows how long before the Conquest. The last of these, **PARACHIQUE**, has recently developed into a motorised port with its own fishmeal factory; the others are all very simple, their inhabitants mostly using sailing boats to fish, and often going out to sea for days at a time.

SECHURA itself is not a large place, though the tall twin towers of its seventeenth-century church have a definite air of return to civilisation. Local legend has it that the church here was built over a pre-Incaic temple, from which an underground tunnel leads out to the ocean and where no doubt treasure was once reputed to be hidden. To the south of the town – between the sea and road – a long line of white crescent **dunes**, or *lomas*, reaches into the distance: another link with the past according to local people who claim that they were used by Incas as landmarks across the desert. If you want to take a closer look at the dunes it's possible to hire four-wheel drive cars by asking around the town. Just a few kilometres to the east there's a huge, supposedly enchanted, star-crescent dune – reached along soft sandy tracks which are too much for most vehicles. If you want to stop overnight here it's possible to **camp** anywhere (including the beach), or there's a small **hostal**. The town's **food market** is a good one and there are also several **restaurants**, the best probably *Don Gilberto's* on the main plaza. Unless the desert excites you, however, there's a lot more life and interest in PIURA, a fast 52km bus ride to the north.

PIURA AND AROUND

The city of **PIURA** feels very distinct from the rest of the country, cut off to the south by the formidable Sechura desert, to the east by the Huancabamba mountains. The people here, too, seem primarily Piurans rather than Peruvians, and the town itself has a strong oasis atmosphere, entirely dependent on the vagaries of the Rio Piura – known since Pizarro's time as the *Rio Loco*, 'Crazy River'. Despite this precarious existence, Piura is the oldest colonial town in Peru. And this century – when alone it has weathered two serious droughts and seven major floods (the last in 1983) – it has grown into a *departmento* of over a million people, around a quarter of them actually living in the city. With temperatures of up to 37° from January to March the region produces more limes than any other. It has also spawned a particularly wide-brimmed straw sombrero, worn by everyone from the mayor to local goat-herders.

Francisco Pizarro spent ten days here in 1532 on his way to that fateful meeting with the Inca overlord, Atahualpa, at Cajamarca. Beginning life as San Miguel de Piura, the town had well over 200 Spaniards by 1534, including the first Spanish women. All were hungry for a slice of the action – and treasure – but although Pizarro kept over 57,000 pesos for himself, he only gave 15,000 to the Piurans; the cause of some considerable resentment, this probably marked the origin of the town's isolationist attitude. Pizarro did, however, encourage the development here of an urban class, drawn from the sick or invalided, and destined for trade rather than war. As early as the 1560s there was a flourishing trade in the excellent indigenous Tanguis cotton, and Piura today still has a third of the nation's production.

The **modern town** is divided in half by the river, although you'll find most of the action and all the main hotels, bars, restaurants, etc. on the west bank. Within a few blocks from the middle bridge is the main square, a very attractive **Plaza de Armas** shaded by tall tamarind trees planted well over a hundred years ago. On the plaza you can see the 'Statue of Liberty', nicknamed *La Pola* (the pole) by Piurans, and, as usual in Peru, the **Cathedral**. Though not especially beautiful it's quite striking in the impressive bronze nails decorating its main doors and in its tasteless gilt altars and intricate wooden pulpit.

Perhaps more interesting from a traveller's point of view are the museums. On Avenida Tacna is the **Museo Grau**, the nineteenth century home of Miguel Grau – one of the heroes of the War of the Pacific (1879–80) in which Chile successfully took control of Peru's valuable nitrate fields in the south and permanently cut Bolivia's access to the Pacific. A British-built ship – the *Huascar* – was Peru's only successful blockade runner, and a model is displayed here, along with various military artifacts and a small archaeological section. It is open Mon.– Sat., 9am–6pm. Stronger on the region's archaeological finds – and in particular the ceramics from Vicus (see below) – is the museum in the **Municipalidad** (3rd floor; open Mon.-Fri., mornings only); whilst there's a third museum, with quite extensive Incaic sections, at Avenida Loreto 818.

Other points to wander out to while you're in town are two neatly laid out **parks** dedicated to the *Conquistadores*, Pizarro and Cortes, and the old bridge connecting the main part of Piura with the less salubrious east-bank **Tacala** quarter. Tacala is renowned for the quality and strength of its fermented *chicha* beer and on Friday afternoons you'll find the bars here packed out with thirsty folk beginning the weekend with a tangy jar.

As far as **nightlife** goes, there are a couple of theatres which often have good visiting shows (details from the tourist office), but the in places to hang out are a handful of nightclub-discos – try *El Tiburon*, 2km south along the Pan American Highway, or *Hector's Bar*, nearer the centre at Av. Sanchez Cerro 408. Most Piurans, however, tend to spend their evenings strolling around the main streets, chatting in the plazas, and drinking in the relatively cheap **bars** along roads like Jiron Junin.

There are a few **local specialities**, probably the most popular being *natilla*, a rather tasty sweet toffee. Apart from this you can buy very well-made strawhats (invaluable for the desert), ceramics made in the village of Simbila, and a variety of leather crafts. The best place to buy stuff like this is the town's **model market**, one block before the Pan American North begins.

Hotels are well spread over Piura but most of them, including some of the more reasonably priced, are within a few blocks of the Plaza de Armas: an area roughly delineated by Av. Sanchez Cerro, Av. Grau, Av. Loreto and the river. The *Hotel San Jorge* on Plaza Grau and *San Martin* on Avenida Cuzco are among the best cheap possibilities. The **Correo** is actually on the Plaza de Armas, and there's a **money-change** section in the bank on the ground floor of the *municipalidad*. **Tourist information** and maps can be obtained from the official office on Calle Libertad (No. 945; tel. 326761) or from a desk at the airport. The main **festival** time is *Piura Week*, which takes place during the first 14 days of October: you'll find the town in high spirits, but beds scarce and cheques difficult to change. Most of the buses – including those to Paita, Tumbes and Chiclayo – leave from a station by the Plaza Grau.

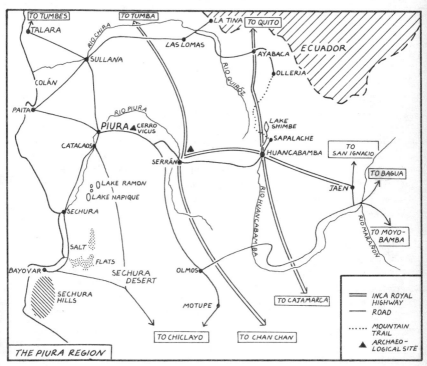

Catacaos

Just 12km south, down the Pan American Highway, **CATACAOS** is well worth some of your time. It's a friendly, dusty little place with a public TV in the main plaza – a gift from the mayor – and an excellent market just off it, which sells everything from food to craftgoods, even filigree gold and silverwork. A good buy are the hammocks hanging colourfully about the square, and the town itself is the best place around to have lunch, famous for its **picanterias** (spicy seafood restaurants) which serve up all sorts of local delicacies. Among these are *tamalitos verdes* (little green maize pancakes), fish-balls, *chifles* (fresh-made banana or sweet potato crisps) and superb goat (*seco de cabrito*). While you're here you can also try the sweet medicinal drink *algarrobina*, made from the berries of a desert tree. A last peculiarity of the village – not meant to be eaten! – are the amazing metallic-looking lizards: young boys try to sell them to everyone who arrives.

There are regular *colectivos* to Catacaos from the Avenida Tacna.

Vicus

At **CERRO VICUS**, 27km east of Piura on the old route to Chiclayo, there is an interesting pre-Incaic site 500m to the left of the main road. According to the kilometre milestone (which is calculated from Trujillo) this is at km 449.

There are no buildings associated with **the site**, probably due to the occasional heavy rains – which can destroy adobe ruins – but there are a number of L-shaped tombs, some up to 15m deep. These graves contained ceramics and metal artifacts revealing several styles – early Mochica the most predominant, superbly modelled in a variety of human, animal and architectural forms; there are good examples in the Piura museum and in Lima, Trujillo and Lambayeque.

To reach Cerro Vicus you can take any of the Olmos buses or *colectivos*. Ask to be dropped off at km 449 (making sure they don't drive past), then walk across the sand to the tombs on the hill. Most buses, and some trucks, will stop if you wave them down beside the road for the return trip to Piura.

SERRAN AND HUANCABAMBA

One of the more adventurous routes around Piura takes you into the hills to the east and – after some 215km and up to 15 hours by bus or truck – to the remote village of **HUANCABAMBA**. According to the chronicler Cieza de Leon, the Inca Topa Yupanqui (1471–93) expanded his empire into this region, taking 'five moons' to subdue the local tribe. The subsequent Inca lord, Huayna Capac, was also forced to return here to restore order.

Up until the Spanish Conquest, the town of Huancabamba was an important crossroads in the Royal Highway. This traversed the Andes, connecting the Inca Empire from Santiago (Chile) to Quito in Ecuador: at Huancabamba one sideroad went down to the coast, linking with the ancient desert highway at Zaran (modern Serran), the other east to Jaen along the forested Marañon watershed, a trading link with the fierce jungle headhunters of the Aguaruna tribe. Even before the Incas arrived the Huancabamba had an extremely active trade – ferrying goods such as feathers, animal skins, medicines and gold from the jungle Indians to the coastal cultures of the Mochica, and later, Chimu.

It was at **SERRAN**, then a small Inca administrative centre, where in 1532 Pizarro waited for Hernando de Soto and a small troop whom he had sent up the Inca road on a discovery mission. Some of this highway was wide enough for six horsemen to ride abreast and it took de Soto just two days and a night to reach the town of Cajas, not far from Huancabamba. Here they gained a first insight into the grandeur and power that the Incas clearly possessed, although, under orders from Atahualpa, the 2,000–warrior garrison had slunk away into the mountains. The Spaniards, given free rein, were not slow to discover the most impressive Inca building – a sacred convent of over 500 mamaconas (virgins of the sun) who had been chosen at an early age to dedicate their lives to the Inca religion. They raped at will, provoking the Inca representative with de Soto to threaten that they would die for such sacrilege committed only 300km from Atahualpa's camp.

This was exactly the information de Soto had been seeking. And after a brief visit to the adjacent, even more impressive, Inca town of Huancabamba – where a tollgate collected duties along the Royal Highway – he returned to rejoin Pizarro. With him de Soto brought the Inca envoy, who invited the Spaniards to Atahualpa's camp at Cajamarca. On behalf of the lord Inca he presented two stone fortress-shaped fountains, some 'fine stuffs of wool embroidered with gold and silver', and a quantity of goose-flesh scent. In return Pizarro made somewhat symbolic gifts of a crimson cap and cheap glass jewellery.

You can still see the ruins of the Inca settlement of **Zaran**, just a short walk from the modern settlement; but **Cajas** seems to be temporarily lost in the region around Huancabamba and Lake Shimbe. Presumably it lies somewhere along the old Inca highway.

In places near the modern village of **HUANCABAMBA** you can make out stretches of this: ancient stone slabs, quite easy to spot alongside the modern road. The actual Inca town here has vanished but, being well made of stone, it too must be around. Today, the village, which is apparently slipping down its hill on very watery foundations, is famous throughout Peru for its **curanderos** – healing wizards or curers, who utilise herbal and hallucinogenic remedies in conjunction with ritual bathing in sacred lagoons such as Lake Shimbe, 2,000m and 7 hours' mule ride above the town. These *curanderos* are visited by Peruvians from all walks of life who want to cure ailments which don't respond to modern medicine.

The name *Huancabamba* means 'valley of the stone spirit guardians': quite fitting, since you can still see the tall pointed stones guarding fields in the sheltered valley. The lake area above the town is much less hospitable, around 4,000m above sea-level, and with sparse marshy vegetation. It is usually possible to hire mules and a guide to take you up to the lake – or even on the five-day trek, keeping close to the old Royal Highway, to AYABACA and the nearby Inca fortress of AYAPATE. These routes, though, are only for the really explorer-minded, and you should come equipped with maps from Lima (see p. 8). It's not a good idea to do it alone or without a local guide.

AYABACA can also be reached by road by **bus or truck**, a 15–hour journey if you're lucky. As for HUANCABAMBA these leave from around Piura's market area. Both towns have small **hostals**, but don't expect comfort. **Information** on both places, and a booklet on the Ayapate fortress (*Las Ruinas de Ayapate* by Mario Polia, 1972) can be obtained from the University in Piura.

NORTH TO TUMBES: PAITA, TALARA AND CABO BLANCO

The Pan American, north from PIURA, goes well wide of **PAITA** – though the town, set on a small peninsula at the mouth of the Rio Chira, has for many centuries been its port and nearest main settlement. With good roads to both PIURA (50km) and SULLANA, it is still a major centre – the country's fifth port – but is best known to many Peruvians as the former home of **Manuela Saenz**, the tragic mistress of Simon Bolivar during the Wars of Liberation. After the 1828 skirmishes with Colombia (of which Bolivar was dictator) Manuela was ostracised by Peruvian society, dying here in poverty in 1856. You can visit her house in the old quarter of town.

Overlooking Paita to the north is a small Spanish fortress built to protect the bay from pirates, and just beyond it the once elite bay of **Colan**. This is still a good place to swim, though the old wooden beach huts which used to echo with the chatter of wealthy land-owning families are now pretty well destroyed. They were washed away in 1983 by the swollen river Chira amid the dramatic floods of that rainy season. Other good beaches nearby include YACILA, HERMOSA and ESMERALDA.

Although only 40km from Piura, **SULLANA** is a major transport junction; quite a large town overlooking the usually dry, but occasionally flooded, river-bed. Here the Plaza de Armas and the old church of La

Santisima Trinidad are worth a quick stroll while you're switching transport – but otherwise, or if your ride takes you straight through, the town has little of interest to travellers. It's at Sullana, however, that you'll emerge if you have just entered Peru at the LA TINA border.

TALARA, some 70km north along the Pan American, is distinctly attractive – taking its name and function from Peru's most important coastal oilfield. It was just a small fishing hamlet until 1940, though its deep-water harbour and tar-pits had been used since Pizarro's time for caulking wooden ships. Pizarro in fact chose the site to build the first Spanish settlement in Peru but it proved too unhealthy and he was forced to look elsewhere, eventually hitting on what is today the city of Piura.

Talara's oil reserves, now a national refinery, were directly responsible for the last military coup in 1968. President Belaunde, then in his first term of office, had given sub-soil concessions to the multinational company IPC, declaring that 'if this is foreign imperialism what we need is more, not less of it'. A curious logic, based on his impressions of superior conditions at the plant, it led to the accusation that he had signed an agreement 'unacceptable to true Peruvians'. Within two months of the affair, and as a consequence (if not perhaps the underlying cause), he was deposed and exiled. One of the initial acts of the new revolutionary government was to nationalise IPC and declare the Act of Talara null and void. Today the town is highly industrialised, with fertiliser plants as well as the oil business. If you need to stop over there are a few reasonable **hotels** in the commercial centre. The nearest unpolluted beach is 2km away at LA PENA.

Thirty km or so beyond, with the road still running away from the beach, there is a short turn-off to EL ALTO and the old fishing mecca of **CABO BLANCO**. It is just off the cape here that the cold Humboldt Current meets the warm equatorial El Niño – a stroke of providence which creates an extraordinary abundance of marine life. Thomas Stokes, a British resident and fanatical fisherman, discovered the spot in 1935, and it was a very popular resort in the post-war years. Hemingway stayed some months in 1951, whilst two years later the largest fish ever caught with a rod was landed here – a 710 kilo black marlin. Changes in the offshore currents have brought decline in recent years but there are still international competitions and it is much reputed for swordfish. The club has one of the few official **campsites** in Peru, and there are a handful of **hotels** too.

From here to Tumbes the Pan American cuts across a further stretch of desert, for the most part keeping tight to the Pacific coastline. It's a straight road, but not a dull one, with immense views along the rolling surf and if you're lucky the occasional school of dolphins playing close to the shore. To the right of the road looms a long hill, the *Cerro de Amotape*, the largest bump along the entire Peruvian coast which isn't actually a proper Andean foothill. Amotape was a local chief whom Pizarro had killed in 1532 – an example to potential rebels; just to the north of this wooded hill, the ancient Inca highway can still be seen (though not from the road) on its way down the coast.

TUMBES AND THE BORDER CROSSINGS

Usually considered a mere pit-stop for overland travellers, the city of **TUMBES** has a significant and interesting history. It was the first town to be 'conquered' by the Spanish and has maintained its importance since – originally as the gateway to the Inca Empire, more recently through its strategic position on the controversial frontier with Equador. Despite two regional wars – in 1859 and 1941–2 – this is still felt to be an issue that has yet to be settled. Maps of the frontier vary depending on which country you buy them in, and the dispute occasionally breaks out on the surface – the last time in 1981 when military skirmishes closed the border for a month.

Predictably, Tumbes has a strong army presence and is very much a border town, most of its 85,000 population seemingly engaged in either transport or petty trading across the frontier. In many ways the people here are quite cut off from mainstream Peru, connected only by the Pan American Highway, and considerably nearer to Quito than to Lima. It is a surprisingly elegant place, however, at least in the centre with its broad plaza and long **Malecon** promenade built along the high riverbanks – the kind of town where although there is nothing much to do there is always something going on. In the rural areas around, nearly half of Peru's tobacco leaf is produced. Down the coast are some of the best **beaches** in the country, among them CALETA DE LA CRUZ, reputed to be the bay where Pizarro first landed. You can get out here by *colectivo* from the central plaza; there are restaurants and *rooms* to let if you want to stay.

Central Tumbes is itself well-endowed with restaurants and **hotels**. The *Hotel Estoril*, two blocks off the main plaza, is as good as any: cheap and surprisingly clean. The best place to try some of the traditional local food is probably *Peko's* where they regularly serve both *ceviche de conchas negras* (black scallop ceviche) and *caldo de bolas de platano* (banana-ball soup). Either of these can be washed down – at your peril – with *chinguirito*, a cocktail of coconut juice and fiery aguardiente. The travelling crowd tends to hang out around the central plaza, drinking ice-cold beers at *Monkey's Restaurant*: when there's a war on, all Ecuadorians are called monkeys – *monos* – by Peruvians. The official money exchange, the **Banco de la Nacion**, is also just off the main square, although the border and sometimes the town are usually milling with **black market** dealers. Be wary: these are renowned for trying to sell *soles* at a higher rate than the bank!

Pizarro and the Inca city of Tumbes

Pizarro didn't actually set foot in Tumbes when it was first discovered in 1527. He preferred to cast his eyes along the Inca city's adobe walls, its carefully irrigated fields, and its shining temple, from the comfort and safety of his ship. However, with the help of translators he set about learning as much as he could about Peru and the Incas during this initial contact. An Inca noble visited him aboard ship and even dined at his table. The noble was said to be especially pleased with his first taste of Spanish wine and the present of an iron hatchet.

The Spaniards who did go ashore – a Captain Alonso de Molina and his black servant – made reports of such grandeur that Pizarro refused at first to believe them, sending instead the more reliable Greek cavalier, Pedro de Candia. Molina's descriptions of the temple, lined with gold and silver sheets, were confirmed by Candia. He also gave the people of Tumbes their first taste of European technological might – firing his musket to smash a wooden board to pieces. With this Pizarro had all the evidence he needed; after sailing another 500km down the coast, as far as the Santa valley, he returned to Panama and then on to Spain to obtain royal consent and backing for his projected conquest.

The Tumbes people hadn't always been controlled by the Incas. The area was originally inhabited by the Tallanes, related to coastal tribes from Ecuador who are still known for their unusual lip and nose ornaments. In 1450 they were conquered for the first time – by the Chimu. Thirteen years later came the Incas, organised by Topac Inca, who bulldozed the locals into religious, economic and even architectural conformity in order to create their most northerly coastal terminus. A fortress, temple and sun convent were built, and the town colonised with loyal subjects from other regions – a typical Inca ploy which they called the *Mitimaes* system. The valley had an efficient irrigation programme, allowing them to grow, among other things, bananas, maize and squash.

It didn't take Pizarro long to add his name to the list of Tumbes conquerors. But after landing on the coast of Ecuador in 1532 with royal warrant to conquer and Christianise the land of Peru, his arrival at Tumbes was a strange affair. Despite the previous friendly contact, some of the Spanish were killed by Indians as they tried to beach, and when they reached the city it was completely deserted with many buildings destroyed, and, more painfully for Pizarro, no sign of gold.

It seems likely that Tumbes's destruction, prior to Pizarro's arrival, was the result of intertribal warfare directly related to the Inca Civil War. This, a war of succession between Atahualpa and his half brother, the legitimate heir Huascar, was to make Pizarro's role as conqueror a great deal easier. Tumbes itself he had taken without a struggle. Leaving a contingent behind to turn it into a 'real town', he set off down the coast, sending a squad under Hernando de Soto to survey the mountainous inland area.

The **ruined Inca city of** Tumbes lies 5km south-west of the modern town and although there's not a lot that you can make out these days it's a pleasant walk and both the temple and fortress are recognisable. The ruins are actually dissected by the modern Pan American Highway. Cows and goats from the nearby hamlet of San Pedro wander freely amongst the ancient adobe walls, devastated by centuries of intermittent flooding.

If you've never seen a mangrove swamp, **PUERTO PIZARRO** too is worth a visit, 7km further on. Buses and *colectivos* go regularly from Tumbes (by the *Roggero* bus depot) to this ancient fishing port. It had a commercial harbour until swamps grew out to sea, making it inaccessible for large boats and permanently disconnecting Tumbes from the Pacific. You can take short boat trips out to see the *rhizopora* mangle tree's dense root system and the wildlife, take part in organised shark-fishing and waterskiing, or just dangle your own hook and line into the warm water.

The Tumbes border
Crossing the border (open 8.30–12 and 2–6) is relatively simple in either direction. On the Peruvian side, at **Aguas Verdes**, there are two huts opposite one another on each side of the road. If you're facing the bridge into Ecuador, the hut on the right is where you get an exit (or entry) stamp for your passport, the hut on the left is the customs office. Once past these buildings it's a short walk to **Huaquillas**, the Ecuadorian border town and the immigration office where you'll get your entry (or exit) stamp.

In both directions the authorities sometimes require that you show an onward ticket (bus or plane) out of their respective countries. Unless you intend to recross the border inside a week or two it's not worth taking out any local currency. You won't be able to get a decent rate for *soles* in Ecuador or *sucres* in Peru, and inflation is such that even a fortnight can make quite a difference.

There are **buses** and **colectivos** several times an hour between Tumbes and Aguas Verdes, or you can take a **taxi** for less than $5.

La Tina: the alternative border
The crossing at **LA TINA**, to the east of Tumbes, is a longer route out of Peru but a fairly spectacular one – particularly in the scenery on the Ecuadorian side. The main disadvantage is the road up from SULLANA, an unbelievably bumpy 8–hour ride. **Buses** and **trucks**, however, travel daily in both directions – and though the service tends to be erratic (frequent breakdowns) everyone gets there in the end. The route became quite popular in 1983 as travellers tried to avoid some of the rain-devastated zones between Piura and Tumbes but it is usually a somewhat eccentric option.

Crossing over from LA TINA to the Ecuadorian town of LA MACARÁ there is a 2km walk (or overpriced taxis) at the International Bridge over the Macará river. If you're coming in the other direction, a somewhat adventurous possibility, **onward from La Tina**, is the Inca fortress of **AYAPATE** near the town of AYABACA, to the east along the Ecuadorian frontier. It is possible to get transport from Las Lomas; for more details see p. 230.

TRAVEL DETAILS

Buses and/or colectivos
From Chiclayo   Piura/Tumbes (several daily; 4hrs/10hrs); Trujillo/Lima (several daily; 3hrs/14hrs); Cajamarca (several daily; 8hrs); Chachapoyas (daily; 17hrs); Huancabamba (every Tue. and Fri.; 15–20hrs).
From Piura   Tumbes (several daily; 4–6hrs); La Tina; (every morning from Sullana; 6–8hrs); Aguas Calientes (at least hourly; 20mins).

From Tumbes   Aguas Calientes (at least hourly; 20mins); Lima (2 or 3 a day and night buses; 24hrs).

Flights
From Chiclayo   Daily to Lima, Trujillo, Piura and Talara; Tue. and Sat. to Rioja/Moyabamba; Mon. and Fri. to Tarapoto.
From   Piura   Daily   to   Lima,   via **Chiclayo**.
From Tumbes   Daily to Lima.

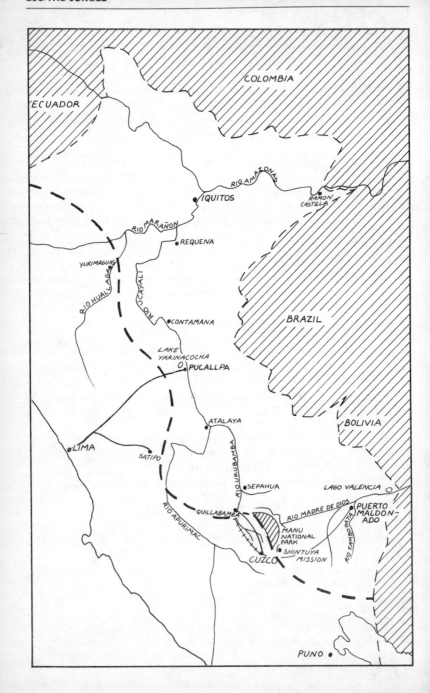

Chapter seven
THE JUNGLE

Few people think of Peru in terms of jungle. Yet despite the inroads of colonists and the ever-advancing lumber industry, almost two-thirds of the country is still covered by dense **tropical rain forest** – the beginnings of a vast Amazon flood plain which emerges from a myriad of Andean streams and extends right across the South American continent until it reaches the Atlantic over 4,000km away. Known to Peruvian outsiders as *El Infierno Verde* – 'the Green Hell' – this is a zone which until recent decades has known only plants, insects, birds, wild animals and scattered native tribes. The rivers fall through great rapids – *pongos* – like the Manseriche and Mainique, and beyond the main waterways much is still unexplored. Jaguars, ant-eaters and tapirs roam the forests, restricted only by their fear of native hunters; huge anacondas live in the swamps, cayman (the South American crocodile) along most riverbanks; and trees like the giant Shihuahuaco, strong enough to break an axe-head, grow as high as 50m.

The forests look endless from both land and air, but in fact are disappearing faster than anyone predicted: bulldozers, and colonists' cattle rapidly turning the wet jungle into arid desert. Beyond the main towns of **Iquitos, Pucallpa** and **Puerto Maldonado**, however, there are still few settlements of any size, and the jungle population remains dominated by around 35 **indigenous tribes**. Each of these have their own distinct language, customs and dress, though after centuries of external influence (missionaries, gold-seekers, rubber barons, soldiers, oil companies, anthropologists, tourists . . .) many jungle Indians also speak Spanish, and few live completely traditional lives. Some, brought into the market economy by selling produce to patrons or missionaries, now prefer to wear Western clothes and drink instant coffee. Others, increasingly pressurised, have been forced to struggle for their cultural and territorial rights, or to retreat well beyond the new frontiers of 'civilisation'.

For most of these traditional or semi-traditional tribes, the jungle offers a semi-nomadic existence. Communities are scattered, with groups of between ten and 200 people, and their sites shifted every few years. For subsistence they depend on small cultivated plots, fish from the rivers and game from the forest. The latter include wild-pigs, deer, monkeys and a great range of edible birds, whilst among jungle-fish are *sabalo* (a kind of salmon), *carachama* (an armoured fish) and the giant *zungaro* and *paiche* – the latter, at up to 200kg, the world's largest freshwater species. Life is by no means easy, yet the native groups here have kept it together for several millennia and generally spend no more than three to four days a week engaged in subsistence activities.

It's difficult to say for sure but many archaeologists reckon that the initial spark for the evolution of Peru's **High Cultures** came from the jungle. Evidence from Chavin, Chachapoyas and Tantamayo all seem to back up such a theory, and the **Incas** were certainly unable to dominate the jungle tribes – their main contact one of peaceful trade in treasured items like plumes, gold, medicinal plants and the sacred coca leaf. At the time of the **Spanish Conquest** fairly permanent settlements seem to have existed along all the major jungle rivers, the people living in large groups to farm the rich alluvial soils. Only with the arrival of the Europeans – and the incursions of the nineteenth-century rubber boom – do they appear to have broken up into smaller and scattered groups.

Prior to the onslaught of the rubber collectors, the Peruvian jungle had deterred major colonisation. Alonso de Alvarado, in 1537, had led the first Spanish expedition, cutting a trail through from Chachapoyas to Moyabamba, but most **expeditions** ended in utter disaster – defeated by the ferocity of the tribes, the danger of the rivers, climate and wild animals, and perhaps as much by the inherent surrealism of the forest. Throughout the centuries, too, there have been significant uprisings. In 1742 a group of tribes drove out all non-natives from their territories and chased the army back into the Andes as far as Tarma. And as recently as 1919 the Campa Indians were blockading the rivers and ejecting missionaries and foreigners from their ancestral lands.

The **rubber boom,** however, from the 1880s to just before the First World War, had a more prolonged effect. Treating the natives as little more than slaves, the Rubber Barons – men like the notorious Fitzcarraldo – made overnight fortunes and large sections of the forests were explored and subdued. It was a process which fell into decline when the British explorer Markham took Peruvian rubber plants – via Kew Gardens – to Malaysia, out-competing the dispersed South American methods of collection. But over the last decades its precedent has been more dangerously and irreversibly repeated in the intrusion of oil corporations and lumber companies, and the colonisation in their wake of large areas of land by mountain peasants. Over the next decades (see p. 292) forest Indian tribes face the very real danger of losing their land and culture completely, and the earth of seeing a diminishing and vital part of its ecology disappear.

JUNGLE ESSENTIALS AND PRACTICALITIES

Ignored by most travellers, the Peruvian jungle is the most exciting of all the country's regions – and the most exotic in every respect. If you go even a little off the beaten track this is *real* travelling, and an environment extraordinarily intense in its mesh of plant, insect and animal life. It is also, of course, an environment not to be taken lightly – the image of poisonous snakes, jaguars and mosquitoes is based on fact. However, once you're there, the myth usually seems to be dispelled as you realise that these dangers don't actually come hunting for you. And if you just want to take a look at the place, exploring the immediate environs of Puerto Maldonado, Pucallpa or Iquitos, you can do so with relative ease.

THINGS YOU'LL NEED TO TAKE If you don't intend to go much beyond the frontier towns there's little that you'll have to take except the usual baggage. Be sure, though, to include the following. *Malaria pills (starting the course in advance); cool daytime clothes; normal evening clothes (including socks, long sleeves, etc. because of mosquitoes); light shoes; waterproof covering (a piece of plastic will do); torch with extra batteries; water-tight box for camera equipment.*

Anyone intending to leave the towns behind for a couple of days or more, however, should be much better prepared. The chances are that you'll be travelling in a canoe and you'll need to keep all of your gear in plastic bags (just in case). Add the following:

A strong multi-purpose knife and tin-opener; medical kit including sticky plasters, bandages, antiseptic cream, antihistamine cream (for insect bites) Imodium or Lomotil against the Inca trots; blanket (preferable to a sleeping bag); hammock (perfect for sleeping but not absolutely essential); mosquito net and repellent (try 'Black Flag'); pair of plastic sandals (leather boots aren't much use — you spend half the time taking them off and putting them on again); candles; lots of boxes of matches (and an emergency fuel lighter — in case the matches get wet); some rope or strong string (never fails to come in handy); tinned fish; water biscuits; fresh fruit, noodles or rice; some beans; cooking pot and eating utensils; coffee or tea; toilet paper (leaves tend to be crawling with biting ants); and, if you're without a guide, a machete.

Apart from a good knife and the medical kit all of these things can be bought in any large jungle town.

HAZARDS The most likely is **river sickness**, a general term for the effect of the sun's strong rays reflected off the water. After several hours on the river, particularly at midday without the shade of a hat, you may get the first irksome symptom — the trots — sometimes followed by nausea or shaking fever; in extreme cases this can last for a day or two. If you're travelling *Lomotil*, etc. will help, otherwise just treat by drinking fluids. Water-born **parasites** are quite common, so it's best to boil all drinking water and to get a check-up when you return home, and **jiggers**, small insects which live in cut grass, can also be a very irritating problem. They stick to and bury their heads into your ankles before slowly making their way up your legs to the groin; itching furiously, you can either pick them out one by one as the natives do, or apply sulphur cream (ask for the best ointment from a *farmacia* in the jungle town). It's unlikely that you will encounter any **snakes**. If you do, nearly all of them will disappear as quick as they can — only the *shushupe* (a bush-master) is fearless. If anyone does get bitten, the first thing to remember is to keep calm — most deaths result from shock, not venom. Try to kill the snake for identification, but more important apply a temporary tourniquet above the bite and find medical help. Some natives have remedies even for a potentially deadly *shushupe* bite.

TRANSPORT The two most common forms of river boats are **canoes** and **launches**, either with a Briggs and Stratton *peque-peque* 9hp engine or more powerful outboard motor. The latter is obviously faster and more manoeuvrable but a peque-peque works out a lot cheaper; in the end your decision will probably be based on the price, your confidence in its captain, and his readiness for embarkation. If you're going to be travelling together for more than a day, it's a good idea to make sure you can get along well and that he really does know the rivers. Anyone who intends **hitching** along a river system should remember that the further you are away from the town the harder it is to lay your hands on **petrol** (even if you come across Shell drilling in the middle of the forest!). However much money you may offer, no-one will take you up river if they're really short on gas — and most of the people are most of the time. Taking along your own supply, say a 5-gallon container, is a little difficult but it wouldn't be a bad idea if you're going somewhere really remote. In the last resort it's also possible to build or get hold of a **balsa raft** and paddle downstream from village to village, but this has obvious dangers (rapids, etc.), may well leave you stuck for the night on the river-bank in some god-forsaken place, and isn't really advisable without the help of someone who knows the river extremely well.

GETTING LOST in the forest is no fun and can happen very easily. Just by straying a hundred metres from camp, the river or your guide you can find yourself completely surrounded by a seemingly impenetrable canopy of plant-life. It's almost impossible to walk in a straight line through the undergrowth and one trail looks very much like the next to the unaccustomed eye. Your best bet, apart from shouting as loud as you can, is to find moving water and follow it downstream to the main river where someone will eventually find you waiting on the river-bank. If you get caught out overnight the two best places to sleep are beside a fire on the river-bank or high up in the boughs of a tree which isn't crawling with biting ants.

GUIDES A basic rule of thumb in the forest or on the rivers is to make sure that reliable guidance is always available – wherever you venture try to be with a local guide. They don't need to have official status – in fact natives are often the best guides – but should be experienced in the region and willing to help out. There are several ways of enlisting this kind of help: by paying through the nose for a 'reputable' **jungle tour**; by going to the port of a jungle town and searching for someone who will rent out his **boat and services** as a guide; or by travelling within the boundaries of friendly human settlements, **hopping** along the rivers from one village to the next with someone who is going that way anyway and who will be able to introduce you to the villagers at each stage. The latter option is obviously the most adventurous and will normally involve long waits in remote settlements waiting for someone else to take you further up river. Whichever, bear in mind that the jungle is an essentially laid-back place: if there's one thing certain to raise the hackles of a *selvatico* (jungle dweller) it's a gringo with a loud voice and pushy manner.

PERMITS To enter certain zones such as the *Manu National Park* or *Lago Valencia*, you'll need to obtain permission first – for details of which see the relevant sections. It's not usually difficult to get a permit unless there's a good reason, like suspected hostility from restless natives. In 1980 a German-led wild-life expedition entered the Manu Park without permission and were attacked by Indians – the first thing they knew about it was a sheet of arrows flying towards their canoe.

BOOKS For additional information, and an interesting account of a trip into the Manu Park, you might want to pick up Tanis and Martin Jordan's *South American River Trips, II* (Bradt Publications: see p. 286). The Jordans made their trip into Manu on a motorised rubber raft which perhaps, in view of the above, isn't a very good idea!

Probably the most important preparation though is a **mental** one: you should be prepared to respect (not fear) the rivers, the forest and its inhabitants. The jungle is actually home for a large number of people, and by arriving ready to accept what comes you'll find most avenues open to you.

CAMPA FACE PAINTING STAMP

MADRE DE DIOS

Still very much a frontier zone, centred on the growing gold-dust town of **Puerto Maldonado,** Madre de Dios is both the wildest and the most accessible region of the Peruvian tropical forest. There's an airstrip at Maldonado, a slippery road up from Cuzco (two to three days by truck), and it's also possible to approach by river from the Shintuya Mission (five or six days; see p. 247).

Like all jungle regions, human activity here is closely linked to the river system: in this case the **Rio Madre de Dios,** fed by two western tributaries which roll off the Paucartambo Ridge just north of Cuzco. The ridge divides the tributaries – *Manu* and *Alto* – from the Urubamba watershed, and delineates the **Manu National Park,** one of the region's greatest attractions and still very much an expedition zone. Outlined on pp. 247–8, the Manu is usually approached by road from Cuzco and, permission having been obtained, entered by canoe.

At Puerto Maldonado, four or five days downstream, the Madre de Dios meets with the **Tambopata river** – and flows on (a day's ride away) into Bolivia. Like the Rio Manu, Tambopata's rich forest flora and wild-life have been turned into a National Park, though it is increasingly under threat from colonists and an expensive place to visit. More accessible, and the target for many travellers stopping over in Maldonado, is the huge expanse of **Lago Valencia** – another extraordinary wild-life locale where, if you feel like it, you can even fish for pirana.

Off the main waterways, within the system of smaller tributaries and streams, live a variety of different **native groups.** All are depleted in numbers due to contact with this century's Western influences and diseases, but several have maintained their isolation. A traditionally dangerous region, with a manic climate (usually searingly hot, but with sudden icy winds), it has only been systematically explored since the 1950s and was largely unknown until Fitzcarraldo founded Puerto Maldonado in 1902. Occasional 'uncontacted' groups still turn up, although they are usually segments of a larger tribe split or dispersed with the arrival of the Rubber Barons, and they are fast being secured in controllable mission villages. Most of the native tribes which remain in, or have returned to, their traditional territories now find themselves forced to take on seasonal work for the colonists who have staked claims around the major rivers. In the dry season, from May through to November, this usually means panning for gold – the region's most lucrative commodity. In the rainy season the Brazil-nut (or, rather, *Peru-Nut*) collections take over. Lumber, too, is well established – indeed most of the accessible large cedars have already gone.

PUERTO MALDONADO

Resembling nothing so much as a Wild-West frontier settlement, **PUERTO MALDONADO** is a slightly weird sort of place. No more so, perhaps, than you might expect arriving here by truck or boat, but odd nonetheless. Most of the people, riding coolly about on Honda–50s, are second generation colonists but there's a constant stream of new and hopeful arrivals – rich and poor boys from all parts of South America and even the occasional gang from the US. The lure, inevitably, is gold. Every rainy season the swollen *rios* deposit a heavy dust of it along the river-banks and those who have been fast enough to stake claims on the best stretches have made their traditional fortunes.

It was rubber, in fact, which led to the town's establishment by Fitzcar- raldo – though the old baron too, when he blundered upon this site, was actually after gold. Somewhere in the jungle hereabouts, is reputed to be the legendary El Dorado-style city of **Paititi**, the great quest of Spanish explorers through the centuries. **Fitzcarraldo**, whilst working rubber on the Urubamba river, caught the Paititi bug – hearing rumours from local Campa Indians of an Inca fort protecting vast treasures, possibly around the Rio Purus. Setting out along the Camisea, a tributary of the Upper Urubamba, he managed to reach its source – and there walked over to a new watershed which he took to be the Purus. Leaving men to clear a trail, he returned to Iquitos and, in 1884, returned down the Camisea on a boat called *La Contamana*. Reaching the source, he took the boat to pieces and, with the aid of over a thousand Campa and other Indians, carried it across to the 'Purus'. As he cruised down, attacked by tribes at several points, Fitzcarraldo slowly began to realise that this river was not the Purus – a fact confirmed when he eventually bumped into a Bolivian rubber collector. What he had discovered, though, was a trail link connecting two of the greatest Amazonian watersheds. In Europe the discovery was heralded as a great step forward in the exploration of South America. For Peru it meant more rubber and a simple route for its export via the Amazon to the Atlantic, and the beginning of the end for the Madre de Dios's indigenous tribes. For Werner Herzog, of course, it meant quite a different story. . .

The town
The main street of Puerto Maldonado, **Leon de Velarde**, immediately establishes its stage-set feel – lined with bars, general stores, ironmongers and a pool-room. At one end is the **Plaza de Armas**, a bizarre Chinese pagoda-type clocktower at its centre, a modern *municipalis* along one side where a TV is sometimes set up by the window for the people to watch an all-important event like a football game. The streets, invariably muddy, show few signs of wealth despite the gold-dust. For the Indians

who now and then come upstream to sell a few grammes at the *Banco Minero*, though, they present a strange spectacle. You sometimes see a small group, having traded for a few essentials like cloth, fish-hooks or machetes, leaning on the outside of restaurant windows, watching with amazement at the 'strange' meals and the way people eat.

Most of the **trucks from Cuzco** arrive at Puerto Maldonado market. It's a laborious two– or three-day journey down from the glacial high-lands; after passing into cloud-covered high forest – the *ceja de selva* – the muddy track winds its slippery way through dense tropical vegetation, via the small settlement at QUINCEMIL. If you arrive **by plane** (less than one hour's flight from Cuzco) the moment you step out onto the runway a blast of hot, humid air is an instant reminder that this is the Amazon Basin. After collecting your luggage from the shack which serves as an airport building, the high cost of a taxi or *colectivo* into town ($2–$6) is another indication that this is the jungle.

There are several **hotels** to choose from. The best is probably *Hotel Wilson* on Avenida Gonzalez Prada, next to the Aero Peru office, but $10 a night is a lot to pay for a cold shower and an electric fan in each room. *Hotel Moderno*, near the plaza, is modest but friendly and much better value or there are any number of other places – most of them within half a block of Leon de Velarde.

You should have no problem finding a good **restaurant** and the food in Puerto Maldonado is tastier than in any other jungle town. Delicious river fish are always available, even in *ceviche* form, and venison or wild-pig, too, fresh from the forest (try *estofado de venado*). Undoubtedly one of the best places is *El Danube Azul* (on the corner of the plaza and Leon de Velarde), run by a friendly lady called Elba who will generally help out with any problem, and arrange daily set meals at a very reasonable price if you're sticking around for a week or so. The *Savoy restaurant* on Leon de Velarde, near the corner with Avenida Gonzalez Prada, serves traditional soup breakfasts but will also fix you up with a fried egg sandwich. More than for its food, though, this restaurant is worth visiting, its walls covered in paintings of a typical *selvatico* style developed to represent and romanticise the main dream-like feature of the jungle – looming jaguars, brightly plumed macaws talking to each other in the tree-tops and deer drinking water beside a still lake. Further up the main street, the morning **market** has excellent juices, fresh fruits and vegetables.

There is very little nightlife in this laid-back town. Most people just stroll around, sit and chat in the plaza or in bars along the main drag. At weekends and fiesta times, however, it's possible to sample what for most people is one of the jungle's greatest delights – **chicha music**. Loud and very easy to move to, you can usually pinpoint a venue just by following the sound of an electric bass guitar. The best place is probably the large pavillion off Jiron Daniel, less than three blocks from the plaza;

shows normally continue into the very early hours of the morning and any *gringas* who go along can expect to be hounded for a dance without respite.

Maldonado's **post office** is on the corner of Leon de Velarde and Jiron Jaime Troncoso. **Money** in dollars cash can often be changed privately (ask in your hotel); for travellers' cheques there are two **banks** in the plaza, *Banco Credito* and *Banco de la Nacion* (both open weekday mornings). The quickest way to get around the town and its immediate environs is by **hiring a moped** (from $1 an hour – or less by the day). You'll find a reasonable (and central) place in an alley-way opposite the Hotel Wilson on Av. Gonzalez Prada. Most of the machines are two-seaters so you can split the costs; if you're zipping outside the town make sure that there's ample gas in the tank. There are two main routes to follow: along Avenida Fitzcarraldo you come out at the cattle-ranches on the far side of the airstrip, turning off on *28 de Julio* you can take the road as far as you like in the direction of Quincemil.

If you're considering a river trip, or just feel like crossing to the other side for a walk, follow Jiron Billingshurst down from the Plaza to the **port** – one of the town's most active corners. There's a standard **ferry service** across the river, but for most major river trips (including Lago Valencia) you'll need to ask permission from the **Captain's Office** on Leon de Velarde, between Av. Gonzalez Prada and 2 de Mayo. This is normally quite straightforward if often a battle to communicate against the radio's *chicha* music! Something not commonly done by gringos, though a possibility, is to travel **by river into Bolivia** on one of the sugar boats which leave more or less every other week. Before embarking on this, however, you'll have to sort out your passport and visa with the police and *migraciones* offices near the Plaza de Armas.

LAGO VALENCIA AND OTHER RIVER TRIPS

Puerto Maldonado has not really been developed for tourism, and with the high cost of living you'll probably want to set about arranging a **river expedition** pretty quickly. You can do this in two ways: by organising your own boat and boatman, or, considerably more expensive, taking an arranged excursion up to one of the nearby tourist lodges.

The **lodges** – *The Explorer's Inn* at the Tambopata Nature Reserve, and *Cuzco Amazonica* an hour down the Madre de Dios – are both very much the preserve of scientists, film-makers and rich tourists. *The Explorer's Inn* runs from around $36 a night for the privilege of Western luxury amid over 5,000 hectares of virgin forest, and the chance to watch over 500 species of birds – one-sixth of all known in South America. *Cuzco Amazonica*, set up by a French-Peruvian venture in 1975 as 'a journey within your journey', is a similar kind of set-up but even more pricey and luxurious (upwards of $50 a night) with cocktail bars and all imaginable comforts. If you can afford it, trips out there can be arranged either in Cuzco (Procuradores 48; tel. 5047) or Lima (Av. Arequipa 4964; tel. 462 775). Alternatively, if you're more interested in wild-life than cocktails – but still high on cash – an American woman called Barbara, who knows the region extremely well, takes people out on **trips**. Her prices are reputed to be about $45 a day but are probably negotiable: contact is easiest made through Elba at the restaurant *El Danube Azul* (see above). Fortunately it is still possible to get **your own expedition** together without spending a fortune. For limited excursions into the wilderness all you need is a boat, boatman, the Captain of the Port's permission, and basic essentials like a mosquito net, blanket and some food (see p. 238). If you've got at least three days to spare (two nights minimum) much the most rewarding trip is down to **Lago Valencia**, an ancient ox-bow lake near the frontier with Bolivia (detailed below). A shorter trip – 5 hours up or about 2 hours down – is to **Tres Timbales**, a small community on the Rio Tambopata, where you can spend two or three spell-binding days watching for wild-life, walking in the forest and fishing; from here, too, you can visit the native village of EL INFIERNO – which has become a little touristy in recent years. Much nearer still (less than 1 hour down, 1½ hours back up) is **Lago Sandobal**, a large lake in the forest where the Ministry of Agriculture have started farming paiche fish; by taking a ferry over the Tambopata it's also possible to walk here in around an hour. Alternatively there are dozens of other possible trips which the boatmen will discuss with you and negotiate.

Obviously one of the most important aspects of any boat trip is finding the right **boatman**. All you can really do is ask around in the town and go down to the port to speak to a few of the guys who have canoes; get some price quotes and, if possible, check out their canoes and motors. Someone I've found very good is Alberto Amachi – a friendly man with many years experience on all of these rivers. His services as boatman and guide come at $40 a day, regardless of the size of the party; the boat takes ten people with relative ease.

Wherever you end up going you're likely to stop off at a **tribal village** for at least half-an-hour or so. Given this, it's more thought-provoking to know a little bit about who they are. Downstream, the most populous indigenous group are the *Huarayos*. Originally semi-nomadic hunters and gatherers, the Huarayos were well-known warriors. They fought the Incas and, later on, the Spanish expedition of Alvarez Maldonado – eventually establishing fairly friendly and respectful relationships with both. Under Fitzcarraldo's reign in the region, they apparently suffered greatly. Today they live in fairly large communities and have more or less abandoned their original bark-cloth robes in favour of shorts and T-shirts. Upstream live several native tribes known collectively as the *Mashcos* but actually comprising at least six separate linguistic groups – the Huachipairi, Shireneris, Amaraceiris, Sapitoyeris, Arasayris and Toyeris. All of them typically use long bows – over a metre and a half – and equally lengthy arrows. Most settlements will also have a shotgun or two these days since less time can be dedicated to hunting when they are panning for gold or working lumber for colonists. Traditionally the Mashcos also wore long bark-cloth robes, had long hair and the men often stuck eight feathers into the skin around their lips – making them look distinctly fierce and cat-like. Having developed a terrifying hatred of white people during Fitzcarraldo's era they were eventually conquered and 'tamed' by missionaries and the army about 30 years ago.

Lago Valencia
Leaving Puerto Maldonado by canoe with a *peque-peque* motor it takes the best part of a day to reach this huge lake. On the way you can stop off to watch some workers panning for gold on the Madre de Dios and visit a small settlement of *Huarayo* Indians; about half-an-hour beyond, you turn off the main river into a narrow channel which connects with the lake.

Approaching towards sunset it's quite common to see cayman basking on the muddy banks, an occasional puma, or the largest rodent in the world, a capybara, scuttling away into the forest. Up in the trees around the channel live hundreds of amazing Hoatzin birds, or *gallos* as they call them locally – large ungainly creatures with orange and brown plumage, long wings and distinctive spiky crests. The strangest feature of the Hoatzin are the claws at the end of its wings; using these to help it climb up into overhanging branches beside the rivers and lakes, it has almost lost the power of flight.

Easing into the lake itself, the sounds of a canoe engine are totally silenced by the weight and expanse of water. There's a *police control post* on the right as you leave the channel, where you must register passports and your Port Captain's permit. Beyond, reached up a slippery path above a group of dug-out canoes, is the lake's one real settlement. A cluster of thatched huts about a larger schoolhouse, under 50 people live here – a schoolteacher, a lay priest, the shop-owner and a few fishing families. Alberto Amachi usually takes groups to stay in a small camp further down, a seasonal nut-collectors *campamento* comprising just one cooking hut with an adjacent sleeping platform.

By day most people take a stroll **into the forest** – something that's both safer and more interesting with a guide, though whichever way you do it you'll immediately sense the energy and abundance of life. Quinine trees tower above all the trails, outflanked only by the Tahuari hardwoods, trees so tall and solid that jungle *shamans* describe themselves in terms of their power. Around their trunks you'll often see *Pega-Pega*, a parasitic ivy-looking plant which the shamans mix with the hallucinogenic

Ayahuasca into an intense aphrodisiac. Perhaps more useful to know are the liana vines. One thin species dangling above the paths can be used to take away the pain from a shushupe bite. Another, the *Maravilla* or *Palo de Agua*, issues a cool stream of fresh water: you chop a section, say half a metre long, and put it to your lips. You may come upon another vine, too – the sinister *Matapalo* (or *Renaco*) which sometimes extends over dozens of trees, sucking the sap from perhaps a square kilometre of jungle. Hideously formed, *Rencals* are a place where demons dwell, zones where native children can mysteriously vanish.

There are plenty of other things to do at Lago Valencia. You can **canoe up the lake** for a spot of fishing, passing beaches studded with groups of lazy-looking turtles sunning themselves in line along the top of fallen tree trunks – when they notice the canoe each one topples off, slowly splashing into the water, one after another. It takes a bit more to frighten the white cayman away, many of which can be seen soaking in the sun's strong rays along the margin of the lake. Sometimes over 2m in length, they look a daunting sight although they are apparently harmless unless you happen to tread on one! At night it's possible to glide along the water, keeping close to the bank looking for the amber glint reflected from a pair of cayman eyes as the beam from your flashlight catches them. This is how the locals hunt them, fixing the crocs with a beam of light then moving closer with a shotgun at the ready. Unless you're really hungry, however, it's just as satisfying to find their gleaming eyes in the pitch darkness; the only sound on the lake will be the grunting of corvina fish vibrating up from the bottom of the canoe.

In the way of **bird-life** Valencia is also well endowed. In addition to the Hoatzin there are kingfishers, cormorants, herons, egrets, pink flamingos, skimmers, macaws, toucans, parrots and gavilans. And behind the wall of trees along the banks hide deer, wild-pigs and **tapir**. If you're lucky enough to catch a glimpse of a tapir you'll be seeing one of South America's weirdest creatures – almost the size of a cow with an elongated rubbery nose and spiky mane. In fact, the tapir is known in the jungle as a *sachavaca* (forest cow – *sacha* is Quechua for forest and *vaca* is Spanish for cow). The easiest **fish** to catch are the pirana – all you need is some line, a hook and a chunk of unsalted meat (brought from Puerto Maldonado). Throw this into the lake and pull out a pirana!

MANU NATIONAL PARK

MANU is an unspoilt corner of the Amazon Basin, a National Park throbbing with life at the foot of the Andes. It is accessible only by river and only to the right kind of person or party: no settlers, no hunters and no missionaries. Within its boundaries there is cool cloud-forest phasing down to dense tropical jungle – a unique, varied and untouched environment, whose only permanent residents are the teeming forest wild-life, a few virtually uncontacted native groups who have split off from their major tribal units (*Yaminahuas, Amahuacas*, and *Matsiguengas*) and the Park guards. There's also a biological research station situated just inside the park on the beautiful lake Cocha Cashu, where flocks of macaws pass the time cracking open Brazil nuts with their powerful custom-made beaks.

To make a trip into the Park is a serious step requiring all the proper expedition preparations. Though not obligatory, a wise first step to assure yourself of entry is written permission from the Ministry of Agriculture in Lima. The *South American Explorers' Club* is able to advise on this, and further information can be obtained from Sr. Ruis, an engineer responsible for the new Park project – *El Plan Maestro de Manu* (which will eventually open the area up to a regulated form of tourism); Sr. Ruis works at La Molina Agricultural University on the outskirts of Lima. The next stage of preparations is in Cuzco – the springboard city for Manu. Here you can buy most of the stores and equipment you'll need (there's nothing available at Shintuya or in the Park itself), and get up to date information from the Park office at Quera 235 (near the Hostal del Inca). Trucks leave Cuzco from Avenida Huascar every Monday, Wednesday and Friday for SHINTUYA (24 hours; $6), but you'll have to ask the driver to stop at SALVACION (just before Shintuya) where there is a Park guard who charges around $1 a day for the anticipated duration of your stay.

Arriving in **Shintuya**, a small mission settlement on the edge of the Park, it's basically a matter of searching out a canoe and a reliable boatman/guide. If you take along some of your own petrol – say 20 gallons – this should be relatively easy. From Shintuya it's one or two days down the Alto Madre de Dios, then up the Rio Manu, to the main guards' outpost near the Park boundary at **Pakitsa**. This is where the real adventure begins. **Manu** covers an area larger than Northern Ireland and is one part of the jungle where you won't bump into missionaries, colonists or gold-panners. It's as much a reserve for the Indians as it is for the wild animals and so anyone or anything you do come across should be treated with the utmost respect. A few expeditions have been attacked in Manu over the past ten years. In each case there were reports suggesting that those concerned were unnecessarily tampering with the native way of life – stealing food, molesting Indian women or vandalising Indian property.

It is possible to go from Manu directly on to Puerto Maldonado via the Madre de Dios river. Although you're more likely to find a boat going downriver at Shintuya, you might be lucky enough to catch one at the junction of the Rio Alto Madre de Dios and the Manu river. The journey takes between two and five days, so, with no settlements of any size en route, you should be prepared to feed yourself.

THE URUBAMBA RIVER

Traditionally the home of the *Matsiguenga* and *Piro* Indians, the **Urubamba river** is one of the most glorious and exciting in Peru. Going north from Cuzco the only way to break into the Amazon Basin is by following the Urubamba down from the Incas' Sacred Valley to the humid lower slopes around the town of **Quillabamba** – the end of the railway line. Still unnavigable beyond, the Urubamba is trailed by a dirt road to the small settlement of **Kiteni**, where it merges with the Rio Koshireni and where the road finishes. From here on, river is the only means of transport. The **Pongo de Mainique**, dreaded white-water rapids, are less than a day downstream – the last physical barrier between the Andes and the Amazon.

QUILLABAMBA

Travelling by train from Cuzco, jungle vegetation begins to cover the valley sides from Machu Picchu onwards; it gets steadily warmer, the plant life thickens, and the train gradually descends the Urubamba valley. The first sights of **QUILLABAMBA** are the old tin roofs and adobe outskirts, coca leaves drying in their gardens. The main town is up above on the top of a high cliff, a stiff climb up from the railway station over a bridge then up a series of steps; the **Plaza de Armas** is just a few blocks ahead at the top.

A cock-fighting, market town growing fat on the proceeds of illicit cocaine production, Quillabamba's main attraction to tourists is a quick look at the *selva*. The only Peruvian jungle town accessible by railway, it is a good place to get kitted out for going deeper into the jungle. The market sells all the necessities like machetes, fish-hooks, food and hats, and it's quite an enjoyable town in which to relax, spending afternoons down by the river, eating ice-cream, or in one of the bars. The *Hotel Cuzco* is a good one (near Plaza Grau, the market square), *Hotel Comercio* slightly cheaper, or there are basic hotels uphill between the *Plaza de Armas* and the market. The best restaurant, beyond comparison, is *Astral* on the plaza, where they serve excellent typical dishes, cheap set menus and good drinks.

To get to KITENI 5–8 hours into the jungle, **buses** (the *Alto Urubamba* service) and **colectivos** (trucks or faster station wagons) leave Plaza Grau every morning between 8 and 10. The road keeps more or less to the course of the Urubamba. For Cuzco, the Hidalgo bus leaves Quillabamba from the market area a few times a week; trucks tend to be more frequent, though slower (from block 5 of San Martin), or there are three trains a day (departing 5.30am; 1.05pm; and 10.50pm), arriving in about 7 hours.

KITENI AND THE PONGO DE MAINIQUE

By the time you reach **KITENI**, the Urubamba river is quite wide and, with the forest all around, the valley is hotter, more exotic and much greener. A small *poblado*, Kiteni was until recently just a Matsiguenga Indian village. And with its ramshackle cluster of buildings, all wooden except for the schoolhouse, it is still a one-street town with more mules than cars.

Arriving, the truck or bus stops at a chain across the dirt track. Here you have to register with the *Guardia* in their office on the right, before walking into town. Straight down the road, at the other end of town (about 100m away) is the scruffy dormitory type *hostal*, the *Hotel Kiteni* – a cheap, friendly place, attractively situated beside the bubbling Rio Koshireni, and serving good set meals; there are no doors for security, though my gear has always been safe here. Next to the Hotel Kiteni there's an *oroya* (stand-up cable car) for people to pull themselves across the river; a 10 minute stroll on the far bank takes you to a new *albergue* which offers seclusion, greater security, spoken English and excellent food for only a few dollars a night.

Kiteni's main pull – beyond the feel of a small jungle settlement – is as a staging post for the awe-inspiring **PONGO DE MAINIQUE** – possibly the most dangerous 2km of potentially navigable river in the entire Amazonian system. Tours down the Urubamba to the *pongo* can be arranged with *Fitzcarraldo Adventure Travel* in either Cuzco (Calle San Augustin 737; tel. 4229) or Quillabamba (Av. San Martin 411) for around $30 a day per person. Other private entrepreneurs may approach you in either Quillabamba (notably in the *heladeria* on the main square) or Kiteni for a trip to the pongo and perhaps a little camping and fishing. The merits of these trips are best judged by the price you have to pay and the confidence you have in the guide. It is cheaper to get a canoe or launch which is going through the rapids anyway: boats are often more than willing to take extra passengers for a relatively small fee; or, if there are enough of you, it might be economical to hire a canoe (preferably with a powerful outboard motor) for a couple of days – from around $35 a day, including boatman. To arrange any of these options you'll do best hanging around the port at Kiteni – the beach behind the *Guardia's* huts. It's just a matter of being there early every morning asking every boat that leaves if it's going to the pongo – have all your baggage at hand for the moment when they say yes. Boats tend to arrive from down stream in the afternoons and it's often worth checking with them when they intend going back down. A boat with a powerful motor takes about 5 or 6 hours to reach the pongo, a *peque-peque* canoe will usually need around 10.

Just before the pongo there's a community of settlers at SAN IDRIATO.

These people, known as the Israelites, founded the village around a biblical sect. The men leave their hair long and, like Rastas, they twist it up under expandable peaked caps. Not far from San Idriato there's a basic tourist lodge, right at the mouth of the rapids – an amazing spot and quite cheap.

You'll have heard a lot about the *Pongo de Mainique* before you get there – from the boatmen, the local Matsiguenga Indians, colonists or the Israelites. Impossible to pass during the rainy season, between the months of November and April, it is dangerous at any time of year. As you get close in you can see a forested mountain range directly in front of you. The river speeds up and closer still it's possible to make out a great cut made through the range over millennia by the powerful Urubamba. Then, before you realise, the craft is whisked into a long canyon with soaring rocky cliffs on either side; gigantic volcanic boulders look like wet monsters of molten steel; stone faces can be seen shimmering under cascades; the danger of the pongo slips by almost unnoticed – the walls of the canyon absorbing all your attention. The main hazard is actually a drop of about 2m which is seen and then crossed in a split second. Now and again boats are overturned at this drop – usually those that try it in the rainy season – but even then natives can somehow come upstream in small unpowered dug-outs!

Beyond the pongo the river is much gentler, but on all major curves there is white water as far down as the Camisea tributary (about two days on a raft). Settlements along the river are few and far between – mostly native villages, colonists or missionaries. If your boat is going straight back through the pongo to Kiteni you'll have to make a quick choice about whether to try your luck going downstream or return to the relative safety and luxury of town. If it's going further down anyway, the next large settlement is SEPAHUA where there's a *hotel*, a few shops and bars, and an airstrip with fairly regular flights to Satipo (for road connection with Lima). Sepahua, however, is a couple of days down stream by motorised canoe or about four days on a raft: to be dropped off in between could mean waiting for a week on the river bank for another boat or raft to hitch with and so, to be on the safe side, you'll need food for at least ten days. From Sepahua it's possible to carry on downstream for another couple of days to ATALAYA, another small and isolated jungle town (cheaper flights to Satipo). At Atalaya the Urubamba meets the Ene-Tambo river to form the Ucayali. It's another few days from here to PUCALLPA and five or six more to IQUITOS on the Amazon.

PUCALLPA AND LAKE YARINACOCHA

Both Pucallpa and Iquitos – the northern jungle towns – have good connections with Lima and elsewhere. They're considerably more developed than anything that's come before in this chapter; their indigenous Indian life is getting more and more artificial, and with it their tourism gets increasingly packaged.

Pucallpa, however, is one of Peru's fastest growing cities (pop. 80,000; cf. 9,000 in 1950) and an interesting – if, to outsiders, sad – place in its own right. With its newly acquired status as the capital of an independent *departmento*, its oil refineries and massive lumber industry, it is a city which more than any other seems to represent the modern phase of the jungle's exploitation. For travellers the big attraction in this region is the nearby **lake of Yarinacocha** – another huge and beautiful ox-bow, where you can swim and rest up, watch schools of dolphin and (if you've the money) take wild-life expeditions.

From Pucallpa, if you've a fascination for the old **steamboat** transport of the last century, it is possible to travel the 1,000km downriver to Iquitos.

PUCALLPA

Long an impenetrable refuge for Cashibo Indians, **PUCALLPA** was 'tamed' and developed as a rubber gatherers' camp at the beginning of this century. In 1930 it was connected to Lima by road, since when its expansion has been intense and inevitable. Most of the parquet floors in Lima originate from the lumber industry here, saw-mills surround the city and spread up the main highway towards Tingo Maria and the mountains, and an impressive floating harbour has been constructed at the new port of La Hoyada It was, until 1980, a province in the vast *departmento* controlled by Iquitos, but months of industrial action eventually led to the creation of a separate province – Ucayali. With the end of financial restrictions from Iquitos, and the turn towards the Pacific (Iquitos exports down the Amazon to the Atlantic), this change is a significant one.

Although in many ways a lively and vibrant city, there is little here of great interest to travellers – most of whom get straight on a local bus for Yarinacocha (15km out: buses leave from the market square). If you stop over a while, though, it's difficult not to appreciate Pucallpa's relaxed jungle feel – nor the optimism in a city whose thick red mud-splattered streets are fast giving way to tarmac and cement. The town is full of

hotels, old and new. Most of the better ones are grouped around the last few blocks of Jiron Tacna and Jiron Ucayali – near the Parque San Martin. At the upper end of the scale *Hotel Mercedes* (Raymondi 610; tel. 6190) and *Hostal Confort* (Coronel Portillo 381; tel. 6091) are the definite choices; slightly cheaper is the *Hotel Amazonas* (Coronel Portillo 729; tel. 6080), and considerably so the basic *Hotel Europa* and *Hostal Los Angeles* (both on Ucayali). **Restaurants** too are plentiful, including a number of excellent *chifa* places – *Chifa Mang Keong* (in the Hotel Mercedes) and *Chifa Pucallpa* (on the corner of Tacna/San Martin) two of the best among them. *El Rinconcito Loretano* (on the 8th block of Tacna) is good for local dishes like the delicious *sarapatera* (soup in a turtle shell), and Pucallpa is also famous for producing Peru's first canned beer – *San Juan.* The **post office** is at San Martin 418; **phonecalls** can be made with *Entel Peru* at Uncayali 357; and there's a **tourist information** office at Dos de Mayo 11(tel. 6585).

Outside the town, the port at LA HOYADA is quite a lively spot, whilst at BARBON COCHA (6km up the main highway) there's a small lakeside settlement and zoological park. If you've an hour or so to while away in the town itself both the modern and old **markets** have interesting and varied stalls.

Transport connections
Connected by 850km of road to Lima, Pucallpa is served by several **bus companies** – all of whom go via HUANUCO (roughly the halfway point at 12 hours). The full journey is reckoned at 24 hours but can take a fair bit longer. Companies include *Tepsa* and *Leon de Huanuco*.

Both *AeroPeru* and *Faucett* operate regular **flights** connecting Pucallpa with Lima and Iquitos; and on Thursdays *Faucett* also fly from here to Tarapoto.

The **steamboat journey** between Pucallpa and Iquitos – taking at least a week and sometimes nearer two – is detailed on p. 254.

LAKE YARINACOCHA

Easily reached by bus from Pucallpa, **LAKE YARINACOCHA** is beyond doubt the more attractive place to stay. A contrast to the southern jungle lakes, its waters are excellent for swimming and there is considerable settlement around its banks. Riverine channels lead off towards small villages of Shipibo Indians, there's an artists' community called Nueva Eden (led by the charismatic wood sculptor Augustino Rivas), two luxurious tourist lodges, and the slightly bizarre *Summer Institute of Linguistics.* The latter is the headquarters of an extremely well-equipped, US-funded missionary organisation – their aim is to bring God to the natives by translating the New Testament into all Indian languages. At present they're working on some 43, 'each as different from each other as Chinese is from Greek'.

The main centre, though, and the place where most travellers stay, is the lake's port of **CALLAO**, a town known locally as the 'shangri-la de la Selva', its bars and wooden shacks ticking over with an almost continuous mesh of *chicha* music. Towards the lake are most of the liveliest **bars** (try *El Grande Paraiso*), **restaurants** and **hotels** (best of which is *Los Pescadores*), or, taking care of thieves, you can **camp** anywhere along the lake. Back on the main plaza is the settlement's most recent achievement, the **Moroti-Shobo Crafts Co-operative** – a project organised by Oxfam but now made over to the Shipibo and Conibo Indians. Always on display here, and reasonably priced, are beautifully moulded ceramics, carved wood and dyed textiles.

Trips to see **wild-life**, visit **Indian villages** or just to **cross the lake** are touted on the waterfront. The standard day excursion goes to the Shipibo village of SAN FRANCISCO, now almost completely geared towards tourism, but from around $20 a day you can hire a *peque-peque* canoe and boatman to yourself; these canoes can take up to eight or nine people and you can share costs, though if you want to go further afield (say on a three-day excursion) expect prices to be up to $50 a day.

The **tourist lodges** on the lake are as expensive as ever but they're wonderfully positioned and a good target for an evening drink. The easiest to reach is *La Brisa*, along a footpath leading around the right-hand side of the lake as you face it from the port. Set up years ago and run by a friendly American couple – the Nixons – it's a palatial structure though built more or less on native lines, raised high off the ground on stilts. A double room here will set you back over $20 a night, but the food (and drink) is good and quite reasonably priced. The other lodge, German-run and over the other side of the lake, is *La Cabaña* – quite possibly the first jungle lodge built in Peru. Prices and accommodation (in bungalows) are similar to La Brisa, though it is a smaller place with less atmosphere. It can be reached only by boat. Both lodges run organised trips, again on a fairly costly basis.

DOWNRIVER TO IQUITOS

Travelling **from Pucallpa to Iquitos on a small steamboat** sounds more agreeable than it actually is. Very few Peruvians, except of course river-men, would ever dream of it – over 1,000km of water separate these two large jungle towns, with very little in between – neverending bends in the river and verdant forest hemming you in on either side. On the other hand, if you're going to Iquitos anyway, you might as well relax in a hammock for a few days and arrive in the style rubber barons were accustomed to.

Steamboats generally leave Pucallpa from LA HOYADA port while the smaller launches and canoes tend to embark at PUERTO ITALIA. The cheapest, and by far the most effective, way of finding a boat is to go down to one of these ports and simply ask around. Try to fix a price and a leaving date with a reputable-looking captain – the normal cost seems to be around $25 per person, including all food for the trip. It can cost more if you want a cabin but you'll probably be more comfortable, and certainly cooler, with a hammock strung under some mosquito netting. If the captain asks for money up-front don't give the whole whack to him; you may never see the man or his boat again. Additionally, even when everything looks ready for departure, don't be surprised if there is a delay of a day or two – embarkations are frequent but extremely irregular. Food on board can be very unappetising at times so it may be worth your while taking along some extra luxuries like a few cans of fish, a packet or two of biscuits and several bottles of drink. Depending on how big the boat is and the number of stops it makes (something which should be checked with the captain beforehand) the journey normally takes between four and six days. Being a commercial port and on one of the illicit cocaine trails there's also a certain amount of paperwork to go through: you'll have to show your documents to the port police (PIP) and get permission from the naval office (your captain should help with all of this).

En route to Iquitos the boats often stop at the two main settlements of CONTAMANA and REQUENA. In theory it's possible to use these as pit-stops – hopping off one boat for a couple of days while waiting for another. However, you may end up stuck for longer than you bargained for. CONTAMANA, on the right bank of the Ucayali, can be reached fairly easily in a day from Pucallpa. There isn't much here but it's OK to camp and food can be bought without any problem. REQUENA, a larger settlement, is another couple of days downstream. This is a genuine jungle town developed by the rubber boom on an isolated stretch of the Rio Ucayali, and within a day's journey from Iquitos. There are a couple of basic *hostals* although you can also camp on the outskirts of town. For those going downstream, Requena is a better stopping-off point than Contamana since boats leave regularly for Iquitos for around $10 per person. A few hours north of Requena, just a few huge bends away, the Rio Marañon merges with the Ucayali to form the Amazon.

IQUITOS AND THE AMAZON

There can be few sights as magnificent as the **Amazon river**, seen from the island city of Iquitos. Surrounded in all directions by brilliant green forest and hemmed in by a maze of rivers, streams and lagoons, it's not difficult to imagine the awe with which Francisco Orellana must have looked out when he discovered it for the Old World only 450 years ago. Already several kilometres wide at Iquitos, by the time the Amazon runs into the Atlantic it is powerful enough to produce an estuary over 100km from end to end.

Connected to the rest of the world only by river and air, **Iquitos** has an obvious travellers' pull. It's the kind of place, too, which lives up to all your expectations of a jungle town, with its elegant reminders of the rubber boom years and the atmospheric shanty-town suburb of **Puerto Belen** – one of Herzog's main film sets in *Fitzcarraldo*. Around the town there are some great island and lagoon beaches, a fair range of adventurous excursions, and the possibility of continuing up the Amazon into **Colombia** or **Brazil**.

IQUITOS

By far the largest of Peru's jungle towns, **IQUITOS** began life in 1739 as a small Jesuit mission – a particularly daunting one, for the missionaries here faced the task of converting the fierce Yagua Indians, renowned as marksmen with their long poison-dart blow pipes. Its strategic position, however, accessible by large ocean-going ships from the 4,000km distant Atlantic, ensured its growth and by the end of the nineteenth century it was *the* great rubber town of South America. From that era of grandeur a number of structures survive, like the majestic Iron House in the Plaza de Armas, but the town itself has oscillated through the century between prosperity and the depths of depression. At present, buoyed by the export of timber, petroleum, tobacco and Brazil nuts, and dabbling heavily in the trade of wild animals, tropical fish and birds, and an insecticide called *barbasco*, long used by natives as a fish poison, it is in a period of quite wealthy expansion. The riverfront now stretches right the way from the old port and market of Belen over to a new floating harbour some 3km downriver.

Like most of the jungle towns, much of Iquitos's appeal lies in the possible excursions into the forest around – which are detailed in the following section. It is, though, an interesting old city in its own right, many of its turn of the century buildings decorated with Portuguese *azulejo* tiles, some brilliantly extravagant in their Moorish inspiration.

The **Iron House** in the Plaza de Armas was created by Eiffel for the 1898 Paris exhibition and shipped out by one of the rubber barons, whilst outside it, in the shadow of the Mamey trees, lurks an unexpected statue by **Rodin**. There's an **acquarium**, too, on Ramirez Hurtado (off the plaza), a small **zoo** (on Ricardo Palma), and an interesting little **Amazonian Museum** (corner of Fitzcarraldo/Tavara; open 9–1 and 4–7) devoted to the region's natural history and tribal culture.

Most memorable, however, is **Puerto Belen**, which looms out from the main town at a point where the Amazon joins the Rio Itaya. Consisting almost entirely of wooden huts raised above the water on stilts or floating on rafts, it has earned the marvellous travelese credit of 'The Venice of the Peruvian Jungle'! Actually more Far Eastern than Italian in appearance it can have changed little over its hundred years or so of life – still a poor shanty settlement and still trading in basics like bananas and yucca. Filming Fitzcarraldo here, Herzog merely had to make sure that no motorised canoes appeared on screen. Virtually everything else, and the style of *barriada* dwellings. looks like an authentic slum town out of the last century. If you want to look around, canoes can be hired very cheaply from the waterfront by the Plaza de Armas or at Puerto Belen itself.

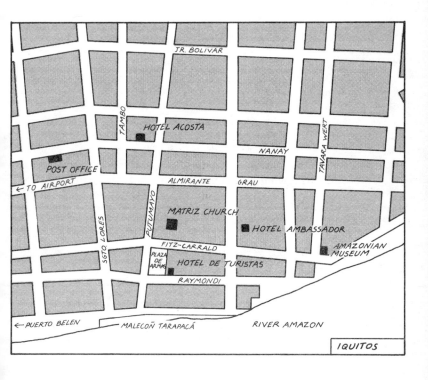

Hotels and practical details

Like every other jungle town Iquitos is comparatively expensive, though the standard of its **hotels** is actually a lot better than most. A room in an average sort of place like the *Hotel Peru* (Prospero 318; tel. 234 961) will include a shower and fan. Other central hotels, all of a similar standard, include the *Maria Antonia* (Prospero 616; tel. 234 761), *Hostal Alfert* (Garcia Sanz 1), *Ambassador* (Pevas 616; tel. 233 110) and *Acosta* (Huallaga/Cesar Calvo; tel. 233 110) There is no shortage of **restaurants** either, again with some good *chifas: Al Paso* (San Martin/Tacna) and *Man Keong* (Putumayo 239). *El Meson* is very popular for local fish dishes, whilst, slightly out of the jungle style, there's also a *Pizza Parlour* on Putumayo and *Texan Snack Bar* at Raymondi 390). Nightlife includes both **discos** and **creole peñas**. Among the former are *Ebony's 2001* (Sargento Lores 700), *El Meson* (Napo 116), *George's* (Huallanga 692) and *El Zorba's* (Mallecon Maldonado 167). For good, live, Peruvian music both *Peña Colpa* (Cesar Calvo de Aranjo 1396) and the more central *Peña Villanueva* (Ramirez Hurtado 672) are highly recommended. The local drink, incidentally, is *Chuchuasi*, made from a tree bark soaked in rum and reputedly aphrodisiac.

Getting around within Iquitos you'll probably want to make use of the rattling **motor cycle rickshaws** – very cheap by taxi standards.

The **post office** is at Malecon Tarapaca 382 (Mon.-Fri. 7–7; Sun. 8–12). **Tourist offices** are stationed at Napo 382 (near the Plaza de Armas), on a 2nd floor office at Prospero 418, and inside the state Turistas Hotel. The Prospero branch has a *Division de Artesanias* where, if you're seriously interested in buying regional handicrafts, you can obtain a list of local producers.

For **flights** to Lima and Pucallpa, *Aero Peru* has an office at Prospero 250 (tel. 232 513) and *Faucett* at Arica 130 (tel. 233 291). The Peruvian Airforce, *Grupo Ocho*, who run sporadic flights to Leticia in Colombia (see p. 000), are at Loreto 243. *Cruzeira do Sol* and other small companies also fly into Leticia and Brazil: contact travel agents for prices and schedules.

Companies worth checking out for **river transport** – either to Pucallpa or Yurimaguas, or down the Amazon into Brazil – include: *Comercial Bellavista* (Malecon Tarapaca 594–596; tel. 231 311), *Linea Amazonica* (Sargento Lores 258; tel. 2455), *Negocios Amazonica Peruanos* (Coronel Portillo 464; tel. 231 432) and *Naviera Amazonica Peruanos* (Sargento Lores 415; tel. 233 871).

The office for all **passport and visa** paperwork is at Arica 447 (tel. 235 371).

Lastly it might be useful to know the **words** *pakucho* (the local form of gringo), and *shushupero* ('drunk'; from the deadly shushupe snake).

TRIPS AROUND IQUITOS

Expeditions around Iquitos are probably the most developed in the Peruvian jungle – fun but, once again, expensive. However, within quite **easy striking distance** the town offers an unusually wide – and often surprising – range of attractions.

On the western edge of the town an affluent of the Rio Nanay forms a long lake called MORONA COCHA, a popular resort for swimming and waterskiing; whilst further out (just before the airport) another lake, RUMOCOCHA, has facilities for fishing and hunting. Beyond this, still on the Rio Nanay, is the popular weekend beach of SANTA CLARA and, 16km on, the village of SANTO TOMAS. This is a worthwhile trip, well connected by local bus. A centre for agriculture and fishing, the village is renowned for its jungle artesania – and has another beach where you can swim and canoe. If you've the chance, try to coincide with Santo Tomas's fiesta (Sept. 23rd–25th), a massive party of dancing and *chicha* music.

Another place you can get to quite easily – by canoe from Belen or the main waterfront – is PADRE ISLA an island actually in the midst of the Amazon, opposite the town. Over 14km long, it has beautiful beaches during the dry season. Or, lastly, there is the QUISTOCOCHA LAGOON, a couple of hours walk along the airport road – turning left at the last fork in the road before the airport. Now taken over by the Ministry of Fishing for the breeding of giant *paiche*, it has a small zoo.

Further afield

If you feel like **more adventurous excursions** you'll have to arrange an expedition with the boatmen at Belen or on the main waterfront. Trips of three days to over a week can be made from around $40–50 a day for the boat (eight-ten people). Negotiable points might include the Boras and Huitoto Indian homeland on the RIO AMPIYACU, the Ticuna's at CUSHILLOCOCHA, or the Koto's (or *Orejones'*) on the RIO NAPO – the last a potential route into Ecuador (six days to the border at Cabo Pantoja: very hard going).

Alternatively, of course, there are the **tourist lodges** to fall back on – particularly abundant in Iquitos. Most of the agencies have offices on Calle Putumayo, and all have their own lodges and offer a variety of long and short excursions. One of the best companies, *Amazon Lodge Safaris* (Putumayo 165, tel. 233 032), has a lodge on the Rio Yanayacu and offers a day trip for $35 a person. Their boat leaves Iquitos at 9.30am, stopping off at Belen en route to the lodge for a 'typical' lunch. In the afternoon a guide takes you on a jungle walk to visit Jivaro Indians, then you return via the lodge to Iquitos on their new 80–ton sight-seeing ship.

Most of the other lodges offer similar tours at similar prices, and if you've got more money than time they serve a useful function. But in many ways they're disappointing. There are better approaches to visiting a native village, for instance, than outnumbering its inhabitants with tourists – who, for many of the 'genuine' Indian villages, now provide the main source of income. Operators included *Explorama Tours* (Putumayo 150) with a lodge on the Rio Yanomomo, *Wagon's Amazon Tours* (Jr. Lima 577) on the Rio Itaya, and *Amazon Camp* (Putumayo 196) on the Rio Momon.

THE THREE-WAY FRONTIER: PERU, BRAZIL AND COLOMBIA

Leaving Peru – or for that matter arriving – **by the Amazon river** is an intriguing trip of its own. The Colom bian frontier is about two or three days downstream from Iquitos and boats run fairly regularly from the harbour or waterfront. Check with the commercial river transporters and keep an eye out for the highly recommended river-boat *Oro Negro*, which costs $25 to the border, inclusive of food but not drink. Before leaving its advisable to complete Peruvian passport formalities at the *Oficina de Migraciones* at Arica 447. Theoretically this is possible at **RAMON CASTILLA**, the last settlement in Peru, but it takes more time and trouble.

Only rarely are boats permitted to travel directly from Iquitos to the Colombian frontier town of LETICIA, and so you'll normally have to take a local ferry (10mins) across the river from RAMON CASTILLA on the opposite bank. **LETICIA**, growing rich on tourism and contraband (mostly cocaine), has more than a touch of the wild west about it. There are no official *tramites* like paper-stamping here, though you should carry your passport at all times. If you intend going on into Colombia from here you'll need to have picked up a Colombian tourist card from the consulate at Iquitos (or, coming from Brazil, at Manuas). If you stay, be warned that it's an expensive town by Peruvian (and Colombian) standards. Best of the basic **hotels** are *Residencia Monserrate* and *Residencia Leticia:* the cheapest place to eat, and the most varied food, is at the riverside market. If you want to go on into Colombia the cheapest access is by taking a canoe to PUERTO ASIS, where you can plug into the **bus** transport system.

The Brazilian border is only another 5km downstream from Leticia, at **TABATINGA**. Here there are customs checks and entry *tramites:* if you're entering Brazil you may be asked to show an exit ticket or $500. Tabatinga has a few hotels and restaurants, and an airport, but it's a much smaller place than Leticia and essentially a staging post for carrying on downstream into Brazil. There are boats to MANAUS, a five-day journey (often very crowded) costing about $30.

The only other way of crossing these three borders is by **flying** – a much less interesting approach though not necessarily a more expensive one. Flights from IQUITOS-LETICIA are operated by the Peruvian Airforce (*Grupo Ocho*) and by *Cruzeira do Sol* and a number of private companies for approximately $50. Flights from IQUITOS-TABATINGA are also run by some of the private firms for around $150.

TRAVEL DETAILS

To Puerto Maldonado *By truck* from Cuzco (fairly regular; 2–3 days). *By Truck* from Cuzco to Shintuya Mission (Mon., Wed. and Fri.; 24hrs) and from there to P.M. *by boat* (5–6 days). *By air* from Cuzco (daily flights; 1hr).

To Quillabamba *By train* from Cuzco/Machu Picchu (2 daily; 6½/2½hrs).

To Pucallpa *By bus* from Lima (daily; 24hrs: via Huanuco, 12hrs). *By air* from Lima and Iquitos (more or less daily flights; 1hr). *By steamboat* from Iquitos (fairly regular; 4–6 days journey but allow at least 10 days to include organisation/documentation, etc.

To Iquitos *By air* from Lima and Iquitos (daily; 1hr). *By steamboat* from Pucallpa (as above). Also *boats and flights* to/from Leticia (Colombia) and Tabatinga (Brazil): see above section for details.

Part three
CONTEXTS

THE HISTORICAL FRAMEWORK

Pre-conquest Peru

Beginnings and pre-history (40,000 BC–1200 BC)

Theories concerning **mankind's arrival in South America** lay emphasis on nomadic bands of hunters and gatherers sweeping across the then land-bridged Bering Straits from Asia, then turning down through the rockies and over the plains of North America. These bands crossed into the Americas at the time of the last successive ice ages (some **40–15,000 BC**) when a combination of ice-packs and low sea-levels exposed a neck of solid 'land', and followed herds of game animals from Siberia into what must have been a relative paradise of fertile coast, wild forest, mountain and savannah.

Over countless generations successive tribes, each with their own language and ethnic identity, swept through Central America, some groups made their way down along the Andes, into the Amazon and out onto some of the more fertile areas of the **Peruvian and Ecuadorean coast;** others found their niches en route. In a number of tribes there seem to be cultural memories of these migrations, encapsulated in their traditional mythologies – though these aren't really transcribable into written histories. There is, however, archaeological evidence of human occupation in Peru dating back to around **20,000 BC.** Concentrated in the **Ayacucho Valley,** these early Peruvians camped in caves or out in the open. Around **12,000 BC,** slightly to the north in the **Chillon valley** (just above modern Lima), comes the first evidence of significant craft skills – stone blades and knives for hunting. At this period there were probably similar groups of hunter tribes in the mountains and jungle too, but the climate conditions of these zones make it unlikely that any significant remains will ever be found.

The difficulties of traversing the rugged terrain between the highlands and coast evidently proved little problem for the early Peruvians. From **8,000 to 2,000 BC, migratory bands** of hunters and gatherers alternated between camps in the lowlands during the harsh mountian winters and highland summer 'resorts' – their actual movements well-synchronised with those of wild animal herds. One important mountain encampment from this '**Incipient Era**' has been discovered at **Lauricocha,** near Huanuco, at an altitude of over 4,000m. Here the art of working stone – eventually producing very fine blades and arrow points – seems to have been sophisticated, while at the same time a growing cultural imagination found expression in cave paintings – depicting animals, hunting scenes and even dances. Down on the coast at this time other groups were living off the greener *lomas* belts of the desert in places like **Chilca** to the south, and in the mangrove swamps around **Tumbes** to the north.

An awareness of the potential encapsulated in plants began to emerge around **5,000 BC** with the **cultivation** of seeds and tubers; to be followed over the next two millennia by the introduction, presumably from the Amazon, of gourds, Lima beans, then squashes, peanuts and eventually cotton. Toward the end of this period a climatic shift turned the coast into a much more arid belt and forced those living there to try their hand at **agriculture** in the fertile river beds; a process to some extent reflected in the mountains. With this development permanent settlements sprung up all along the coast, notably at **Chicama, Asia** and **Paracas,** and in the sierra at **Kotosh.** The population began to mushroom, and with it came a new consciousness, perhaps influenced by cultural developments within the Amazon Basin to the east: **Cultism** – the burial of dead in mummy form, the capturing of trophy heads, and the building of grand religious structures – made its first appearance. At the same time there were also overwhelming technological advances in the spheres of weaving, tool-making and ornamental design.

The Chavin cult: the Formative Era (1200 BC–AD 200)

From around 1200 BC to AD 200 – the '**Formative Era**' – agriculture and village life became established. Ceramics were invented, and there were the beginnings of a slow disintegration in regional isolation.

This last factor was due mainly to the widespread dispersal of a religious cult, the **Chavin movement.** Remarkable in that it seems to have spread without the use of military force, the cult was based on a conceptualisation of nature-spirits, and of an all-powerful feline creator god. This widespread feline image rapidly exerted its influence over the northern half of Peru and initiated a period of inter-relations between fertile basins in the Andes and some of the coastal valleys. How – and where – the cult originated is uncertain, though it seems probable that it began in the eastern jungles, possibly spreading to the Andes (and eventually the coast) along the upper Marañon river.

The Chavin cult was responsible for excellent progress in the work of **stone-carving** and **metallurgy** (copper, gold and silver) and, significantly, for a ubiquity of temples and pyramids which grew up as cultural centres where the gods could be worshipped. The most important known centre was the temple complex at **Chavin de Huantar** in Ancash, though a similar centre was built at **Kotosh** near Huanuco – whose influence seems to have spread over the northern highlands and coast from Chiclayo down as far as the Paracas Peninsula (where it had a particularly strong impact). There were immense local variations in the expressions of the Chavin cult: elaborate metallurgy in the far north; adobe buildings on stone platforms in the river valleys; excellent ceramics from **Chicama** and the extravagant stone engravings from Chavin itself. In the mountains life must have been very hard, based on subsistence agriculture and pilgrimages to the sacred shrines – most of which probably originated around ideas formulated by an emergent caste of powerful priest-chiefs. On the coast there was an extra resource – seafood – to augment the meagre agricultural yields.

Towards the **end of the Chavin phase,** an experimental period saw new centres attempting to establish themselves as independent powers with their own personalities. This gave birth to **Gallinazo** settlements in the Viru valley; the incredible **Paracas culture** on the south coast (with its excessively beautiful and very advanced textile technology based around a cult of the dead); and the early years of **Tiahuanaco** development in the Lake Titicaca region. These three cultural upsurges laid the necessary foundations for the flourishing civilisations of the subsequent Classical Era.

The Classical Era: pre-Inca cultures (200–1100)

A diverse period – and one marked by intense development in almost every field – the **Classical Era** saw the emergence of numerous distinct cultures, both on the coast and in the sierra. The best documented, though not necessarily the most powerful, are the **Mochica** and **Nazca** cultures (both probably descendents of the coastal Paracas culture) and the **Tiahanuco.**

The **Mochica culture** has left the fullest evidence of its social and domestic life, all aspects of which, including its work and religion, are vividly represented in highly realistic pottery. The first real urban culture in Peru, these people maintained a firm hierarchy with an elite group combining both secular and sacred power. Ordinary people cultivated land around clusters of dwelling sites, dominated by sacred pyramids – man-made *huacas* dedicated to the gods. The key to the elite's position was presumably their organisation of large irrigation projects, essential to the survival of these relatively large population centres in the arid desert of the north coast. In their religion, nature and the world of the ancestors seem the dominant elements; occasional human sacrifices were offered and trophy-heads were captured in battle. The peak of their influence came around 500–600, with cultural and military control of the coast from Piura in the north to the Nepena valley in the south.

More or less contemporaneous with the Mochica the **Nazca culture** bloomed for several hundred years on the south coast. Thought to be responsible for the astonishing lines and drawings etched into the Pamoa de San José little is known for certain about Nazca society or general way of life. The Nazca did, however, build an impressive temple complex in the desert at Cahuachi (see p. 129), and their burial sites have turned up thousands of beautiful ceramics whose abstract designs can be compared only to the quality and content of earlier Paracas textiles.

Named after its sacred centre on the shore of Lake Titicaca, the **Tiahuanuco culture** developed at much the same time as the Mochica – with which, initially at least, it peacefully co-existed. Tiahuanuco textiles and pottery nevertheless spread along the desert, modifying both Mochica and Nazca styles and bending them into more simplified shapes and abstract patterns. The main emphasis in Tiahuanuco pottery and stone-work was on symbolic elements featuring condors, pumas and snakes – more than likely the culture's main gods, representing their respective spheres of the sky, earth and underworld. In this there seem obvious echoes of the same deified creatures of the earlier Chavin cult.

Although initially peaceable, the Tiahuanuco influence is associated in its decadent phase with **militarism.** Originating either at Huari, in the sierra near Ayacucho, or on the central coast, this forceful tendency extended from AD 650 to AD 1100 and was dominated by what today is called the **Huari-Tiahuanuco culture.** The ruins at Huari cover some 8 square km and include high-walled enclosures of field-stones laid and plastered with mud, decorated only by a few stone statues along Tiahuanuco lines. Whether or not this was the actual inspirational centre, by around AD 1000 Huari-Tiahuanuco features were dominant in the art forms over virtually all of Peru.

An increasing prevalence of **inter-tribal warfare** characterised the ultimate centuries of this era – culminating in the erection of defensive forts, a multiplication of ceremonial sites (including over 60 large pyramids in the Lima area) and, eventually, the uprooting of Huari-Tiahuanuco influence on the coast by the youthful emergence of three mini-empires – the **Chimu,** the **Cuismancu** and the **Chincha.** In the mountains its influence mysteriously disappeared to pave the way for the separate growth of relatively large tribal units such as the **Colla** (around Titicaca), the **Inca** (around Cuzco) and the **Chanca** (near Ayacucho).

Partly for defensive reasons, this period of isolated development also sparked off a **city-building urge** which became almost compulsive by the start of the Imperial Era in the twelve century. The most spectacular urban complex was **Chan Chan** (near modern Trujillo) built by the **Chimu** on the opposite side of the river to earlier Mochica temples but indicating a much greater sophistication in social control – the internal structure of their clan-based society reflected in its intricate layout. By now, with a working knowledge of bronze manufacture, the Chimu flung the arms of an empire from Chan Chan to Tumbes in the north and Paramonga in the south – a domination of nearly half of the entire Peruvian coastline. To the south they were bounded by the **Cuismancu,** less powerful, though capable of building similar citadels (such as Cajamarquilla near Lima) and of comparable attainments in craft industries. Further down the coastline the **Chincha** – known also as the *Ica culture* – produced fine monuments and administrative centres in the Chincha and Pisco valleys too. The lesser rainfall on the southern coast, however, didn't permit the Chincha State – nor (to an extent) the Cuismancu – to create urban complexes of anything like the size of Chan Chan.

The Incas (c.1200–1532)

With the **Inca Empire** came the culmination of this city-building phase, and the beginnings of a kind of Peruvian unity – the Incas gradually taking over each of the separate coastal empires. One of the last to go – almost bloodlessly, and just 60 years before the Spanish conquest – were the Chimu, who for much of this 'Imperial Period' were a viable and powerful rival.

Based in the valleys around Cuzco, the Incas were for the first two centuries of their existence much like any other of the larger mountain tribes. Fiercely protective of their independence, they maintained a somewhat feudal society, tightly controlled by rigid religious tenets, though often disrupted by inter-tribal conflict. The founder of the dynasty – some time around 1200 – was one **Manco Capac,** who passed into Inca mythology as a culture hero. Historically, however, little definite is known about Inca developments or achievements until the accession in 1438 of Pachacuti, and the onset of their great era of expansion.

Pachacuti, most innovative of all the Inca emperors, was the first really to expand their traditional tribal territory. The beginnings of this were not in fact of his making but the response to a threatened invasion by the powerful, neighbouring Chanca Indians during the reign of his father, Viracocha. Viracocha, feeling the odds to be overwhelming, left Cuzco in Pachacuti's control, himself withdrawing to the refuge of Calca along the Urubamba river. Pachacuti, however, won a legendary victory — traditional Inca chronicles recording that the very stones of the battlefield rose up in his defence — and, having vanquished the most powerful force in the region, shortly took the Inca crown for himself.

Within three decades Pachacuti had consolidated this power over the entire sierra region from Cajamarca to Titicaca, defeating in the process all main imperial rivals except for the Chimu. At the same time the capital at **Cuzco** was spectacularly developed, with the evacuation and destruction of all villages within a 10km radius, a massive programme of agricultural terracing (watched over by a skyline of agro-calendrical towers), and the construction of unrivalled palaces and temples. Shrewdly, Pachacuti turned his forcible evacuation of the Cuzco villages into a positive scheme — relocating the Incas in newly colonised areas. He extended this practice too, towards his subjugated allies, binding them into the Inca armies while their chiefs remained as hostages and honoured guests at Cuzco.

Inca territory expanded north into Ecuador, almost reaching Quito, under the next Emperor — **Topac Yupanqui** — who also took his troops down the coast, overwhelming the Chimu and capturing the holy shrine of Pachacamac. Not surprisingly the coastal cultures influenced the Incas perhaps as much as the Incas influenced them — particularly in the sphere of craft industries. With Pachacuti before him, Topac Yupanqui was nevertheless an outstandingly imaginative and able ruler. During the 22 years of his reign — 1471–93 — he pushed Inca control southwards as far as the Rio Maule in **Chile;** instigated the first proper census of the empire and set up the decimal-based administrative system; introduced the division of labour and land between the State, the gods and the local *allyus;* invented the concept of Chosen Women (*Mamaconas*); and inaugurated a new class of respected individuals — the Yanaconas. An empire had been unified not just physically but also administratively and ideologically.

At the end of the fifteenth century the Inca Empire was thriving probably as well as any this planet has ever witnessed. Its politico-religious authority was finely tuned, and could extract what it needed from its millions of subjects and give what was necessary to maintain the status quo — be it brute force, protection or food. The only obvious problem inherent in the Inca system of unification and domination was one of overextension. When **Huayna Capac** continued Topac Yupanqui's expansion to the north he created a new Inca city at **Quito,** one which he personally preferred to Cuzco and which laid the seed for a division of loyalties within Inca society.

This came to a head even before Huayna Capac's death. Ruling the empire from Quito, along with his favourite son Atahualpa, he had installed another son, Huascar, at Cuzco. In the last year of his life he tried to formalise the division — ensuring an inheritance at Quito for Atahualpa — but this was totally resisted by Huascá, legitimate heir to the Lord Inca and the empire, and by many of the influential Cuzco priests and nobles. In 1527, with Huayna Capac's death, civil war broke out. Atahualpa, backed by his father's army, was by far the stronger and immediately won a major victory at the Rio Bamba — a battle

Lord Incas

MANCO CAPAC (Culture hero c.1200)
SINCHI ROCA
LLOQUE YUPANQUI
MAYTA CAPAC
CAPAC YUPANQUI
INCA ROCA
YAHUAR HUACA

VIRACOCHA INCA
PACHACUTI (1438–71)
TOPAC YUPANQUI (1471–93)
HUAYNA CAPAC (1493–1525)
HUASCAR (1525–32)
ATAHUALPA (1532–3)

which, it was said, left the plain littered with human bones for over a hundred years. A still bloodier battle, however, took place along the Apurimac river at Cotabamba in 1532. This was the decisive victory for Atahualpa, and with

his army he retired to relax at the hot baths near Cajamarca. Here, informed of a strange-looking alien band, successors of the bearded adventurers whose presence had been noted during the reign of Huayna Capac, they waited.

Colonial Peru

Francisco Pizarro was one of 26 soldiers who stumbled upon and named the Pacific Ocean in 1513, while on an exploratory expedition in Panama. From that moment his determination, fired by native tales of a fabulously rich land to the south, was set. Within 11 years he had found himself financial sponsors and set sail down the Pacific coast with the priest Hernando de Luque and Diego Almagro.

With remarkable determination, and having survived several disastrous attempts, the three explorers eventually landed at *Tumbes* in 1532. A few months later a small band of Spaniards, less than 170 men, arrived at the Inca city of *Cajamarca* to meet the leader of what they were rapidly realising was a mighty empire. En route to Cajamarca, Pizarro had learned of the Inca civil wars and of Atahualpa's recent victory over his brother Huascar. This rift within the empire provided the key to success that Pizarro was looking for.

The day after their arrival, in what appeared to be a lunatic endeavour, Pizarro and his men massacred thousands of Inca warriors and captured Atahualpa. Although ridiculously outnumbered, the Spaniards had the advantages of surprise, steel, cannons and, above all, mounted cavalry. The **decisive battle** was over in a matter of hours: with Atahualpa prisoner, Pizarro was effectively in control of the Inca empire. Atahualpa was promised his freedom if he could fill the famous ransom room at Cajamarca with gold. Caravans overladen with the precious metal arrived from all over the land and within six months the room was filled: a treasure, worth over one and a half million *pesos*, which was already enough to make each of the conquerors extremely wealthy. Pizarro, however, chose to keep the Inca leader as a hostage in case of Indian revolt, amid growing suspicions that he was inciting his generals to attack the Spanish.

Atahualpa almost certainly did send messages to his chiefs in Cuzco: orders to execute his brother Huascar who was already in captivity there. Under pressure from his worried captains, Pizarro brought Atahualpa to trial in July 1533, a mockery of justice in which he was given a free choice: to be burned alive as a pagan or strangled as a Christian. They baptised him before death.

With nothing left to keep him in Cajamarca, Pizarro made his way through the Andes to Cuzco where he crowned a puppet emperor – *Manco Inca* – of royal Indian blood. After all the practice that the Spaniards had had in imposing their conquest culture on both the Moors in Spain and the Indians in Mexico, it took only a few years to replace the Inca empire with a working colonial mechanism. Now the Inca civil wars were over the natives seemed happy to retire quietly into the hills and get back to the land. However, more than wars were responsible for the almost total lack of initial reaction to the new conquerors. The **native population** had dropped from some 32 million in 1520 to only 5 million by 1548 – a decline due mainly to new European diseases such as smallpox, measles, bubonic plague, whooping cough and influenza.

Queen Isabella of Spain indirectly laid the original foundations for the political administration of Peru in 1503 when she authorised the initiation of an **encomienda system,** which meant that successful Spanish conquerors could extract tribute for the crown and personal service in return for converting the natives to Christianity. They were not, however, given titles to the land itself. As Governor of Peru, Pizarro used the *encomienda* system to grant large groups of Indians to his favoured soldier-companions. In this way the basic colonial land-tenure structure was created in everything but name. 'Personal service' rapidly came to mean subservient serfdom for the native population, many of whom were now expected to herd animals introduced from the Old World (cattle, hens, etc.) on behalf of their new overlords. Many Inca cities were rebuilt as Spanish towns, although some, like Cuzco, still retain native masonry for their foundations and even walls. Other Inca sites, like *Hucanuco Viejo*, were abandoned in favour of more hospitable lower altitudes. The Spanish were drawn to the coast for strategic as well as climatic reasons – above all to maintain constant oceanic links with the homeland via Panama.

The **foundation of Lima** in 1535 began a multi-layered process of satellite dependency which continues even today. The fat of the land (originally mostly gold and other treasures) was sucked in from satellite regions all over Peru, processed in Lima, and sent on from there to Spain. Lima survived on the backs of Peru's municipal capitals which, in turn, extracted tribute from the scattered *encomenderos*. The encomenderos depended on local chieftains (*curacas*) to rake in service and goods from even the most remote villages and hamlets. At this lowest level there was little difference between Inca imperial exploitation and the economic network of Spanish colonialism. Where they really varied was that under the Incas the surplus produce circulated among the elite within the country, while the Spaniards sent much of it to a distant monarch on the other side of the world.

In 1541 Pizarro was assassinated by a disgruntled faction among the Conquistadors who looked to Almagro as their leader, and for the next seven years the nascent colonial society was rent by civil war. In response, the first **Viceroy** – Blasco Nuñez de Vela – was sent from Spain in 1544. His task was to act as Royal Commissioner and to organise the colony in favour of Spain; his fate to be killed by Gonzalo Pizarro. But Royalist forces, now under Pedro de la Gasca, eventually prevailed – the surviving Pizarro brother was captured and executed and crown control firmly established.

A developing society

Meanwhile **Peruvian society** was being transformed by the arrival of new generations: *creoles*, descendants of Span-

iards born in Peru, and *mestizos*, of mixed Spanish and native blood, created a new class structure. In the coastal valleys whose population had been decimated by European diseases, slaves were imported from Africa. There were over 1,500 black slaves in Lima alone by 1554. At the same time, as a result of the civil wars and periodic Indian revolts, over a third of the original conquerors had lost their lives by 1550. Nevertheless, on the ground, effective power remained in the hands of the independent *encomenderos*.

In an attempt to dilute the influence of the *encomienda* system, the Royalists divided the existing 20 or so municipalities into **Corregimentos,** smaller units headed by a *corregidor*, or royal administrator. They were given the power to control the activities of the *encomenderos* and exact tribute for the crown – soon becoming the vital links in provincial government. The pattern of constant friction between *encomenderos* and *corregidores* was to continue for centuries, with only the priests to act as local mediators.

Despite the evangelistic zeal of the Spanish, religion changed little for the majority of the native population. Although Inca ceremonies, pilgrimages and public rituals were outlawed their mystical and magical base endured. Each region quickly reverted to the pre-Inca cults which were deep-rooted in their culture and cosmology. Over the centuries the common folk learned to absorb symbolic elements of the Catholic faith into their beliefs and rituals – allowing them, once again, to worship relatively freely. Magic, herbalism and divination have continued strongly at the village level as well as successfully pervading modern Peruvian thought, language and practice. The Peruvian World Cup football squad in 1982 enlisted (in vain) the magical aid of a *curandero*. At the elite level, the Spanish continued their fervent attempts to convert the entire population to their own ritualistic religion. They were, however, more successful with the rapidly growing *mestizo* population who shared the same cultural aspirations.

Miraculous occurrences became a conspicuous feature of the popular Peruvian Catholic Church; the greatest example being Our Lord of Miracles which originated amongst the black population of colonial Lima. In the devastating earthquake in 1665, an anonymous mural of the Crucifixion on the wall of a chapel in the poorest quarter was supposedly the only structure left standing. This direct sign from God took hold among the local population, and Our Lord of Miracles, remains the most revered image in Peru. Thousands of devotees process through the streets of Lima and other Peruvian towns every October, and even today many women dress in purple throughout the month to honour Our Lord of Miracles.

In return for the salvation of their souls, the native population was expected to surrender their bodies to the Spanish. Some forms of service (*mita*) were simply continuations of Inca tradition – from keeping the streets clean to working in textile mills. But the most feared was a new introduction, the *mita de minas* – **forced work in the mines**. With the discovery of the 'mountain of silver' at Potosi (now in Bolivia) in 1545 and of mercury deposits at Huancavelica in 1563 it reached new heights. Forced off their small-holdings, few Indians who left to work in the mines ever returned. Indeed the mercury at Huancavelica were so dangerous that the quality of their toxic ore could be measured by the number of weekly deaths. Those who were taken to Potosi had to be chained together to stop them escaping: if they fell lame their bodies were cut from the shackles by sword to save precious time. Some 3 million Indians worked in Potosi and Huancavelica alone – some of them had to walk over 1,000km from Cuzco to Potosi for the privilege of working themselves to death.

In 1569, **Francisco Toledo** arrived in Peru to become Viceroy. His aim was to reform the colonial system so as to increase royal revenue while at the same time improving the lot of the native population. Before he could get on with that, however, he had to squash a rapidly developing threat to the colony – the upsurgence of a **neo-Inca State**. After an unsuccessful uprising in 1536, Manco Inca, Pizarro's puppet emperor, had disappeared with a few thousand loyal subjects into the remote mountainous regions of Vilcabamba, northwest of Cuzco. With the full regalia of high-priests, virgins of the sun and the golden idol *punchau*, he maintained a rebel Inca State and built himself impressive new palaces and fortresses between Vitcos and Espiritu Pampa – well beyond the reach of colonial power. Although not a substantial threat to the colony, Manco's forces repeatedly raided nearby settlements and robbed travellers on the roads between Cuzco and Lima.

Manco himself died at the hands of a Spanish outlaw, a guest at Vilcabamba who hoped to win himself a pardon from the crown. But the neo-Inca State continued under the leadership of Manco's son, Sairi Tupac, who assumed the imperial fringe at the age of ten. Tempted out of Vilcabamba in 1557, Sairi Tupac was offered a palace and a wealthy life in return for giving up his refuge and subversive aims. He died a young man, only three years after turning to Christianity and laying aside his father's cause. Meanwhile Titu Cusi, one of Manco's illegitimate sons, declared himself emperor and took control in Vilcabamba.

Eventually, Titu Cusi began to open his doors. First he allowed two Spanish friars to enter his camp and then, in 1571, negotiations were opened for a return to Cuzco when an emissary arrived from viceroy Toledo. The talks broke down before the year was out and Toledo decided to send an army into Vilcabamba to rout the Incas. They arrived to find that Titu Cusi was already dead and his brother, **Tupac Amaru,** the new emperor. After fierce fighting and a near escape, Tupac Amaru was captured and brought to trial in Cuzco. Accused of plotting to overthrow the Spanish and of inciting his followers to raid towns, Toledo saw that Tupac Amaru was beheaded as soon as possible – an act which was disavowed by the Spanish crown and caused much distress in Peru.

Toledo's next task was to establish firmly the viceregal position – something which outlasted him by some two centuries. He toured highland Peru searching for ways to improve crown control, starting with an attempt to curb the excesses of the *encomenderos* and their tax-collecting *curacas* (hereditary native leaders), by implementing a programme of **reducciones** – the physical resettlement of Indians in new towns and villages. Hundreds of thousands of peasants, perhaps millions, was forced to move from remote hamlets into large conglomerations or *reducciones* in convenient locations. Priests or *corregidores* were placed in charge of them, undercutting the power of *encomenderos*. Toledo also established a new elected position – the local mayor (or *varayoc*) – in an attempt to displace the curacas (hereditary native leaders). The *varayoc*, however, was not necessarily a good colonial tool in that, even more than the *curacas*, his interests were rooted firmly in the *allyu* and his own neighbours, rather than in the wealth of some distant kingdom.

Seeds of independence

When the Hapsburgs gave way to the Bourbon kings in Spain at the beginning of the eighteenth century, shivers of protest seemed to reverberate deep in the Peruvian hinterland. There were a number of serious **native rebellions** against colonial rule during the next hundred years. One of the most important, though least known, was that led by Juan Santos Atahualpa, a *mestizo* from Cuzco. Juan Santos had travelled to Spain, Africa and some say to England as a young man in the service of a wealthy Jesuit priest. Returning to Peru in 1740 he was imbued with revolutionary fervour and moved into the high jungle region between *Tarma* and the *Ucayali River* where he roused the forest Indians to rebellion. Throwing out the whites, he established a millenarian cult and, with an Indian army recruited from several tribes, successfully repelled all attacks by the authorities. Although never extending his powers beyond Tarma, he lived a free man until his death in 1756.

Twenty years later there were further violent native protests throughout the country against the enforcement of *repartimientos*. Under this new system the peasants were obliged to buy most of their essential goods from the *corregidores*, who as monopoly suppliers sold poor quality produce at grossly inflated prices.

In 1780, another *mestizo*, José Gabriel Condorcanqui, led a rebellion calling himself **Tupac Amaru II.** Whipping up the already inflamed peasant opinion around Cuzco into a revolutionary frenzy, he imprisoned a local *corregidor* before going on to massacre a troop of nearly 600 Royalist soldiers. Within 12

months Tupac Amaru II had been captured and executed but his rebellion had demonstrated both a definite weakness in colonial control and the high degree of popular unrest. Over the next decade several administrative reforms were to alter the situation, at least superficially: the *repartimiento* and the *corregimento* systems were abolished. In 1784, Charles III appointed a French nobleman – Teodoro de Croix – as the new viceroy to Peru and divided the country into seven intendencies containing some 52 provinces. This created tighter direct royal control, but also unwittingly provided the pattern for the Republican state of federated *departmentos*.

The end of the eighteenth century saw profound changes throughout the world. The North American colonies had gained their independence from Britain; France had been rocked by a people's revolution; and liberal ideas where spreading everywhere. Newspapers and periodicals began to appear on the streets of Lima, and discontent was expressed at all levels of society. A strong sense of **Peruvian nationalism** emerged in the pages of *Mercurio Peruano* (first printed in the 1790s), a concept which was vital to the coming changes. Even the architecture of Lima had changed in the mid-eighteenth century, as if to welcome the new era. Wide avenues suddenly appeared, public parks were opened and palatial salons were given over for the discourse of gentlemen. The philosophy of the enlightenment was slowly but surely pervading attitudes even in remote Peru.

When, in 1808, Napoleon took control of Spain, the authorities and elites in all the Spanish colonies found themselves in a new and unprecedented position. Was their loyalty to Spain or its rightful king? Who was the rightful king now?

Initially there were a few unsuccessful, locally-based protests in response both to this ambiguous situation and to the age-old agrarian problem, but it was only with the intervention of outside forces that independence was to become a serious issue in Peru. The American War of Independence, the French Revolution and Napoleon's invasion of Spain all pointed towards the opportunity of throwing off the shackles of colonialism, and by the time Ferdinand returned to the Spanish throne in

1814, Royalist troops were struggling to maintain order throughout South America. Venezuela and Argentina had already declared their independence, and in 1817 San Martin liberated Chile by force. It was only a matter of time before one of the great Liberators – **San Martin** in the south or **Bolivar** in the north – reached Peru.

San Martin was the first to do so. Having already liberated Argentina and Chile, he contracted an English naval officer, Lord Cochrane, to attack Lima. By September 1819 the first rebel invaders had landed at Paracas. Ica, Huanuco and then the north of Peru soon opted for independence, and the Royalists, cut off in Lima, retreated into the mountains. Entering the capital without a struggle, San Martin proclaimed Peruvian **Independence** on July 28th 1821.

The Republic

San Martin immediately assumed political control of the fledgling nation. Under the title 'Protector of Peru' he set about attempting to devise a workable **constitution** for the new nation – at one point even considering importing European royalty to establish a new monarchy. A libertarian as well as a liberator, San Martin declared freedom for slaves' children, abolished Indian service and even outlawed the term 'Indian'. But in practice, with Royalist troops still controlling large sectors of the sierra, his approach did more to frighten the establishment than it did to help the slaves and peasants whose problems remain, even now, deeply rooted in their social and territorial inheritance.

The development of a relatively stable political system took virtually the rest of the nineteenth century, although Spanish resistance to independence was finally extinguished at the Battles of Junin and Ayacucho in 1824. By this time San Martin had given up the political power game, handing over to **Simon Bolivar,** a man of enormous force with definite tendencies towards megalomania. Between them, Bolivar and his right-hand man Sucre, divided Peru in half, with Sucre as first president of the upper sector, renamed Bolivia. Bolivar himself remained dictator of a vast Andean Confederation – encompassing Colombia, Venezuela, Ecuador, Peru and Bolivia – until 1826. Within a year of his withdrawal, however, the Peruvians had torn up his controversial constitution and voted the liberal General La Mar as president.

On La Mar's heels raced a generation of *caudillos*, military men, often *mestizos* of middle-class origins who had achieved recognition (on either side) in the battles for Independence. The history of the early Republic consists almost entirely of internal disputes between the *creole* aristocracy and dictatorial *caudillos*. Peru plunged deep into a period of domestic and foreign plot and counterplot, while the economy and some of the nation's finest natural resources withered away.

Generals **Santa Cruz** and **Gamarra** stand out as two of the most ruthless players in this high stakes power game: overthrowing La Mar in 1829, Santa Cruz became President of Bolivia and Gamarra of Peru. Only four years later the liberal *creoles* fought back with the election of General Orbegoso to the presidency. Gamarra, attempting to oust Orbegoso in a quiet palace revolution, was overwhelmed and exiled. But the Liberal constitution of 1834, despite its severe limitations on presidential power, still proved too much for the army – Orbegoso was overthrown within six months.

Unable to sit on the side lines and watch the increasing pandemonium of Peruvian politics, Santa Cruz invaded Peru from Bolivia and installed himself as 'Protector' in 1837. Very few South Americans were happy with this situation, least of all Gamarra who joined with other exiles in Chile to plot revenge. After fierce fighting, Gamarra defeated Santa Cruz at Yungay, restored himself as President of Peru for two years, then died in 1841. During the next four years Peru had six more presidents; none of any notable ability.

Ramon Castilla was the first president to bring any real strength to his office. On his assumption of power in 1845 the country began to develop more positively on the rising wave of a booming export in *guano* fertiliser. In

1856 a new moderate constitution was approved and Castilla began his second term of office in an atmosphere of growth and hope – there were railways to be built and the Amazon waterways to be opened up. Sugar and cotton became important exports from coastal plantations and the *guano* deposits yielded a revenue of $15,000,000 in 1860. Castilla abolished Indian tribute and managed to emancipate the slaves without social and economic disruption by buying them from their 'owners' – *guano* income proved useful for this compensation.

His successors fared less happily. President Balta (1868–72) presided over the construction of most of the railways, but overspent so freely on these and a variety of other public and engineering works that he left the country on the brink of economic collapse. In the 1872 elections an attempted military coup was spontaneously crushed by a civilian mob, and Peru's first civilian president – the *laissez-faire* capitalist Manuel Pardo – assumed power.

The War of the Pacific

By the late nineteenth century Peru's foreign debt, particularly to England, had grown out of all proportion. Even though interest could be paid in *guano* there simply wasn't enough. To make matters considerably worse, Peru went to war with Chile in 1879.

Lasting over four years this '**War of the Pacific**' was basically a battle for the rich nitrate deposits located in Bolivian territory. Peru had pressured its ally Bolivia into imposing an export tax on nitrates mined by the Chilean-British corporation. Chile's answer was to occupy the area and declare war on Peru and Bolivia. Emerging victorious both on land and at sea, Chilean forces had occupied Lima by the beginning of 1881 and the Peruvian president had fled to Europe. By 1883 Peru 'lay helpless under the boots of its conquerors', and only a diplomatic rescue seemed possible. The **Treaty of Anco,** possibly Peru's greatest national humiliation, brought the war to a close in October 1883. Peru was forced to accept the cloistering of Bolivia high up in the Andes, with no land link to the Pacific, and the even harder loss of the nitrate fields to Chile. The country seemed in ruins: the *guano* virtually exhausted and the nitrates lost to Chile, the nation's coffers empty and a new generation of *caudillos* ready to resume the power struggle all over again.

The twentieth century

Modern Peru is generally considered to have been born in 1895 with the forced resignation of General Caceres. But in fairness the seeds of industrial development had been laid under his rule, albeit by foreigners. In 1890 an international plan was agreed to bail Peru out of its bankruptcy. The **Peruvian Corporation** was formed in London and assumed the £50,000,000 national debt in return for 'control of the national economy': they took over the railways, navigation of Lake Titicaca, vast quantities of *guano*, and had free use of seven Peruvian ports for 66 years as well as the opportunity to start exploiting the rubber resources of the Amazon. Under Nicolas de Pierola, some sort of stability had begun to return by the end of the nineteenth century.

In the early years of the twentieth century, Peru was run by an oligarchical clan of big businessmen and great landowners. Fortunes were made in a wide range of exploitative enterprises, above all sugar along the coast, minerals from the mountains and rubber from the jungle. Meanwhile, the lot of the ordinary peasant worsened dramatically.

One of the most powerful Oligarchs, **Leguía,** rose to power through his possession of franchises for the New York Insurance Company and the British Sugar Company. He became a prominent figure representing the rising bourgeoisie in the early 1900s – and in 1908 he was the first of their kind to be elected President. Under his rule the influence of foreign investment increased rapidly, with North American money taking pride of place over British. It was with this capital that Lima was modernised – park, plazas, the Avenida Arequipa, the Presidential Palace all date from this period. But for the majority of Peruvians, Leguía did nothing. The lot of the mountain peasants worsened, and the jungle Indians lived as near slaves on the rubber plantations. Not surprisingly, his time in power coincided with a large number of Indian rebellions, general discontent and the rise of the first labour movement in Peru. Elected for a second term, Leguía became still more dictatorial, changing the constitution so that he could be re-elected on another two occasions. A year after the beginning of his fourth term he was ousted by a military coup – in 1930 – more as a result of the Wall Street Crash and Peru's close links with US finance than for his other political failings.

During Leguía's long dictatorship, the **labour movement** began to flex its muscles. A General Strike in 1919 had established an 8–hour day and ten years later the Unions formed the first National Labour Centre. The World depression of the early 1930s hit Peru particularly badly; demand for all its main exports (petrol, silver, sugar, cotton and coffee) fell off drastically. Finally, in 1932, the Trujillo middle class led a violent uprising against the sugar barons and the primitive conditions of work on the plantations. Suppressed by the army, nearly 5,000 lives are thought to have been lost, many of the rebels being taken out in trucks and shot among the ruins of Chan Chan.

The rise of **APRA** – the American Popular Revolutionary Alliance – which had instigated the Trujillo uprising, and the growing popularity of its leader, Haya de la Torre, kept the nation busy during the Second World War. Allowed to participate for the first time in the 1945 elections, APRA chose a neutral candidate – Dr Bustamante – in place of Haya de la Torre whose fervent radicalism was considered a vote loser. Bustamante won the elections with APRA controlling 18 out of 29 seats in the Senate and 53 out of 84 in the Chamber of Deputies. The first act of the Senate was an expression of pleasure at the Labour party's victory in Britain.

Postwar euphoria was short-lived however; inflation was totally out of hand and apparently unaffected by Bustamante's exchange controls. During the 1940s the cost of living in Peru rose by 262 per cent. With anti-APRA feeling on the rise, the president leaned more and more heavily on support from the army, until General Odria led a coup d'état from Arequipa in 1948 and formed a military junta. By the time Odria was through with office, in 1956, a new political element threatened oligarchical control – the young **Belaunde** and his *National Youth Front* (later *Accion Popular*) demanding 'radical' reform. Even with the support of APRA and the army, Manuel Prado barely defeated Belaunde

in the next elections: the unholy alliance between the Establishment and APRA has been known as the 'marriage of convenience' ever since.

The economy remained in dire straits. Domestic prices continued to soar and in 1952 alone there were some 200 strikes and several serious riots. Meanwhile much more radical feeling was aroused in the provinces by **Hugo Blanco,** a charismatic *mestizo* from Cuzco who had joined a trotskyist group – the *Workers Revolutionary Party* – which was later to merge with the *FIR* – the *Revolutionary Left's Front*. In La Convencion, within the Department of Cuzco, Blanco created nearly 150 syndicates, whose peasant members began to work their own individual plots while refusing to labour for the hacienda owners. Many landowners became bankrupt or opted to 'bribe' labourers back with offers of cash wages. The second phase of Blanco's 'reform' was physically to take over the haciendas, mostly in areas so isolated that the authorities were powerless to intervene. Blanco was finally arrested in 1963 but the effects of his peasant revolt outlived him: in future Peruvian governments were to take agrarian reform far more seriously.

Back in Lima, the elections of 1962 had resulted in an interesting dead-lock with Haya de la Torre having 33 per cent of the votes, Belaunde 32 per cent and Odria 28.5 per cent. Almost inevitably, the army took control, annulled the elections and denied Haya de la Torre and Belaunde the opportunity of power for another year. By 1963, though, neither *Accion Popular* or *APRA* were sufficiently radical to pose a serious threat to the establishment. Elected president for the first time, Belaunde quickly got to work on a severely diluted programme of agrarian reform, a compromise never forgiven by his left-wing supporters. More successfully, though, he began to draw in quantities of foreign capital. President De Gaulle visited Peru in 1964 and the first British Foreign Secretary ever to set foot in South America arrived in Lima two years later. Foreign investors were clamouring to get in on Belaunde's ambitious development plans and obtain a rake off from Peru's oil-fields. But by 1965 domestic inflation had so severely damaged the balance of payments that confidence was beginning to slip away from Belaunde's international stance.

By now, many intellectuals and government officials saw the agrarian situation as an urgent economic problem as well as a matter of social justice. Even the army believed that **Agrarian Reform** was a prerequisite for the development of a larger market without which any genuine industrial development would prove impossible. On October 3rd 1968, tanks smashed through the gates into the courtyard of the Presidential Palace. General Velasco and the army seized power, deporting Belaunde and ensuring that Haya de la Torre could not even participate in the forthcoming elections.

The new government, revolutionary for a **Military Regime,** gave the land back to the workers in 1969. The great plantations were turned virtually overnight into producers' co-operatives, in an attempt to create a genuinely self-determining peasant class. At the same time guerilla leaders were brought to trial, political activity was banned in the universities, indigenous banks were controlled, foreign banks nationalised and diplomatic relations established with East European countries. By the end of military rule, in 1980, the Agrarian Reform had done much to abolish the large capitalist landholding system.

Even now, though, a shortage of good land in the sierra and the lack of decent irrigation on the coast means that less than 20 per cent of the landless workers have been integrated into the co-operative system – the majority remain in seasonal work and/or the small farm sector. One of the major problems for the Military Regime, and one which still plagues the economy, was the **fishing crisis** in the 1970s. An overestimation of the fishing potential led to the build-up of a highly capital-intensive fish-canning and fish-meal industry, in its time one of the world's most modern. Unfortunately, the fish began to disappear because of a combination of ecological changes and overfishing – leaving vast quantities of capital equipment inactive and thousands of people unemployed,

Although undeniably an important step forward, the 1968 military coup was always an essentially bourgeois revolution, imposed from above to speed up the transformation from a land-based oligarchy to a capitalist society. Paternalistic, even dictatorial, it did little to satisfy the demands of the more extreme peasant reformers, and the military leaders eventually handed back power voluntarily in democratic elections.

Political update

After 12 years of military government, the 1980 elections resulted in a centre-right alliance between *Accion Popular* and the *Popular Christian Party.* **Belaunde** resumed the presidency having become an established celebrity during his years of exile and having built up, too, an impressive array of international contacts. The policy of his government was to increase the pace of development still further, and in particular to emulate the Brazilian success in opening up the Amazon – building new roads and exploiting the uncounted wealth in oil, minerals, lumber and agriculture. But inflation (over 150 per cent) remains an apparently insuperable problem, and Belaunde has fared little better in coming to terms with either the parliamentary Marxists of the *United Left* or the escalating guerilla movement led by *Sendero Luminoso.*

Appearing from nowhere in 1980, **Sendero Luminoso** (the Shining Path) have persistently discounted the possibility of change through the ballot box and adopted armed struggle as the only means to achieve their 'anti-feudal, anti-imperial' revolution in Peru. Following the line of the *Gang of Four*, Sendero are led by Abimael Guzman (or Comrade Gonzalo) whose ideas they claim to be in the direct lineage Marx-Lenin-Mao-Gonzalo. Gonzalo himself – originally a philosophy lecturer from Ayacucho – hasn't been seen in public for several years, but his organisation, thought to have some 7,000 secret members, has remained very active. Rejecting Belaunde's style of technological development as imperialist and the United Left as 'parliamentary cretins', they carry out attacks on business interests, local officials and police posts, and anything regarded as outside interference in the self-determination of the peasantry. On the whole members are recruited from the poorest areas of the country and from the *Quechua* speaking population, coming together for their paramilitary operations and melting back into the obscurity of their communities.

Although strategic points in Lima have been attacked – police stations, petrochemical plants and power lines – Sendero's main centre of activity is in the sierra around Ayacucho and Huanta, more recently spreading into the remote regions around Vilcabamba – site of the last Inca resistance, a traditional hideout for rebels, and the centre of Hugo Blanco's activities in the 1960s. By remaining small and unpredictable, Sendero has managed to wage its war on the Peruvian establishment with the minimum risk of major confrontations with government forces.

The **government reponse** has been to tie up enormous amounts of manpower in counter-insurgency operations whose main effect seems to be to increase popular sympathy for the guerillas. In 1984 more than 6,000 troops,

marines and anti-terrorist police were deployed against Sendero, and at least 3,000 people, mostly peasants, are said to have been killed. 'Disappearances', especially around Ayacucho, are an everyday occurrence, and most people blame the security forces for the bulk of them. Belaunde's popularity has slipped disastrously. In August 1984 even the chief of command of the counter-insurgency forces joined the criticism of the government's failure to provide promised development aid to Ayacucho. He was promptly dismissed for his claims that the problems were 'the harvest of 160 years of neglect' and that the solution was 'not a military one'.

Most recently, new urban-based terrorist groups have begun to make their presence felt, like the *Tupacamaristas* in Villa El Salvador, a shanty town outside Lima. Belaunde lost office in the April **1985 elections** with APRA taking power for the first time and the *United Left* also getting a large percentage of the votes. Whether or not this change in the balance of power will cause *Sendero Luminoso* to change its stance towards parliamentary matters is uncertain.

INCA LIFE – AND ACHIEVEMENT

In less than a century, the Incas developed and knitted together a vast empire peopled by something like 20 million Indians. They established an imperial religion which didn't drastically clash with those of their subject tribes; erected monolithic fortresses, salubrious palaces and temples; and, astonishingly, evolved a viable economy – strong enough to maintain a top-heavy elite in almost godlike grandeur. To understand these achievements and get some idea of what they must have meant in Peru 500 or 600 years ago, you really have to see for yourself their surviving heritage: the stones of Inca ruins and roads; the cultural objects in the museums of Lima and Cuzco; and their living descendants who still toil the soil and talk *Quechua* – the language used by the Incas to unify their empire. What follows is but the briefest of introductions to their history, society and achievements.

Society and the politics of control

The Inca Empire rapidly developed a **hierarchical structure.** At the highest level it was governed by the **Sapa Inca,** son of the sun and direct descendant of god. Under him were priest-nobles – the royal **allyu** or kin group which filled most of the important administrative and religious posts – and, working for them, regional allyu chiefs, **curacas** or orejones, responsible for controlling tribute from the peasant base. One-third of the land belonged to the Emperor and the State; another to the High Priests, gods and the sun; the last was for the allyu themselves. Work on the land, then, was devoted to maintaining the Empire rather than mere subsistence, though in times of famine store-houses were evidently opened to feed the commoners.

Life for **the elite** wasn't, perhaps, quite as easy as it may appear: their fringe benefits were matched by the strain and worry of governing an empire, sending armies everywhere and keeping the gods happy. The Inca nobles were nevertheless fond of relaxing in thermal baths, of hunting holidays and of conspicuous eating and drinking whenever the religious calendar permitted. Allyu chiefs were often unrelated to the royal Inca lineage, but their position was normally hereditary. As lesser nobles they were allowed to wear earplugs and special ornate headbands; their task was to squeeze and protect the commoners but they themselves were free of labour service.

The hierarchical network swept down the ranks from important chiefs in a decimalised system. One of the larger *curacas* (lesser nobles) might be responsible for 10,000 men; under him two lower chiefs were each responsible for 5,000, and so on until in the smallest hamlets there was one man responsible for ten others. Women weren't counted in the census. For the Incas, a household was represented by the man and only he was obliged to fulfil tribute duties on behalf of the allyu. Within the family the woman's role was dependent on her relationship with the dominant man – be he father, brother, husband or eldest son.

In their conquests the Incas absorbed **craftsmen** from every corner of the Empire. Goldsmiths, potters, carpenters, sculptors, masons and *quipumayocs* (accountants) were frequently removed from their localities to work directly for the Emperor in Cuzco. These skilled men lost no time in developing into a new and entirely separate class of citizens. The work of even the lowest servant in the palace was highly regulated by a stiff demarcation of labour. If a man was employed to be a woodcutter he wouldn't be expected to gather wood from the forests; that was the task of another employee.

Throughout the Empire young girls, usually about 9 or 10 years old, were constantly selected for their beauty and serene intelligence. Those deemed perfect enough were taken to an *acclahuasi* – a special sanctuary for the 'Chosen Women' – where they were trained in specific tasks, including the spinning and weaving of fine cloth and the higher culinary arts. Most Chosen Women were destined ultimately to become *mamaconas* (Virgins of the Sun) or the concubines of either nobles or the Sapa Inca himself. Occasionally some of them were sacrificed by strangulation in order to appease the gods.

For most Inac **women** the allotted role was simply that of peasant/domestic work and rearing children. After giving birth a mother would wash her baby in a nearby stream to cleanse and purify it and return virtually immediately to normal daily activities, carrying the child in a cradle tied on her back with a shawl. As they still are today, most babies were breastfed for years before leaving their mothers to take their place in the domestic life-cycle. As adults their particular role in society was dependent first on sex then on hierarchical status.

Special regulations affected both the **old** and **disabled.** Around the age of 50, a man was likely to pass into the category of 'old'. He was no longer capable of undertaking a normal work-load, he wasn't expected to pay taxes, and he could always depend on support from the official store-houses. Nevertheless, the community still made small demands by using him to collect fire-wood and other such tasks – in much the same way as the kids were expected to help out around the house and in the fields. In fact the children and old people often worked together, the young learning directly from the old. Disabled people were obliged to work within their potential – the blind, for instance, might de-husk maize or clean cotton. Although always maintained fairly from official stocks an Inca law bound the deformed or disabled to marry similarly unfortunate persons, e.g. dwarfs to dwarfs, blind to blind, legless to legless.

In Inca eyes the known world was their empire and **absorption** therefore limitless. They divided their territories into four basic regions or **suyos** each radiating from the central plaza in Cuzco: *Chincha Suyo* (north-west), *Anit Suyo* (north-east), *Cunti Suyo* (south-west) and *Colla Suyo* (south-east). Each suyo naturally had its own particular problems and characteristics but all were approached in the same way – initially being demoralised or forced into submission by the Inca army, later absorbed as allies for further conquests. In this way the Incas never seemed to over-extend their lines to the fighting front. The most impressive feature of an Inca army must in fact have been its sheer numbers – a relatively minor force would have included 5,000 men. Their armour usually consisted of quilted cotton shirts, a small shield painted with designs or decorated with magnificent plumes. The common warriors – using slingshots, spears, axes, and maces – were often supported by bowmen drafted from the 'savages' living in the eastern forests; and when the Spanish arrived on horseback the Incas were quick to invent new weapons: large two-handed hardwood swords and *bolas* (wooden balls connected by a string) good for tangling up the horses legs. The only prisoners of war traditionally taken by a conquering Inca army were chieftains, who lived comfortably in Cuzco as hostages against the good behaviour of their respective tribes. Along with the chiefs, most of the important portable idols and *huacas* of conquered peoples were 'looked after' in Cuzco as sacred hostages. Often the children of the ruling chieftains were also taken to Cuzco to be indoctrinated in Inca ways.

This very pragmatic approach toward their subjects is exemplified again in the Inca policy of **forced resettlement.** Whole villages were sometimes sent into entirely new regions, ostensibly to increase the crop yield of plants like coca or maize and to vary their diet by importing manioc and chilis – though it was often criminals or rebellious citizens who ended up in the hottest, most humid regions. Large groups of people might also be sent from relatively suspect tribes into areas where mostly loyal subjects lived, or into the newly colonised outer fringes of the Empire; and many trustworthy subjects were moved into zones where restlessness might have been expected. It seems likely that the whole colonisation project was as much a political manoeuvre as a device to diversify the Inca economic or dietary base. New regions came under imperial influence and dangerous elements lurking within an otherwise fragile empire were at least geographically dispersed.

Inca economy: building and agriculture

The main resources available to the Inca Empire were agricultural land and labour, their mines (producing precious and prestigious metals such as gold, silver or copper) and fresh water, abundant everywhere except along the desert coast. With careful manipulation of these resources, the Incas managed to keep things ticking over the way they wanted. Tribute in the form of **service** – *mita* – played a crucial role in maintaining the Empire and pressurising its subjects into ambitious building and irrigation projects. Some of these projects were so grand, that they would have been impossible without the demanding whip of a totalitarian state.

Although a certain degree of local barter was allowed, the State regulated the distribution of every important product, including the use of its astonishing **highways** – the key to its economic success. Some of the tracks were nearly 8m wide and at the time of the Spanish Conquest the main Royal Highway ran some 5,000km from the Ancasmayo river in Colombia down the backbone of the Andes to the coast at a point south of present day Santiago in Chile. The Incas didn't know of the wheel but gigantic llama caravans were a common sight tramping along the roads, each animal carrying up to 50 kilos of cargo. Every corner of the Inca domain was easily accessible via branch roads, all designed or taken over and unified around one intent – to dominate and administer an enormous Empire. Runners were posted at *chasqui* stations and *tambo* rest-houses which punctuated the road at intervals between 2 and 15km. Fresh fish was relayed on foot from the coast and messages were sent with runners from Quito to Cuzco (2,000km) in less than six days. The more difficult mountain canyons were crossed on bridges suspended from cables braided out of jungle *lianas* (creeping vines) and high passes were – and still are – frequently reached by incredible stairways cut into solid rock cliffs.

The primary sector in the economy was inevitably **agriculture** and in this the Incas made two major advances: large terracing projects created the opportunity for agricultural specialists to experiment with new crops and methods of cultivation; and the transport system allowed a virtual revolution in distribution. Megalithic agricultural **terracing projects** were going on continuously in Inca-dominated mountain regions. The best examples of these are in the Cuzco area – at Tipón, Moray, Ollantaytambo, Pisac and Cusichaca. Beyond the aesthetic beauty of Inca stone terraces – demonstrating the transformation of the material world into an envisaged cultural ideal – they have distinct practical advantages. Stepping hillsides minimises erosion from landslides, and by using well-engineered stone channels gives complete control over irrigation. Natural springs emerging on the hillsides became the focus of an intricate network of canals and aqueducts extending over the surrounding slopes which themselves had been converted into elegant stone terraces. An extra incentive to the Inca mind must surely have been their reverence of water, one of the major earthly spirits. The Inca terraces are often so elaborately designed around springs that they seem to be worshipping as much as utilising water.

The construction industry assembled the most permanent Inca heritage of all – vast **building projects** masterminded by high-ranking nobles and architects, and supervised by expert masons with an almost limitless pool of peasant labour. Without paper the architects resorted to imposing their imagination onto clay or stone, making miniature models of the more important constructions – good examples of which can be seen in the Cuzco Archaeological Museum. The Inca masonry, however, can still be seen in situ throughout Peru – most spectacularly at the fortress of Sascayhuaman above Cuzco, and on the coast in the Achirana aqueduct, which even today still brings water down to the Ica valley from high up in the Andes. In the mountains, Inca stonework gave a permanence to edifices which would otherwise have needed constant renovation. The damp climate and mould quickly destroyed anything but solid rock. Spanish and modern buildings have often collapsed around well-built Inca walls – through both the weather and earthquake activity. Strangely though, unlike earlier cultures, most stones carved or engraved by the Incas were small portable objects like dishes or amulets.

The **Inca diet** was essentially vegetarian, based on the staple potato but encompassing a range of other foods like quinoa, beans, squashes, sweet potatoes, avocados, tomatoes and manioc. In the highlands emphasis was on root crops like potatoes which have been known to survive in 18 degrees of frost at over 5,000m. On the valley floors and lower slopes of the Andes maize cultivation predominated. The importance of maize both as a food crop and for making *chicha* increased dramatically under the Incas; previously it had been grown for ceremony and ritual exchange – as a status crop rather than a staple. The use of **coca** was restricted to the priests and Inca elite. Coca is a mild narcotic stimulant which effectively dulls the body against cold, hunger and tiredness when the leaves are chewed in the mouth with a catalyst such as lime or calcium. Its leaves possessed magical properties for the Incas – they could be cast to divine future events, offered as a gift to the wind, the earth or the mountain apu, and they could be used in witchcraft. Today it's difficult to imagine the Incas having great success in restricting coca growing and use; even with helicopters and machine guns the authorities are unable to control its production.

In **artesania,** high standards were achieved in **pottery** around Cuzco, with pieces well-polished and baked to perfection – but Inca designs generally lack imagination and variety, tending to have been mass-produced on techniques evolved by previous cultures. The most common pottery was the *aryballus* – a large jar with a conical base and a wide neck thought to have been used chiefly for storing chicha. Its decoration was usually geometric, often associated with the back-bone of a fish – the central spine of the pattern was adorned with rows of spikes radiating from either side. Fine plates were made with anthropomorphic-shaped handles, and large numbers of cylindrically tapering goblets – *keros* – were manufactured, though these were often of cedar wood rather than pottery.

The refinements in **metallurgy,** like the ceramics industry, were mostly developed by craftsmen absorbed from different corners of the Empire. The Chimu were particularly respected by the Incas for their superb metal-work. Within the Empire bronze and copper were used for axe-blades and tumi knives; gold and silver were restricted to ritual use and for nobles. The Incas smelted their metal ores in cylindrical terracotta and adobe furnaces which made good use of prevailing breezes to fire large lumps of charcoal. Molten ores were pulled out from the base of the furnace. Although the majority of surviving metal artifacts – those you see in museums – have been made from beaten sheets there were plenty of cast or cut solid gold and silver pieces. Few of these survived due to being melted down by the Conquistadores, who weren't after all interested in precious objects for their artistic merits.

Religion

The Incas smoothly incorporated the religious features of most subjugated regions. The setting for beliefs, idols and oracles, more or less throughout the entire Empire, had been preordained over the previous 2,000 years: a general recognition of certain creator deities, and a whole pantheon of nature related spirits, minor deities and demons. This customary form of worship varied a little but everywhere the Incas (and later the Spanish) found the creator god amongst other animistic spirits and concepts of power related to lightning, thunder and rainbows. The Incas merely superimposed their variety of mystical, yet inherently practical, elements onto those that they came across.

The main novelty introduced by Inca religious domination was their demand to be recognised as direct descendents of the creator-god **Viracocha.** A claim to divine earthly perfection was, to the Incas, a valid excuse for military and cultural expansion. There was no need to destroy the *huacas* and oracles of subjugated peoples; on the contrary, certain sacred sites were intrinsically holy in the sense of being powerful spots for communication with the spirit world. When ancient shrines like Pachacamac, near Lima, were absorbed into the Empire they were simply turned over to worship on Imperial terms.

The sun is considered the Inca's traditionally worshipped deity and the visible head of the State religion – Viracocha was a less direct, more ethereal, force. The sun's role was naturally overt, as life-giver to an agriculturally-based Empire, and its cycle intricately related to agrarian practice and annual ritual patterns. To think of the Inca religion as essentially sun worship though would be far too simplistic. There were distinct layers in **Inca cosmology:** the level of creation, the astral level, and the earthly dimension. The first, highest level corresponds to Viracocha as the creator god and culture hero who brought life to the world and society to mankind. Below this, on the astral level, are the celestial gods – the sun itself, the moon and certain stars (particularly Venus and the Pleiades, patrons of fertility). The earthly dimension, although that of man, was no less magical – endowed with important *huacas* and shrines which might take the form of unusual rocks or peaks, caves, tombs, mummies and natural springs.

The astral level and earthly dimension were probably fairly ubiquitous in Peru before the Incas rose to power. The creator and who he favoured was the critical factor in their claims to divine right of Imperial government, and the hierarchical structure of religious ranking also reflects the division of the religious spheres into those that were around before, during and after the Empire and those that only stayed as long as Inca domination lasted. At the very top of this **religio-social hierarchy** was the *Villac Uma*, the High Priest of Cuzco, usually a brother of the Lord Inca himself. Under him were perhaps hundreds of high priests, all nobles of royal blood who were responsible for ceremony, temples, shrines, divination, curing and sacrifice within the realm, and below them the ordinary priests and Chosen Women. The base of the hierarchy though, and probably the most numerous of all religious groups, were the **curanderos,** local curers practising herbal medicine and magic, and making sacrifices to small regional *huacas*.

Most **religious festivals** were calendrically-based and marked by processions, sacrifices and dances. The Incas were aware of lunar time and the solar year, although they generally used the blooming of a special cactus to gauge the correct time to begin planting. Sacrifices to the gods normally consisted of llamas, cuys or chicha – only occasionally were Chosen Women and other adults killed. Once every year, however, young children were apparently sacrificed in the most important sacred centres.

Divination was a vital role payed by priests and *curanderos* on all levels of the religious hierarchy. Soothsayers were expected to talk with the spirits and often utilised a hallucinogenic snuff from the Vilca plant to achieve a trance-like state and communion with the other world. Everything from a crackling fire to the glance of a lizard was seen as a potential omen and treated as such by making a little offering of coca leaves, coca spittle or chicha. There were specific problems which divination was considered particularly accurate in solving: retrieving lost things; predicting the outcome of certain events (the oracles were always consulted prior to important military escapades); receiving a vision of contemporaneous yet distant happenings; and the diagnosis of illness.

NIGHT SKY DESIGN FROM MOCHICA CERAMIC

ARCHITECTURAL CHRONOLOGY

20,000–10,000 BC	First evidence of **human settlement** in Peru.	Cave-dwellings in the **Ayacucho Valley;** stone artifacts in the **Chillon Valley.**
8,000–5,000 BC	**Nomadic tribes,** and more permanent settlement in fertile coastal areas.	Cave paintings and fine stone tools.
5,000–2,000 BC	Introduction of **cultivation** and stable settlements.	Early agriculturalist sites include **Huaca Prieta** in the Chicama Valley, **Paracas** and **Kotosh.**
1200 BC–200 AD	Formative era and emergence of the **Chavin Cult,** with great progress in ceramics and metallurgy.	Temple complex at **Chavin de Huantar,** important sites too at **Kotosh** and **Sechin.**
300 AD	Technological advances marked above all in the Viru Valley – the **Gallinazo Culture** – and at Paracas.	Sites in the **Viru Valley,** at **Paracas,** and the growth of Tiahuanuco culture around **Lake Titicaca.**
200–1100 AD	**Classical Cultures** emergent throughout the land.	**Mochica** culture and Temples of the Sun and Moon near Trujillo; further **Tiahuanuco** development; **Nazca lines** and **Cahuachi** complex on the coast; **Wilkawain** temple; **Huari** complex, and **Tantamayo** ruins.
1200	The age of the great city builders.	Well-preserved adobe settlements survive at **Chan Chan** (near Trujillo) and and **Cajamarquilla** (Lima).
1438–1532	Expansion of the **Inca Empire** from its base around Cuzco north into Ecuador and south into Chile.	Inca sites survive throughout Peru, but the greatest are still around **Cuzco** – **Sacsayhuaman** and **Machu Picchu** above all. **Inca Highway** constructed from Colombia to Chile; parts still in existence.
1532	**Pizarro** lands at Tumbes, captures Atahualpa.	
1533	**Atahualpa executed,** Pizarro reaches Cuzco.	**Colonial architecture** draws heavily on Spanish influences, though native craftsmen leave their mark too. Church building above all – at **Arequipa** (Santa Catalina Convent) and around Cuzco. The Spanish city of **Cuzco** incorporates much Inca stonework.
1535	**Foundation of Lima.**	
1536	**Manco Inca** rebels.	
1545	Silver deposits of **Potosi** discovered.	

		Meanwhile the rebel Incas build new cities around **Vilcabamba.**
1572	Spanish invade final Inca refuge at Vilcabamba; **Tupac Amaru executed.**	
1742	Juan Santos Atahualpa leads first **peasant revolt.**	Throughout colonial rule building follows European fashion, especially into **baroque:** churches, mansions and a few public buildings constitute the majority.
1780–1	**Rebellion** under Tupac Amaru II.	
1819	San Martin's forces land at Paracas.	
1821	Peru declares **Independence.**	
1823	**Simon Bolivar** arrives; Peru and Bolivia devided.	University of Trujillo founded by Bolivar.
1824	Final defeat of the Royalists at Junin and Ayacucho.	
1870s	Construction of the railways and other engineering projects. First exploitation of Amazonian rubber.	High-altitude **railways** are remarkable engineering feats.
1879–83	**War of the Pacific** bankrupts the country: Chilean troops occupy Lima.	
1890–1930	Peru effectively under control of foreign capital	Much modernisation in **Lima** (Presidential Palace, etc.), grandiose public buildings elsewhere.
1932	Violent **APRA uprising** in Trujillo – APRA outlawed.	Massive urban growth in Lima (from 1930s onwards).
1945	APRA candidate **Bustamante** wins presidential election.	
1948	Military coup.	
1956	APRA-army alliance wins elections.	
1963	Accion Popular leader **Belaunde elected.**	**Barriadas** – organised shanty towns – begin to appear (and escalate) in Lima.
1968–80	**Military rule** – Belaunde exiled – extensive Agrarian Reform.	
1980	Return to democracy. **Belaunde re-elected.**	New **development of jungle** – lumber, oil companies and settlers threaten traditional tribal life and ecology; construction of 'Marginal Highway' into central Amazon resumed.
1985	New presidential elections:	APRA takes the scene.

BOOKS

Peruvian writers

Mario Vargas Llosa *Aunt Julia and the Scriptwriter* (£2.95), *The Time of the Hero* (Penguin, o/p), and others. The best known and the most brilliant of contemporary Peruvian writers, Vargas Llosa is essentially a novelist but has also written many books and articles commenting broadly on Peruvian society, has run his own TV current affairs programme in Lima, and even made a (rather average) feature film. *Aunt Julia,* the latest of his novels to be translated into English, is a fabulous book, a grand and comic novel spiralling out from the stories and exploits of a Bolivian scriptwriter who arrives in Lima to work on Peruvian radio soap-operas. In part too it is autobiographical, full of insights into Miraflores society and goings on. Essential reading – and perfect for long Peruvian journeys.

Ciro Alegria *Broad and Alien is the World* (Merlin Press, £3.50). Another good book to travel with, this is a distinguished 1970s novel about life in the Peruvian highlands.

Manuel Scorza *Drums for Runcas* (Sear & Wallburg, US). Radical novel dealing with the miners' struggle in the sierra. Like Llosa, Scorza writes in a style following the Latin American tradition of magical surrealism. Highly recommended.

Julio Ramon Ribeyro, Jose Mario Arguedas. Ribeyro is one of Peru's best short story writers, Arguedas is an *indigenista* – writing for and about the native peoples. Neither are yet translated into English but their Spanish editions are readily available in Lima.

Cesar Vellejo *Collected Poems of Cesar Vellejo* (Penguin, £3.50). Peru's one internationally renowned poet – and deservedly so. *Peru: The New Poetry* (Red Dust), US) includes a fairly broad selection of other modern Peruvian poets.

Inca and ancient history

John Hemmings *The Conquest of the Incas* (Abacus, £4.95). The authoritative narrative tale of the Spanish Conquest, very readably brought to life from a mass of original sources.

William Prescott *The Conquest of Peru* (o/p). Hemmings's main predecessor – a nineteenth-century classic that remains a good read.

J. Alden Mason *Ancient Civilisations of Peru* (Penguin, o/p). Now somewhat out of date, but nevertheless a good summary of the country's history from the Stone Age through to the Inca Empire.

G.H.S. Bushnell *Peru* (Thames & Hudson, o/p). From an archaeological perspective, this surveys social and technological change in Peru between 2,500 BC and 1500 AD – clear and well illustrated though again becoming out of date.

Ann Kendal *Everyday Life of the Incas* (Batsford, o/p). Accessible, very general description of Peru under Inca domination.

Victor Von Hagen *The Realm of the Incas* (1957, o/p). An easy introduction to the history/architecture of the Incas but now considerably outmoded.

Gene Savoy *Vilcabamba – The Lost City of the Incas* (1971, o/p). Exciting

account of one of Savoy's most important explorations.

Elizabeth Benson *The Mochica* (Thames & Hudson, 1971, o/p). Brief sketch of the Mochica civilisation through its vast and astonishingly realist ceramic heritage.

Garcilasco de la Vega *The Royal Commentaries of the Incas* (London & Austin, 1966, o/p). Most good libraries have a copy of this – the most readable and fascinating of contemporary sources, written shortly after the Conquest by a 'Spaniard' of essentially Inca blood.

Modern history and society

Luis Martin *The Kingdom of the Sun* (Scribner, US, 1974). Best available general history, concentrating on the post-Conquest period and bringing events more or less up to the present.

H. Dobyns and P. Doughty *Peru: A Cultural History* (Oxford Univ. Press; paperback) 1976. Similar breadth to the above – though a heavier, much more comprehensive tome.

F. Bruce Lamb *The Wizard of the Upper Amazon* (Houghton Mifflin, US, 1975; paperback). Masterful reconstruction of the true life story of Manuel Cordoba Rios – 'Ino Moxo', the famous herbal healer from Iquitos. A fairly compelling read.

Harold Osborne *Indians of the Andes* (RKP, 1951, o/p). Long out of print, but an interesting, well-travelled study.

Peter Lloyd *The 'Young Towns' of Lima* (Camb. Univ. Press, 1980; paperback). Excellent account of the barriadas and urbanisation in Peru. Quite academic.

Travel

Ronald Wright *Cut Stones and Crossroads: A Journey in the Two Worlds of Peru* (Viking Press, 1984, £9.95). An enlightened travel book – and probably the best general writing on Peru over the last couple of decades.

Dervla Murphy *Eight Feet in the Andes* (John Murray, 1983, £9.95). Enjoyable enough account of a rather adventurous journey Dervla Murphy made across the Andes with her young daughter and a mule. Not a patch on her Indian books, though.

Hiram Bingham *Lost City of the Incas* (Lima reprint). Marvellous tale of Bingham's discovery of Machu Picchu in 1911. Available quite widely in Cuzco and Lima bookshops.

George Woodcock *Incas and Other Men* (Faber, 1959, o/p). Still a good introduction to Peru 36 years on – an enjoyable, light-hearted tour, mixing modern and ancient history and travel anecdotes.

Nicole Maxwell *Witchdoctor's Apprentice* (Collier Books, US, 1973). Maxwell worked as a missionary in the Peruvian Amazon in the 1950s, and this, despite the twee American title, is a fascinating record.

Leonard Clark *The Rivers Run East* (Hutchinson, 1954, o/p). Dare-devil exploration in the grand old style, racy and at times quite intriguing (though some of the ethnographic detail needs to be taken with a pinch of salt).

Christopher Isherwood *The Condor and the Cows* (Methuen, 1949, o/p). Diary of Isherwood's South American trip after the last war, most of which took place in Peru (the condor of the title is a symbol of the Andes). Like Theroux (see below) Isherwood eventually arrives in Buenos Aires, and to a meeting with Jorge Luis Borges.

Paul Theroux *The Old Patagonian Express* (Penguin, £2.95). Theroux didn't much like Peru, nor Peruvians ('the only way to handle a Peruvian is to agree with his pessimism'), but for all the self-obsessed pique, and Evelyn Waugh-like disgust for most of humanity, at his best – being sick in trains – he is highly entertaining.

Peter Matthiessen *At Play in the Fields of the Lord* (Bantam; paperback). Celebrated American novel which catches the energy and magic of the Peruvian selva.

Specific guides

Hilary and George Bradt *Backpacking and Trekking in Peru and Bolivia* (Bradt, £4.50). Detailed and excellent coverage of some of Peru's most rewarding hikes – worth taking if you're remotely interested in the idea, and good anyway for background on wild-life and flora, etc.

Tanis and Martin Jordan *South American River Trips, II* (Bradt, £4.95). Useful practical sections on river trips in general, along with detailed accounts of a number of Peruvian possibilities – some no longer entirely advisable (see p. 240).

Peter Frost *Exploring Cuzco* (Bradt,

£5.50). A very practical and stimulating site-by-site guide to the whole Cuzco area. Unreservedly recommended if you're spending more than a few days in the region.

Jim Bartle *Trails of the Cordillera Blanca and Huayhuash* (Bradt, £4.95). Excellent trail guide for what is probably the best walking country in Peru.

All of these guides are available in Lima through the **South American Explorers' Club** (Av. Portugal 146), from **specialist bookshops** in Britain and the US (in London try the **Travel Bookshop,** 13 Blenheim Crescent, W11), or by post through **Bradt Enterprises** (41 Nortoft Rd, Chalfont St Peter, Bucks, SL9 0LA, England). The *Travel Bookshop* is also a good source for most of the out of print travel/history books detailed above.

WILD-LIFE AND ECOLOGY

Peru may well have the most diverse array of wild-life of any country on earth; its varied ecological niches relate to an incredible range of climate and terrain. And although mankind has occupied the area for perhaps as long as 20,000 years, there has been less disturbance, until relatively recently, than in most other parts of our planet. For the sake of organisation this piece follows the country's usual regional divisions – coastal desert, Andes mountains and tropical jungle – though a more accurate picture would be that of a continuous intergradation, encompassing literally dozens of unique habitats. From desert the land climbs rapidly to the tundra of mountain peaks then down again into tropical rain-forest, phasing gradually through a whole series of environments in which many of the species detailed below overlap.

The coast

The **COASTAL DESERT** is characterised by an abundant sea life and by the contrasting scarcity of terrestrial plants and animals. The *Humboldt Current* runs virtually the whole length of Peru, bringing cold water up from the depths of the Pacific Ocean and causing much moisture to condense out over the sea, depriving the mainland coastal strip and the lower western mountain slopes of rainfall. Along with this cold water large quantities of nutrients are carried up to the surface, helping to sustain a rich planktonic community able to support vast numbers of fish, preyed upon in their turn by a variety of COASTAL BIRDS AND MAMMALS. **Gulls, Terns, Pelicans, Boobies, Cormorants** and wading birds are always present along the beaches. One beautiful specimen, the **Inca Tern,** although usually well camouflaged as it sits high up on inaccessible sea cliffs, is nevertheless very common in the Lima area. The **Humboldt Penguin,** with grey rather than black features, is a rarer sight – shier than its more southerly cousins it is normally found in isolated rocky coves or on off-shore islands. Competing with the birds for fish are schools of **dolphins, sea-lion** colonies and the occasional coastal **otter.** Dolphins and sea-lions are often spotted off even the

most crowded of beaches or scavenging around the fishermen's jetty at CHORRILLOS, near Lima.

One of the most fascinating features of Peruvian bird-life are the vast high-density colonies: although the number of species is quite small, their total population is enormous. Many thousands of birds can be seen nesting on islands like the BALLESTAS off the **Paracas Peninsula** (see p. 141) or simply covering the ocean with a flapping, diving carpet of energetic feathers. This huge bird population, and the *Guanay Cormorant* in particular, is responsible for depositing mountains of *guano* (bird droppings) which form a traditional and potent source of natural fertiliser.

In contrast to the rich coastal waters **THE DESERT** lies stark and barren. Here you find only a few trees and shrubs; you need endless patient sitting or the building of a hide to see wild animals other than birds. The most common animals are feral **goats,** once domesticated but now living wild, and **burros** (or donkeys) introduced by the Spanish. A more exciting sight is the attractively coloured **coral snake** – shy but deadly and covered with a black and orange hooped skin. Most animals are more active after sunset, when out in the desert you can hear the eerily plaintive call of the *Huerequeque* (or **Peruvian Thick-Knee** bird), and the barking of the little **desert fox** – alarmingly similar to the sound of car tyres screeching to a halt. By day there are several species of small birds – a favourite being the vermillion-headed **Peruvian Flycatcher.** Near water – rivers, estuaries and lagoons – desert wild-life is at its most populous. In addition to residents such as **Flamingos, Herons** and **Egrets,** many migrant birds pause in these havens between October and March on their journeys south and then back north.

In order to understand the coastal desert you have to bear in mind the phenomenon of *EL NINO,* a periodic climatic shift caused by the displacement of the cold Humboldt Current by warmer equatorial waters which last occurred in 1983. This causes the plankton and fish communities either to disperse to other locations or to collapse entirely. At such a period the shore rapidly becomes littered with carrion since many of the sea-mammals and birds are unable to survive in the much tighter environment – scavenging condors and vultures, on the other hand, thrive, as does the desert where rain falls in deluges along the coast, with a consequent bloom of vegetation and rapid growth in animal populations. When the Humboldt Current returns, the desert dries up, its animal populations decline to normal sizes (another temporary feast for the scavengers), and at least ten years will usually pass before the cycle is repeated. Generally considered a freak phenomenon, *El Niño* is probably better understood as an integral part of coastal ecology; without it the desert would be a far more barren and static environment, virtually incapable of supporting life.

The mountains

In the **PERUVIAN ANDES** there is an incredible variety of habitats. That this is a mountain area of true extremes is immediately obvious if you fly across, or along, the Andes towards Lima – the land below shifting from high Puna to elfin wood, cloud forest to riparian (stream) valleys and eucalyptus woods (introduced from Australia in the 1880s). The complexity of the whole makes it incredibly difficult to formulate any overall description which isn't essentially misleading: climate and vegetation vary according to altitude, latitude and local characteristics. Generally, though, the vegetation is sparse and the climate extreme, allowing relatively few species to adapt to life here permanently. Additionally, much of the Andes has been settled for over 2,000 years – and hunter-tribes go back another 8,000 years before this – so most of the larger predators are rare, though still present in small numbers in the more remote regions. Among the most exciting you might actually see are the **mountain cats**, especially the **Puma** which lives at most altitudes and in a surprising number of habitats. Other more remote predators include the shaggy-looking **Maned Wolf** and the likeable **Spectacled Bear** which inhabits the moister forested areas of the Andes and actually prefers eating vegetation to people.

The most visible animals in the mountains, besides sheep and cattle, are the *cameloids* – the wild **Vicuña** and **Guanaco,** and the domesticated **Llama** and **Alpaca.** Although these species are clearly related, zoologists disagree on whether or not the Alpaca and Llama are domesticated forms of their wild relatives. Of the two wild cameloids, the Vicuña is the smaller and rarer – living only at the highest altitudes (up to 4,500m). **Andean Deer** are quite common in these higher valleys and with luck you might even come across the rare **Mountain Tapir.** Smaller animals tend to be confined to particular habitats – rabbit-like **Viscachas,** for example, to rocky outcrops; **squirrels** to wooded valleys; and **Chinchillas** (Peruvian 'chipmunks') to higher altitudes.

Most birds also tend to restrict themselves to specific habitats. The **Andean Goose** and **duck** are quite common in marshy areas along with many species of waders and migratory waterfowl. A particular favourite is the elegant, very pink, **Andean Flamingo** which can usually be spotted from the road between Arequipa and Puno where they turn Lake Salinas into one great red mass. In addition, many species of *passarines* can be found alongside small streams, perhaps the most striking of them being the **Dipper** which hunts underwater for larval insects along the stream-bed, popping up to a rock every so often for air and a rest. At lower elevations, especially in and around cultivated areas, the **Ovenbird** (or *Horneo*) constructs its nest from mud and grasses in the shape of an old-fashioned oven; while in open spaces many birds of prey can be spotted: the comical **Caracaras, Buzzard-Eagles** and the magical **Red-Backed Hawks** among them. **Andean Condors,** the birds most often associated with these mountains, are actually one of the more difficult species to see – although not especially rare they tend to soar at tremendous heights for most of the day, landing only on high, inaccessible cliffs or at carcasses after making sure that no-one is around to disturb them. A glimpse of this magnificent bird soaring overhead on its 3m wing-span will only come about either by frequent searching with binoculars or a lucky break as you climb to hilltops in relatively unpopulated areas.

Tropical jungle

Descending the eastern edge of the Andes you pass through a number of distinct habitats including puna, shrub-woods, cloud-forest, high and then lowland rain-forest. In spite of the rich and luxuriant appearance of the **RAIN-FOREST** it is in fact extremely fragile. Almost all the nutrients are recycled by rapid decomposition, with the aid of the damp climate and an incredible supply of insect labour back, into the vegetation – thereby creating a nutrient-poor soil which is highly susceptible to large-scale disturbance. When the forest is cleared, for example, usually in an attempt to colonise the area and turn it into viable farm-land, there is not only heavy soil erosion to contend with but also the fact that there are only enough nutrients in the earth for five years' good harvests and 20 years' poorer farming at the most. Natives of the rain-forest have evolved cultural mechanisms by which, on the whole, these problems are avoided: they tend to live in small, dispersed groups, move their gardens every few years, and obey sophisticated social controls to limit the chances of over-hunting any one zone or any particular species.

The most distinctive attribute of the **AMAZON BASIN** is the overwhelming abundance of plant and animal species. Over 6,000 species of plants have been reported from one small 110–hectare tract of forest, and there are at least a thousand species of birds and dozens of types of monkeys and bats spread about the Peruvian Amazon. There are several reasons for this marvellous natural diversity of flora and fauna. Most obviously, it is warm, there is abundant sunlight and large quantities of mineral nutrients are washed down from the Andes – all of which help to produce the ideal conditions for forest growth. Secondly, the rain-forest has an enormous structural diversity, with layers of vegetation from the forest floor to the canopy 30m above providing an infinity of niches to fill. Thirdly, since there is such a variety of habitats as you descend the Andes, the changes in altitude mean a great diversity of localised ecologies. And lastly, because the rain-forest has been more stable over longer periods of time than temperate areas (there was no Ice Age here, nor any prolonged period of drought) the fauna

has had freedom to evolve, and to adapt to often very specialised local conditions.

But if the Amazon Basin is where most of the plant and animal species are, it is also the most difficult place to see them. Movement through the thick vegetation is extremely limited and the only real chance for extensive observation is along the rivers from a boat. The river banks and flood-plains are richly diverse areas: here you're likely to see **Caimans, Macaws, Toucans, Oropendulas, Terns, Horned Screamers** and the primitive **Hoatzins** – birds whose young are born with claws at the wrist to enable them to climb up from the water into the branches of overhanging trees. You should catch sight, too, of one of a variety of **hawks** and at least two or three species of **monkeys** (perhaps the *Spider Monkey*, the *Howler* or the *Capuchin*). And with a lot of luck and more determined observation you may spot a rare **Giant River Otter, River Dolphin, Capybara** or maybe even one of the **jungle cats.**

In the **FOREST** proper you're more likely to find mammals such as the **Pecary** (wild pig), **Tapir, Tamandua Tree Sloth** and the second largest cat in the world, the incredibly powerful **Spotted Jaguar.** Characteristic of the deeper forest zones too are many species of birds, including **Humming-birds** (more common in the forested Andean foothills), **Manakins** and **Trogons,** though the effects of widespread hunting make it difficult to see these around any of the larger settlements. Logging is proving to be another major problem for the forest wild-life, since with the valuable trees dispersed among vast areas of mixed tree species in the rain-forest, a very large area must be disturbed to yield a relatively small amount of lumber. Deeper into the forest, however, and the further you are from human habitation, a glimpse of any of these animals is quite possible.

As preparation for all this, **LIMA ZOO,** in the Parque de las Leyerdas, is well worth a visit. It contains a good collection of most of the animals mentioned above, particularly the predators, and since there are no handy field-guides (a book based on 'Mammals of Peru' would be a very neat aid for travellers) this is about the best way to familiarise yourself with what you might see during the rest of your journey. Be prepared, however, to see animals kept in appalling conditions. You might also check out the **Natural History Museum** in Lima and the Ministry of Agriculture's *'Vida Silvestre'* section for publications and off-prints on Peruvian flora and fauna.

Among the few directly relevant books currently in print are:

M. Koepke *The Birds of the Department of Lima* (Livingston Press, Wynnwood, PA, 1970).

Parker, Parker and Plengue *A Checklist of the Birds of Peru* (1981) – a useful summary with photos of different habitats.

R. M. de Shounnsee and Phelps *The Birds of Venezuela* (Livingston Press, 1978).

CONFLICTING INTERESTS IN THE JUNGLE

Within the next 20 years Peru's **forest Indian tribes** may cease to exist in any meaningful way. Daily, at present, their land and culture are being eroded. All along the main rivers and jungle roads, settlers (and missionaries) are flooding into the area – and in their wake, forcing through land title agreements to which they have no conceivable right, are the major lumber companies and multi-national oil corporations. In large tracts of the jungle the fragile *selva* ecology has already been destroyed; in others the tribes have been more subtly disrupted by establishing their dependence on outside consumer goods and trade. But most importantly, the sustainable Indian economy is being disrupted and made redundant – leaving behind it, after the initial timber and chemical exploitation, nothing but irredeemable waste. Forest land does not respond well to prolonged intensive cultivation.

Since the early 1970s the Indians – and in particular the **Campa Ashaninka communities** from the much threatened Ene river area – have been co-ordinating opposition. Representatives, working sometimes in conjunction with the Indian aid groups *CIPA* and *Acotepa*, have gone more and more regularly to Lima to gain publicity and put indigenous Indian claims to land titles on the **Ene** and **Tambo** – the only regions left to them after four centuries of 'civilising' influence. In publicity terms they have met with some success. The exploitation of the forests has become a political issue, fuelled ironically in Peru (and outside) by the bizarre events surrounding Werner Herzog's filming of *Fitzcarraldo* – a film *about* exploitation of Indians, yet whose arrogant and exploitative making so angered local communities that at one stage a whole production camp was burnt down. And the Indians, certainly, have undergone a radical growth in political awareness. In real terms, though, they have made no progress. President Belaunde, whose promises of Indian rights led to many thousands of Campas making their way down to polling stations by raft to vote for him, has merely speeded up the process of colonisation. The 1974 *Law of Native Communities*, which specifies indigenous land rights, has been almost totally ignored. And at present in the Ene region alone, the Indians face multi-national claims to over a million hectares of their territory.

Below, an eloquent witness to the problems, and to the way of life that colonists and corporations are rushing to destroy, is an account by a local **Amarakaeri Indian** from the south-east province of Madre de Dios. This account was originally given as testimony to a human rights meeting in Lima. It is reprinted by permission of *Survival International*.

We Indians were born, work, live and die in the basin of the Madre de Dios River of Peru. It's our land – the only thing we have, with its plants, animals and small farms: an environment we understand and use well. We are not like those from outside who want to clear everything away, destroying the richness and leaving the forest ruined forever. We respect the forest; we make it produce for us.

Many people ask why we want so much land. They think we do not work all of it. But we work it differently from them, conserving it so that it will continue to produce for our children and grandchildren. Although some people want to take it from us, they then destroy and abandon it, moving on elsewhere. But we can't do that; we were born in our woodlands. Without them we will die.

In contrast to other parts of the Peruvian jungle, Madre de Dios is still relatively sparsely populated. The woodlands are extensive, the soils poor, so we work differently from those in other areas with greater population, less woodland and more fertile soils. Our systems do not work without large expanses of land. The people who come from outside do not know how to make the best of natural resources here. Instead they devote themselves to taking away what nature gives and leave little or nothing behind. They take wood, nuts and above all gold.

The man from the highlands works all day doing the same thing whether it is washing gold, cutting down trees or something else. Bored, he chews his coca, eats badly, then gets ill and leaves. The engineers just drink their coffee and watch others working.

We also work these things but so as to allow the woodland to replenish itself. We cultivate our farms, hunt, fish and gather woodland fruits, so we do not have to bring in supplies from outside. We also make houses, canoes, educate our children, enjoy ourselves. In short we satisfy almost all our needs with our own work, and without destroying the environment.

In the upper Madre de Dios River wood is more important than gold, and the sawmill of Shintuya is one of the most productive in the region. Wood is also worked in other areas to make canoes and boats to sell, and for building houses for the outsiders. In the lower region of the River we gather nuts – another important part of our economy. Much is said about Madre de Dios being the forgotten Department of Peru. Yet we are not forgotten by people from outside nor by some national and foreign companies who try to seize our land and resources. Because of this we have formed the *Federation of Indian Peoples of Madre de Dios* to fight for the defence of our lands and resources.

Since 1974 we have been asking for legal property titles to the land we occupy in accordance with the Law of Indian Communities. The authorities always promise them to us, but so far only one of our communities has a title, and that is to barely 5,000 hectares.

You may ask why we want titles now if we have not had them before. The answer is that we now have to defend our lands from many people who were not threatening us in the past.

In spite of journeys to Puerto Maldonado to demand guarantees from the authorities, they do not support us by removing the people who invade our land. On the contrary, when *we* defend our land, forcing the invaders to retreat, they accuse us of being wild, fierce and savage.

Equally serious are invasions by gold mining companies. The Peruvian State considers the issue of mining rights to be separate from that of land rights, and there are supposed to be laws giving priority to the Indian communities for mining rights on their lands – but the authorities refuse to enforce them. Many people have illegally obtained rights to mine our lands, then they do not allow us to work there. Others, without rights, have simply installed themselves.

There are numerous examples I could give; yet when my community refused entry to a North American adventurer who wanted to install himself on our land, the Lima *Commercio* accused us of being savages, and of attacking him with arrows. Lies! All we did was defend our lands against invaders who didn't even have legal mining rights – without using any weapons, although these men all carried their own guns.

We also suffer from forms of economic aggression. The prices of agricultural products we sell to the lorry drivers and other traders in the area have recently been fixed by the authorities. For example, 25lb of yuca used to sell for 800 *soles*. Now we can only get 400 *soles*. Such low prices stop us developing our agriculture further, and we are not going to be able to sell our products outside because we can no longer cover our costs and minimal needs. On the other hand, the authorities have fixed the prices of wood and transport so that the amount that we can earn is continually diminishing. And the prices we have to pay for things we need from outside is always rising.

There are also problems with the National Park Police. They no longer allow us to fish with 'barbasco' [fish poison] in the waters of our communities, although they are outside the National Park. They say that barbasco will destroy the fish. But we have fished this way for as long as we can remember, and the fish have not been destroyed. On the contrary: the fish are destroyed when people come from outside and overfish for commercial sale, especially when they use dynamite.

Our main source of food, after agriculture, is fishing – above all the *boquichico* which we fish with bow and arrow after throwing barbasco. We cannot stop eating, and we are not going to let them stop us from fishing with barbasco either!

There are so many more problems. If our economic position is bad, our social situation is even worse. Traders reach the most remote areas, but medical facilities don't, even now with serious epidemics of malaria, measles, tuberculosis and intestinal parasites in the whole region. Our children go to primary schools in some communities, but often the schools are shut. And there are no secondary schools.

The commercial centres in the gold zone are areas of permanent drunkenness. Outsiders deceive and insult us and now some of our people no longer want to be known as Indians or speak our languages; they go to the large towns to hide from their origins and culture.

We are not opposed to others living and benefitting from the jungle, nor are we opposed to its development. On the contrary, what we want is that this development should benefit us, and not just the companies and colonists who come from outside. And we want the resources of the jungle to be conserved so that they can serve future generations of both colonists and Indians.

If you want to know more about – or keep up to date on – the cause of forest Indians in Peru the best people to contact are **Survival International,** a charity established to publicise and support worldwide the struggles of tribal people towards self determination. *Survival* have groups throughout the US and Britain, who support aid projects in tribal land rights, health and education, publish literature and reports, and provide speakers, bookstalls and exhibitions, etc. Their two main national branches are:

LONDON: 29 Craven Hill, WC2 (tel. 01–839 3267).
WASHINGTON: 2121 Decatur Place NW, DC 20008 (tel. 202–265 1077).

PERU'S WHITE GOLD

Peru's coca industry netted an estimated $3 billion in 1984 – 20 per cent of the country's Gross National Product

At isolated stations like Ayaviri on the desolate Peruvian altiplano, ragged children clamber daily into the train waving oranges and sweet corn. Behind them follow their stout mothers thrusting woollen jumpers and socks towards tourists as they shout – alpaca! alpaca! Generally unable to sell anything, most mountain Indians find it virtually impossible to make a living from weaving or agriculture any more. If you want to make money you're better off 'cooking' **cocaine.** Illegal 'kitchens', makeshift coke refineries, have become the main means of livelihood for many ordinary peasant families.

Coca has travelled a long way since the Incas distributed this 'divine plant' across fourteenth-century Andean Peru. Originating as a gift from the gods, coca was used to exploit slave labour under Spanish rule: without it the Indians would never have worked in the gruelling conditions of colonial mines such as Potosi. The isolation of the active ingredient in coca, cocaine, in 1859 began an era of intense medical experimentation. Its numbing effects have been appreciated ever since by dental patients throughout the world, and even Pope Leo XIII enjoyed a bottle of the coca wine produced by an Italian physician who amassed a great fortune from its sale in the nineteenth century. The literary world, too, was soon stimulated by these white powdery crystals: in 1885 Robert Louis Stevenson wrote *Dr Jekyll and Mr Hyde* during six speedy days and nights while taking this 'wonder drug' as a remedy for his tuberculosis, and Sir Arthur Conan Doyle, writing in the 1890s, used the character of Sherlock Holmes to defend the use of cocaine. On a more popular level, coca was one of the essential ingredients in Coca Cola until 1906. Today, cocaine is the most fashionable – and expensive – of drugs.

From its humble origins as the 'divine plant' of the Incas, cocaine has become very big business. Unofficially, it may well be the biggest export for countries like Peru and Bolivia, where coca grows best in the Andes and along the edge of the jungle. While most mountain peasants always cultivated a little for personal use, many have now become dependent on it for obvious economic reasons: coca is easily the most profitable cash crop and is readily bought by middlemen operating for extremely wealthy cocaine barons. A constant flow of semi-refined coca – *pasta,* the basic paste – leaves Peru aboard Amazon river boats or unmarked light aircraft heading for the big-time laboratories in Colombia. From here the pure stuff is shipped or flown out, mostly to the USA via Miami or Los Angeles, finding its way eventually into the apartments of middle-class Westerners.

Reputed to be a 'fun drug', few people care to look beyond the wall of illicit intrigue which surrounds this highly saleable contraband. In the same vein as coffee or chocolate, the demand for this product has become another means through which the privileged world directly dictates and controls the lives of Third World peasant farmers. As more Peruvian Indians follow world market trends by turning their hands to the growing and 'cooking' of coca, their more staple crops like cereals, tubers and pulses are cultivated less and less.

It's a change brought about partly by rising expectations, partly by circumstance. Agricultural prices are state-controlled, but manufactured goods and transport costs rise almost weekly, preventing the peasants from earning a decent living from their crops. Moreover, the soil is poor and crops grow unwillingly. Coca, on the other hand, grows readily at the most barren heights and needs little attention. Revered by the Indians for centuries for its stimulant and hunger-suppressing effects, the plant now promises wealth as well.

The kitchens are in cottages or backyards, and the equipment is simple – oil drums, a few chemicals, paraffin and a fire. Bushels of coca leaves are dissolved in paraffin and hydrochloric acid, heated and stirred, eventually producing the pasta, which is then washed in ether or acetone to yield powdery white cocaine.

For this work the peasant receives the equivalent of $7, better than the average daily wage of about 60 cents. He may produce kilogrammes of cocaine, which goes to the dealer. This man supplies the chemicals, and perhaps some of the leaves, and lives in town. He is well off, selling the cocaine in Peru for about $12 a gramme – an enormous profit. Dollars are accepted, but the Peruvian sole is not, at least not by the dealers in quantity.

By the time the cocaine reaches New York or Berlin, each gramme costs between $80 and $120 despite adulteration by 'cuts' such as milk powder or washing soda.

In the Department of Puno, on the shores of Lake Titicaca, the Capachica peninsula pokes like a crooked finger into the lake. No buses run there, and the dirt road is closed by a chain. Men lounging near by mutter: 'No entry': controlled by the Peruvian underworld, this peninsula is the site of many kitchens. No Civil Guard has visited it for years; the last occasion produced nothing but sniper fire. Since then the Civil Guards in Puno have become the richest in all Peru, a waiter says. Even the presence of the PIP, the secret police, merely keeps the kitchens outside the town limits. Transport is by the back roads at night.

The dealers invest much of their profits in legitimate enterprises, particularly clubs and restaurants, and 90 per cent of the cocaine is exported, as few Peruvians can afford it. The peasant farmers, on the other hand, have temporarily given their land-base, time and energy for the benefit of the dealers and hedonistic Westerners. While the coke trade is internationally deplored, the Peruvian peasant digging with his foot-plough no doubt dreams of the chance to keep his radio supplied with batteries and maybe one day buy a truck, a more permanent key to wealth in the Andes. Anonymously connected to a fickle world market, the coca-grower's lot is to hope that the chain of demand never falls drastically in relation to the supply.

With thanks to Dan Richardson for original research.

PERUVIAN RECIPES

Peruvian cooking – even in small restaurants well away from the big cities – is appealing stuff. The seven recipes below are among the classics, fairly simple to prepare and (with a couple of coastal exceptions) found throughout the country. If you're travelling and camping you'll find all the ingredients listed readily available in local markets; alternatives are suggested for trying them in North America or Europe. All quantities given are sufficient for four people.

Ceviche
A cool, spicey dish, eaten on the Peruvian coast for at least the past thousand years.
1 kilo soft white fish (lemon sole and plaice are good, or you can mix half fish, half shellfish)
2 large onions (sliced)
1 or 2 chilies (chopped)
6 limes (can use lemons but not so good)
1 tbsp olive oil
1 tbsp fresh coriander leaves (chopped – parsley is a poor substitute)
salt and pepper
Wash and cut fish into bite-sized pieces. Place in a dish with sliced onions. Add the chopped chili and coriander. Make a marinade using the lime juice, olive oil, salt and pepper. Pour over fish and place in a cool spot until the fish is 'soft cooked' (from 10 to 60 minutes). Serve with boiled potatoes (preferably sweet) and corn on the cob.

Papas at la Huancaina
An excellent and ubiquitous snack – cold potatoes covered in a mildly *picante* cheese sauce.
1 kilo potatoes (boiled)
1 or 2 chilies (chopped)
2 cloves of garlic (chopped)
200 grammes soft goat's cheese (feta is ideal, cottage cheese alright)
6 soda crackers (try *TUC*)
1 hard boiled egg
1 small tin of evaporated milk
Chop very finely all the above ingredients except for the potatoes (or liquidise). The mixture should be fairly thin and smooth though not too runny. Pour sauce over thickly sliced potatoes. Arrange on a dish and serve garnished with lettuce and black olives. Best served chilled.

Palta Rellena
Stuffed avocados – another very popular snack.
2 avocados (soft but firm)
1 onion (chopped)
2 tomatoes (chopped)
2 hard boiled eggs (chopped)
200 grammes cooked chicken or tuna fish (cold and either chopped or flaked)
2 tbsp mayonnaise
Cut avocados in half and remove stones. Scoop out a little of the flesh around hole. Gently combine all other ingredients before piling into the centre of each avocado half.

Causa
About the easiest Peruvian dish to reproduce outside the country, though there are no real substitutes for Peruvian tuna and creamy Andean potatoes.
1 kilo potatoes
200 grammes tuna fish
2 avocados (the riper the better)
4 tomatoes
4 tbsp mayonnaise
salt and black pepper
1 lemon
Boil potatoes and mash to a firm, smooth consistency. Flake tuna fish and add a little lemon juice. Mash avocados to a pulp, add the rest of lemon juice, some salt and black pepper. Slice tomatoes. Press one quarter of potato mixture in a deep dish and cover with a spoonful of mayonnaise. Put one quarter of the tuna fish over this, then a quarter of the avocado mixture on top. Add a layer of sliced tomato. Continue the same layering process until you have four layers of each. Cut into rough slices. Serve (ideally chilled) with salad, or on its own as a starter.

Locro de Zapallo
A vegetarian standard found on most set menus in the cheaper, working-class restaurants.
1 kilo pumpkin
1 large potato
2 cloves of garlic
1 tbsp oregano
½ cup of milk
2 corn on the cob
1 onion
1 chili (chopped)
salt and pepper
200 grammes cheese (Mozarella type works well)

Fry onion, chili, garlic and oregano. Add half a cup of water. Mix in the pumpkin as large cut lumps, slices of corn on the cob and finely chopped potato. Add milk and cheese. Simmer till a soft, smooth consistency then add a little more water if necessary. Serve with rice or over fish.

Pescado a la Chorillana
Probably the most popular way of cooking fish on the coast.
4 pieces of fish (cod or any other white fish will do)
2 large onions (chopped)
4 large tomatoes (chopped)
1 or 2 chilies (chopped into fairly large pieces)
1 tbsp oil
½ cup of water
Grill or fry each portion of fish until done. Keep hot. Fry separately the onions, tomatoes and chili. Add the water to form a sauce. Pile the hot sauce over each portion of fish and serve with rice.

Asado
Roast. An expensive meal for Peruvians, though a big favourite for family gatherings. Only available in flashier restaurants.
1 kilo or less of lean beef
2 cloves of garlic
200 grammes butter
1 tin of tomato puree
salt and pepper
2 tomatoes
1 chili (chopped)
Cover the beef with pre-mixed garlic and butter. Mix tomato puree with salt, pepper and soy sauce. Liquidise tomatoes with chopped chili. Spread both mixtures on the beef and cook slowly in a covered casserole dish — perhaps for 4 or 5 hours. Traditionally the *asado* is served with *pure de papas* which is simply a quite runny form of mashed potatoes whipped up with some butter and a lot of garlic. A very tasty combination.

MOCHICA RAY MOTIF

ONWARDS FROM PERU

As illustrated by the incredible expansion of the Inca Empire, Peru is ideally situated to begin (or continue) an extended tour of the South American continent. Its **Pacific coastline** offers easy access by road north into **Ecuador,** towards the Gulf of Guayaquil and the fascinating Galapagos Islands, or south into the cooler climates of **Chile.** The southern *sierra* leads naturally across the **Titicaca Basin** into **Bolivia** from where it's relatively simple to travel overland to **Brazil** or **Argentina.** Flowing down the eastern side of the Peruvian Andes, the **Amazon** (downriver from Iquitos) connects with **Brazil** and **Colombia,** as well as an alternative ('scenic') route into **Ecuador** via the Rio Napo. Whichever way you go onwards from Peru the journey can't fail to cover a variety of startlingly different landscapes, climates and cultures. In the same breath no other South American country offers as broad a range of attractions as Peru, and it's hard to advise you to leave. Perhaps the most popular overland trip is south or east via Bolivia.

Twice the size of Spain, **BOLIVIA** sits on top of the Andes, cut off from the Pacific but rolling down its high plains into the south-east corner of the Amazon Basin. Politically very unstable, Bolivia's power games have been complicated by the intrigues of its booming cocaine industry and although **Sucre** is the legal capital, **La Paz** is in practice the centre of government and commerce. Fortunately it's generally safe and easy to travel around the country whatever might be happening in La Paz. The country is easily entered by **bus or boat train** from **Puno** in Peru, or **by air** from **Lima** and **Cuzco.** Many travellers continue by train across the Andes to Antofagasta on the Chilean coast, although a more popular route is the breathtaking railway ride from Santa Cruz via Corumba to São Paulo on the Brazilian Atlantic. **Tourist cards,** usually valid for 90 days, are available for all nationalities except those of Communist countries (who'll need to approach embassies or consulates). Most of Bolivia's health hazards are similar to those in Peru and the relevant **inoculations** are the same – typhoid, paratyphoid, yellow fever, gamma-globulin, and anti-malaria pills if you intend to visit the jungle zone.

Smaller but longer than Peru, the narrow strip of **CHILE** reaches right down the Pacific coastline to Tierra del Fuego. An extremely beautiful country with deserts in the north and tall pine forests in the south, its controversial and oppressive politics belie the friendliness of the people. Since President Allende's marxist coalition was violently overthrown by the army in 1973, the country had been dictatorially run by General Pinochet, apparently with a lot of CIA help. Although it's possible to approach Chile by **air** from **Lima,** the **bus trip to Santiago** is a much more rewarding journey (particularly if you break it at **Arequipa, Arica** and **Antofagasta**). Chile also has rail links with both Bolivia and Argentina. **Tourist cards** for a 90–day period are available from Chilean consulates and many airline offices throughout South America – only African nationals and citizens of communist countries need visas. Healthwise Chile is generally safer then Peru though typhoid **inoculations** are still recommended.

BRAZIL is an attractive goal, particularly for anyone into long river journeys or the jazzy rhythms of good live music (in or out of the February fiestas). Virtually the same size as the USA, Brazil is the fifth biggest country in the world. The Amazon Basin's tropical forest takes (or took) up much of the land, though it is bounded to the north by the Guiana Highlands and in the south by the Brazilian mountains. Most of its 120 million people, however, are concentrated on the narrow coastal belt, a mixture these days of heavy industry, beach resorts and dire poverty. Having been run by a military government for the last 20 years, the Brazilian electorate are eagerly awaiting the return to democratic civilian rule, planned, in a limited way, for 1985. To approach Brazil from Peru can require some planning. Rio can be reached by **air** from **Lima,** but from **Iquitos** flights rarely go further than Manaus. **Overland** the easiest route is through Bolivia to Santa Cruz, then by train to São Paulo. A more adventurous journey takes the most obvious route – **down the Amazon** from **Pucallpa** and **Iquitos** to Manaus, or even as far as Belem on the Atlantic; some of these can also be routed along the amazing trans-

Amazonica highway. **Visas** are necessary for most nationalities including US, but not for Western European tourists. All visitors, however, are required to provide evidence of sufficient funds to survive in and eventually get out of the country (standard stamp for 90 days). **Inoculations** recommended for Brazil include: typhoid, paratyphoid, cholera, yellow fever, and (for children) poliomyelitis; anti-malaria pills and water sterilising tablets are also a good idea. Bubonic plague too has caused increasing devastation in restricted zones over recent years – best to make enquiries about this at Brazilian tourist offices when you arrive.

COLOMBIA is an invigorating country with diverse mountain and jungle terrain and with both the Pacific and Caribbean coasts. Liberals and conservatives have battled for power since the Second World War; at present it's a conservative president. More recently there's been a growth in active terrorism and extremist splinter groups – though this rarely affects conditions for travellers. Robbery, however, might: be careful. From Peru most people approach Colombia **by air** from **Lima** to Bogota, or **overland through Ecuador** (two or three days). From **Iquitos,** however, Colombia's Amazon zone can be entered **by river** at Leticia – a tough river trip to 'civilisation' at Puerto Asis, but superb for wild-life. Only an onward ticket is needed for Western European passport holders, though US citizens require a **visa** from an embassy or consulate (on provision of two photos and return/onward ticket) or two-week transit visas which are issued on board aircraft. For Australians and New Zealanders a visa is also necessary and it's important to apply in plenty of time. **Inoculations** recommended include: typhoid, paratyphoid and gamma-globulin (anti-malaria pills are useful for certain areas).

ECUADOR, a relatively small country squeezed out towards the Pacific, away from the Amazon, by Colombia and Peru, is dominated by two beautiful high-land ranges separated by a central valley. The population is essentially split between the fertile coast and the sierra, with very little settlement in the eastern jungles and extensive rural migration to the two main cities – Quito and Guayaquil. After a long history of military coups, President Roldos took power in 1979 with an aim to transform the economy and reform Ecuadorean society. After his untimely death in an air crash back in 1981, he has been succeeded by the like-minded vice-president, Osvaldo Hurtado. A simple overland approach from Peru via **Tumbes** or **La Tina** takes you in a day to Guayaquil. From here there's a magnificent railway to **Quito** in the mountains. Virtually all nationalities are given a **tourist card** for up to 90 days on arrival, though sometimes travellers are asked to provide evidence of $20 for every day they intend staying in the country. The usual inoculations are recommended: typhoid, paratyphoid, gamma-globulin and yellow fever, along with anti-malaria pills for everywhere but the highlands.

Lastly, a few **books** you might find of use outside Peru. For **South America as a whole** the *South American Handbook* (Trade and Travel Publications, £12.95) is the standard – a bible for most overland travellers, and adequate (if not always too culturally illuminating) for each of the continent's nations. Along similar lines, and also with its good points, is Geoff Crowther's *South America on a Shoestring* (Lonely Planet, £6.95). Individually, in **Ecuador,** Rob Rachowiecki's *Climbing and Hiking in Ecuador* (Bradt Publications, £8.50) is trusty – and newly researched, while for **Mexico** John Fisher's *Rough Guide* (RKP, £4.50) is very good. *Rough Guides* to Brazil, and perhaps eventually Chile, are planned.

For **guides and maps** to all South American countries two of the best sources – both in Britain – are *Bradt Enterprises* (mail order only: 41 Nortoft Rd, Chalfont St Peter, Bucks SL9 0LA) and *McCarta* (122 Kings Cross Rd, London WC1).

LANGUAGE

Although Peru is officially a **Spanish-speaking** nation, a large proportion of its population, possibly more than half, actually regard Spanish as their second language. When the Conquistadores arrived, **Quechua,** the official language of the Inca Empire, was widely spoken everywhere but the jungle. Originally known as *Runasimi* (from *runa*, person, and *simi*, mouth) the name *Quechua* – which actually means 'high Andean valleys' – was coined by the Spanish. *Quechua* was not, however, the only pre-Columbian tongue. There were, and still are, well over 30 Indian languages within the jungle area and, until the late nineteenth century, *Mochica* had been widely spoken on the north coast for at least 1,500 years.

With such a rich linguistic history it is not surprising to find non-European words intruding constantly into any Peruvian conversation. *Cancha*, for instance, the Inca word for courtyard, is still commonly used to refer to most sporting areas – *la cancha de basketball*, for example. Other linguistic survivals have even reached the English language: *llama, condor, puma* and *pampa* among them. Perhaps more interesting is the great wealth of traditional **creole slang** – utilised with equal vigour at all levels of society. This complex speech, much like cockney rhyming slang, is difficult to catch without almost complete fluency in Spanish; though one phrase you may find useful for directing a taxi driver is *de fresa alfonso* – literally translatable as 'of strawberry, Alfonso' but actually meaning 'straight on' (*de frente al fondo*).

Once you get into it **Spanish** is the easiest language there is – and in Peru people are eager to understand even the most faltering attempt. You'll be further helped by the fact that South Americans speak relatively slowly (at least compared with Spaniards in Spain) and that there's no need to get your tongue round the difficult lisping pronunciation.

The rules of **pronunciation** are pretty straightforward, and once you get to know them strictly observed:

A somewhere between the A sound of back and that of father

E as in get

I as in police

O as in hot

U as in rule

C is soft before E and I, hard otherwise: *cerca* is pronounced serka.

G works the same way, a guttural H sound (like the *ch* in loch) before E or I, a hard G elsewhere – *gigante* becomes higante

H is always silent

J has a guttural H sound similar to that of G: *jamon* is pronounced hamon

LL sounds like an English Y: *tortilla* is pronounced as torteeya

N is as in English unless it has a tilde (accent) over it, when it becomes NY: *Mañana* sounds like manyana

QU is pronounced like an English K: *Quechua* becomes Kechua

R is rolled, RR doubly so

V sounds more like B, *vino* becoming beano

X is slightly softer than in English – sometimes almost S – except between vowels in place names where it has an H sound – i.e. Mexico or Oaxaca

Z is the same as a soft C, so *cerveza* becomes serbesa

Below is a list of a few essential words and phrases, though if you're travelling for any length of time some kind of dictionary or phrasebook is obviously a worthwhile investment – some specifically Latin American ones are available (see below). If you're using a **dictionary,** bear in mind that in Spanish CH, LL and N count as separate letters and are listed after the Cs, Ls and Ns respectively.

Basics

Yes, No, O.K.
Please, Thank you
Where, When

Si, No, Vale/O.K.
Por Favor, Gracias
Donde, Cuando

What, How much	Que, Cuanto
Here, There	Aqui, Alli
This, That	Esto, Eso
Now, Later	Ahora, Mas Tarde
Open, Closed	Abierto/a, Cerrado/a
With, Without	Con, Sin
Good, Bad	Buen(o)/a, Mal(o)/a
Big, Small	Gran(de), Pequeño/a
More, less	Mas, Menos
Today, Tomorrow	Hoy, Mañana
Yesterday	Ayer

Greetings and responses

Hello, Goodbye	Ola, Adios
Good Morning	Buenos Dias
Good Afternoon/Night	Buenas Tardes/Noches
How are you?	Como esta (usted)?
Not at all/You're welcome	De nada
I (don't) understand	(No) Entiendo
Do you speak English?	Habla (usted) Ingles?
I (don't) speak Spanish	(No) Hablo Castellano
What (did you say)?	Como?
My name is . . .	Me llamo . . .
What's your name?	Como se llama usted?
I am English/American	Soy Ingles(a)/Americano(a).
See you later	Hasta Luego
Sorry	Lo siento/disculpeme
Excuse me	Con permiso/perdon

Needs – hotels and transport

I want	Quiero
I'd like	Quisiera
There is (is there?)	Hay (?)
Do you have . . . ?	Tiene . . . ?
. . . the time	. . . la hora
. . . a room	. . . un cuarto
with two beds/double bed	con dos camas/cama matrimonial
Do you know . . . ?	Sabe . . . ?
I don't know	No se
Give me . . .	Deme . . .
(one like that)	(uno asi)
Where does the bus to . . . leave from?	De donde sale el omnibus para . . . ?
Is this the train for Puno?	Es este el tren para Puno?
I'd like a (return) ticket to . . .	Quisiera un billete (de ida y vuelta) para . . .
What time does it leave (arrive in . . .)	A que hora sale (llege en . . .)
What is there to eat?	Que hay para comer?
What's that?	Que es eso?
What's this called in Spanish	Como se llama esto en Castellano?

Numbers and days

1	un(o)/a	9	nueve	20	veinte	90	noventa
2	dos	10	diez	21	veintiuno	100	cien(to)
3	tres	11	once	30	treinta	101	ciento uno
4	cuatro	12	doce	40	cuarenta	200	doscientos
5	cinco	13	trece	50	cincuenta	500	quinientos
6	seis	14	catorce	60	sesenta	700	setecientos
7	siete	15	quince	70	setenta	1000	mil
8	ocho	16	diez y seis	80	ochenta	2000	dos mil

1985 mil novocientos ochenta y cinco
First – primero/a;   second – segundo/a;   third – tercero/a.
Monday, lunes;   Tuesday, martes;   Wednesday, miercoles;   Thursday, jueves;
Friday, viernes;   Saturday, sabado;   Sunday, domingo.

Most functional of the phrasebooks is probably the *Berlitz Latin-American Phrasebook:* Pan also publish such a book, or try the University of Chicago *Dictionary of Latin-American Spanish* (Pocket, $1.95).

INDEX

UPDATE 1986

One year on from publication, a few changes, openings/closures and developments. Thanks to all readers who sent in accounts and additional/revised information: please keep writing!

Basics

p6 The Peruvian **currency** is no longer just the sol (which at the time of writing stands at 25,000 *soles* to the pound). The new APRA government, under Alan Garcia, has created a new monetary unit, the **inti** (Quechua for 'sun'), equivalent to 1,000 *soles*. Most restaurants and hotels now give their bills in *intis* rather than *soles*, in essence just chopping off the three noughts.

The main notes now available are: 1 *inti*/1,000 *soles*, 5 *intis*/5,000 *soles*, 10 *intis*/10,000 *soles*, 50 *intis*/50,000 *soles* and 100 *intis*/100,000 *soles*.

p10 Trains seem to have tightened up on some of their schedules – even to the extent of sometimes leaving *earlier* than time-tabled. They still leave late too, but to be on the safe side arrive at least one hour before the official departure.

p22 Customs. Although **coca leaves** are a very common commodity in the mountains, their legality is in a state of flux at present, and they are certainly illegal to export from Peru into most European and North American countries. The same holds true for the apparently innocuous **coca tea-bags** which are served in most places in Cuzco.

Chapter one

p53 Artesania *Antisuyo* has moved to Jiron Tacna 460, Miraflores, parallel to Block 44 of the Aveinida Arequipa; Tel. 452-557.

p57 Pachacamac. Taxis from Lima Centro to the ruins of Pachacamac can be arranged from around $25-30; at this price the driver should take you through the site and, importantly, back to Lima.

Chapter two

p72 Cuzco map. The *Aeroperu* office has moved to the Avenida del Sol (on opposite side to Faucett Airlines); the Post Office is also on Av. del Sol (same side as but further downhill from Aeroperu).

p75 The *Colonial Palace Hotel*, on Quera opposite the Hostal del Inca, is a flashy new place set in a colonial building – expensive but good.

p86 The *South American Cafe* no longer sells food or drink unfortunately; it does, however, sell some of the finest new and antique Peruvian weavings.

p91 The Co-operative **mini-bus service for Pisac** and the Sacred Valley is in fact *a few hundred metres* down Recoleta from the heart of Cuzco.

p95 A couple of points on **the Inca trail**: firstly, it's rapidly earning a bad reputation for robbery (sometimes armed), so it's certainly not advisable to do it alone; and secondly, some tour operators in Cuzco (offices mainly in Calle Procuradores) will provide guides/porters from around $3 a day, plus initial arrangement fee of $5 each (this service also provides additional security on the walk).

p99 At **Aguas Calientes** a new *Albergue Juvenil Machu Picchu* – actually an upmarket Youth Hostel – provides some of the best accommodation for around $5 per night (reductions for Youth Hostel members).

Chapter three

p114 Pisco. The town's best restaurant now seems to be *Ace de Oros* (on the Plaza de Armas near the Chifa). The *Restaurante Las Vegas* still serves excellent food – though the service is often poor for gringos. Beside the main church, on the corner of the plaza, there's a very friendly bar.

p115 Paracas National Park has introduced a $3 entrance fee for tourists.

p124 Nazca. Maria Reiche gives a talk on the Nazca Lines in the lounge of the Hotel de Touristas most evenings at around 7pm.

The *Hotel Montecarlo* now offers half hour flights over the Nazca lines at only $20 for anyone who stays there.

p126 Another company taking **flights** over the lines, *Aeroica*, has opened an office on the street between Hotel Montecarlo and the Plaza de Armas.

There are two very cheap, and quite basic, **hostals** on the Plaza de Armas. The Banco Interbanc (on the Plaza de Armas) change dollars and travellers cheques . . . when they've got sufficient cash; in general it's probably not a good idea to rely on **changing money** in Nazca.

129 Another good **local Nazca guide** is Carlos Acosta (Bolognesi 687; Tel. 100). He offers similar trips at similar prices and also incorporates an interesting visit to an ex-hacienda, now a farming co-operative near to the Chauchilla cemetery.

p134 Arequipa map. The Casa Moral is in fact on the opposite side of the road.

p139 Arequipa. Two more **hotels** – both upmarket but pretty good value at around $6 – are the *Hotel Jerusalen* (Jerusalen 601; Tel. 222502), which is large, clean and with excellent service and the *Hotel Crisnar* (Moral 107), a little more central.

Manolo's Restaurant is a very good fast-service joint – excellent for teas, snacks or full meals.

p150 Puno. The *Hotel Embajador* (Av. Los Incas 289; Tel. 592) is a good modern hotel, very close to the station and market.

p150 Puno. *Club 31* has improved its catering facilities – probably now the best, cheapest and quickest place for breakfasts.

p151 An excellent, English-speaking **guide to the Floating Islands and Chullpa Tombs**, Andres Lopez Pacosonco, can be contacted through *Suri Tours* (Tel. 592).

p152 The Evangelical School has moved off the main Uros Island – Huacavacani – due to problems it caused by creating a split between Catholic and Evangelical islanders.

p155 Routes to Bolivia. You need to change only about $15 to $20 into Bolivian currency at the border – just enough to get you on to La Paz (through the black market rates in La Paz are nothing like as good as they used to be).

Chapter seven

p244 The **Explorer's Inn** now charges from $45 per night. It does, however, offer crocodile spotting, a climb up a ladder to the high jungle canopy, and aluminium canoes which visitors can take solo onto nearby lakes.

p250 Kiteni. The 'new' Albergue was closed in January 1986, and it's not clear when or if it'll re-open, so don't bank on any quality accommodation in this little settlement, the *Hotel Kiteni* is friendly, but extremely basic – no toilets and only the river to wash in.

HELP US UPDATE
We've added an interim 1986 update to this first edition of **The Rough Guide to Peru**. Next edition, when the main body of the guide will be two years old, we'll be making more extensive revisions – and hopefully adding further places, possibilities and accounts.

To do this, and to keep sharp all the basic info on hotels, bars, opening hours, etc, it helps enormously to get feedback from anyone using the book. A couple of lines on a postcard can be invaluable; a detailed hiking or expeditionary route, even more so. All **letters** we include or make use of will be acknowledged, and for the best ones we'll send a **free copy** of the next edition (or if you prefer any one of the other Rough Guides).

Please write to: Dilwyn Jenkins
            The Rough Guides
            Routledge & Kegan Paul
            11 New Fetter Lane
            London EC4P 4EE

TRAVEL ADS

Adverts are a new feature of the *Rough Guides*, and are being introduced mainly to keep down the costs of research and production, and hence of the books themselves. We hope, though, that the kind of ads which we print – for specialist companies, trekking organisers, student, youth and cheap flight outlets – will also be a useful service. We're certainly not interested in promoting package firms and credit cards!

When replying to an ad, we would appreciate you mentioning *The Rough Guides* thanks.

THE
Dilwyn Jenkins
TOUR OF PERU

Peru is one of the
most exciting and diverse
countries in the world. Any short
tour must be supremely well run to
allow travellers to really get to grips
with the country and its people. All Dilwyn
Jenkins Tours are led by experts with extensive
experience of living and travelling in Peru, and
with a network of reliable local contacts. You'll
be staying in small local hotels and using public
transport — getting to know not only your own
small group but also the local people.

Book through STA Travel
Tel: 01-581 1022 for your brochure.

21 days from £440